The
HOME
VISITOR'S
Guidebook
SECOND EDITION

The

HOME
VISITOR'S
Guidebook
SECOND EDITION

PROMOTING OPTIMAL
PARENT & CHILD DEVELOPMENT

by Carol S. Klass, Ph.D.

·P·A·U·L·H·
BROOKES
PUBLISHING CO®

Baltimore • London • Sydney

Paul H. Brookes Publishing Co.
Post Office Box 10624
Baltimore, MD 21285-0624

www.brookespublishing.com

Second printing, August 2005.

Typeset by Integrated Publishing Solutions, Grand Rapids, Michigan.
Manufactured in the United States of America by
Victor Graphics, Baltimore, Maryland.

The names of the family members described in the vignettes and interviews
recorded in this book have been changed to protect their identities.

Permission to reprint the following quotations is gratefully acknowledged:

Page 3: Reprinted with the permission of Scribner, an imprint of Simon & Schuster
Adult Publishing Group, from I AND THOU by Martin Buber, translated by Ronald
Gregor Smith. Copyright © 1958 by Charles Scribner's Sons.

Page 231: Quotation from THE COLLECTED POEMS AND PLAYS OF RABINDRANATH
TAGORE (New York, Macmillan, 1937) reprinted by permission of the estate of Rabindranath Tagore.

Page 297: Text from p. 61 from BLACKBERRY WINTER by MARGARET MEAD.
COPYRIGHT © 1972 by MARGARET MEAD. Reprinted by permission of HarperCollins
Publishers Inc. WILLIAM MORROW.

Photographs on pages xxiii, 3, 37, 79, 127, 171, 203, 257, 315, and 341 are courtesy
of Marilyn Nolt, 508 Noble Street, Souderton, PA 18964. Phone/fax: 215-721-9055.
e-mail: noltphotos@mail.com.

Library of Congress Cataloging-in-Publication Data

Klass, Carol Speekman.
   The home visitor's guidebook : promoting optimal parent and child
development by Carol S. Klass.—2nd ed.
   p.   cm.
   Rev. ed. of: Home visiting / Carol S. Klass. ©1996.
   Includes bibliographical references and index.
   ISBN-13: 978-1-55766-611-6
   ISBN-10: 1-55766-611-3
   1. Parenting—Study and teaching.   2. Child development—Study and teaching.
   3. Home-based family services.   4. Social case work.   I. Klass, Carol Speekman.
   Home visiting.   II. Title
   HQ755.7 .K59 2002
   649'.1'071—dc21   2002038478

British Library Cataloguing in Publication data are available from the British Library.

Contents

About the Author

In her long career, Carol S. Klass, Ph.D., has taught college, worked as an early intervention specialist and mental health consultant, and served as a field-based mentor of early educators. She has designed and directed two early intervention programs for young children with high needs and three professional development programs for early childhood educators. Dr. Klass has used ethnographic action research to improve her own practice and the practice of the early educators with whom she has worked.

Her books include *The Autonomous Child: Day Care and the Transmission of Values* (Falmer Press, 1986) and *The Child Care Provider: Promoting Young Children's Development* (Paul H. Brookes Publishing Co., 1999). Her works in progress include a book of oral narratives of early childhood educators and a book for parents. Dr. Klass provides training seminars and keynotes and teaches as an adjunct professor. She is a sunrise walker, cook, gardener, mother of two sons, and grandmother of one granddaughter, and she always knows the phase of the moon.

Foreword

This second edition of Carol Klass's valuable book is as welcome as was the original. The dilemmas, delights, and challenges experienced by a practitioner entering a family home are again set forth recognizably and articulately. This basic, yet sophisticated, primer will be of great value to anyone attempting work with parents and their young children in a home-visiting model. Whether the reader is an occupational therapist, a childhood educator, a mental health professional, or a professional from another background, this book—overall and in specific chapters—makes welcome contributions to understanding the complex nature of home visiting. It addresses the expected struggles involved in learning how to do this work well and comfortably.

The continuing need for services that support families is often met through home visiting. In this new edition, Dr. Klass expands considerably on descriptions of the many aspects of environments, situations, and internal and external stressors that place young children and their families at risk. The material presented is wide-ranging and includes discussion of such disparate things as maternal depression, drug exposure and drug use, community and domestic violence, parental discord and absence, general societal toxicity, and other obstacles to a child's optimal development. These are important variables of which practitioners need to be aware.

The numbers of children developing in such vulnerable environments grow larger, while economic support for the services they need shrinks. This is true despite the fact that research since the 1970s has made it abundantly clear that the experiences infants and toddlers have within their caregiving relationships and within the social and cultural contexts in which their families are embedded make crucial contributions to their development, affecting their developing sense of self and sense of others, their internal beliefs and values, their general competencies, and their sense of possibility. Children developing in stressful, unresponsive, understimulating, or violent environments, whose parents must struggle to achieve any sense of stability for their family, require many kinds of services. Offering needed services competently can enhance and shift the climate of relationships within which the child grows and even some aspects of the environment in which the family is embedded. These services constitute a serious and hopeful response to infants', toddlers', and parents' personal needs; community needs; national needs; and overarching human needs.

The most promising and frequent effort offered to meet this need has been home visiting programs that are universally accessible and programs that serve at-risk families. They are designed to nurture, educate, treat, support, and care about young children and their families. Healthy Start, Even Start, Smart Start, and Early Start programs of various kinds with different goals are reaching into communities across the country. The rapid proliferation of these programs highlights the need to support and promote their best functioning. Home visitors—with a range of motivations, skills, supports, training, and knowledge—are central in providing these services. Whatever the explicit goals of these programs, and they are myriad, all are devoted to working with parents to make positive differences in their lives and the lives of their small children. At its best, the work is intended to create a personal world and way of relating that is more positive and rewarding for parent and child than existed when the visitor first entered their lives.

This book speaks to all of these different practitioners with their particular goals and illuminates what they have in common, including challenges. Both in overall concept and in revealing, detailed vignettes, Dr. Klass has something useful, insightful, or practical to say. Whether she is focusing on the complexities of parent–child–visitor relationships or on child development, the book is clear and useful. Her chapters on child development are models. They present developmental progression from the point of view of both the child and the parent. She shows simultaneously what each emerging level of development in an area means to the child's skills, understanding, and sense of self and what each emerging developmental level might mean to, demand of, enrage, or engage the parent.

As she describes aspects of the mutual experience of parent, child, and home visitor, Dr. Klass thoughtfully describes the repeated dilemmas posed to the home visitor. She understands the simultaneous and sometimes conflicting needs of all the parties, including the home visitor. How can the home visitor attend effectively to both mother and child, and how can the home visitor support the efforts of the mother to do the same with the home visitor and the child? Dr. Klass's insights are complemented by practical ideas on how to solve such dilemmas. This perspective is threaded throughout the book and simultaneously acknowledges the difficulty of the work and offers help.

This updated edition specifically expands the discussion of culture, particularly as it shapes families' beliefs and values and the many important ways these values and beliefs are expressed. It emphasizes the need to recognize and acknowledge the roots of difference and an appreciation of these differences. Discussions of ethnicity, economic status, cultural transition, and the definitions of *family* and *role* are among the many aspects of diversity included. All of these inform, but also underline, the need for home visitors not only to appreciate these things in others but to become highly aware of their own often unarticulated systems of belief.

Dr. Klass's book stems from her more than 30 years of experience with young children and their various caregivers, from her supervision in a variety of programs, and from her ability to make keen observations. It stems as well from her splendid knowledge of infant-toddler development and infant–parent interaction; from her thoughtful understanding and articulation of the experiences of doing this work; and from her careful analysis of the complex relationships between the parent(s), the child, and the home visitor. She uses this understanding of the relationship context to portray in vivid and useful ways the many aspects of the parent–home visitor relationship. She does this skillfully enough that the book is relevant to the beginner with little specialized training and also to those professionally trained in some or many of the required skills.

The book is coherent and flows from the author's understanding of well-researched bodies of knowledge. It represents as well a useful distillation of a wide range of thinking about supportive therapy, interpretive therapy, and therapeutic intervention. The same useful distillation is true for the book's developmental material.

Dr. Klass offers an opportunity for practitioners to reflect on what they do and why and how they might do it better in a wholly engaging and available form. Her informed perspective also stresses the need for the clarification of limits and possibilities of what a particular home visitor should feel reasonably responsible for and competent to provide in terms of skills, training, and goals.

Overall, Dr. Klass's book offers a source of understanding, knowledge, and support to home visitors. At the same time, it offers a model for how seriously and carefully the role of the home visitor must be conceptualized, delimited, and supported by supervision. It is only by being as thorough and as careful about home visiting as Dr. Klass is that these efforts can be of as much benefit as possible and do no harm.

This new edition will not only prove useful to individual practitioners but also contribute to the spirited discussion in this burgeoning field. It is a strong voice for the need to provide appropriate, ongoing, thorough training; a sound knowledge base; and the crucially necessary supervisory support to the home visitor working with children and their families.

The work of helping parents and children find new strengths, new hopes, and new possibilities could not be more important. It needs to be treated as well and as seriously in the world as it is in this book.

Jeree H. Pawl, Ph.D.
Former Director
Infant-Parent Program
University of California,
San Francisco

Preface

Kaon arrives at the home of Jamal, age 13 months, who lives with his mother, Djuanna. This is Kaon's second year as a home visitor for Jamal and Djuanna. Kaon takes Jamal's file, which lists his birth date and his mother's name on the outside. In her bag, Kaon has two hard-paged books, a canister with a slit on its top, and two dozen poker chips.

As Kaon walks toward this family's front door, she thinks about her plans and wonders if Djuanna has settled her dispute with her mother-in-law. Will she once again need to use time in this visit to process this dispute? She knows that no matter how carefully she has planned this visit, she cannot anticipate what will happen until after she enters that front door. She sees Djuanna peeking from the living room curtain as she walks toward the front door.

Experienced home visitors know that each home visit is unique. In fact, with the same family, each visit is different from the last one. They know that their consistent challenge is to balance their interactions with the parents and with the child or children. They also know that family events between visits may be positive and productive but may also be problematic. The parent might need to process these events instead of focusing on the child's development. Some parents and children live in extended families, so a grandparent or sibling might join the visit. If a family has multiple stresses, home visitors do not know if anyone will be home when they arrive. Kaon likes her job. She likes that home visiting can be messy and unpredictable but knows that she makes a difference in families and their children's future.

As I wrote this book, my aim was to try to make sense of the ever-changing, complex nature of the home visitor's work. I wanted to demonstrate how over time, home visitors can develop close, personal relationships with parents and, in fact, make a difference in the lives of young children and their families. I have been very fortunate to have spent several years working with talented home visitors who I repeatedly observed and interviewed both informally and formally. This book is grounded in several years of home visits, interviews with home visitors and parents, extensive reading in child development theory and literature on home visitors, and my own professional experience in the field of child development.

I use a developmental frame to guide the discussion in this book. Five assumptions are central to home visiting. First and most important is that development occurs within and through relationships. Babies and young children develop within their relationships with their parents. When home visitors are effective, parent development also occurs within the relationship with the home visitor.

Second, all relationships involve mutuality. Parents influence their young children, and their children influence them. Home visitors influence parents, and parents also influence home visitors. A mother's soft voice soothes her baby, and her baby's smile and cooing stimulates her to sing softly. A home visitor's support and guidance may encourage a parent to give her toddler some clear limits, and the parent's success may give the home visitor confidence to initiate new topics.

Third, young children develop as a whole. There is unity in development. No developmental realm—communicative, cognitive, social-emotional, physical, moral, or spiritual—can be understood apart from other realms. Development is an integrated process. Each domain of development has significant implications for development in other domains.

Fourth, development is characterized by increasing complexity and qualitative change. As babies and young children develop, new and more complex behavior builds on previous behavior. Development is not linear. Rather, qualitative changes in development occur. For example, at 3 months, babies begin to coo, smile, and have extended periods of alertness; between 7 and 9 months, babies share attention and intention—they experience intersubjectivity.

Finally, child and parent development are intertwined with their social environment beyond the family.[1] Friends and relatives, neighborhood and workplace, child care center, local community resources, and national economy and policy all have an impact on the everyday life of young families. Thus, an effective home visitor's perspective includes not only the specific family visited but also the family's informal and formal support systems.

As I was writing the second edition of this book, I realized how much of my own professional history was coming into play. Since the mid-1960s, I have helped adults in their work with babies and young children in several roles and programs. Working with parents, teachers, family child care providers, and home visitors, I have had the opportunity to observe the subtleties and complexities of adults' everyday interactions with young children. As I reflected on what I observed, I began to understand the meanings of these ever-changing interactions. I have seen wide differences, but along with these differences, I have seen commonalities in patterns of adult–child interactions across contexts.

Since the late 1970s, I have combined work with parents, child care providers, and teachers with qualitative research, much of which has focused on adult–child interactions. When I conducted a participant observation case study of child care programs, I found that patterns of child care teachers' interactions with young children emphasized individual as opposed to social learning and, on a small scale, reproduced our nation's ethic of individualism.[2] In an early intervention program for the Illinois Department of Children and Family services, I hired and provided ongoing training in rural counties and factory towns to women, who, in their homes, cared for babies and young children at risk of maltreatment. In this project, I found that I could understand how the life history of talented family child care staff intersected with their skill in relating to young children.[3]

In 1988, as research coordinator for the Parents as Teachers (PAT) national center, I began observing several PAT home visitors conduct home visits and wrote a case study on the parent educator's role.[4] That was the beginning of the work that led directly to this book. When I left PAT, I took a job as an early intervention specialist at a children's hospital. I helped child care providers and parents of young children who had behavior difficulties at home and in the classroom. In my work with parents and child care providers, I learned that the taken-for-granted daily routines and adult–child interactions could be adapted so that young children could succeed. As I revised this book for the second edition, I participated in reflective one-to-one supervision with urban child care providers of children 2 weeks to 3 years old. I never get tired of observing and assisting adults learning to interact meaningfully with children in ways that may influence the children's developmental potential.

In all these positions, I have shuttled back and forth between scholarly literature and my own clinical experience and research. Core themes have been relationship, child and parent development, and the complex interplay between child development, parent development, and the social environment. As I read scholarly work, I could see the ideas being worked out in the nitty-gritty reality of parenting and early education. Problems that perplexed parents, child care providers, and home visitors were addressed in scholarly literature, but I found that scholarly information usually was not easily accessible to parents or people in early education

I have tried to integrate my clinical and research experience, developmental theory and research, and the everyday encounters between young children, home visitors, and parents. If I am successful, home visitors will be able to see themselves in some of the vignettes and learn new ways to understand and practice home visiting.

NOTES

1. Current literature uses the term *ecological* to describe the reciprocal relationship between people and their environment. Bronfenbrenner, Garbarino, and Cochran have each conducted extensive research on the interplay of child and parent development, and multiplelevels of environement—personal, community, and national. Bronfenbrenner, 1979; Cochran, Larner, Riley, Gunnarsson, & Henderson, 1990; Garbarino, 1992; Garbarino, Dubro, Kostelny, & Pardo, 1992.

2. Klass, 1986, pp. 99–117.

3. Klass, 1985.

4. Klass, 1990.

REFERENCES

Bronfenbrenner, U. (1979). *The ecology of human development: Experiments by nature and design.* Cambridge, MA: Harvard University Press.

Cochran, M., Larner, M., Riley, D., Gunnarsson, L., & Henderson, C.R., Jr. (1990). *Extending families: The social networks of parents and their children.* New York: Cambridge University Press.

Garbarino, J. (1992). *Children and families in the social environment.* New York: Aldine de Gruytyer.

Garbarino, J., Dubrow, N., Kostelny, K., & Pardo, C. (1992). *Children in danger: Coping with the consequences of community violence.* San Francisco: Jossey-Bass.

Klass, C.S. (1985). *A profile of caregiving: Life history interviews of family day care providers.* Paper presented at the American Education Research Association annual meeting, New Orleans.

Klass, C.S. (1986). *The autonomous child: Day care and the transmission of values.* London: The Falmer Press.

Klass, C.S. (1990). *Anotomy of the personal visit: A case study of the Missouri Parents as Teachers Program.* St. Louis: The Missouri Parents as Teachers National Center.

Acknowledgments

I am very grateful for the emotional and cognitive support that my husband, sons, and close friends gave me as I was writing this book revision. My husband, Dennis E. Klass, initially edited each chapter and, before my final revisions, once again read and edited each chapter. Dennis helped me speak more directly and clearly.

I also appreciate the assistance that Jessica Allan, my acquisitions editor, gave me during all phases of my work on this revision.

To my very close friend
Marion M. Wilson
1927–2002

Marion was a teacher, coordinator, and administrator for 48 years in a multi-racial, consolidated school district. During her last 25 years, she was director of early education. She led more than 100 early educators in multiple programs that she initiated. For example, in the early 1970s, she initiated the first preschool in a public school system in the United States and one of the first early childhood special education programs in St. Louis.

Marion was a reader for the first edition of this home visiting guidebook. She urged me to speak more strongly about the negative aspects of home visiting. With her guidance, I ended each chapter with a section on "difficulties and dilemmas."

Marion died as the type was being set for this edition.

Introduction

Marquisha is a 39-year-old mother of six children, ages 3–21 years. I interviewed her after she had completed 2 years in Even Start. During these 2 years, her home visitor, Cynthia, visited her and her children twice a month. Marquisha was deeply affected by her experience with Cynthia and told me the following.

> The home visiting program has made a wonderful difference in how I feel about myself. Talking to Cynthia, she treats you like a bigger sister, more or less, like your friend. She's just like the big sister I never had. Talking to her, I can talk about my problems if I'm going through any problems. I know Cynthia respects me and cares a lot. I told her, "You know something, I needed somebody a long time ago that cared about me the way you care about me. Care enough to boost me up instead of letting me down." Cynthia is a person you can talk to because she's looking at you. You can see that she is understanding your feelings from the expression that she shows, that she really cares. A person that you can look straight in the face and talk to. You know, when I talk to people, I don't hold my head down. Cynthia is a person you can look at, talk to because she's looking at you. You can see that she really cares. I had never really met nobody that cares about me, other than my mother. I knew my mother loved me and everything else. I knew she loved me with all her heart—but a person that I can talk to and tell my problems to, Cynthia knows how to answer me. Maybe it's not everything I want to hear, but I know what Cynthia's saying is true.
>
> Before this program, I mean, I had little reason to live. I was just like in my bed all the time, just grogging around. Then, I signed up for this program with Cynthia. If it wasn't for Cynthia, I'm telling you, I wouldn't have a business. The day Cynthia walked in that door, I still think about it. I mean, even when I'm laying down sometimes at night, I think if Cynthia had never come, I would never be where I'm at right now. I look at Cynthia sometimes and say, "Boy, that is a woman!" Made a big difference in my life, and for my kids, for every last one of them. I love the way my kids love to play with Cynthia. I learn something about my kids every time she comes over. And my 3-year-old says, "Come on Mom, let's play like Cynthia did." I'm learning every day.

Later, I told Cynthia how Marquisha had said that she was an important person in her and her children's lives. "Yes," Cynthia replied, "She often tells me that. And I know that Marquisha is probably one of the two people in my life that I truly have influenced in a way that allowed them to make dramatic changes." Cynthia knows that very few of her families will respond as dramatically as did Marquisha. She said that it is harder to know what her visits mean to some people. But she does know that she is making a difference.

This book is about home visiting, an evolving profession in which adults strive to assist other adults in improving their everyday family lives. Modern home visiting began in the 1960s as one part of America's "war on poverty." In the early 1960s, child development research gave evidence that the first 5 years of life are the years of most rapid intellectual development and have great consequences for later development. Developmental literature moved from a uni-dimensional focus on the child's development to a bi-directional focus on parent and child. At the same time, literature on cultural deprivation claimed that our nation's poverty cycle might be broken by compensatory education that would allow children living in poverty to be better prepared for schooling. This social science literature coincided with the civil rights movement and President Johnson's anti-poverty political agenda. Federal assistance became available for impoverished families with young children in the form of federal grants to states for child care programs, Head Start, and early intervention programs.[1] Home visiting became a central program component of early intervention programs such as the Child and Family Resource Program sponsored by the Administration for Children, Youth and Families; Ira Gordon's Home Learning Center Approach to Early Stimulation in Gainesville, Florida; and David Weikart's Ypsilanti Perry Preschool Project in Ypsilanti, Michigan.

The 1970s brought a marked increase in single-parent homes, teenage parenting, and employed mothers of children younger than age 6. As a response to qualitative changes in social values, economic realities, and changes in the traditional family, family support programs have grown across the United States.[2] Home visiting became a primary means of service delivery in many of these programs. Most home visiting programs have the child as their primary focus and have prevention and intervention goals such as preventing low birth weight newborns, preventing child abuse and neglect, promoting healthy child development, and improving school readiness.

Although home visiting is a relatively new profession, it was a part of earlier United States history. The latter half of the 19th century was marked by increasing industrialization, massive European immigration to America, and rapid urbanization. As a response to this immigration and urbanization, settlement houses emerged and developed programs to support the family. Settlement houses were one of the first movements of the Progressive era. Wealthy women raised funds for these centers. Supervised matrons who maintained day nurseries regularly visited children's homes and taught night classes in English, homemaking skills, and child care. The settlement house programs were the beginning of America's family support movement, dedicated to socializing recent immigrants to normative American values of middle class family life.

By the beginning of the 20th century, the hallmark of the Progressive era was social reform. The first White House Conference on Children in 1909 was part of this movement toward social reform. G. Stanley Hall had begun the child study movement, and Hall's ideas were integrated into the newly begun Parent–Teacher Associations (PTAs). When they began, PTAs primarily focused on parent education. In the 1920s, with the popularization of the progressive education theory of Dewey and the psychological theories of Freud, Gesell, and Watson, parent education flourished. As parent education expanded, family support for immigrants declined. The 1920s also was the decade when nursery schools, which embraced parent education, were begun for middle class children. Until the 1970s, parent education focused on current social scientific theory; parent educators were experts teaching parents what was needed if parents were to raise successful children.

Today, our theory is different. We recognize that parents are the experts about their own children and that effective home visiting is a partnership between professional and parent, not the expert teaching the parent.

APPROACH

This book attempts to portray the complexity and the developmental possibilities in home visiting. Home visiting programs vary according to the population served, the program agenda, the strategies used to implement the agenda, the intensity and duration of service, and the types of people who conduct the home visits.[3] The vast majority of home visiting programs are primarily prevention-oriented and serve families with children, from pregnancy through age 5 years. This book discusses home visiting that helps parents to understand child development and to develop appropriate parenting skills. Home visiting programs with other goals can benefit from many parts of this book, especially the first three and last two chapters.

This book integrates theory and research from the field of infant mental health. Charles and Paula Zeanah identified several key concepts in infant mental health.

• Multiple interrelated contexts within which infants develop

• Process and content of infant development

• Risk and protective factors as they impact developmental trajectories

- Infant psychopathology
- Social competence and resilience[4]

Emde (2000) wrote of two important perspectives on the developmental contexts for infant mental health.

First, we must think about infant mental health in terms of the development of competencies. It involves, for example, increasingly organized complexity in the acquisition of abilities to learn and to accumulate knowledge, to regulate one's emotions, and to build social skills within relationships. It also involves the child's ability to gain satisfaction during exploration, social exchanges, and play. Second, we must think about infant mental health in terms of successful adaptation in the midst of challenges and opportunities. Successful behavioral adaptation involves the ability to respond meaningfully to changing circumstances across time—simply put, the ability to be flexible.[5]

These key concepts and perspectives are prevalent in this book.

Quality programs are family centered because they believe that parents are the true experts regarding their child's and their family's needs. Families are treated with dignity and respected as implementers strive to create partnerships with parents. When programs can be community-based, they are delivered in both physical and psychological proximity to where young children live. Effective programs coordinate their services with those of other agencies and organizations in the community.

This book is designed for home visitors and those adults involved in supervision, pre-service, and in-service professional development of home visitors. I have tried to write this book in a manner in which home visitors can see themselves in the vignettes and conversations with home visitors; the vignettes illustrate the key ideas and practices discussed. As readers understand the home visitors whose work is described in the book, they may understand themselves better. Many of the vignettes are based on my extended study of one home visitor, Janice. For 2 years, I observed Janice as she completed monthly home visits with two families. Then, for 2 additional years, I observed her as she conducted home visits with three additional families. Please note that the vignettes are taken from interviews conducted in the early 1990s and may not always reflect current terminology and practices.

As I began writing this book, I also began working with Cynthia, the director of an Even Start program. Cynthia also is an exceptionally skilled and insightful home visitor, and I have included vignettes from my work with Cynthia, primarily in the first two chapters.

Because I have been engaged in professional development of adults since the 1980s, I am aware that one learns best when highly skilled models are available to the learner. Janice and Cynthia are exemplary home visitors whom I believe can make the home visiting process most clear. I have observed many other home visitors, not all of whom are as skilled as Janice and Cynthia. Some vignettes in the book depict additional home visitors, and some vignettes depict child care providers or other caregivers with whom I have studied in the past. Everyone can learn to improve his or her understanding and skill.

Home visiting can be unpredictable, messy, difficult work. Some families are not able to relate to friendly home visitors, whether they are professional or paraprofessional home visitors. Both Janice and Cynthia have had families in their caseloads who refused home visits, and each has experienced an array of struggles with families that remain in their program. Success is not a given, even for experienced, talented home visitors. Though I did not witness these struggles, these women's descriptions of some of these difficulties are included in this book. In addition, each chapter ends with a description of difficulties and dilemmas that home visitors may encounter in their work.

Parents as Teachers (PAT) is a partnership between home and school that is based on the belief that experiences in the early years are critical in laying the foundation for later school success. PAT aims to support parents in their role as their child's first and most influential teacher. In my home state of Missouri, the legislature has mandated and appropriated funds for each of the 543 school districts to serve 40% of district families with children who are birth to 3 years. PAT is a universally accessible nondeficit program. The program entails regularly scheduled home visits by trained parent educators, group meetings with other parents, periodic monitoring, and formal developmental screening of children from birth to 36 months.

In the United States, a large proportion of home visiting programs serve at-risk families such as low-income families and teen parents. This book primarily discusses home visiting for all families, for our basic assumption is that the primary principles and approaches of home visiting are the same for everyone, across social class, age, ethnicity, or any other distinguishing characteristic of a family. For example, effective home visitors show respect, develop rapport, empathically listen, and support every family with whom they work. I acknowledge that the home visitor's task often becomes more complex and challenging when working with families with multiple, complex problems, a pattern that occurs with greater frequency in low-income, teen, and minority families. I address these complexities as part of the first chapter on parent–home visitor relationships and the second chapter on home visiting approaches. In addition, chapters in Section I and II end with a discussion of difficulties and dilemmas that home visitors experience. Home visitors can experience these difficulties and dilemmas with any family; however, not surprisingly, they will confront many of these challenges more often with at-risk families.

OVERVIEW OF TOPICS

Section I, Home Visiting: The Basics, focuses on the complexities of the home visitor role. The first chapter, The Parent–Home Visitor Relationship, discusses the relationship between the parent and the home visitor, which is the scaffolding that makes it possible for parents to gain new understanding of their child and to strengthen their parenting practices through their home visiting experience. Chapter 2, The Home Visitor's Approach, discusses two levels of skills needed for effective home visiting. First, the chapter discusses communication and interpersonal skills that encourage, maintain, and promote the parent–home visitor relationship. The later portion of this chapter examines the complexities and difficulties of working with families at greatest risk in our society— minority, low-income, and teen families. The chapter also examines a collection of knowledge and skills that are less process-oriented, but essential to the home visiting process.

In Chapter 3, Working with Diverse Families, I discuss effective home visiting with culturally diverse families. After defining the meaning of culture, race, and ethnicity, I discuss ethnic differences, bilingual families, poverty, and difficulties and dilemmas in working with this population.

Because my professional work over the past 25 years has been mainly with Caucasian and African American families, I have limited my discussion of minority families to African Americans, but home visiting programs can support families of all populations. Because of the target population with whom I have worked, the people discussed in this book are primarily urban and suburban families; however, home visiting is a needed form of family support in rural areas, as well.

Chapter 4, Professional Development, ends Section I with a discussion of ways in which home visitors can gain greater knowledge, understanding, and skill. Professional education and supervision are discussed as contexts for gaining new knowledge, understanding, and reflection on one's practice, individually and through sharing with peers, mentors, and supervisors.

Section II, Promoting Healthy Parent and Child Development, covers the topics that home visitors find most important for effective home visiting to occur. The discussion has a developmental thrust, for regardless of program agenda, every home visitor of families with young children needs a strong developmental knowledge base. At the same time, not all areas of development are detailed, for there are many excellent child development texts available.

The organization of Chapters 5–8 is three tiered. First, the chapters trace child development from birth to 5 years. Then, the chapters discuss appropriate understanding and parenting skills, and finally, how home visitors can promote parents' understanding of their children and appropriate parenting practices. Chapter 5, Developing a Sense of Self: The Foundation of Social and Emotional Development, discusses how sense of self encompasses social and emotional development and affects all other developmental areas.

Once their infant becomes a toddler, parents often are most interested in talking about guidance and discipline, the topic of Chapter 6. Mundane, everyday routines often are the setting for many parents' difficulties in guidance and discipline, yet it is an area that often is taken for granted and unexamined. Chapter 7, Communication and Language, examines how children learn to talk and communicate. Chapter 8, Play, Learning, and Development, explains how play is the primary way of learning for infants and young children.

Section II continues with a discussion of routines, rituals, and celebrations in Chapter 9 and sibling relationships in Chapter 10. Chapter 11 discusses salient factors that cause a family to be psychologically vulnerable: marital discord, separation and divorce, mother's mental illness, domestic and community violence, and child maltreatment. Patterns of parent action as well as family dynamics as they affect young children are discussed. There is also a discussion of resilient children.

Section III, Person and Profession, asks the question: What kind of people are these home visitors? In my work, I consistently find that very skilled professionals often are people who experience their work life as being very meaningful, who express themselves creatively in their work; and interestingly, their work often intersects with dominant strands of their childhood history. Chapter 12 briefly portrays themes that characterize the personal history of Janice and Cynthia, two PAT home visitors, their values and attitudes, and the meaning they find in their work.

Working with caregivers of infants and young children has helped me to better understand the subtle, ever-changing nature of early development and the caregiving process. Throughout this book, I have tried to be mindful of how young children, parents, and home visitors each are developing, and in turn, how each can influence the other's development. I designed this book to be useful to home visitors, their supervisors, and teachers. At the same time, I know that the discussion is not complete. I hope that it can be a useful step in the growth of an evolving profession in our society.

NOTES

1. Lazar and Darlington provided an overview of early intervention programs of the 1960s and 1970s and of accompanying research on these programs. Lazar & Darlington, 1982.

2. Weissbourd provided a provocative overview of traditional parent education and a history of the development of family support programs. Weisbourd, 1987.

3. Varying dimensions of home visiting and different types of programming were discussed in Behrman, 1993.

4. Zeanah & Zeanah, 2001, p. 14.

5. Emde, 2000, p. 22.

REFERENCES

Behrman, R.E. (Ed.). (1993). *Home visiting: The future of our children*. Los Altos, CA: Center for the Future of Children, David and Lucile Packard Foundation.

Emde, R.N. (2001). A developmental psychiatrist looks at infant mental health challenges for Early Head Start: Understanding context and overcoming avoidance, *Zero to Three, 22*(1), 21–24.

Lazar, I., & Darlington, R. (1982). Lasting effects of early education: A report from the Consortium for Longitudinal Studies, *Monographs of the Society for Research in Child Development, 47*(2, Serial No. 195), 2–3.

Weissbourd, B. (1987). A brief history of family support programs. In S.L. Kagan, D.P. Powell, B. Weissbourd, & E.F. Zigler (Eds.), *America's family support programs* (pp. 38–56). New Haven, CT: Yale University Press.

Zeanah, C.H., & Zeanah, P.D. (2001). Towards a definition of infant mental health. *Zero to Three, 22*(1), 13–20.

I

Home Visiting

The Basics

1

The Parent–Home Visitor Relationship

The true community does not arise through people's having feelings for one another (though indeed not without it), but through first, their taking their stand in living in mutual relations with a living Center, and second, their being in living mutual relation with one another.

Martin Buber (1923/1958, p. 45)

At the core of home visiting is the relationship between parents and the home visitor. This chapter examines components of the parent–home visitor relationship that maximize the chances for promoting parent development. In turn, the parents' development enhances their relationship with the child, which is the foundation for the child's development. A basic premise of this book is that development occurs both through and within the relationship—which consists of patterns of interaction over time. Just as the everyday patterns of parent–child interaction are the most powerful influences on baby and child development, so, too, the parent–home visitor relationship is pivotal to parent development.

A central characteristic within the parent–child relationship and the parent–home visitor relationship is that each person influences the other at every moment and in important ways over time. The central characteristic of these relationships is *mutuality*, also termed *reciprocity*.[1] What A does influences B, and what B does influences A. For example, when a young baby is very irritable and difficult to sooth, the parent's feelings of competency are affected, which in turn can decrease the parent's ability to provide calm, warm, loving care. Then, the baby feels the parent's tension and becomes more irritable. Thus, the cycle continues.

The parent–home visitor relationship is dynamic; it varies both in nature and in effect as a result of the personal characteristics of the parents and the home visitor and the dynamics of the larger environment. The personality, values, and attitudes of the parents and home visitor affect their relationship. Furthermore, the parent–home visitor relationship is influenced by characteristics of larger social systems, such as the parents' neighborhood and the race, ethnicity, schooling, and social class of the parents and the home visitor.[2] All of these factors are at work as the parents and home visitor co-create their relationship.

This chapter first discusses key elements in forming the parent–home visitor relationship. Second, the chapter examines the progression of the relationship. Third, it discusses the meaning and significance of the personal relationship for the parent. Finally, it explores dimensions of home visitors' relationships with teenage parents.

FORMING THE PARENT–HOME VISITOR RELATIONSHIP

In home visitors' work with a family, four elements are central. In good home visiting, these elements are made explicit in initial contacts with a family:

1. *Expectations:* In forming a relationship, home visitors discuss with parents their expectations and the parents' expectations.

2. *Agenda:* Home visitors describe what they want to do with the parent and the child.

3. *Roles:* In the initial phase of home visiting, home visitors and parents clarify their roles—those behaviors associated with the specific roles of parent and home visitor in their relationship.

4. *Setting:* The setting of a home visitor's work in the parents' personal space raises issues different from other work settings such as an office, classroom, or clinic.

Expectations: Parent and Home Visitor

All relationships include expectations of ourselves and of other people. At the outset, it is important for home visitors to state clearly their expectations and to invite parents to share theirs. The home visitor's role is fairly new in our society, so what people think might happen during and after the visit can be ambiguous; thus, it is helpful for the home visitor and parent to say explicitly what each expects. Expectations are multiple. The home visitor asks, "What do I expect of myself, what do I expect of the parent, and what do I think the parent expects of me?" And the parents ask, "What do I expect of myself, what do I expect of the home visitor, and what do I think the home visitor expects of me?" Intertwined with these expectations are the parents' and home visitor's expectations for the child and what will happen to the child as a result of their work together.

A big area of a person's expectation in this relationship is expertise and authority. Sometimes home visitors and parents may have different ideas about where the authority lies. In the family support programs described in this book, the home visitor assumes that parents are the experts in their child's development and aims to support, affirm, and promote the parents' relationship with their child. Some parents, however, may assume that the home visitor is the expert and is coming into their home to teach them the right way to parent. In other words, parents may give total authority to their home visitor as teacher and put themselves in a subordinate role. This expectation violates the kind of relationship that makes the parent—home visitor partnership work. In these situations, it is not the task of home visitors to challenge the parents' expectations; however, home visitors do not have to accept the authority that the parents project onto them. Rather, home visitors may need to adjust their approach—for example, by being very specific about goals and the approach to take and trusting that, over time, the parents' experiences in working together with the home visitor will influence the parents' original expectations.

During the initial phase of home visiting, the home visitor can encourage parents to express their expectations for their baby or child and talk about their priorities regarding their child's behavior and skills. It also can be helpful to ask specifically how parents would like to use their time with their home visitor. The home visitor can use what the parents say to establish rapport and to build a partnership with the parents. Some parents' goals or priorities may seem developmentally unrealistic, and home visitors can discuss these issues with the parents in an open and respectful manner as they share developmental information. Within these discussions, the home visitor can communicate clearly that parents are always the decision makers in matters about their child. Home visitors also need to ensure that parents know that all conversation during a home visit is confidential.

Because the home visitor's role is ambiguous, many parents enter the relationship with uncertainties. Some parents have little experience with opening their home to others. They may worry about their privacy being violated or about the adequacy of their home being judged. Sally is a young mother with learning disabilities who joined Even Start (a family support program) when her son was 3 months old. Sally was in and out of juvenile detention centers as an adolescent and quit school in the eighth grade. Given her troubled background in her family of origin and adolescence, she had misgivings about being visited at her home. She shared her concerns about her adequacy as a parent with her home visitor.

> It's hard to explain. I was a first-time mother, and I was real nervous. I mean, I babysat and stuff like that, but I never had a baby for 24 hours a day. I didn't know if I'd do things right. I used to think I was bad and couldn't do it. I could never raise a child. But just being in the program, I think I am as good as any parent, maybe even better than some.

Similarly, Rob, a parent in a Parents as Teachers (PAT) Program, expressed his initial wariness of the home visiting program:

> I was just skeptical. I don't know. Probably because I work with the fire department, and it is involved with school districts. And I'm just skeptical about your tax dollar . . . .Is this just another program to get more employment for the school district staff? And I'd have to schedule being home during the visits, and I thought that might be a pain to do.

Because parents initially may have uncertainties, home visitors need to clearly state their purpose and expectations and invite parents to share their expectations to help parents to gain confidence in themselves and in this new experience. Knowing that parents may be expecting a report card, home visitors can look for opportunities to praise a parent and child.

Experienced home visitors are confident. They trust the power of the process of developing the relationship. When beginning in this role, however, home visitors also may have uncertainties. The comments of Janice and Lynette, two home visitors in a PAT program, illustrate initial discomforts and developing skills. Janice said,

> It is always difficult to begin a relationship, no matter how long you have been doing this, no matter how comfortable you feel with all the families you have been serving over the years. Your heart beats a little faster when you walk into someone's home for the first time because you want to be accepted by them, and you are never sure what it is going to take to have that happen. When I first began, I was a motor mouth, but in the past couple of years, I've learned that it is okay to have quiet time when no conversation is going on between the parent and me, or between the child and me. And this helps the parent feel a sense of calm. And when they feel that you are calm with whatever is going on in their family, they feel more calm about what is going on—for example, being calm when the baby starts crying or the toddler starts being negative. If we act like this is something we expect kids to do, that it's no big deal, then the parent does not feel embarrassed and nervous about it. [Of all] the changes we have felt [the most important is] one of comfort with what we are doing—our own self-confidence.

Before the birth of Janice's children, she taught third grade. Given the newness of the home visitor role when she started, Janice's own expectations were not very clear. She did not have the self-confidence that she had in her teaching, where she knew what she was supposed to do. With experience, she began to understand her relationships with parents and to trust her skills. Then, she could maintain a slower, calmer pace during her home visits. Lynette also changed with experience:

> Since I had been a kindergarten teacher, I knew I was comfortable with the kids. So at first, I would "fill the time" in play activities with the child. And I know that sometimes we feel like we are expected to go in there and tell the answers. And at first, I thought I needed to have the answers, since that was expected of me.

Home visitors bring their prior work experiences into their new role as home visitor, and this influences their interactions with parents. All adults experience uncertainty in new occupations, and home visiting is no exception. Having a clear understanding of the program agenda and the tasks involved assists the home visitor's transition into this new role.

The Agenda: What Is My Job?

Among the first tasks of home visitors is to understand clearly the agenda of the program in which they work. The program agenda varies with the population being served and within the overall agenda of the agency or institution, and whether professionals or paraprofessionals do the home visiting.[3] Is the program universally accessible? Is it for teenage parents only? Is it for parents with low incomes who are at risk? Is it for families with low birth weight babies? Is the agenda primarily to lessen existing difficulties or to prevent the occurrence of problems? Possible agendas might be to promote the health of babies and young children, to ensure the child's physical and psychological safety, to promote the cognitive skills of at-risk children in low-income families, to help parents develop an understanding of child development and appropriate parenting skills, and to work toward prevention of child abuse and neglect. Still, regardless of the agenda, nothing can be accomplished until a trusting relationship is formed.

Within program agendas, the home visitor chooses activities determined by a continuum of priorities ranging from giving information, to understanding how a family is doing, to deciding what resources can be brought to bear, to being a surrogate parent to a teenage mother. Competent home visitors know their agenda when they are in the home. It is impossible to pay attention to everything. Home visitor Janice explains her goals and the agenda that she sees as basic to her work.

> I think parents appreciate someone coming in who sees lots of children the age of theirs and who can help them be objective, but who also helps them appreciate that these are really great kids. And even though they are great, I think parents want to be sure that they are great. Parents also appreciate the screening we do and knowing appropriate kinds of things for themselves and their children to do—things that will maintain their children's interest, things that nurture their development without pushing. I think they really are looking for appropriate ways to nurture their child.

Janice understands that parents can take in information when they are affirmed, and the strongest affirmation is taking pleasure in their child.

Respective Roles: Who Is Responsible for What?

In forming a relationship with parents, home visitors try to ensure that parents understand the behaviors associated with the roles of home visitor and parent. The most important dynamic of family support programs is developing mutual respect and partnership between parents and home visitors. Historically, parent education put the parent educator in the role of expert directing the parent. In contrast, the home visitor in family support programs is an empathic listener, consultant, resource, guide, advocate, and partner. For example, in the traditional parent education model, the professional chooses a topic such as sleeping and then lectures on appropriate parenting practices to promote healthy sleep patterns in the child.[4] The modern home visitor first learns how the baby or young child is sleeping and how the parent assists the child's sleep. Then, the home visitor shares developmental information and possible parenting strategies as related to the lived experience of the parents and child. The topic may be the home visitor's or the parents' choice. The directives of traditional parent education are replaced in home visiting by joint problem solving—a working alliance. Parents are the experts in their children's development, active participants in home visits, and the final decision makers with regard to nurturing their children. Home visiting is a helping relationship defined by collaboration between the home visitor and the parents.

Competent home visitors work on two levels. They are completely engaged in interactions with the parents and child while they track the process; that is, they observe the interactions during the visit and are aware of their own reactions and feelings. Sometimes unpredictable intrusions within a visit can be very difficult to manage. When home visitors can relate to the family and simultaneously be aware of their own feelings and make decisions based on these feelings, they are more likely to be successful. Cynthia illustrates this concept of working on two levels:

> For over 2 years, I have been working with Marquisha and her large family, her sister, and [between them] their 12 children, between 2 and 22 years old. I was sitting on the couch with Marquisha. Her 18-year-old daughter [Rashonda] stood next to us with several envelopes in her hand. She took the envelopes and held them up to the light and read the dollar amounts. Well, then it occurred to me, they were welfare checks, and she was looking at hers and reading the amount—and her mother's and her aunt's and her cousin's. Her mother knew I was there to visit and was very embarrassed. She said, "Rashonda, stop doing that. Quit reading other people's mail." But Rashonda kept doing it.
>
> By that time, I was aware of my own feelings. I was irritated with the 18-year-old. It's like, "Why are you doing this? Why are you embarrassing your mother? Rashonda, go in the back of the room, and just leave us alone." And she kept doing it, and then she'd look at me and say, "I'm not opening the mail, am I, Cynthia?"

Well at this point, I was aware of feeling baited. "Okay, Cynthia, what are you going to do about it? How are you going to handle this?" In my head, I knew I had to decide "What am I going to do? I know I have a good relationship with this family, a decent relationship, but it's not the strongest in the world. I was being challenged by the 18-year-old. Her mother is embarrassed. So what do I do?"

I just stuck with what I know best, which is to be myself, and I answered honestly, but I was conscious of "Don't let your anger show. Just be honest." So what I said to Rashonda was, "Nope. You are not opening up the envelopes, but you still are invading people's privacy." And that is all I said. Then, I turned back to her mom, and we continued our conversation. Rashonda put the envelopes down. She didn't leave the room. She sat down and just kind of listened and played with her baby. By the time I left, it was okay. We were back on track.

Cynthia feels secure in her relationship with this family. A professional with 20 years of experience, she is confident and trusts her judgment, even when everything seems to be falling apart. Had she scolded Rashonda, Rashonda probably would have fled the room, enraged. Her honest, respectful reply not only ended Rashonda's behavior, but also gave Rashonda permission to remain and learn what Cynthia had to offer. This two-level process using internal and external dialogue is a skill that develops over time, with experience and ongoing supervision.

The Setting: Working in the Parents' Space

Home visitors enter into a family's private space, of which many families are protective. Some parents may not understand why the home visitor is there and may not feel safe. Given their uneasiness, parents carefully watch their home visitor from the moment he or she gets out of the car. Home visitors can help parents feel comfortable when they themselves are relaxed, genuine, and able to find a common ground on which to make their first contact. Once the adults are able to have a relaxed exchange, home visitors can describe their role and begin to learn what the parent would like from their visits. Home visitors understand that they cannot accomplish anything until they know the family, the family knows them, and a relationship is established. They also know this process takes time.

As a guest in parents' homes, effective home visitors take cues from parents, for example asking the parents' permission before touching or picking up their baby. Similarly, it would be inappropriate to enter other rooms in the home unless the home visitor is invited to do so. Janice explained how she tries to follow the parents' lead:

I try to come in as the guest in the home, not as somebody that is in charge of this hour. I always try to keep in mind that it is the parent's home; thus, as much as possible, I try to follow the parent's lead. If the parent sits on the floor first, I sit on the floor. Wherever she sits first is where I sit first. Once I introduce an activity, usually we both sit on the floor with the child. But, if the parent initially is most comfortable remaining on the chair, I'll respect that decision. Then, in a few minutes, I'll invite the parent to join the child and me.

But just as important as my own agenda and planned activity, I invite parents to share observations of their child, happenings within the family, concerns, or questions. The visit always is for the family, and I try and keep foremost that I am interested in how parents would like to use our time together.

Janice's behavior communicates to the parent respect and genuine interest. Janice knows that the language of her behavior as well as what she says will communicate to parents who she is and what these visits are going to entail.

When home visiting is not sought out by a family, a first visit can be very difficult. Cynthia described her first visit with a family she has worked with for 2 years:

I have been working with two sisters in their late thirties and their children, who range in age from 19 years to, when I first met them, a newborn. So there are 12 children between the sisters who live in this household, and the older children of these sisters also have children. So, at any given moment, there are up to 20 people in and out of this household.

On my first visit, I knocked on the door. This was a referral from the child protection agency. They [the sisters] did not want to see me. They did not want me in their home. They did let me in. It was dark in the home. There was a couch and a loveseat in this fairly large room, a small TV on the shelf. One of the moms let me in, and I introduced myself. I did my spiel about [how] I am from Parents as Teachers, and this is what we do. I'll bring these games, and we are going to talk about development—the whole spiel.

She kind of looked at me and turned about and walked away. And she didn't come back for 5 minutes. You know, you are just kind of standing there. [I was] like, "Well, now what do I do?"

So pretty soon she comes back with her other sister, and I had to go through this spiel again. She wanted her sister to know about this, but she really wanted somebody there with her while I was there.

It didn't take long for Cynthia to realize that this was not going to be a typical visit, and her planned agenda had to be disregarded. Although she felt awful, she persevered.

And no one asked me to sit down. I had been told to take my cue from the parent. They just left me standing there. So, I finally thought, "That's not going to work. I'm not going to be able to take my cue here." Either I leave or I ask to sit down, which is what I did. "Would it be okay if I sat down?" They replied, "Oh well, all right. Go ahead."

Well, then they brought the kids out, and the sisters sat on one side of the room. And I was over on the other side with the children. The TV was blaring. I didn't have the nerve to ask them to turn it down because I thought, "You know, I'm just getting started with this. I'm not going to ask them to do that." So I kind of sat there and played with the children, a 3- and a 4-year-old. We talked, and I got some books out and read some books. The parents sat on the other side of the room, and they watched me.

Then, someone knocked at the door. A third adult came in, and the three of them sat over there and had their own conversation and said things I couldn't quite hear. They would laugh, and I thought, "I'm not paranoid, but I know they're talking about me, and they don't want me here. I'm going to leave and never come back." And so I read stories, played with the children, and watched a little TV.

Cynthia described this family's life as being on the edge of chaos; yet, she knew she was making a difference.

Now the family has moved from Parents as Teachers into Even Start. Neither mom had finished high school. They are in adult education; they bring their children to the child care center, and I make two visits a month.

At the end of the my second year working with this family, the evaluator asked one of these parents, "Why are you in this program?" and she said, "Because Cynthia just won't go away." And I think there is some truth in that. I just wouldn't give up. There were a lot of times I wanted to, but I saw that spark of interest. I know they wanted to do something for themselves and for their kids. I just kept coming back. Last year, they only attended the adult education center 1 out of 4 days. This year, one of the sisters has been attending 3 out of 4 days and even has gotten several attendance awards for perfect weekly attendance.

Over time, Cynthia has communicated to the sisters that she cares and that they and their children are important. Cynthia knows that parents, regardless of how problematic their behavior may seem, want the best for their children and for themselves. This knowledge gives Cynthia the commitment and courage to persevere. In turn, the sisters have learned that they have a friend who truly cares. They have experienced what Jeree Pawl stated is "one of life's greatest privileges—the experience of being held in someone's mind."[5]

PROGRESSION OF THE PARENT–HOME VISITOR RELATIONSHIP
Establishing Appropriate Boundaries

Each home visiting program has its own goals, agenda, and time limitations. Regardless of the program agenda, the process of implementing an agenda is through patterns of interaction over time—through an *extended* relationship. There can be a blurring of the appropriate boundaries of parent–home visitor interaction. Working in a family's home adds to the role ambiguity. Once parents feel they have a trusting relationship with their home visitor, within the privacy of their own home, parents may extend the discussion beyond the explicit goals and tasks of the home visiting program to include personal problems that are preoccupying them.[6] These topics may involve family conflict such as with a spouse or parents, internal stresses such as depression, or external problems such as housing or inadequate income or employment.

Some home visitors have a hard time distinguishing what they can do and what they are unprepared to handle, as well as a hard time knowing how to maintain carefully their boundaries of involvement with families. Some home visitors try to solve others' problems when they do not have the expertise; doing this violates family support program goal of empowering parents. When parents discuss highly personal matters or external problems beyond the home visiting agenda, home visitors can listen empathetically and, when appropriate, strive to help the parents seek other services in the community to meet their needs. When a home visitor encounters a parent who shares his or her personal troubles, the home visitor can seek advice or help from peers and/or supervisors, a sign of a mature professional aware of his or her professional limitations. Multiple, complicated family problems can be so great that they interfere with parents' attention to their child and often are beyond a home visiting program that does not include broader social services.[7] (See Chapter 2 for a discussion of networking with community resources.

Cynthia discussed how she strives to maintain boundaries:

I see myself in a helping relationship without taking over. I listen because if the parent brings something up, it is foremost on the parent's mind, so you at least listen to it. A lot of times, home visitors get hooked up trying to solve everything. But most people don't want you to tell them what to do anyway. So, I'll listen to the parent, and sometimes you can tell they just needed to get that off their chest, and then they can go on. And sometimes you need to let them talk about it more and explore options with them. When you are working with families, you are there to help them problem solve, not do things for them.

Cynthia understands that one of her most effective approaches is listening to her parents, even when they go beyond the planned agenda of discussing their child and their parenting. At the same time, she understands that her role is not to rescue parents who are immersed in problems. I interviewed Cynthia and explored further the issue of boundaries:

Carol: In those families in which there are substantial problems, like serious emotional problems or external problems like housing, do you find that you also are making decisions about when is it time to get a professional with expertise that you don't have?

Cynthia: Oh sure! But I still listen. I make the decision that this is not my realm of expertise, and I need to help this family get other resources. I'll say to the parent, "You know, I am not really experienced with this kind of thing. I am not a counselor. I don't feel I really can help you with this, but I know someone who can." Then, I offer possible services. I'll tell them that if they would like to talk more about this—because it really seems to be bothering them—here is the number of someone who can help. For the most part, I give them the information and let them self-refer. On a few occasions, I thought the situation was really bad, and I called the psychologist who works with families in our district, and he then called the parent.

Cynthia knows specifically what her agenda is and what her areas of expertise are. If a parent shares a problem beyond the scope of Even Start, Cynthia is able to think on two levels, talking with the parent while thinking through whether the parent's problem is a situation requiring just listening and support, listening and help with problem solving, or listening and networking with community resources. Having built trust into her relationships with parents, Cynthia actively listens to whatever the parent chooses to share; yet, she is able to let parents know when they have entered areas beyond her expertise. In turn, parents appreciate Cynthia's honest statements regarding her own limitations, for this acknowledgement communicates genuineness and respect of the parent.

Janice, who has been a home visitor with working-class families since 1986, shared her perspective:

When a parent puts out something that I don't feel equipped to discuss, I have to remember sometimes all she wants me to do is listen and that I can provide an important service to her by just listening very empathetically and not offering anything other than my ears, really; a friendly gesture; and a suggestion of whom she might contact.

We have to be real honest with parents and let them know where we are good and where we are not. And that the things I know, I know pretty well. I really know child development and understand parenting, but I don't know anything about housing. And if they have a housing issue, they need to call Mrs. Smith at such and such bureau because I know she is good and can help them. I think when parents hear that we are real honest on that, they will trust us more on the issues where we do have expertise.

Like Cynthia, Janice understands that when a parent is troubled, listening empathetically can be the support needed. At the same time, Janice is quick to recognize when a parent's problem is beyond her expertise; then, she tells the parent who could be of assistance.

During seminars that I have conducted on parent–home visitor relationships, experienced early educators across program types—people who work in home visiting, social work, speech and language, occupational and physical therapy and nursing—have shared their successes and the barriers they have had as they have dealt with boundary issues. Table 1 depicts these successes and boundaries.

Building on Strengths

Home visitors recognize parents as experts regarding their own children. In their interactions, home visitors recognize the important job of parenting and can acknowledge this parental expertise. From the outset, home visitors identify parents' strengths, affirm them, and strive to use these strengths as the building blocks for their relationship and for the parents' development. Janice described her approach:

Especially in early parts of my relationship, I make sure I can praise things the parent does. And that makes them realize right up front that not only do I enjoy their baby, but I think they are doing a good job. Even if there are some things they are not doing, I really praise the things they are. And at the end of my visit, when I give them our handouts, I'll say, "You probably are doing this already." In as many subtle ways as possible, I try to find the strength of the parent and build on that.

My goal is for parents to trust themselves, to trust what they know, to trust their judgment because they have a foundation of child development information and parenting information that our program provides for them so that they feel strong in what they do. And you know, interestingly, when parents feel strong in what they do, they are more likely to ask for help when they need it.

Table 1.   Boundary issues in home visiting

Successes	Barriers
Home visitors set clear goals.	Parents are not accessible.
Home visitors are nonjudgmental.	Parents have low self-esteem.
Home visitors are active listeners.	Home visitors have unmanageable case-loads.
Home visitors are supportive and empathic.	Parents do not follow through with home visitors' suggestions.
Home visitors are persistent and don't give up.	Parents experience difficulties with extended family members.
Home visitors know who and where to refer parents to and explain to parents available community resources.	Physicians say the child is fine, but home visitors know this is not true.
Programs have bilingual staff members.	Parents are overwhelmed because their homes are a revolving door for professionals helping their children.
Programs have a lending library of books with videotapes, audiotapes, video players, and audio players.	Homes have inadequate space and are filthy with rats and cockroaches.
Programs budget for a taxi service for parents.	Parents' homes are in dangerous neighborhoods and pose safety issues.
Home visitors work with grandparents.	Parents have unrealistic expectations for their children or spouses.
Home visitors give parents options.	Home visitors don't understand the family's culture or ethnicity.
Home visitors are culturally and ethnically sensitive.	Home visitors impose their own personal or social values on parents.
Home visitors help parents develop a list to use when talking to a professional of another discipline.	Home visitors do too much for parents.
Home visitors employ role play with parents to practice calling a professional of another discipline.	Home visitors need an interpreter to communicate with parents.
Home visitors help parents schedule needed visits with professionals of other disciplines.	Parents deny a child's special needs.
Programs feature effective mentoring and supervision.	Parents refuse to admit a family problem.
Home visitors help parents read confusing documents, such as legal documents.	

Karyn, a first-time mother of a 24-month-old, described what Janice's home visits meant to her:

> She never left the house without telling me, "You are doing an important job. It is very hard work, and you are doing it well." I always waited for her to say that.

When working with troubled families, home visitors can feel uneasy, even overwhelmed, with a family's many difficulties, and they may find it difficult to spot the positive and build on it. In these situations, home visitors may need to give themselves and parents time to get to know one another and to build a relationship. The child often can serve as a common ground to begin a conversation. At first, maybe the only common ground will be a television show or an event within the community. When home visitors are genuine and interested, over time they develop a relationship in which they can see, acknowledge, and affirm parents' interests and strengths.

Sharing One's Own Family Life

Just as home visitors learn to develop boundaries for areas they can address and those that are beyond their expertise, so too do home visitors develop sensitivities as to when sharing their own family life is appropriate. The parent–home visitor relationship involves balancing professional neutrality with the parent–home visitor alliance. Initiating descriptions of one's own family life that are unrelated to the family one is visiting are *not* appropriate; however, when a parent expresses a concern or asks a question, a home visitor's brief vignette from his or her own family life can communicate understanding, support, and validation of the parent. The effective home visitor tries to keep the child's and parent's development as the focus; thus, any personal sharing must be integral with ongoing concerns, questions, or happenings within the family being visited. Janice's discussion with Shelly is illustrative:

Shelly: Erin [age 24 months] loves the playground at the park. She's getting better with the slides. She holds on pretty good. But on the swing, she doesn't have the concept to wait until the swing stops to get off.

Janice: I remember it was hard for me when my boys were small. I used to find myself saying, "Be careful" again and again and again. It's hard because I also wanted them to try and to be competent.

Shelly: I try and remember to say to Erin, "Pay attention to what you are doing."

Once Janice shared this personal vignette, Shelly then elaborated on her concern. The two adults brainstormed together how Shelly could ensure Erin's safety while encouraging her to climb and swing competently. Janice explained to me her rationale for sharing her own family life with parents:

I think personal sharing helps rapport. Not that I am always spinning off about my family, but every now and then I am willing to share about my own life or about my own child that matches up with something in their lives. I mean, I don't care what family it is, I try to pull something out of my life. For example, this week, with one really low-income family, the mother was working as a nurse's aide part time in a nursing home. And I didn't have anything in common with this woman except that my husband's aunt is in a nursing home. And I was able to say to her how important the people are to our family that do the kind of work that she does. And just pulling together that nursing home experience, validating her importance to my life, did something for us. It made her see me as a person, which is what I think I need to be to parents for them to pay attention. I heard a phrase at one of our staff meetings that I really believe—that parents need to know that we care before they care what we know.

Janice wants the parents she works with to know that she cares and respects them. When something in a parent and child's life together triggers Janice's thoughts of her own family, her sharing is another way she communicates the meaningfulness of this family's life. Janice aims to have mutuality in her relationship with parents, a mutuality in which parents' comments have meaning to her in the same way that she hopes her comments are meaningful to them.

Parents are disclosing so much of their private life to me that if I don't disclose something about me to them, they are going to think it is too one-sided. I am in their home, asking about their baby, asking about their opinions, and if I don't share something, if I don't let them at least partway into my life, it seems like there is too much distance. And that's not fair to them. I don't go overboard and talk a lot about my kids, but I want them to know that I am a mother and that I have experienced some of these things. And as I get the sense that there is some closeness developing between us, then I feel more comfortable discussing some touchy issues. I am not as comfortable getting into problem areas with somebody I do not know very well, and I don't think it works either.

Janice accepts and trusts her own family experience. She is sensitive to balancing the parents' levels of disclosure with her own sensitive disclosure of selfhood, a disclosure of *only* that which matches what the parents are sharing. As she shares her own experience, she is assisting parents in accepting and trusting their experience.

ESTABLISHING RECIPROCAL, POSITIVE FEELINGS BETWEEN PARENTS AND HOME VISITORS: A PERSONAL RELATIONSHIP

Whether or not they know it, parents make decisions every moment they interact with their babies and young children. Home visitors are in the home only an hour per week or per month, but the parents spend a great deal more time with the child. So, it is not what home visitors tell the parent or the decisions they think are best for the child that in the end will make a difference. The child is affected by the decisions the parents make in the morning, at bedtime, when the television is on, at the store and so on. When parents are making decisions that help the child's development, then the program is successful. Regardless of a home visiting program's agenda, parents are the final decision makers in their child-rearing practices. When home visiting programs are successful, parents' new understanding and skills allow them to be informed decision makers when making deliberate decisions such as what kind of toys to buy for their child, and everyday decisions become habitual and are taken for granted, such as what to say while diapering and feeding a baby.

Parents' informed decision making emerges from their extended interactions with their home visitor, from their personal relationship.[8] In personal relationships, each person influences the other continuously over time. Just as the toddler learns to say *please* and *thank you* because she has learned from her parent over time, so too as a result of their relationship with their parent educator, the parents become comfortable talking to their 4-month-old son as they change and feed him. Shelly talked about the home visitor's continued influence.

> We always look forward to Janice coming—oh, what is she going to tell us this month, and what is going to be going on [in the visit]? And I can't wait to show her what we can do. And, you know, Janice will say something and then leave. And in a few days, Erin would be doing it, and I will think, "Oh, I knew she was going to do this."

Janice had been visiting Shelly, Rob, and their daughter Erin for 2 years—since Shelly's third trimester of pregnancy. Patterns have developed in Shelly and Rob's relationship with Janice. They look forward to her visit when they can share Erin's new skills, and they sense that Janice truly enjoys relating to them and their child. They remember Janice's descriptions of the new developmental strides they can expect in their child. In her discussions with Janice, Shelly sometimes describes an experience she and Erin have had and then tells Janice what she remembered that Janice had told her during a prior home visit—sometimes as long ago as the previous year.

How does this personal relationship between parents and home visitors develop? The relationship evolves from extended interactions over time. Several home visitors in a PAT program identified key themes in forming their relationship with parents. Lela works with working-class and low-income mothers and fathers.

> First, parents have to trust you, and that takes time. I try and build a rapport so that they can talk to me about things they are concerned about, topics like sleep problems, discipline, or toilet training, with comfort, and not feel-

ing like they are being failures as parents. And they need to know that I am not there to judge them, that I'm there as a support person. And if there is any information I can get them that they need, I'll be glad to do that. And sometimes I even bring in personal experiences in my own life so that they'll know that, hey, a lot of other parents experienced this problem too.

Several themes emerge in Lela's description. Parents need to feel comfortable enough to talk about whatever is going on their lives. They can do this if Lela has developed rapport with them, so that they can trust Lela. Like Janice, Lela feels that occasional sharing of her personal experience supports parents in the knowledge that they are not alone in their concerns.

Ernestine also works with working-class and low-income families. Ernestine explained her relationships with parents as follows:

I think I gave genuine concern and even sometimes stated, "I am concerned" or "I care." And what we focus on often depends on the family. What is going on in that family? And I try to be available to listen to whatever is going on in that family's life that the parent chooses to tell me. As I listen, I make sure I give them eye contact and sometimes even restate what they have said to help them know I understand.

Ernestine sees *genuineness, concern, caring,* and *active listening* as central to her relationships with parents. The parents feel her genuine concern and caring because often they share whatever is going on in their family life—a clear sign of their trust. Although she always enters a home with activities and ideas to discuss with parents, she is quick to adjust her agenda when parents want to share their concerns. Mutuality is a part of these relationships; both parent and home visitor control the agenda of the visit.

Janice discussed how she tries to praise what she sees parents and their child doing as she strives to help them trust themselves and "feel strong in what they do." Extended observations of Janice's home visits illustrate her approach:

Greg (age 19 months) is playing with a large tub of beans and assorted spoons and cups. As he puts a spoon into a cup, he says, "Spoon in cup." His mother, Karyn, repeats his statement.

Janice says, "You are so good at saying his words." As she praises Karyn, Janice provides developmental information and developmental interpretation: "Then, he hears the correct pronunciation. He knows you understand him, and you are encouraging him to talk."

Greg's parents explained how they would describe Janice to a friend who knew nothing about PAT:

Karyn: She is the best, like a surrogate mother to me. She is warm, and I always feel comfortable with her. She is so encouraging. And I feel free to call her when I need her helpful knowledge, even though we have moved out of the district. I don't have enough words for her. She is very warm—like a friend. And she gives information in a way that you can accept or reject it.

Don: And she has a genuine interest in Greg. She doesn't lecture. She tells you what she thinks—not "go do this or that." And when playing with Greg, I used to take the lead. Now, Greg takes the lead, for Janice taught me that he could feel more connected and accepted if he took the lead.

Karyn and Don described Janice as warm and comfortable, easy to talk to, and someone whom they see as a friend who has a genuine interest in their child and whom they can call on when needing help. They acknowledge that Janice shares a wealth of information, yet it is *they* who choose what they think is relevant for their family. Although they are aware that Janice has influenced their parenting, they also are aware that they are the decision makers.

From this discussion of home visiting and comments from parents and home visitors, several themes arise that are basic to forming personal relationships between parents and home visitors.

- Parents feel the home visitor's genuine concern and caring.
- The home visitor enjoys the parents' child.
- The home visitor is warm, and the parents feel comfortable, as if relating to a friend.
- The home visitor actively listens to whatever the parents choose to discuss.
- The home visitor is nonjudgmental and validating, praising the parents' actions when appropriate.
- The parents are the decision makers.

For further information on the parent—home visitor personal relationship, see Chapter 2.

SHARED DELIGHT IN THE CHILD

When home visitors show they enjoy playing with a child or when they delight in a child's new skill, parents experience this enjoyment as affirmation of themselves. Janice consistently expresses her delight in a baby or young child's achievement. As Erin easily puts together a puzzle, Janice tells Erin's mother and father, "I can't tell you how exciting it is to see how she just does it with such ease for her young age!" After this visit, I remarked to Janice how delighted she seemed to be in Erin's play. Janice replied, "But it is fun!" Erin's father, Rob, shared his experiences with Janice as follows.

> She always is so enthused about what Erin is doing. It's not like a job to her, I don't think. I think it's just something she really enjoys doing, and she gets paid for it. The last time you both [Janice and Carol] were here, and Erin [age 25 months] started jumping rope—and the surprise that came over both of your faces when she started jumping. When you left, we were like, "Did you see their faces?" Like it was no big deal to us.

Janice spoke of how important it is that parents know that she enjoys their child as much as they do, and she sees this enjoyment as helping them feel closer to her. When she has her final visit with each family, Janice shares her pleasure and appreciation with parents. On this last visit, she gives parents a summary sheet that highlights one thing from each of her visits. She explained this process to me.

> On the summary sheet, I write, "Thank you for sharing this special time in your life with me," and then some little blurb about their child and that they are doing a good job as a parent. I'm really sincere in saying that. I enjoy going and seeing them. And it is a special time in their lives. And they have every right to keep it private, but they have shared it with me, and I appreciate that.

Janice understands that she can connect most readily with young parents through her genuine enjoyment of their children. As she celebrates a baby or young child's accomplishment with parents, she also is encouraging parents' skill in observing their child's development.

When parents consistently experience a home visitor's enjoyment and delight in their child, they often enjoy telling their home visitor stories of happenings between visits. This sharing and joint pleasure is reminiscent of grandparents' and parents' shared joy in their children. Several parents have told me that they always are eager to tell Janice stories about their child because they never feel as if they are bragging. As Shelly stated, "If I tell somebody else, they'll just think I'm trying to show off my child, but I know Janice really cares and really enjoys Erin in the same way as I do." Given the close bond Rob and Shelly feel toward Janice, they eagerly tell her about family happenings—a trip to their uncle's farm, a family birthday party, a parent's illness—in a manner reminiscent of sharing with a relative who has stopped by for a visit. As they describe these events, they often invite Erin to tell Janice about some specific aspect of the event, and Erin usually does so in a simple manner typical of toddlers.

FATHER INVOLVEMENT IN HOME VISITS

Beginning in the 1970s, the role of many fathers changed dramatically. The father's traditional place in the family was as the financial provider and guardian of the family values. Many fathers today are committed to being the children's nurturer and wife's partner in homemaking. Research indicates that fathers as well as mothers bond to their baby shortly after birth and contribute significantly to their child's emotional, social, and intellectual development—although males feel, think, and act differently than do females.[9]

Fathers are more likely to engage in play activities with their young children than with caregiving (e.g., feeding, diapering), and to engage in activities that promote assertiveness rather than activities that promote dramatic play or cooperation.[10] Play activities often include physical play—movement games such as bouncing—though many fathers enjoy reading stories to their young children. Mothers most often focus on social-emotional stimulation in their play with babies, whereas fathers most often focus on assertiveness. Young children benefit from having both their father and mother involved in child rearing.

Home visitors do not always find it easy to include fathers in their home visits. Janice always tries to conduct her first home visit at a time when both mother and father can be present. When she gives the mother the parent handout, she urges her to share it with the child's father. Some mothers that I have observed in Janice's home visits enjoy telling Janice about how the father plays with the baby or what concerns the father may have. Many home visitors work in the evening or on Saturdays so that they can meet with both mothers and fathers. Given the increasing number of working mothers of children under 3 years of age, evening and Saturday visits can be essential.

WORKING WITH PREGNANT
MOTHERS AND THEIR FAMILIES

Becoming pregnant and having a baby is one of the most transforming experiences women can have. Throughout pregnancy, selfhood is redefined. Women experience changes in their relationship to their body and their relationship with their spouse, to their parents, and to other significant people in their lives. If a woman is working, she is confronted with a host of decisions regarding whether she will continue to work and in what manner she will work.

Pregnancy can be planned or accidental, nonvolitional, avoided, or even terminated. When a woman continues a pregnancy and keeps her baby, she chooses to not only make the transition to motherhood but to face changes in other relationships and experiences in her life. She gains extraordinary new responsibilities and undergoes tremendous physiological changes. Sleep, appetite, and hormonal surges often affect the woman's mood. She gains extra weight, and her body changes shape.

As the woman adapts to pregnancy, she begins to imagine herself as a mother and to hold representations of her baby in her mind. For babies and mothers to be positively attached, mothers must embrace their pregnancy and recognize that their unborn baby will be a separate and unique person. Optimally, these beginnings allow mothers to create an emotionally secure and loving environment for their babies. Mothers and their unborn babies begin their dance of attachment. The fetus hears her voice and body sounds and feels her movements. The mother feels the fetus's movements and talks softly, strokes her stomach, and sings to the fetus. This prenatal attachment supports the baby's emotional development.

Pregnancy often brings joy and excitement; however, women—and even their husbands—often feel anxious and ambivalent, even when pregnancies are planned and wanted. Many first-time pregnant mothers feel emotionally unprepared for pregnancy and motherhood. The woman's experience of pregnancy is tied to the biological changes of fetal development and her own body. Though the baby is not visible, the greatest amount of fetal development takes place in the first trimester of pregnancy. At this time, the fetus is most vulnerable to toxic influences. Often, morning sickness, mood changes, and irritability can accompany the hormonal changes within the woman's body.

In the second trimester, the growth of the fetus is more visible. The mother typically experiences less morning sickness, is less moody, and is less concerned with miscarriage (which is most common in the first trimester). Women have different responses to their bodily growth. For some, their sense of loss of body control is frightening; others enjoy the visible changes to their body and rejoice in the feeling of the fetus's movement at 4–5 months. Beginning at about 15 weeks, women can see their baby using ultrasonographic methods.

In the third trimester, the fetus is primarily formed, and the mother gains the most weight. Winnicott speaks of this period as the beginning of "primary maternal preoccupation."[11] The mother often daydreams and fantasizes. Intense and ambivalent feelings emerge at the time of labor and childbirth. Though long awaited, most women know that childbirth will be the most painful experience of their life. Women who are informed about it and are in some control of the childbirth process often are more emotionally resilient.

Although brain development is most rapid during the third trimester, it begins long before that. Overall, the structural development of the brain is completed before birth; however, the functional development of the brain depends, in many instances, on the baby's experience. In other words, the development of brain activation is the result of a consistent transaction between genetically coded programs that form the structures and connections and the influence from the environment.[12] At the same time, we know that the fetus is substantially affected by the extra-uterine world, for example, the mother's nutrition, drug use and/or abuse, or experiences of chronic stress. Research suggests that a mother's stress during pregnancy can adversely affect fetal brain development.[13]

Pregnant women live in a complex network of family and culture and often need support from husbands, extended family, and friends. Each woman's experience of pregnancy is strongly affected by her relationships with her husband, her previous children, her extended family, and her friends. Though there is surprisingly little literature on fathers' psychological experiences during pregnancy, their feelings also are quite powerful, and they, too, are confronted with substantive transitions when becoming fathers. As with mothers, fathers, too, assume responsibility for the care of their new babies. Though in many cases women do the majority of child care, fathers can join in the process by changing diapers, feeding babies, and transporting babies to child care.

Expectant fathers often feel excited, proud, and protective. Just as the mother may feel ambivalent and anxious, so too many fathers may feel intimidated by their new responsibilities and the new changes in their wives and other children. Some men are anxious about their wives' or babies' health. Some have difficulty accepting their wives' preoccupation with the baby or their having less time alone with their wives. In sum, both parents experience considerable transformation during pregnancy and childbirth.

Home visitors' first task with pregnant mothers is to provide support, encouragement, and shared delight. They also can be a source of very helpful information. They can help pregnant mothers learn how to safeguard their own health, for example, by avoiding alcohol, tobacco, and other drugs; getting regular exercise; attending prenatal visits; and eating nutritious meals. They can encourage parents to learn about any family history of birth defects, hereditary conditions, miscarriages, or unexplained stillbirths.

Home visitors also can tell parents that their attachment to their baby begins as soon as they begin to feel a connection to their fetus. The stronger the parents' attachment is to their baby prenatally, the more secure the baby will be after birth. By the 24th week of gestation, babies begin hearing. We now know that hearing relaxing music can calm both mothers and their fetuses. Home visitors can help parents understand that fetal hearing can be a direct avenue for attachment.

When home visitors begin working with families in the early stages of pregnancy they can ensure that mothers gain appropriate prenatal care. As they visit the pregnant mother, they can discuss physician's visits and the baby's development in utero. They can also ask open-ended questions to motivate pregnant mothers to share any stresses or changes they may be experiencing. For first-time pregnant mothers, the home visitor can explain the usual schedule of visits to the physician: every 4 weeks during the first trimester, every 2–4 weeks during the second trimester, and every 1–2 weeks during the third trimester.

HOME VISITORS' RELATIONSHIP WITH TEEN PARENTS

The United States has the highest teenage birth rate of any Western industrialized nation.[14] Home visitors are very likely to encounter families headed by teen parents, so they need to understand the developmental characteristics of both the adolescent parents and their babies and young children. Many teens lack adult understanding and skills. Others have had to grow up early and may be wise beyond their years. While being a parent to their baby or young child, teenage parents are in the midst of characteristic adolescent issues, such as striving for independence from their families and longing for peer companionship.

Difficulties in parenting and poor developmental outcomes for children are common by-products of teen parenting. Osofsky and Thompson identified patterns often found in teen mothers and their children:

- *Teen mothers may be less responsive to their babies.*
- *Teen mothers may have less verbal interaction with their babies.*
- *Babies of teen mothers may have poorer cognitive and linguistic skills.*
- *Babies of teen mothers may be poorly attached to their mothers.*
- *As preschoolers, children of teen mothers often seem to have behavior problems.[15]*

Teens often have difficulties establishing appropriate boundaries with their babies and young children. The teen mother's mental health and intelligence are two factors that affect her maternal skills, responsiveness to her baby, and perceptions of the baby.[16] Poorer quality parenting is also associated with rapid subsequent pregnancy.[17]

Having a baby often interferes with a teenager's educational attainment and limits his or her economic self-sufficiency. Teenage parents often share the characteristics of lower socioeconomic status (SES) families, for example, difficulties of accessibility and multiple external and internal problems. In fact, children of unmarried teenage parents are very likely to be poor.[18] Many home visiting approaches with teenagers are similar to those used when working with families with lower SES. Like lower SES families, teenager-parented families are not all alike, and some manage better than others.

A Look into the Teenage Brain

To understand the behavior of teenage parents, it helps to understand the brain. Significant brain development occurs during a child's first 5 years (see Chapter 5), but the brain undergoes a second wave of development during the child's teenage years. Teenagers are more likely than adults to respond with a strong gut response for several reasons.[19] First, adults' emotions are tempered by the prefrontal cortex, which has practically no activity among teens.[20] Magnetic resonance imaging (MRI) reveals that brains of adults show activity in both the prefrontal cortex and the limbic system. The brains of teenagers only show activity in the limbic region; the prefrontal cortex, which is in charge of executive functions such as language, decision making, and judgments, does not show activity. In other words, the prefrontal cortex has decreased activity between 10% and 20% since childhood.[21] The inactive prefrontal cortex hampers the brain's ability to handle ambiguous information and affects the brain's ability to soften or prolong strong emotions. Second, the serotonin level declines in most adolescents, leading to increased impulsivity and the inability to process information in a mature way. Finally, during the teenage years the limbic region of the brain—the source of raw emotions such as anger—develops. The limbic region includes 1) the amygdala, a small almond-shaped structure in the brain that governs the fight-or-flight response and allows a person to rapidly detect and respond to danger, and 2) the frontal cortex, which helps temper emotional responses. Because teens' frontal lobes are not fully developed, they are not active when teens experience stress.

Focus on Self

As with parents experiencing multiple stresses, a teenage parent's immaturity and needs may be so great that he or she may not recognize the child's needs. Especially at the outset, a home visitor's conversation may have to be teen-centered rather than baby-centered. The home visitor role often expands to include counselor, referral source to community resources, friend, role model, and surrogate parent.[22] Carrie described her home visiting work with teenage parents as follows.

> We wear two hats—surrogate parents and parent educators aiming to provide developmental guidance. We have a dual approach, but both are one. Our teens always have their own agenda. They mostly are interested in meeting their own needs, which can be gigantic. One of our most difficult challenges is to move from parent need to focus on the parent's child. We understand that as we move mother along, we bring her baby along. As we help moms feel their feelings, they can recognize their babies' feelings—that the best way to understand their toddlers' fear is to understand their own fear. And whenever a teen is in crisis, we are their referral source. Recently, a pregnant girl was badly malnourished, her hair was coming out, and she had massive headaches. Six months ago, she had had an abortion [and now was pregnant again]. Addressing this teen's immediate needs took me 2 hours. These crises make our work very episodic.

Many teen parents come from troubled families. Not only are they very young, but their childhood homes often have characteristics of troubled families: disorganization, family conflict, poverty, and/or substance abuse. Given their immaturity and social-emotional problems, many of these teens have difficulty tuning into their babies. Cynthia knows that if she is going to help a teen parent, she must have a personal relationship with that parent.[23] She explained:

> In working with these teen families, the key is time and number of contacts, because the more you are there, and the more you get to know that parent, and the more you can connect with the parent as a person in her own right, not as the mother of a child, the more you can have a personal relationship. The relationship is the key. And once you can establish that you see them as a person and one of their roles as a human being is to be a mother of this child, but that they have other things that they do that you care about, that helps.

Changing Family Roles

Adolescence is a time of transition. Teen parents must redefine themselves as parents at the same time they redefine their relationships with their own parents and siblings. Because most teen mothers have limited money, they tend to live with members of their childhood family and do not marry their babies' fathers. In 1994, 76% of teenage girls who gave birth were unmarried, compared with 15% in 1955.[24] Mothers of teenage parents often are relatively young women themselves who may still have young children at home and may work full time. Strain is added when a teenage daughter adds a newborn to the family, and conflicts arise.

Though home visitors strive to focus their work on the teen mother, it is important that they also relate to the grandparent whose home they are visiting and who often is a central player in child rearing. This process entails a difficult balance of strengthening the young mother's role while respecting and affirming the grandparent's role. Cynthia discussed how she approaches these families.

> When you have a teen parent and her mother at odds, in conflict over how to raise that baby, that gets real sticky, and you have to be very careful. One of my rules of thumb is always talk to the parent of the child, the teen. I will direct my talking to the teen parent. If the grandmother is there and offers things, I will interact with the grandmother. But I always try to come back to the parent of the baby and reinforce that role. A lot of times teenagers really don't want to be the parent of that baby, and it is easier to let grandmother take over—and grandma takes over, and sometimes that causes tension. Yet, there are some extended families where everyone works pretty well together to raise that child.

The task becomes even more difficult when the home visitor's views contradict those of the grandparents. Home visitors don't want the teen mother to feel caught in the middle or for the grandparent to feel threatened. There is no ready solution in these situations. Expressing respect and genuine interest and actively listening to all family members is helpful. Janice shared her approach in these situations:

> I try and help parents recognize and value the grandparent's perspective because many times young parents will talk with you about the frustration they feel about the grandparent spoiling their baby or being overly intrusive or any number of things. What I always try to do is to frame it in terms of the grandparent's love and interest . . . if there is a way the parent can think about it in terms of a loving relationship, even if it is an uncomfortable loving relationship, if they can think about it as love. And yes, it is still their baby, and they still have the power to do things their own way, but acknowledge the grandparent's perspective.
>
> I remember one teenage mom whose child was getting to the age of wanting to touch and explore, and the grandmother was determined that this coffee table was going to stay where it was with the artificial flowers on top, and the child would learn not to touch it. I empathized with the mother,

and as it played out over several months, the mom would say to me, "When I am here by myself with the baby, I move all that stuff up. When my mom is here, we have to have it down. But those are the times that I try to take the baby somewhere else to play or try to stay closer to her." Then, after several months, I went back, and everything was gone. The grandmother just joked about it, "Yeah, we just sort of got rid of the whole thing." How they worked that out internally in their family, I don't know, but I felt my role was to try to encourage the mom to talk continually with her parent and make this a mutual decision allowing for the child's safety and exploration in whatever way they could work it out in that family.

Janice knew that the baby's grandmother was engaged in the baby's care and needed to be recognized and valued. Janice gave the teen mother support and developmental information and encouraged her to discuss her baby's needs with her mother when there was a disagreement between them. With Janice's help, the teen was able to be the decision maker regarding her baby.

Because problems of overcrowded space and the many extended family members interrupting a home visit can be common with teen families, it may be more effective to conduct visits out of the teen's home. In these situations, often the most productive work with the teenage parent is in more neutral territory, such as the teen's high school or the home visiting program's office. At the same time, effective home visiting programs also try to reach the extended family members. Some home visiting programs have found that grandparent support groups are useful in giving grandparents a setting to meet each other, express their frustrations, and gain support and possible ideas to improve their relationships with their teenage children. One home visiting program has monthly meetings for teens and their entire extended families with transportation, dinner, and child care. Then, adults attend three 20-minute sessions offered by a variety of social service and health professionals in the community—for example, one session on health resources in the community, one session on guidance and discipline of young children, and one session on sibling rivalry.

Need for Expression

Teenagers often do not express themselves in mature ways and need help with social skills. Beyond home visiting, home visitors may meet weekly in small groups with the teens at their school. Carrie and Diane described their work with teens:

Carrie: They have a real difficult time expressing themselves and usually are not sure what the problem is, so one of our jobs often is just to observe behaviors. For example, a mother who normally talks all of a sudden seems very quiet and is kind of off by herself, away from her friends. That usually indicates she is dealing with a pretty heavy problem. So we might approach her and ask an open-ended question, and then she shares with us her problem.

You usually can tell that they are trying to express themselves, but often there is so much anger in their family that they start screaming at each other. Mother, the daughter, and the baby's daddy will start hollering, and then they get real depressed because they never have been able to convey what they needed to express. So, in group we talk a lot about what did you really want to say, and we talk about the different ways of being able to say it.

Diane: And with many of our mothers, we try to get them counseling. Social skills play a big part in what we do—what is the appropriate way to act. You know, a lot of our teen mothers feel like they don't have a family. The majority of these kids sort of have been left on their own to raise themselves, and it is amazing! When you talk to them about how they want to raise their babies differently, their ideas often are more structured than the home life they came from.

Education

Usually teen parenting responsibilities are incompatible with typical adolescent activities such as attending school and having a social life with peers. Some programs have worked with school districts to have their programs integrated with the junior high and high schools so that teenage parents more easily can finish their schooling. Sarah is the mother of a teenage parent. She was once a teenage mother herself. She explained that attitudes toward teenage parents have changed a lot since she was in high school.

When I was young, forget it! You got pregnant—you left school. It was an embarrassment. You couldn't go to school. I think Weston [High School] really has outdone themselves on this because they want the girls to finish; they want them to go ahead and do something with their lives.

Results of Home Visiting

Work with teen parents can be astonishingly draining, and Carrie appreciates having another teen-parent home visitor, Diane, with whom she can share problems, strategies, and successes. Carrie and Diane also gain assistance and support in their weekly 2-hour staff meetings. Providing support and professional development to teen-parent home visitors is essential for providing quality service.[25] Even though the job can seem endless, teenage parents do benefit greatly from home visiting. Terry, a teen parent, explained how home visiting has helped her.

Terry: They understand you. At first, you think you are just the bad kid, and everyone is looking down on you. But they support you and tell you you're still normal.

Carol: Has PAT made a difference in your feelings about Nicholas [your 24-month-old]?

Terry: Yes, because now when I think he has done something wrong, I just know that it is to be expected, and that he is not a mean kid or trying to be rotten. That's what he's supposed to be doing.

It is also important to remember that teenage parents are not a unified group in our society and that some teen parents are more mature and are better able to handle the responsibility of parenting than others. Cynthia sees the fact that a teen parent joined Even Start as indicative of some maturity because Even Start focuses on gaining a high school diploma in addition to parenting a young child. Cynthia explained:

The teens I am working with are ready to leave and are trying to get out of their [childhood] home. They are 17 or 18, for the most part. Many of the teens we have in Even Start are not living with their parents; rather, they are bouncing from house to house. In these instances, they are in control and are assuming the role of parent, in the sense of making a decision of where that child is going to be. But what they tend to do is drop their child off at different places, a friend watches the child for a day, an aunt watches the baby for a day, or a boyfriend, which is difficult for the child as well as the teen parent, yet, it is hard to generalize. We have another teen mom who moved out of her home because her mother is an alcoholic and abusive, so the teen took her two kids and left. She is 18 years old. She tried living in shelters for a short period of time, got a part-time job, and now has her own apartment.

DIFFICULTIES AND DILEMMAS

Home visitors encounter some parents with whom it is very difficult to develop a meaningful relationship and thereby assist them. Two types of parents who are very challenging to work with are parents who are unmotivated and minimally involved with their child and parents whose inner turmoil impedes their awareness of their baby's emotional and developmental needs.

When a parent is unmotivated and minimally involved with his or her child, this parent also probably will not remain in the room during a home visit. Working with these parents can be very demoralizing to a home visitor, who has to be ingenious to capture the parents' attention. In reality, these often are parents who themselves were reared in a troubled family with minimal parenting and probably are somewhat depressed or in some other way overwhelmed with their ongoing problems. For these parents, their young toddler may be viewed as intrusive. They get little joy from parenting.

With unmotivated, minimally involved parents, forming a trusting personal relationship can take extended time and repeated visits. Without a personal relationship, the home visitor never gains the parent's trust or involvement in the home visit. Cynthia's discussion of her experience with unmotivated, minimally involved parents provides some guidelines for working with this type of family.

You may have a parent who sees the child as a burden and wants nothing to do with the child. I have worked with some moms, especially younger moms, who have that attitude but not so much that at some point I can't get them to interact with their child. It all depends on time and the number of contacts you have with the parent. As you get to know that parent, you care more about her as a person and get more involved in your visit.

As I get to know the parent and establish the relationship, and as trust builds, I sometimes get real directive. If they walk out of the room, I just yell, "I need you in here. Help"—that kind of thing. I may say, "This child is driving me nuts. You need to come help me"—something that is kind of funny. And they'll come back and not leave me.

Last year, I worked with a mom who saw her child as a pain in the rear, an imposition. It was a real challenge to work with her. Often, I had to say, "I need you to come back in here with me. This is for you, too, and not just for your child." I would have to be directive. Once I got her back in, I would find a way to relate to her, not necessarily as a mother, but "How is your job?" I have found that when both child and parent are together, the child usually is trying to relate to the parent, whether the parent is connecting or not. And I can use that, "Did you see the way she looked at you? Look at that. Look, she wants you to see what she is doing." Most parents can't resist that.

And sometimes I speak for the child. For example, this mother would deliberately hurt the child. When the child put her hand down to feel the xylophone, the mother took the stick and hit the child's hand with it. And I said, "Oh mom, that hurt me. I was just trying to feel what this was like." And the mom looked at me and said, "That tap didn't hurt her." But what it did was stop the child's play, so I talked about that a little. I said, "It may not have hurt her but, you know, she is not interested in it any more." You have to be careful and not say, "What did you do that for?" or "Look at what you did." At the same time, you have to help parents see how their actions and interactions with their child make a difference. It is difficult, but you have to keep working at it.

Cynthia understands that when she works with an unmotivated, uninvolved parent, she first must connect with the parent as a person, not as a parent. She lets the parent know that she knows the parent does other things and has other interests and problems. She is interested in relating to the parent as a person. Once she develops a personal relationship, she uses several strategies to work with the parent. At times, she is directive. She speaks for the child because she knows that some parents do not understand that their behavior has an effect on their child. Other times, she points out when the child is approaching the parent. Often, these parents are so shut down that they are not aware that their child seeks their attention. Most important, Cynthia is persistent and confident that, with time, she can develop a personal relationship with most parents and thereby begin to help the parent. At the same time, Cynthia recognizes that some parents never will be open to working with a home visitor. In spite of her extensive experience, Cynthia finds accepting this reality to be very difficult.

Some parents rarely focus on the baby as a separate individual because their inner turmoil impedes their awareness of the baby's emotional and developmental needs. Unwittingly, the baby becomes a participant in the parent's conflictual experience. In other words, the baby becomes a representative of a figure within the parent's childhood. Most often, the parent has negated or repudiated this figure, possibly a very harsh mother or a father who sexually abused the child. Frailberg used the metaphor "ghosts in the nursery" to speak of this parent–baby dynamic.[26] During psychotherapy, the therapist provides for the parent a corrective attachment that can be a vehicle for the parent's conflictual internal representations of self in relationship to the parent's original problematic attachment figure.[27] In this type of therapy, the baby always is present, most often on the mother's lap. The baby's behavior is a powerful aspect of the therapeutic intervention.

CONCLUSION

This chapter discusses the formation and progression of parent–home visitor relationships. Two very skilled home visitors, Janice and Cynthia, shared their experiences in establishing and developing relationships with parents, and several parents shared how they view these women. These parents spoke of Janice and Cynthia as their friends, their surrogate mothers, and their confidantes. Janice and Cynthia related that, in their work, it is the parents who are the experts about their child and who are the decision makers regarding how they parent their child. These home visitors explained that they can assist parents' decision making only if they have a personal relationship with them. Parent development occurs through and within parents' relationship with their home visitor, just as child development occurs through and within the child's relationship with his or her parent.

The process of developing relationships is different for different people. This chapter points out some common themes across people, such as the importance of a trusting relationship between parent and home visitor; discussing expectations, tasks, and roles; and maintaining boundaries of involvement. Also discussed is working with families who are parented by teenage mothers. Beyond developing a personal relationship, home visitors use many different approaches to promote parenting. Chapter 2 discusses approaches in effective home visiting, and Chapter 3 explores those approaches that assist in working with parents who are members of cultural subgroups different from that of the home visitor.

2

The Home Visitor's Approach

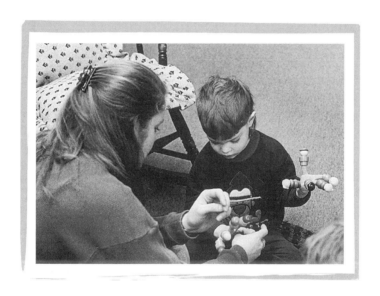

In our endeavor to understand reality we are somewhat like a man trying to understand the mechanism of a closed watch. He sees the face and the moving hands, even hears its ticking, but he has no way of opening the case. If he is ingenious he may form some picture of a mechanism which could be responsible for all the things he observes, but he may never be quite sure his picture is the only one which could explain his observations.

Albert Einstein and Leopold Infeld (1938/1996, p. 31)

Once parents and home visitors have developed the personal relationship described in Chapter 1, home visitors can address their program objectives. The primary purpose of many home visiting programs is to help parents to understand their child's development and to improve their parenting skills. When home visiting is effective, parents see themselves and their child from a whole new perspective and interact with their child in new ways.

This chapter discusses approaches that promote effective home visiting, which can be performed using many approaches, some of which overlap with one another. This chapter examines these approaches in three parts. The first part explores 14 communication and interpersonal skills that encourage, maintain, and promote the parent–home visitor relationship:

1. Individualizing across families
2. Establishing respect and rapport
3. Providing empathic listening and support
4. Active listening
5. Engaging in observation and offering descriptive affirmation
6. Modeling
7. Sharing developmental information
8. Making developmental interpretations
9. Offering suggestions within context
10. Questioning
11. Problem solving
12. Promoting active parent involvement
13. Being comfortable with silence
14. Achieving streams of interaction: Balancing and initiating

The second part discusses five additional skill areas that are essential to effective home visiting:

1. Promoting informal support through social networks
2. Networking with community agencies, institutions, and organizations
3. Promoting the program agenda
4. Maintaining efficient organization and management
5. Being aware of legal and ethical issues

The chapter concludes with the third part on difficulties and dilemmas that emerge when working with parents who are concrete thinkers and with families who live in chaotic conditions.

COMMUNICATION AND INTERPERSONAL SKILLS

This section is divided into 14 aspects of communication; however, in reality, approaches often work in tandem to form the whole. For example, home visitors cannot listen empathically unless they respect parents. They cannot give helpful developmental interpretation of a child's action unless they are keen observers and are knowledgeable about child development. Furthermore, communication is more than just language. In order for babies and young children to learn to communicate, they must have experienced repetitive daily give-and-take exchanges with their parents and other caregivers. In order for parents and home visitors to communicate, they must have a relationship grounded in mutual respect and trust, and their conversations must express such mutuality.

The approaches discussed here are skills that cannot be taught. The home visiting process entails the organic unfolding of a relationship. Recipes do not work. Even for the experienced home visitor, the home visiting process is unique to each family and can be known only as it develops over time. Home visitors can improve their skills through experience in home visiting; through thinking about their experience; and through gaining constructive feedback from peers, mentors, and supervisors. Thus, underlying this discussion is a paradox. Some of these communication and interpersonal skills are essential to forming the parent–home visitor relationship, yet a relationship takes time to develop. More paradoxically, the parents and home visitor need to know one another and have a trusting relationship before some of these approaches can be effective.

Individualizing Across Families

Because each family is unique, effective home visiting means individualizing the approach to address each family's distinctive patterns, and it necessitates different approaches with different families. When home visitors understand that each of the families with whom they work is unique, they can use their observation skills and extended conversations with parents to guide their work. They learn that each family has its own routines, problems, values, standards of behavior, and priorities. Different kinds of communication are suited to different families. For example, once a home visitor becomes aware of a mother's unique style of interaction with her baby and the activities that the mother most enjoys with her baby, then the home visitor can support the mother's participation in these activities with her child.

In order to individualize, home visitors also look beyond the everyday patterns of the family to understand the family's connection with extended family members, neighborhood, workplace, and so forth. For example, when a grandmother is very close to the baby's mother, and regularly provides child care, the home visitor encourages the grandmother to participate in the visits and includes discussion of the grandmother in his or her conversations with the baby's mother. When a child is enrolled in a child care program, the home visitor invites parents to talk about their experiences and feelings about the program. Not only do home visitors make adaptations in their approaches with different families, but they must also make accommodations in their approach with individual families as families change and need different approaches at different times. Janice spoke with me about her perspective on individualizing across families.

Janice: You have to know that when you step through the door, you may find something that is totally different than what you anticipated. It could even be a family that you have visited for 2 years, and you can walk in, and the mom may look different, she talks different, she may simply be different from what she has ever been before. The child may be behaving differently and you know that something is going on with her. I have to change. I have to step back and listen, listen to what it is that is happening in this home right now.

The cues usually come from the parents. You must be able to read their signals. You also must be able to read what the child's needs are at the time. Development may be entirely different than what you anticipated when you came through the door. This is especially true when you are working with a family that has had a premature baby because those babies really are on a different time schedule. You may think that they are going to be developmentally at such a stage because the child was age 3 a month ago, and that is what you expected. And they may be far more advanced than you had expected. There is an incredible call for flexibility.

If you have not been able to blend the parent's agenda with your agenda, you might as well not be there. There are certain things that you want the parent to have access to, such as appropriate expectations for a child at this stage of development. But if that's not what is high on her agenda, pick out the one or two key points you want to get through and forget the rest, and spend most of your time addressing what are her issues for that day, and do the best you can with that. That's why it is incredibly important to be prepared and to know the range of things that are likely to come up with parents and their whole family, really.

Carol: As I listen to you, I sense the ever-expanding lens that your have from your extended experience with a large range of parents and your understanding of the range of parent development and not just child development.

Janice: That's true, but on the other hand, you can pretty quickly pull in the
           range of things likely to come up. Because it is just not that much. You
           know, if I think about what it takes to work with families that have 2-year-
           olds, there are likely to be only so many issues that they are going to be
           facing. I may go to a visit thinking that I am going to talk about toilet train-
           ing, and the issue the parent wants to discuss is about the child's night-
           mares. Well, I'll put my issue aside for the next visit, for we are going to
           talk about nightmares. And I know that this is an appropriate topic within
           the 2-year-old time frame; so I shift topics.

Although Janice enters each home with a planned agenda, she is quick to shift her agenda when either the child is behaving differently from what she had anticipated or the parents have issues they want to discuss. Janice understands the mutuality of her relationship with parents and knows that parent-initiated agendas always come first. In this way, Janice communicates respect, affirmation, and support. She also knows that parents integrate knowledge into their decision making most readily when parents raise the issue themselves. Being experienced and knowledgeable in child development, she knows the range of behavior and potentially problematic issues for each period of development. When parents initiate a concern not on Janice's initial plan, she understands that concern within a developmental frame and can assist the parent spontaneously. At the same time, however, Janice understands that when parents initiate discussion of a concern with which she does not feel equipped to deal, she listens, supports, and, when appropriate, suggests another professional with expertise in the area of the parent's concern. This issue of professional boundaries is discussed in Chapter 1.

Establishing Respect and Rapport

When home visitors communicate that they value and accept parents, parents feel they are respected. When parents feel some mutual understanding, agreement, and connection with their home visitor, the home visitor has established rapport. A home visitor's first task is to find a common ground with the parent and thereby begin to develop rapport. Cynthia described the various topics she discusses in a first visit: commenting on something she sees in the home, something the parent or child is wearing, even television programs or movies. As home visitors have informal conversations with parents, they help parents feel at ease and connected with them. In this process, home visitors convey respect and genuine interest in parents.

When a home visitor has been working with a family for some time, the first few minutes of conversation often are a continuation of a topic discussed in a previous session. For example, Cynthia knows that Sally's mother-in-law, in whose home Sally lives, just began a new job. On arrival, Cynthia asked Sally, "How does your mother-in-law, Donna, like her new job?" Her question sparked a brief conversation about Donna's new job. Then, Sally told Cynthia about how Willy's child care teachers are trying to address the problem of his biting the other children. Cynthia first renews her bond with Sally, who then shares what is on her mind—her son's biting problem. Cynthia then can proceed to discuss Sally's concern.

When Cynthia enters a home, she strives to let the parents know that she understands she is a guest in their home.

> When I first walk in, it's a little awkward because the parents are not sure what to do with me or where to put me. I am aware that this is their home. I want to be invited to sit down or be told where to sit down. In my first home visits, I usually will introduce myself and tell the parents why I am there. Then, I'll say, "Where would you like me to sit?" Then, I am saying, "This is your home; you make the choice of where you want us to meet." I am somewhat direct. Then, I talk to them about some common ground like the weather, or if the child is there, we talk about the child.

Cynthia communicates respect and genuineness in her own way to the parents with whom she works. She is skilled at removing emotional distance between herself and the parents and thereby develops trust and rapport with them.

Empathic Listening and Support

Empathic listening and support are intertwined in home visitors' interactions with parents throughout their home visits. As they carefully listen, home visitors try to see things from the parents' perspective and recognize the parents' feelings. When Sally tells Cynthia that her 20-month-old son Willy had a 104-degree fever over the weekend, Cynthia comments, "That's scary." When Karyn tells Janice that she took Greg (age 9 months) to the eye specialist because he had been scratching his eyes, but the specialist could discover no cause, Janice comments, "All kinds of medical things occur this first year. And when you are concerned, it is good to trust yourself and call the doctor." Janice and Cynthia's empathic responses give support to these mothers and communicate that they understand and value what the parent is sharing.

Once a personal relationship is formed, parents share their frustrations, ambivalence, or anxiety about their child or their parenting. As they listen, home visitors suspend judgment. Sometimes they can help parents understand that these are normal feelings experienced by many parents. Parents then feel accepted and can be more at ease knowing that their feelings are universal. Sharing one's own personal life experiences is another way of showing empathy and support. Visiting Karyn 5 weeks after her baby Greg was born, Janice had the following conversation:

Janice: How was your delivery?

Karyn: It was a C-section. He was so big. They did not give me realistic expectations of my recovery.

Janice: That was one of my big surprises! I was told what to expect of my baby, but nobody told me what my body would feel like.

Karyn: My husband, Don, took off work for 3 weeks, and that helped.

Janice: Do you have any relatives nearby?

Karyn: No, except for Don's sister, who has a 3-month-old and a 3-year-old.

Janice: That's tough, really tough. When my first was born, my mother was with me for 3 weeks. I can still remember when she drove off. Bill and I looked at each other. I almost can feel that now because my feelings were so strong.

Janice expressed to Karyn that she hears her and understands her feelings. This conversation occurred during her second visit with Karyn. Janice's empathic support and personal sharing are significant threads in establishing the rapport that is essential to her effectiveness.

When home visitors value listening, they allow ample time for parents to talk about what is concerning them, to share what has happened since the last visit, to respond to the home visitor's questions, or to ask questions themselves. Home visiting demands total focus. The home visitor's attentiveness and body language communicate support and interest just as words do. As parents talk, home visitors sort through what is being said so that they can respond appropriately. Sometimes what the parent leaves unsaid is just as important as what is said.

Much of our talking includes telling stories. In the telling of stories, we give meaning to our lives.[1] That is, as we talk, we are thinking about our experiences and weaving our experiences into the meanings we make of our lives. When parents and home visitors have developed a personal relationship, parents talk about their child, experiences they have had with their child, and family life in general. The home visitor's ability to listen actively and empathically to what is being said not only affirms parents but also contributes to parents' understanding of themselves and their family. Sometimes it is even helpful to ask parents to explain a word they have used or to invite the parent to say more and, in this manner, to both support and assist the parent's thinking. For example, a mother says that her new baby is well behaved. When asked to say more, the mother describes how helpful it is that her baby can sleep through the night and is not colicky, as was her first child. As she talks, she realizes that the issue is not her first baby's behavior, but rather that her second baby's calm temperament allows her to sleep more and to be more relaxed.

Active Listening

Active listening involves repeating the speaker's content in different words. When home visitors actively listen, they often can rephrase a parent's comment and in this manner, the parent knows that the home visitor has listened and heard what she is saying. For example, when a parent describes her husband's long work hours and the emerging dilemmas these work hours cause, the home visitor might say, "It sounds like you are quite concerned that Damon's work hours are so very long." In some situations it can be helpful for the home visitor to replay to a parent's comment with a "wonderment," that is a statement that rephrases but asks a wonder question to encourage a parent to continue talking. For example, when a parent tells the home visitor that her baby is always bad, the home visitor can say, "I wonder when Justin is bad, what specifically does he do to make you feel he is being bad." It might be that this young parent thinks crying means that her baby is bad. The home visitor then can help the parent understand that all babies cry and suggest what normally triggers a baby's cry.

Home visitors effectively communicate when they use I-messages, that is, begin a statement with *I* followed by a verb. For example, "I am eager to know what new skills Jamal has learned during the past few weeks." When parents hear I-messages, they do not have to second-guess what the home visitor meant in her statement.

Observation and Descriptive Affirmation

Keen observation of both parent and child actions serves three purposes. First, by observing, the home visitor can identify positive parenting behaviors and build on these strengths. In recognizing and supporting the parents' strengths, home visitors support the parents' self-confidence and lessen any feelings of discomfort. Second, home visitors observe to assess the developmental level of the child and adjust their interactions and activities to this developmental level. Being in the home provides an opportunity to be aware of the family's neighborhood and physical resources in the home, such as the amount of space or amount and quality of toys. Third, home visitors can use their observations to describe verbally positive parent and child actions and, in this way, affirm the parent and child. This is a more powerful and specific form of encouragement than using evaluative words such as *good* or *nice job*. Drawing attention to specific positive behavior helps parents and children understand their successes rather than merely recognizing that they are pleasing the home visitor. This use of observation is termed descriptive affirmation. Descriptive affirmation also models for parents an effective strategy—verbally recognizing the child's positive behavior and thereby fostering the child's sense of self-worth. In other words, the home visitor builds on the parent's strengths in the same manner that the home visitor strives to help parents build on their child's strengths.

Within each home visit, Janice describes the positive behavior of both parent and child as she interacts with them.

> Erin (age 31 months) is hammering golf tees into a square of Styrofoam. Her mother, Shelly, comments, "You did a good job hammering that one in."
>
> Janice says, "That's a good way you have praised her, telling her what you are pleased about. You are hooking a little description onto your praise so that she can develop her own concept of what she did. What we want is for her to develop her own sense of pride—helping her recognize her successes."
>
> Later in the session, Erin picks up her toy phone and gives it to her mother as she says, "Call Robbie."
>
> Shelly says, "You want me to call Robbie."
>
> Janice responds, "You are so good at automatically repeating and expanding Erin's speech. You probably are not even aware you are doing it. But Erin knows she is being heard and that you understand her."
>
> Shelly says, "I remember last year when Erin began talking, you suggested I repeat but not correct her."
>
> "That's it," Janice explains. "You are encouraging her speech and at the same time she hears the correct way to speak."

Janice has visited Shelly, Rob, and their daughter Erin monthly since Shelly's third trimester of pregnancy. Her relationship with Shelly continues, even when she is not present at the couple's home. Although Shelly no longer is aware of repeating and expanding her daughter's speech, she does remember that she had learned the skill from Janice the previous year. As Erin plays, Shelly positively describes her action.

In turn, Janice affirms Shelly's parenting. When Shelly repeats and expands Erin's speech, Janice again affirms Shelly's action. Then, Janice interprets the meaning of Shelly's action in terms of Erin's development. During one home visit, my written observations documented that Janice had provided positive description of the child's action 12 times and had given 4 examples of positive description of the parent's action. Janice explained:

> It comes naturally now. I don't even realize I am doing it a lot of the time. To me, it is a combination of parallel descriptive talk to support the child's action or language, but it also helps the child recognize her accomplishment. I always try to point out strong points of the parent and build on that. They are more likely to hear and remember my developmental information when I "hook it" to what they are doing.

Beyond affirming both parent and child by describing positively their actions, Janice frequently provides developmental information, suggestions within context, or interpretation of the developmental meaning of the observed actions. The following sections discuss these additional approaches.

Modeling

Modeling refers to the home visitor's interactions with the child that the parents may imitate, for example, the way the home visitor plays with the child, speaks to the child, asks the child questions, or reads to the child. Modeling can help parents feel safe trying out new ways of relating to their child. Modeling is most effective when it is spontaneous rather than an explicit demonstration. Demonstrations implicitly place the home visitor in the expert role, thereby leaving parents feeling less than adequate. As home visitors interact with a child, they can talk about what they see happening with the parents. They can explain the meaning of the child's actions developmentally or comment positively on the child's involvement. In this way, the parents are involved and are not just observing passively.

During each visit, Janice provides a developmentally appropriate play activity for the young child. Janice actively participates in play with the child and, at the same time, maintains a dialogue with the child's parent as to the developmental meaning of the child's actions.

> Janice sits on the floor with Mia (age 20 months). Janice gives Mia a cloth bag, and Mia dumps out toy kitchen items—cups, plates, utensils, pots, and pans. Mia hands Janice a plastic cup and metal lid. Janice remarks, "This

lid doesn't fit on the cup. There's a pan. I wonder if it'll fit on the pan." Mia puts the lid on the pan. Janice exclaims, "The lid does fit on the pan!"

Mia picks up a fork as she says, "Fork."

Janice says, "A fork. You can take a bite." Mia puts the fork to her mouth as Janice says, "It tastes pretty good." Mia picks up the knife also, but only puts the fork to her mouth.

Janice comments to Tracy (Mia's mother), "It's interesting to note that Mia puts only the fork to her mouth."

Tracy answers, "We usually don't let her have knives."

Janice explains, "She's picked that up."

Janice picks up a cup as she suggests to Mia, "We can pretend to pour juice into my cup and drink it." Mia pours the juice and pretends to drink. Janice continues, "Can you give Mommy some juice, too?" Janice pretends to drink from the cup as Mia pretends to pour juice into a cup for her mother.

Janice comments to Tracy, "A lot of imitating goes on at this age. Children love to role-play family activities like cooking. It's a time when they can be in charge. Pretend play is a natural way small children learn. When she gets a little older, she'll love to dress up in grown-up clothes."

Mia holds up a bottle as she says, "Open."

Janice says, "Can you open it?"

Mia answers, "I can't." Then, Mia says, "Juice."

Janice says, "You are pouring juice into the cup." She asks Mia, "May I have some in my glass, please?" Mia pretends to pour into Janice's glass. Janice smiles and says, "It tastes good." Mia pretends to pour some in her cup and drink from it, and Janice comments, "You're having some, too. Let's give some to Mommy, too." Mia pretends to pour into her mother's cup. Janice then suggests that Mia cook her mother some eggs for breakfast, and the role play continues.

Throughout Janice's play with Mia, she models ways to promote Mia's emerging language: repeating Mia's words and extending them into complete sentences. She also models positive reinforcement. She describes Mia's actions and thereby affirms her competence. As they play, she explains to Tracy the developmental importance of pretend play. She makes certain that Tracy also is included in the play. When Janice writes notes on this visit, she reminds herself to continue discussing Mia's spontaneous pretend play with Tracy.

Developmental Information

One of the home visitor's central tasks is providing information about child development and appropriate parenting practices. Parents hear and remember this information when it relates to ongoing conversations or activities, such as when the information is part of a conversation the parents initiated or as part of the home visitor's observation of parent or child action. Developmental information helps parents understand their child's current behavior and anticipate the next steps in their child's development.[2] Tracy, the young mother in the previous example, explained:

> Now I know the things that are going on. And things that aren't happening shouldn't be happening yet. Like, for instance, when I was worried about Mia [age 25 months] with potty training and that she wasn't doing good, Janice reassured me that they go through stages like that. Things that I don't know, she kinda helps clear up. And it's reassuring with Mia, who now is going through bad times with her temper. And Janice reassures me that they go through stages. And you will have bad times and good times. That kind of stuff reassures me.

Many parents experience concern when their child is behaving in bothersome ways or is not progressing as fast as the parent expected. When Janice explains that children go through stages that can be hard on parents but do not last forever, parents like Tracy are reassured.

Janice frequently provides developmental information as she positively comments on a child or parent's action.

> Janice has just arrived at Marta's home. As she and Marta chat about Thanksgiving, Brianna (age 7 months) crawls about the living room. Marta shares that Brianna began crawling 2 weeks ago. Janice gives Brianna an infant toy, and Brianna sits on the living room floor and begins exploring the toy.
>
> Janice comments, "Brianna sits up so smoothly from that position. 'Miss Motor.' Her motor skills are just wonderful! One of the things that makes crawling challenging when it begins this early is that Brianna's memory is not up to her motor skills. You tell her not to touch, and she won't remember. You will need to have quite a repertoire of distraction tools to redirect her when she moves at this young age."

Janice observes Brianna's skill in moving from a crawling to a sitting position. She delights in Brianna's early motor development, and her delight communicates that she cares and enjoys this infant. Within these comments she shares developmental information—that Brianna's memory is not as advanced as her motor development, so she will not remember her mother's directives. She also makes a simple suggestion, that Marta can use distraction to redirect Brianna.

Developmental Interpretations

Within the activities and conversations of a visit, home visitors can interpret the meaning of a parent or child's action as another way of promoting parents' understanding. When a parent describes her toddler's new constant climbing, the home visitor can explain the developmental significance of this climbing—how the toddler's exploration is a sign of healthy curiosity and a primary way she learns about the world. Similarly, when a home visitor observes a parent's interaction with her child, the home visitor can explain the significance of this interaction. When she hears a parent repeatedly state rules, she can explain how the parent's consistent guidance is giving her toddler security so that he is able to explore and develop increasing independence. Providing developmental interpretations within the context of a home visit is a skill that develops with experience and supervision. Janice is very skilled in making interpretive comments, as she does with Natalie and her daughter Jene (age 5 months).

Natalie: Jene puts her lips out and pouts when upset.

Janice: Jene is saying, "I'm learning how to communicate. I can let you know when I'm unhappy. I don't have lots of tools yet, but I'm good with my mouth."

[Jene is lying on her back, holding a toy ring that she has in her mouth.]

Everything in her mouth. It's so good. She is curious and first learns about items through mouthing them. And there is a connection between mouthing toys and eating later on. She is getting used to different things in her mouth. It will be easier to have different kinds of table foods. Babies who are not used to lots of toys in their mouths may want only milk and mush.

Janice's interpretations of Jene's actions help her mother understand the developmental significance of these actions. Parents' understanding of the developmental meaning of their child's behavior can guide their child-rearing interactions and deepen their enjoyment of the child. When there is more than one child in the home, making interpretive comments to the children about their sibling often helps them understand one another's feelings and actions. Beyond helping the children's understanding, the home visitor is modeling effective parenting.

Janice does not implement parent education in an abstract way; rather, she informs parents as she interacts with them and their children. The central focus of her visits is play activities that she initiates with the child, activities in which she is an active participant. Then, she invites the parent to join the activity.³ Parents usually enjoy their children's delight in having two adult playmates, and these positive feelings promote learning.

Suggestions within Context

Different ways of offering suggestions communicate different messages. How parents hear a message influences their relationship with the home visitor and the effectiveness of the process. When a person gives a direct suggestion, the listener may hear authority and expertise. When a suggestion is given that does not relate to ongoing events, the listener may feel a lack of connectedness. When home visitors want to respect, support, and ensure that parents understand that they always are the final decision makers in their child rearing, they should be very sensitive to the manner in which they give suggestions. Janice discussed her method as follows.

> I try not to make a lot of suggestions, especially direct suggestions. Rather, I try to point out strong points of the parents and build on that. They are more likely to use these comments rather than a suggestion. If I were to give a lot of suggestions, I doubt if they would be remembered. My primary task is empowerment. I might frame a suggestion as, "Some parents have found that it helps if . . . " I don't want them to think I am coming in as the expert; rather, I am coming in to support them. I am under, supporting, not on top of you.

Janice strives to relate to parents as a partner, not as an expert. She often discusses a variety of methods other parents have used in similar situations. When Janice does give a suggestion, she either is answering a parent's question or concern or the suggestion is part of her observation. As Janice watches Greg (age 7 months) roll over and then get into a sitting position, she comments:

> He has excellent motor coordination, the way he went from rolling to sitting. You really no longer can leave him. Have you purchased a gate?

As their relationship develops, Greg's mother, Karyn, feels comfortable sharing her concerns about Greg (now age 27 months) with Janice.

Karyn: Greg loves to dump things into the trash, like my cookbooks. He broke one of my $30 frying pans.

Janice: It's a difficult age. He will get through this. You will get through this. He doesn't have much inner control. He is into "I want it my way."

Karyn: It's driving me crazy.

Janice: Give him his own trash can. He is at the age where he loves to put things into containers.

Janice gives Karyn support and offers a suggestion with developmental information to help Karyn understand Greg's actions. Janice described her growth in this area as follows:

> Initially, especially in my first year, when a parent would ask, "What should I do about this?" I would be quick to tell them what I thought they ought to do. I don't do that anymore. I have found it is much more effective to ask, "What have you tried?" using a whole series of questions, and then, "What else have you tried?" And very often one of the things they have tried is something that I can say, "Well that is really a good idea. I hope you take that one up." And then we talk about it. It makes them feel better if they can have ownership of the idea, if I can reinforce something that they have tried. It has more power than if I would say, "I think you should do . . . " And another method I use is I speak in terms of children in general: "Some children usually benefit from this, others benefit from that, and so on." Then, parents can pick out what they want without feeling threatened or without seeing me as the expert. On the other hand, if there is an issue of the child's safety, such as wearing a seatbelt in the car, I will be very direct.

In asking parents to share prior methods, Janice is letting parents know that she thinks they know many good ways to handle situations. When she speaks of how children benefit from different kinds of experiences, she trusts that it is the parents who are the decision makers and that they merely need some information to assist their decision making.

Questioning

Questions are a natural part of conversation. In home visiting, open-ended questions encourage parents to talk more. Questions are open-ended when more than one answer is possible, for example, "What are some of the things you enjoy doing with your baby?" When a parent makes a statement, home visitors can ask a question to make sure they understand the parent, such as asking the parent to give an example or asking the meaning of a word used. Sometimes a question can help a parent focus on specific issues that are a concern. For example, when a parent says, "He's bad all the time," the home visitor can ask the parent to give an example of the child's behavior that he or she sees as bad. The parent hears that the home visitor is listening and wants to understand. Once examples are given, the parent and the home visitor can discuss the issue.

Especially during a baby's first year, Janice asks questions that track the baby's development. Her first few visits with Marta and her baby, Brianna, illustrate this pattern.

> On Janice's first visit with Marta and Brianna, Brianna was 4 weeks old. On her second visit, Brianna was 4 months old. Janice asked Marta, "How is she sleeping? Does Brianna turn over? How does she respond when you read her books?" On the third visit, Brianna was 5 months old. Janice asked Marta, "What sounds is she making? How does she sleep? What is her feeding schedule?" On her fourth visit, Brianna was 7 months old. Janice asked Marta, "What is her favorite thing to do? How is her eating? How does she fall asleep?"

As Janice asks these questions, she is assessing the baby's developmental strides. Often one of these questions leads to an extended conversation, for example, discussing how the baby's nighttime awakenings cause the parents' drowsiness and impatience during the day, or how the family has needed to adapt to the baby's need for regular feedings.

Problem Solving

When parents ask home visitors a question, they often put the home visitor in the expert role and expect a quick answer. Rather than accept the expert role, home visitors can use the parents' questions or concerns as the first step in joint problem solving.[4] Not only does this joint problem solving help parents address their concern or question, but their participation increases the likelihood that they will remember the information discussed. When a parent shares a concern with Janice, she uses the situation for joint problem solving.

Shelly told Janice that Erin (age 31 months) recently had been very negative, always saying "No" when Shelly asks her to do something. Interspersed with play and conversations with Erin, the adults discussed her new pattern of negativism around toileting and hair washing.

Janice: How do you respond to Erin?

Shelly: I started the star routine on the calendar, and that's helping a little bit. Sometimes, I'm real patient, but other days [I'm not] . . . I finally said to Rob, "When she wants to go, she'll go." Now, I hold a star and say, "Do you want a star?" and she'll say yes, and go to the bathroom.

Janice: That's real smart.

Shelly then described the battle she and Erin had over washing Erin's hair.

Shelly: I don't want to fight with her, but I want to keep the discipline.

Janice: I think you have handled both situations positively. Kids need to under-stand that their parents understand their feelings, but rules are rules. The trick is to know when to ease up and when to stay firm. Are there enough situations where you can give her some space?

Shelly then described situations when she has given Erin choices and comments that she remembered how the previous year Janice had em-phasized the value of giving children choices.

When parents share a concern, Janice always asks the parents how they deal with the issue. In this way, Janice has some time to think, and she gains information. Furthermore, being included in the problem solving means the parent will have ownership of the solution. Janice explained:

I always begin with "What have you tried?" And sometimes the question may change the direction of the discussion. The first issue may not be the most important issue for the parent.

Often some of the parents' actions are appropriate, and Janice can affirm them. As they talk, she provides developmental information and gives suggestions.

When both parents are present, home visitors can invite each par-ent to share his or her understanding of the problem. Sometimes, a few questions help the parents look at the problem from a larger perspec-tive. For example, if one parent is complaining that her son does not re-main at the table during dinner, the home visitor can ask questions to frame the discussion around the family's patterns of eating dinner. The home visitor can ask parents what they would like to have happen. When focusing on desired solutions to the problem, the conversation becomes positive. During a discussion, the home visitor can help the parent understand there usually are several ways to handle every situ-ation. Sharing how other parents have handled a similar situation can be helpful and reassuring. As possible solutions are discussed, both short- and long-term benefits and liabilities can be identified.

Active Parent Involvement

One of the challenges of home visiting is balancing involvement with both parent and children. Active parent involvement increases the like-

lihood that parents will learn and remember child development information and child-rearing strategies that have been a part of the visit. As
parents play with their child, home visitors can help them understand
the developmental meaning of a play activity and how young children
learn through play. Janice discussed her approach as follows.

> Parents will learn best through their own and their home visitor's interactions
> with the child and through their observations of their child engaged in activ-
> ities during the visit. They will understand child development best by having
> it related to what their child is doing at any given moment.
>
> I initiate the activity with the child to provide an opportunity for model-
> ing. Then, usually I invite the parent to join us, unless the activity is built
> around the child exploring something. But even then, I always end my visits
> with a book, and in these situations, I'll invite the parent to read the book. I
> want parents to feel that they are a real integral part of the visit. And also,
> I want to see how they interact with their child. And if a parent is very im-
> mature or developmentally slow, I take her down the path a little more slowly
> and with much smaller steps.

Janice understands that she promotes the parent's learning when
she interacts with the parent and child. The process reinforces the mutuality of the relationship that Janice strives to maintain.

> Janice takes toy musical instruments out of a bag and says to Mia (age 36
> months), "Now we're going to hear a song, and then after the song, we'll
> play the instruments." Janice has a small tape recorder on her lap. She
> helps Mia's little sister, Maggie (age 18 months), push the button, and the
> Itsy Bitsy Spider song plays. As the song plays, Janice and the children's
> mother, Tracy, sing. Mia and the adults do the hand motions with the song.
> During the second song, Janice gives Mia cymbals, Maggie maracas, and
> Tracy a tambourine. She does the hand motions to the song as Tracy
> and the children play the instruments. The two adults and children continue
> the activity for about 15 minutes. As the children play their instruments, Jan-
> ice comments, "Anything that promotes a sense of rhythm is really valuable.
> Children love this kind of activity."

Janice understands that it is important for play activities to be
simple and inviting, yet having parents be active play participants during a home visit is not a simple matter. First, a trusting personal relationship with the home visitor must be in place in order for parents to
feel comfortable playing, and this relationship takes time to develop.
Second, many parents do not expect to play during a home visit and

may feel a little clumsy at first. In fact, some parents will never play, in spite of their home visitors' skill, because their definition of parenting does not include play. Promoting active involvement of the parent is another skill that takes experience to develop.

Comfort with Silence

With experience, the home visitor learns to be comfortable with periods of silence when the parent and home visitor observe the child. When parents learn that their home visitor is comfortable with silence, they know that the home visitor is relaxed, at ease, and at home with them. During these quiet times, parents often make specific observations of their child, similar to what they have observed the home visitor do on previous visits. The home visitor can affirm the parent's observation.

> Home visitor Rachel sits on the floor with 14-month-old Asha and her parents, Ronnie and Tuni. Rachel has been visiting this family since Tuni's third trimester. All three adults are silent as they watch Asha put chips into a canister with a slit in the top. After a few moments, Tuni says, "I'm amazed at how well she grasps these thin chips."
>
> Rachel says, "It's an excellent indication that Asha has learned the pincer grasp: thumb and forefinger. That learning is important for her later learning in holding a crayon and pencil."

Streams of Interaction: Balancing and Initiating

A consistent challenge for home visitors is balancing their interactions with the parents and their interactions with the children. Home visiting involves multiple tasks, such as discussing developmental characteristics and emerging skills of the child, discussing parenting practices and issues, initiating activities with the child and involving parents in these activities. For each visit, home visitors plan a specific activity and a developmental topic related to that activity. At the same time, however, parents and/or children may initiate a topic or activity unrelated to the home visitor's plan. Home visitors then adjust their plans to integrate what the parent or child has initiated.

Interaction with Parents

Janice described a situation in which the mother's agenda became the theme of her visit. Her planned activity was to invite the toddler's exploration of a bag filled with assorted items and to discuss the child's curiosity and intellectual development with the mother.

This was the fifth home visit with a 2-year-old child, and his language . . . well he just wasn't talking very much at all. And all year long I had been very frustrated because I felt like the mother never was involved in really hearing what I was saying. Finally, yesterday his language was something she brought up, and I was thinking, "Thank goodness."

Language didn't quite fit my intent of the activities I brought, but I shifted gears to make the activity a language activity because now this was something she finally was ready to discuss and listen and try things out. And it was great! It was wonderful! I had started out using the bag of items to explore and had intended to talk about intellectual development and the value of exploration.

Well, my original intent to talk about curiosity and intellectual develop-ment became a very minor piece. I emphasized instead the adult's parallel talk and naming for the child, naming what he was pulling out of the bag and describing what he was doing with what he pulled out. I demonstrated naming and parallel talk and then got her to try it. She was a mom that was very much into asking her child questions and giving directives. Just an in-credible number of questions. She couldn't even make a statement without putting it in the tone of a question.

This is not an activity I ever used in this way, but I thought, "I don't care. I'm going to have a language emphasis because finally she is ready to talk about language. She finally is ready to look at herself and see how she can encourage language development with her little boy who really needs to be talking more."

Janice was able to be flexible and shift her original plan in order to use the mother's expressed interest as the basis of the visit's activity and discussion. Because Janice knows child development, she could immediately shift her topic to helping this mother learn how she could facilitate her son's language development. As the toddler pulled items out of the bag, Janice modeled methods to stimulate language, for example, she described what the child was doing as he played and encouraged the child to name the items. Given the interest and con-cern this mother had expressed, Janice was able to encourage her to try some new parenting approaches. Janice has a goal that her work encompasses a partnership between parents and herself. If parents are to benefit from her work, she must be ready to work with them to deal with the concerns they are expressing at the moment.

When I go into a visit, I will have a generalized plan for what I hope will hap-pen, but I always think that it has to fit in terms also of the parents' agenda. I really don't come in with lots of details about what I am going to do in a visit, and my reason is that I want to have some control in the visit but only an element. I want a lot of control to be with the parents. If I've got in my head that I've got to talk about their toddler sharing, that might not exactly fit. I would rather talk about sharing when the mother brings up that the child cannot share with other children. I like to respond to, rather than initiate, these issues.

I can click off developmental information, but I don't think that's nearly as meaningful as pointing it out when I see it, as talking about it when the mother sees it and letting her really believe, as is the case many times, that she is seeing something first, and then we get to talking about it. However, there is also this tricky balance between having the parent bring up an issue and my letting them know in advance that a particular development is likely to occur. The difference is the scope: I mention in advance developments the parents can anticipate. We discuss it in depth when they see it and bring up the issue themselves.

Janice is steeped in developmental knowledge and appropriate parenting strategies. She knows what topics need to be covered for each developmental period, and she understands that she can be an effective promoter of parents' understanding and skills only when the parents' lived experience gives them reason to be interested in the topic. (Part II of this chapter discusses developmental progression, birth to 5 years, in five central areas of home visitors' focus.)

Interaction with Children

In addition to their involvement with parents, home visitors also are relating to young children. Beyond the activities and discussions that the home visitor and parent initiate, children also initiate activities. Child-initiated activities most often occur either at the outset of a visit or after the child is finished with the activity the home visitor has introduced. When Janice enters a home, a child may be playing with a toy or might go get a toy specifically to share with her. Janice frequently engages in play with these toys with the child.

Erin (age 20 months) comes into the living room with a large plastic beach ball that she throws to Janice, who is seated on the floor. As she rolls the ball to Erin, Janice suggests, "Let's roll it." After a few exchanges with the ball, Janice asks Shelly if she has a laundry basket.

Shelly returns with a circular laundry basket that Janice places in front of her. Standing a few feet from the basket, Erin throws the ball into the basket several times. Each time she is successful, Erin jumps up and down as she says, "I got it! I got it!" Her mother hugs her as she says, "I'm so proud of you."

Janice then suggests, "Let's give Mommy a turn." Shelly first playfully bounces the ball as she says, "I have to dribble a bit." Then, she shoots a few baskets.

> Janice holds the basket high as she says to Erin, "Do you want it high or low?" Erin replies, "Low," and then successfully throws the ball into the basket. As Janice raises the basket, she says to Shelly, "It's a totally different game when I put it on the floor and then lift it higher."
>
> Janice now puts the basket on its side as she suggests to Erin, "How about rolling it like when Mommy goes bowling?" Erin does as Janice has suggested, and when the ball goes into the basket, she again jumps up and down saying, "I did it! I did it!" Janice then asks Erin to get a little ball, which Erin does. She throws it into the basket and then suggests, "Mommy's turn."

In this last sequence, Janice improvises to extend the activity with new ideas—introducing the basket, utilizing the basket in several ways, suggesting a different-sized ball. She encourages Erin's mother to join the play, and both mother and child express delight in the activity. I asked Janice to explain her rationale for utilizing children's toys during home visits.

> One of the reasons that I like to use the children's toys is that I think I sometimes can expand on what the child does with that toy in ways that the parent might not have thought about—give them new ideas for stuff that has been around for a while. The other thing it does is it helps parents to further believe that they have made good choices in the toys they have bought for their child. Further, it lets the family realize that the things they want to be a part of the home visit are certainly as important as the things I choose. All along we are trying to promote the idea of following the child's lead, of paying attention to the child's cue.[5] Thus, if I ignore what the child brings in, I am not practicing what I preach, so to speak.
>
> Even the most disadvantaged family has something that their child has been playing with before I arrive. If I can, I'll use it in some way or observe the child playing with it. In cases where the toys are not appropriate, I use safe household objects that the parent probably has but hasn't designated as toys.

Achieving a balance in interacting with parents and their children is a progressively developed skill. Often, the home visitor feels that a child's initiative or a parent's question interrupts the flow. After observing how Janice was able to maintain a discussion with Tracy while having several sequences of exchanges with Tracy's 20-month-old baby, Mia, I asked her to explain what was going on in her mind during her discussion with Tracy.

> Well, I do this deliberately, for I want the parent to see that you can acknowledge the child's desire to be a part of it and still get your point across

without telling the child, "Be quiet. Wait a minute until I am finished," and so forth . . . that you really can juggle both roles—an adult role and interacting with the child as well. And it is a way to help the child feel a sense of being included. Because if you tell the child, "Wait a minute," the child is going to keep bugging you and bugging you and bugging you, and they're coming out looking bad instead of coming out looking good. You play with her doll for a couple minutes. They are satisfied, having been included, and then you go on with your adult conversation.

Janice knows that each moment that she is relating to parent and child she is modeling for the parent. Often, parents have difficulty with their young child's persistent interruptions. In modeling, Janice exposes parents to a way of dealing with a child's interruptions. As parents watch, they see how their child responds. Then, the parents can decide whether what they are observing would be something they would like to try.

Inner Dialogue

When home visitors engage in conversation with parents, they are aware of not only the content of the discussion, but also 1) their own personal feelings and reactions to the ongoing process and contact; 2) the balance of child, parent(s), and home visitor's involvement; and 3) whether the home visitor's culture or gender is interfering with their response. For example, when a parent describes what happened the night before, when her 2-year-old woke up in her bed and began crying, the home visitor recognizes her own bias about children sleeping separate from their parents. The bias is probably based on cultural assumptions that she does not share with the parent.

ADDITIONAL KNOWLEDGE AND SKILLS

The second part of the chapter discusses the knowledge and skills that are essential for promoting the home visiting process. Unlike communication and interpersonal skills, these skills do not occur or interact together; therefore, each area is discussed separately.

Informal Support Through Social Networks

Social ties among parents become networks that are powerful influences motivating behavior, beliefs, and development. Parents' social networks can provide information, emotional and material assistance, and support and encouragement of certain child-rearing attitudes and behavior, as well as role models. In order for infants or young children to flourish, their parents need access to support, encouragement, and assistance—all of which can be provided through social networks.[6] In other words, for parents to fulfill optimally their child's developmental needs, they need the support not only of family members within the household, but also of people in their larger network of social relations. In these relationships, parents learn that they are not alone in their child-rearing responsibilities.

As they work with families, home visitors become sensitive to the differences in social networks of their families and the varied influences these networks have in a family's functioning.[7] Social networks can include extended family, neighbors, friends in the workplace, and others with whom parents associate socially. Both relatives and friends can offer informal support and companionship to parents.[8] The size of parents' personal networks may vary greatly. A parent who is a full-time homemaker with very small children may experience isolation and accompanying loneliness. Many young parents in our society are quite mobile and may be relatively new to the community and, therefore, have minimal personal networks. In these situations, home visitors often can assist parents in developing relationships, for example, informing parents of neighborhood playgroup possibilities, community playgroups or "parents' day out" programs. Some home visiting programs also offer parent group meetings or parent–child sessions, both of which are excellent settings for parents to develop peer relationships. Janice described a method she has used to promote parents' social networking.

> I have done a small group meeting about infancy, and mothers have come together in somebody's home, and we would talk about babies. And we would plan, maybe or maybe not, another similar meeting for this group. But what is more likely to happen is they make it happen for themselves. The kids in one of these groups are 8 or 9 years old now. I had no idea they would continue as a group. Their parents continue to get together as couples for a card club and that was strictly through their contacts in these infant groups.

The family's social network can expand to include child care staff. In the United States, about 60% of children younger than 6 years old receive child care. Enrollment in child care varies by family income— 77% of children enrolled have families that make an income of more than $75,000 a year.[9] The demand for child care has mushroomed with the increase in single parenting and working mothers of children from birth to age 6. When the infant or toddler is enrolled in a child care program, the connections between parents and child care staff become central to the child's healthy development. Young children feel secure when they hear similar messages from parents and their child care teachers. When home visitors value families' social networks, they can sensitively respond to parents' discussion of these experiences. For example, when a parent is having difficulty relating to her infant's child care teacher, the home visitor can listen empathically and engage in joint problem solving with the parent to discover possible strategies to resolve the parent's difficulty.

Extended Family and Social Support

Often, home visitors work with young parents living with their extended family in the same house, next door, or within the same neighborhood. Extended families can offer young children multiple strong emotional attachments with adults committed to their well-being.[10] For families at risk, extended families often can buffer parents and their young children from the impact of stress, for example, availability of child care and pooling of money for food and housing. When home visitors work with several extended families, they recognize that there are considerable differences in the way extended families are organized and relate to each other. The home visitor's task becomes more complex because the home visit may include the extended family members. Cynthia discussed her experience.

> When parents are living with extended family members, sometimes I go on a home visit, and I'll have the grandmother there or an aunt or sister there. What I usually do is leave it to the parent to decide whether or not that person stays, and it also is up to the other person who is there if she or he wants to stay. Sometimes they elect to leave. But what I find is if someone is there, especially if it is the grandmother or the aunt who is helping to raise the child, they'll stay. One of my rules of thumb is always to talk to the parent of the child. When the grandmother is there and offers things, I'll interact with the grandmother, but I always try to come back to the parent of the baby and reinforce that role. Or if it is the father, sometimes the father will be in the bathroom listening but won't come out because he doesn't want to participate actively but will stay in the bathroom and listen. And I respect his decision.

As she relates to young parents, Cynthia remembers that her role is to strengthen the parents' role as decision makers. Thus, Cynthia invites the parents to decide whether extended family members participate in the home visit. She also respects how family members may choose to be involved, whether actively or passively. When extended family members do participate, Cynthia accepts this extension; yet, she maintains her primary focus with the parent. She communicates that she values all family members' roles in rearing the child and at the

same time communicates that she understands that the primary responsibility belongs to the parent.

Sometimes parents disagree with other family members about their
child-rearing practices and share these disagreements with their home
visitor. Cynthia discussed her approach in these situations.

> I have encountered families where everyone has a different approach. As I
> am working with the family and getting to know the people, I get a better
> sense of where they are coming from and what they consider important in
> child rearing. Any time the family has a conflict and I am working with people
> who have opposing views on something, I try to find a common ground.
> And if they are coming from the same family, there usually is a common
> ground. They have shared experiences, and so there is something that they
> both believe in when it comes to raising that child, and I try to use that as
> the beginning point.

Cynthia begins with the assumption that all family members have
shared experiences that give them a common ground on which they all
can agree. Once Cynthia and parents identify this common ground,
Cynthia is able to assist family members in working through their differences. As she discusses differences with family members, Cynthia
also helps them understand that young children feel secure when
hearing similar messages from their family caregivers.

Janice also confronts these situations, and she shared her approach as follows.

> Parents are very likely to talk about grandparents somewhere along the line.
> Some do it much more often than others. Some will do it in a positive mode;
> some will do it feeling frustrated about their experiences.
>
> Regardless of the parent's approach to the grandparent, I try to lay the
> groundwork of the grandparent's perspective. I even did that before I be-
> came a grandparent myself because I think it is important to establish that
> we really honor the whole family, and we understand that grandparents
> have a different perspective and show their love in a different way. But it
> doesn't mean that they should be ignored just because you have a home
> visitor coming in with different ideas. I try to help pull it all together, instead
> of pulling it apart. You can affirm the parents' role but also help them under-
> stand where the grandparents are coming from.

Janice tries to avoid making parents feel caught in the middle between their interest in the home visiting program philosophy and the
rest of the family's beliefs, even though she may be providing new
information and new suggestions that may be contrary to the family's
beliefs.

> I try to back out of that whenever and as much as is possible and let that be the parents' decision as to how to deal with the information. I might sympathize with the parent when she is going through this. . . .As far as discipline is concerned, parents can feel caught in the middle when Dad does not agree with what Mom is doing and Grandmother certainly doesn't agree with what Mom is doing. And Mom thinks she is trying to do something that she has learned through our program. It is easier when a parent can learn a new technique and practice that new technique on her own, before Dad is home or when Grandma is not around, and get pretty good at it. And then when Dad sees it, Mom feels very confident in passing along that suggestion because it has become her suggestion. It is not her home visitor's suggestion. It is something she has seen work with the baby, and she now wants to convince Dad.

Janice strives to help parents respect the grandparents' perspective, even when it is different from their own. Sorting through differences about discipline approaches is not an academic exercise, and there is not a hierarchical value to different people's perspectives. Like Cynthia, Janice always strives to build on the parent's strength. She knows that parents can approach differences best when speaking in their own voice, based on their own successful experience.

Social Supports in the Neighborhood and Workplace

There are settings, such as the family's neighborhood and parents' workplace, in which the child does not participate directly, but which are significant to the parent and thus have an effect on the child. When parents have neighbors who offer companionship, support, nurturance, feedback, and connectedness, parents then have social resources to draw on. With this support, parents are more able to feel confidence and strength to meet the needs of their infants and toddlers. With a strong neighborhood connectedness, parents feel a sense of security, belonging, and peace of mind that gets translated in the ease with which they relate to their young children. Osofsky and Thompson identified three ways that social networks benefit parents:

1. *Parents are able to gain additional information about developmentally appropriate methods.*

2. *Supportive networks offer tangible resources, for example, child care and money.*

3. *Networks serve as buffers against maladaptive parenting and stress from life situations.*[11]

When parents experience support and affirmation at their workplace, they are able to return home and give full attention to their family. When they experience tension or vulnerability at work, they are not as well equipped to relate spontaneously to the day-to-day patterns of life with their spouse and young child. In other words, social networks can spark stress as well as support. When parents have limited access to employment and safe neighborhoods, they also have limited opportunities for social networking. When parents' stress is increased, this stress influences their child's development.

Networking with Community Agencies, Institutions, and Organizations

Informal social networks such as extended family, friends, and neighbors provide young families with many different services. At the same time, however, families sometimes need services from more formal support systems, such as child care, mental health and physical health services, public aid and housing, juvenile justice, shelters for homeless families or battered women, and so forth. These resources are formal services offered both by government agencies (e.g., the Women, Infants, and Children [WIC] program), private nonprofit organizations (e.g., Alcoholics Anonymous), and private for-profit companies (e.g., a child care center run as a for-profit business).

Chapter 1 examines the need for home visitors to know what they can do and what they are unprepared to handle, in other words to recognize boundaries of the program's agenda and the home visitor's expertise. When parents initiate discussion about personal troubles or external difficulties beyond the home visiting agenda and home visitors' expertise, home visitors can listen empathically and assist the parent in getting help from resources within the community. Before home visitors can connect parents with the appropriate community resources, they must to be familiar with community resources. Becoming familiar with these resources extends the tasks of home visitors.

When the administration of a home visiting program is committed to community networking, the home visitor has information and resources available. One PAT program in a suburban, multi-cultural, multi-income district illustrates integrating community resources into a home visiting program. Mariam Skoten, Director of Early Education, discussed her program's use of community human services.

I believe our district's early childhood programs are simply part of a big pie. Therefore, we often become a hub of referrals. Sitting on my staff now is a social worker [Jill] who has an adjunct position with the county department of mental health, who offers this free of charge to school districts. And this social worker is housed at the well-baby clinic in our area. Thus, she serves as an intermediary to the health care provider that many of our families utilize.

It's neat because when a home visitor discovers some health concerns, either vocalized by the family or a concern of the home visitor, they immediately call Jill. And Jill can network expediency of health care, for example. She can break through the bureaucratic system of public health provisions.

Also, we have used on our staff in adjunct positions, our Division of Family Service [DFS]. When a family identifies for us that they have a case worker in this agency, we alert the case worker that we now also are included, and the family gives us permission in writing to do this. And then the case worker and home visitor work together. We have had some situations where our families have been under abuse or neglect with court orders, and again, with the family's written permission, we have become involved in providing alternatives to discipline. We have had DFS workers who actually have transported parents to parent education seminars.

Another tangent that has been really interesting to us is for our teen parents to work in tandem with the public health nurse, who has been identified through the county's department of health to see teen parents judged [to be] at high risk. We work in tandem with them.

We also have connections with our local out-of-home child care centers and nursery schools. We have gotten some scholarships for our PAT general population. There are very few [special programs] in our area that offer out-of-home child care for infants, but we have gotten some scholarships.

Coordination with businesses in the community is an area [where] we need to experience growth. Kiwanis has supported us by financial contributions and increasing the community's awareness of our program. They bought our first VCR. Because we are so included in the total community, when we have a need, we just express that need to our community, and it is often filled through church contributions or donations from civic organizations such as the Kiwanis.

In order to get known, I—and our staff—did a lot of workshops. For example, I did a workshop on PAT for all out-of-home child care center directors and their guests to alert the community to what we were about. And we've sent letters to all the ministers, to all the physicians, in the community. In staff meetings, we keep emphasizing that awareness must be comprehensive, intensive, and ongoing—the community's awareness of us and our awareness of the community.

Mariam sees her district's PAT program as an integral part of the community and as a hub of referrals to human service agencies in her community. She and her staff have developed relationships with professionals in an array of agencies that potentially can serve their young families. Given her close relationships with many agencies, she is able to hire professionals from these agencies as consultants to serve as a bridge between families and the agencies. Just as an agency can provide services to promote the PAT program (e.g., providing transportation so that a parent can attend a group meetings), so too the PAT staff can promote an agency's goals (e.g., by helping parents learn positive discipline strategies.) When community resources are integral to a home visiting program, home visitors gain needed information and support in their work.

Program Agenda

The agenda of home visiting programs is different for different program sponsors and different populations being served.[12] For example, the agenda of Boston's Patrick O'Hearn Elementary School's home visiting program, implemented by parents, is to increase parent involvement.[13] Programs with a primary health focus such as the Prenatal/Early Infancy Project utilize nurses to serve young at-risk mothers. Some programs focus on promoting the parent's role as teacher of their child, such as the Head Start home visiting program.

Home visiting programs vary as to their method of helping home visitors know clearly what their tasks and goals for home visits are. Effective programs have some explicit structuring of services, ongoing supervision, and professional development meetings. PAT and the Portage Project provide home visitors with very concrete lesson plans and home visiting observation record forms.[14] In these two projects, home visitors have a lesson plan for each developmental period from birth through 60 months. When home visitors are just beginning their work, these lesson plans can be helpful guides, as they were for home visitor Lela.

> When I first began, the lesson plans were my bible, and I kept them right on my desk beside the families' folders. Every time I planned a visit, I used them almost to the letter. Now that I have worked a few years, I may go back to them, especially with young babies, to check to see that I didn't miss anything. Now, I have a developmental framework and know what is appropriate for the different ages of the children.

Experienced, skilled home visitors usually have an agenda based on a developmental framework. Janice explained.

> I like [to have] an overall structure of the things I would like to cover, the major issues of each developmental phase. For example, in Phase IV (8–14 months), the major issues are parallel talk and independence. I always try to hook the developmental information to something the baby is doing. I al-

ways have a play activity and spend time playing with the child and then inviting the parent to join the play. I believe that the mom gains the most information through the child as we are doing something with that child. But my focus always is interaction.

Lesson plans initially are important tools to assist PAT home visitors. With time, their primary tool is their developmental framework. Experienced home visitors such as Janice understand that their primary tool and focus always is interaction in the context of a strong personal relationship with parents and their young children. A primary premise of this book is that no home visiting agenda can be successfully implemented without a strong personal relationship between parent and home visitor.

Efficient Organization and Management

Home visitors work with a wide range of people and a wide range of settings. Given the complexity of their work, careful organization of use of time, materials, and record keeping becomes an essential skill.

Use of Time

Home visitors coordinate home visits with schedules of individual families while allowing time for their other responsibilities, such as completion of home visit reports, supervision and staff meetings, and community networking. Given the multiple tasks and different daily schedules of parents, home visitors benefit from careful time management. This scheduling needs to allow time for travel and record keeping. Documentation of a home visit is most accurate if done soon after the visit. At the same time, a schedule needs built-in flexibility to adapt to needed cancellations, such as when an infant is ill.

Janice explained the rationale for limiting the number of consecutive home visits on the same day.

Doing home visiting is a very intensive thing to do . . . .I can do four [visits in one day] as an experienced home visitor. But beyond that I do not believe I am giving a high-quality visit to the last family. In fact, I don't even feel that I am giving as good a quality to the fourth family as I did to the first. You cannot retool your own head to go from one family to another because this is intense work. Even when there are no problems brought forward, it is intense work.

The thing about a home visit [is that] you are essentially on stage every minute you are on the visit. In the classroom, you even get little children occupied for a few moments, and you can turn around and take a deep breath. In home visits with a parent and child, you have no time to take a deep breath. You must be ready to answer, ready to respond, to observe, and to interact.

Janice understands that the total focus demanded during 1 hour of interaction with parents and their young children is a focus that cannot be maintained indefinitely. Over years of experience, she has discovered that four is the maximum number of visits she can effectively complete within 1 day.

Organization of Materials

In order to give a family total focus, home visitors need to have organized and prepared all materials in advance of their visits. Materials can include toys for different developmental periods, parent handouts, and individual family folders. Given the different materials for different families, as well as materials for their use within the agency, home visitors need a very clear, organized, system. Not surprisingly, car trunks often provide an easy-access file, especially for toys and family folders. Janice explained her system.

I spend a lot of time at the beginning of my program year doing initial organization that will make my day-to-day work flow more smoothly. For example, I organize my individual folders for the year for each family that I am going to see. If the child is 6 months old at the beginning of a program year, I will put in not just the handouts I want to use for my very next visit but also the standard handouts I know I will be giving that family for at least 6 months, maybe 10 months. I want to get a whole set of materials in one place so that I don't have to search for handouts each time.

I know there are certain handouts I am going to use time and time again. And also, I will put key information, such as the mother's first name, readily accessible. I don't want to drive up to the house and say, "Uh-oh, what is her first name?" I make certain I know the child's name, the family's name, the young siblings' names, and the mom's first name. I take a glance at the outside of the folder and there it is, along with their telephone number and directions to the house, right on the front.

I also put on the outside of the folder the dates that the child will enter a different developmental phase, so that I will know the key changes in development I can expect. I also color-code with dots on the folder different ages of the children. I also keep certain key handouts addressing certain issues. I would put all my good discipline handouts in, say, an orange folder and all my good language handouts in a blue folder, so that when I want it fast, I can get it. Issues like sleeping, eating, setting limits, toilet training, key issues that appear again and again, across families.

Home visitors figure out their own system of organizing their materials. As long as they have some system that allows them to enter the home unencumbered with a mind full of details, they can give total focus on their interactions with parents and their young children.

Record Keeping

Home visitors will save time in the long run by spending time shortly after each home visit to write notes on what specifically they did during the home visits, any parent concerns, their observations of parents and child, and reminders for the next visit. For example, they might ask themselves, "What information do I need to give the parent next time? What topic did we leave unfinished?" This writing needs to occur after the home visit because it is distracting during the home visit. If the home visitor is writing during the visit, parents most likely will be thinking about what is being written and lose their focus on the ongoing activity or discussion. Similarly, as they are writing, home visitors are missing subtleties of behavior and are not able to respond to either parent or child. Visitors can use these written records as a guide for evaluating one's relationship with a family and planning for the next visit and as a resource during supervision and staff's professional developmental meetings. In some situations, the written descriptions of the child's developmental progress can be invaluable assistance when a referral is needed, for example, for an evaluation for possible special education services.

Legal and Ethical Issues

Confidentiality

As previously discussed, the role of the home visitor can be ambiguous to parents. Meeting in the parents' home invites the parent to relate on a more personal level than work in public settings would. The combination of role ambiguity and the personal nature of the parent–home visitor relationship sometimes invites parents to share personal information that is outside the boundaries of the home visiting program agenda. Personal sharing introduces issues of confidentiality. No doubt each home visiting program has its own policy regarding confidentiality. However, several guidelines cross over all program agendas.

Confidentiality is an ethical obligation in all home visiting. At the outset, home visitors can tell parents that personal information discussed during a visit will remain confidential unless a child or parent is in danger, such as indications of child maltreatment or parent suicidal thinking. Home visitors never should discuss clients in settings separate from supervision or team meetings. Some home visiting programs are part of a larger social service delivery system with other professionals such as physicians, nurses, and therapists. In these situations, home visitors need to share appropriate family information; yet, they can offer only that information needed by the other service professional and in a confidential manner. Knowing what is appropriate information to share sometimes can be difficult. Before home visitors contact community agencies to link families with their services, they need parents' written permission. Confidentiality issues often confront home visitors with dilemmas such as how much confidential information is necessary for a specific referral.

In order for parents to trust their home visitor, they need to feel confident that the home visitor will not discuss their child or their parenting with other people. When home visitors do illustrate how other parents handle a parenting issue or how a child has learned a specific skill, they speak in general terms so that no parent could recognize the people described. In this manner, home visitors demonstrate in their actions and words that they honor confidentiality with all their families.

Maintaining confidentiality also extends to any written materials about a family. Janice explained her approach.

> When parents share personal information, I do not include it in my written records. I may put a key phrase related to the discussion to trigger my memory in future visits, but I never add any details or subjective interpretations about what they talked about. My written records are public records that can be subpoenaed, thus, I try and keep them as objective as possible. I believe every home visitor needs to do their written records with the assumption that every single piece of paper could be subpoenaed for a child custody battle, for example.

Janice is rigorous in maintaining written observations of what she did in each visit, observations of child and parent action, any parent concerns, and reminders to herself for her next visit. She maintains these records as objectively as possible and excludes any personal family data or her own subjective interpretation. In this manner, she maintains confidentiality.

Child Maltreatment

Child abuse and neglect are not protected by the ethical obligation of confidentiality because the home visitor's duty to the welfare of the child comes before the duty to the child's parent. Home visitors are mandated to report evidence of child abuse and neglect. Each home visiting program has its own procedure for reporting child maltreatment. When home visiting programs have a primary intent to develop a partnership with parents, home visitors need to inform parents of their forthcoming report to the child protection agency. Although it is difficult for the first few times, experienced home visitors with strong personal relationships with parents find it most helpful to make the reporting call while they are in the parents' home and with the parents present. In this manner, the home visitors make certain that parents know there are no secrets, and the call is based on their striving to assist the family. These situations never are easy, and feelings of parents and home visitors often are in turmoil. Knowing that they have the strong support of their administrators can give home visitors the courage to relate openly to parents about the child maltreatment report. When this is possible, the home visitor often becomes part of the child protection agency's team in offering help to the family. Home visitors may encounter other family situations in which they do not have a strong personal relationship, and, in fact, suspect that making a hotline call could put them in danger. In these situations, administrators usually make the call. Each state allows hotline calls to be anonymous. When safety is a concern, anonymous calls may be appropriate.

It can be harder for a home visitor to report child maltreatment than a teacher because home visitors have developed a trusting, personal relationship with the parents and know that their report probably will be devastating to the parents. Often, the most difficult situations are in the gray areas when there is no concrete physical evidence of maltreatment, such as neglect in supervision or emotional abuse. Cynthia described an example.

> We had a situation this year where there were many—entirely too many— people living in a home. The water was shut off for a period of time, and I reported it as a situation that had implications of health hazards. The child protection agency then was aware of it and began working with the family to try to get the water turned back on. This home is not the best place for these kids. It is chaos. I really struggle going in there. It's not like I see someone get hit with a belt, or I see a black eye or big bruise; it's just that I know that every day, this home is not a good environment for those kids. I struggle with that on each visit, and then when something happens like the water getting turned off and the adults in the home don't seem to be doing anything about it, I report it because in my mind, maybe now someone will do something about this situation.

Twice a month, Cynthia visited this family. On each visit, she left knowing that the children were living in a very dysfunctional home environment with too many people coming and going. Once Cynthia had a concrete basis to call the child protection agency—no running water in the home—she was able to help this family get resources to improve their daily life.

DIFFICULTIES AND DILEMMAS

Two types of parents with whom it is predictably difficult to work are, first, those parents who are concrete thinkers (i.e., parents who need a specific example to understand an abstract idea) and have difficulty generalizing; and second, those living in chaotic conditions. Lela described her frustrations in working with four parents in her caseload who are concrete thinkers.

> A frustrating thing I am feeling right now is how to deal with the parent who does not grasp things, thinking like a child. I share information with the parent on one visit and the very next visit they ask me about the same issue. Sometimes, I am at a loss as to how to you get through with some parents.

Lela made these comments during a weekly staff meeting, and her co-workers were able to offer several helpful suggestions. For instance, Cynthia finds that it is helpful to be concrete and directive when working with this type of parent. Cynthia visits Sally twice a month. Sally has difficulty managing her very active 18-month-old son. Cynthia used a sensory activity as the setting in which to guide Sally.

> Cynthia places a large plastic tub filled with birdseed, assorted spoons, and plastic containers in front of Willy. As Cynthia removes the lid, she says to Sally, "I brought this for a couple reasons. You know last time you told me Willy was doing so well with spoons, and you and I have been talking about setting limits. You know how he loves to throw things. Plus, sensory play is fun."
>
> Willy immediately picks up some seed and tosses it out of the tub. Sally says, "In the box, baby." Willy begins putting seed into a small container with his hands as Sally softly says, "Good boy! You are so smart! You are taking the seed and putting it into the tub."
>
> Cynthia says, "That describing what he is doing is wonderful. That is what he needs to learn language."

Cynthia knows that parents who think very concretely learn best from their own experience. In her twice-monthly visits, she frequently describes Willy's actions and then tells Sally how important these descriptions are for Willy's developing language as well as his self-esteem. When Sally spontaneously described her child's actions, Cynthia reinforced this important skill as it happened.

Willy throws a small amount of seed, and Cynthia says, "He's still throwing, right?"

Sally responds, "You can tell! Yeah."

"We have to set limits for him," Cynthia says. "When he throws things, what do you do?" Sally shrugs. Cynthia suggests it might help if Cynthia put Willy on her side of the tub so that it would be easier for her to guide him. "It will be easier to catch his hand if you do not want him to throw the seed," she says, "and when you are with him, you are helping him to keep calm. You can take his hand to show him how to use the spoon, too."

Cynthia gives a specific directive with a simple explanation that Sally can understand. Cynthia explained that Sally usually does not remember Cynthia's specific guidance. Cynthia knows that it will take time and repetition for Sally to show her son spontaneously what she wants him to do.

As Sally watches her son play in the seed, Cynthia explains how this play is a calming activity that helps his eye–hand and small-muscle coordination as he dumps and fills. The experience of the moment becomes the teaching moment. Cynthia further described how she works with parents who are concrete thinkers.

Basically, what I do is work at two different levels. I work with the parents at whatever level the parents are. When they are at very concrete levels, I do a lot of demonstration of hands-on activities where the parents practice in order to help them understand a concept or skill.

After I have known the parent for a while, I get better at knowing how the parent learns, whether they need to be told to watch it or to do it themselves, or whether they do better watching a videotape. Usually, I will demonstrate and then have them try it and then coach them through. I talk about what the parent is doing and how the child reacts, and how that relates to the child's learning and development. Because that is what they often have trouble understanding—how their actions help their child learn, not what their child learns but how their child learns.

And in group meetings, we have to have something the parents can hold and touch in order to understand. So, when we are working with self-concept of the children, and how words and negative interactions impact a child, we take a paper doll. And each negative statement becomes a bruise or a tear in the doll. We told them things that they might say to their child, and then they had to judge whether or not that was something that supports the child's self-esteem.

I think the parents [with low intelligence] have to experience for themselves before they are able to provide that kind of activity for their child, let alone relate the activity to child development. Some of them never really quite get it. Most of the people we serve do not live alone; rather they live in an extended family, and that extended family helps to raise that child. So, we do not limit ourselves to just working with the parent during our home visit. We also work with the father, the aunty, the grandmother or grandfather, whoever is home and helps with child rearing.

Cynthia understands that in order for some of her parents to understand a concept or a skill, they must have direct experience, and, in that experience, the home visitor can talk about the meaning of that experience. Cynthia often models for parents and then invites the parents to participate in the activity, coaching them as they play with their children. Some parents need more time than others, as well as repeated concrete experiences, and home visitors realize that they need to exercise patience and persistence. Nothing will happen if the parent and home visitor do not have a trusting personal relationship.

It is very difficult to work with families that seem to be on the edge of chaos, for example, large extended families coming and going throughout the day, or families with multiple, complex external problems and little ability to cope with them. Given Cynthia's respect for each family, once she arrives, she invites the parents to decide whether they wish her to enter into their chaotic world. I asked her how she relates to those families who seem to live in perpetual chaos.

Cynthia: I went into a home with 12 children ranging in age from 18 months to 9 years, two mothers, and three adult men who were visiting the mothers. The men did not want me there, and they tried to intimidate me by singing nasty songs. I know these moms well enough that I thought, "Nope, I am not going to leave. These moms do not want me to leave. They do not think that this is not a good time for me to visit," so I stayed. And finally, one man in particular finally gave up and went outside to smoke.

Carol: But what happens when you cannot get the mom's focused attention because of so many kids?

Cynthia: Then, I hang out and play with the kids. It does not matter if I have Mom's attention. I mean it does matter in the long run, but I will stay. I know that I am the only constant in these women's lives. With this family, I spent the first 6 months playing with the kids, and neither mom would talk to me. Often, they would go to another room and half-listen. This went on for 3 months before they would sit with me and their children. And then they could not sit with me the whole hour. They would get up and go have a cigarette or make a phone call.

Cynthia's persistence is nonwavering; eventually, the parents understand that she does want and expect them to be with her and their children. But first they need to experience Cynthia's care and commitment by her persistent visiting, active play with their children, and consistent invitation for them to join her, even when they do not for so many months. For these two mothers, Cynthia was the first adult who had been absolutely predictable.

> I know they want me to come. Their friends in Even Start teased them for only coming to Even Start 1 in 4 days on most weeks. They replied, "We do not need to come because Cynthia always visits us at home!" It is now so different [from] when I first started visiting them. They screen all their phone calls, but they always answer when I call them.
>
> People see you in a certain light and expect you to do the same thing they are used to. One of the things I do for these chaotic families is that I provide a routine within the time frame that I am in their home. They know we are going to play some kind of game, and I am going to read a story, and then I am going to ask them to read. And the longer I have been there, the more successes I have in getting them on the floor to play with their child. Not every time, but it is much better than at the beginning.

Cynthia is secure in her competence and the parents' desire to give their children the best that they can. Thus, she is willing to try new strategies, even though she does not know whether they will work. What she does know is that she cares and that the parents eventually will understand that she cares; then, with her guidance, they can move forward. Cynthia described a poignant example of her creative initiative.

> One of the moms seemed so depressed that I changed my mode of operation one day. These are not women who would tell me about personal problems such as having a fight with their boyfriend. But I went to this mom's home and decided to change what I normally do. When I got to this home, I said, "I don't want to see the kids. Do you have someone who can watch them while you and I go to McDonald's?" We went to McDonald's, and I bought her a soda. And I just talked to her like a person and said, "You really have been down. Is there some way that I can help?"
>
> And she cried and talked about how she has to do everything for her family and her sister's family [who all live with her]. Everyone is in and out of this house, and the teenagers and boyfriends come in and eat all the food that she has bought for the small children. And she goes to bed at night wondering if they will have food in the morning, and often they do not. And

this happens almost every night. There are a lot of people in this home, up to 20 people, and she is tired, tired of trying to swim up river when there is this current the other way.

That was the only time that she talked to me like that. And what I did for her was to try to hook her up with the child abuse network because they do in-home counseling. I do not know if she will do it. But on the positive side, this mom tested on the sixth- or seventh-grade level last fall. And after 1 year, she now is at the eleventh-grade level. She only comes to Adult Basic Education 1 day instead of 4 days a week, but this is a parent who told me, "The reason I am still here is because you won't leave me alone." But it is hard. I sometimes feel like I have been in a washing machine being pulled in all directions. One time, I arrived in her home and the 3-year-old was fingerpainting the baby's head. The mom was screaming at him, which did not help. Then, we could not find anything in the house to wipe the paint off with—no rags, tissues, nothing.

When I am with this family, I try to bring order, the only order this family experiences. In that living room, for 10 minutes, if I can get everyone around me listening to that book, I have brought order for a small amount of time. And that to me is powerful because I can show it can be done and for the first time, they experience order. These parents are not stupid. They experience this with me, and they remember, and the next time, maybe they will pick up the book and sit down to bring that order.

Cynthia believes that parents can give their child improved parenting if the parents themselves experience a personal relationship with a caring adult who gives them support and guidance. She understands that some of the parents she works with had troubled childhoods and live in extreme chaos with no support. Although she often feels as if she is being pulled in too many directions when visiting these families, she knows that the parents feel they are overwhelmed with responsibilities with little support. Her persistence and predictable, unswerving respect and care allow these parents to know that their struggles to care for their children are valued and that they can make a difference in their young children's lives.

CONCLUSION

This chapter examines two levels of home visiting skills. First, the chapter identifies 14 communication-interpersonal skills. These are high-level skills that improve through experience over an extended time through self-reflection on that experience and through constructive feedback from professional peers and supervisors. These 14 skills encourage, maintain, and promote the parent–home visitor relationship.

Regardless of home visitors' extended experience and skills, forming a relationship can be very messy.

Second, the chapter identifies five areas of knowledge and skill also essential to the home visiting process. Unlike the first 14 skills, these areas do not overlap or occur together. They are more like a collection that can be taught at least partially, for example, knowledge of available community resources, child maltreatment laws, and areas of confidentiality. This is knowledge involving societal rules and resources. To illustrate these two levels of skills, two exemplary home visitors, Janice and Cynthia, share their experiences with families and their understanding of these experiences. To gain clarity, the chapter discusses different approaches separately, even though experts agree that home visiting is an organic, unfolding process in which visitors use several approaches simultaneously. The chapter concludes with a discussion of difficulties and dilemmas involved in working with parents who are concrete thinkers and those families who live in chaotic conditions.

3

Working with Diverse Families

I have a dream that one day this nation will rise up and live out the true meaning of its creed: "We hold these truths to be self-evident: that all men are created equal."

Martin Luther King, Jr. (1963)

Each family has beliefs, values, interaction styles, role expectations, and rituals that reflect its ethnic, racial, religious, or national membership and socioeconomic status (SES). These characteristics influence every aspect of development; however, there are universal features of child development and parent–baby relationships that cross all of these boundaries. For example, young children are attached to their primary caregivers. The United States is a diverse society, and this diversity continually increases. By 2030, children of European origin will make up less than 50% of the population younger than age 5 in the United States.[1] Respecting and accepting a family's diversity is an essential part of home visiting. This chapter begins by discussing working with families of diverse backgrounds, especially those who are disproportionately at risk.[2] Next, it addresses the role of extended family members in the home visiting process. Finally, the chapter addresses poverty and the difficulties of working in violent environments.

CULTURE

Lewis (2000) defined *culture* as the norms, values, attitudes, and behaviors of a group that are transmitted through language and everyday interactions between caregivers and young children. These meanings are learned, shared, and communicated across generations.[3] Daily interactions within the home and among family members reinforce the values and beliefs of culture. Culture is often confused with the concepts of ethnicity and race. Ethnicity is a self-defined identity based on the culture of one's ancestors' national or tribal group. Ethnicity and race are different concepts: A racial group has a distinctive genetic heritage.[4] In the United States, race means a group defined by its members' physical characteristics, such as skin color or hair type. Ethnic groups may be made up of people from several racial groups. For example, people who call themselves *Hispanic* may have skin tones from very light to very dark. There is both similarity and heterogeneity among members of cultural, ethnic, and racial group.

Families are the primary vehicle for the transmission of culture. Young children learn their cultural schemes from their parents and extended families. Aspects of culture important to child development include beliefs about child rearing, children's growth and development, the role of the family, and the meaning of child and parent behavior.[5] Cross-cultural research indicates that significant variation in maternal sensitivity and contingent responsiveness to babies' cues is based on parental cultural beliefs.[6]

Sensitivity is the key to working with parents from diverse cul-

tures. Home visitors must respect cultural differences in feeding practices, sleeping, toilet learning, discipline, and the role of family members as well as beliefs about holding, cuddling, and spoiling babies and
young children. Home visitors need to be sensitive when interpreting
babies' needs, responding to babies, and considering babies' and their
parents' points of view.

The young child's social context within the home is very important for both language learning and emergent literacy. Heath studied
specifically the language patterns of two communities, Trackton and
Roadville, a few miles from one another in the Piedmont Carolinas,
among whom Heath lived and worked with for nearly a decade.[7] Her
work illustrated how different cultures within the home have different
values and practices of language and literacy. Both Trackton, an African American community, and Roadville, a European American community, are working-class communities. Trackton parents did not create reading and writing tasks for their children, nor did they buy
special books for their children. Yet, Trackton children developed literacy skills through a process of group-oriented social interaction, for example, extended family members and neighbors chatting together on
their front porches. In contrast, Roadville homes had abundant reading
materials. Parents read books to their children, gave them workbooks,
and assisted them in learning colors, matching shapes, and letters.
Children both in Trackton and Roadvile talked a lot; however, the children's talking did not transfer well into the existing primary-level practices of the local school. Each community practiced language and literacy in a different manner; yet neither community's practices matched
well with the expectations within the children's school.

Developmental competence is a culturally defined construct. The mean
age expectations in months for milestone attainment among Anglo,
Puerto Rican, and Filipino families illustrates culturally defined developmental competence. (See Table 1.)

When home visitors work with families of cultural backgrounds
different from their own, respect, rapport building, empathic listening,
and support are especially important. Everyone has assumptions about
other cultures that could lead to stereotyping. To provide effective service when working with families of different cultures, however, home
visitors need to be flexible and open-minded and to rigorously avoid
stereotyping.

What people see, hear, and understand is filtered through their
cultural heritage. Home visitors' sensitivity to how their own behavior,
attitudes, and values reflect their age, gender, ethnicity, and social class
is the first step in their ability to relate to families with a culture differ-

Table 1.   Cultural definitions for age (in months) of milestone attainment

	Anglo	Puerto Rican	Filipino
Eat solid food	8.2	10.1	6.7
Training cup	12.0	17.1	21.9
Utensils	17.7	26.5	32.4
Finger food	8.9	9.4	9.5
Wean	16.8	18.2	36.2
Sleep by self	13.8	14.6	32.4
Choose clothes	31.1	44.2	33.1
Dress self	38.2	33.2	39.2
Play alone	25.0	24.8	12.3
Toilet trained/day	31.6	29.0	20.4
Toilet trained/night	33.2	31.8	34.2

From Carlson, V.J., & Harwood, R.L. (2000). Understanding and negotiating cultural differences concerning early developmental competence: The six raisin solution. *Zero to Three, 20*(3), 22; reprinted by permission.

ent from their own. In other words, competent home visitors are dual minded—aware of their own actions, thoughts, and feelings as well as the actions, thought, and feelings of the families with whom they work.

When home visitors work with families who are members of a different culture from their own, they try to do several important tasks at the same time. First, home visitors are aware of their own cultural biases. Second, they work to understand and respect each family's cultural patterns. Third, they try to recognize differences within and not just between different family cultures, and fourth, they see the uniqueness of each family, regardless of its culture. For example, the home visitor understands that the discipline values and practices of the Tsai family represent their Japanese American heritage; however, the Tsai family also has developed patterns of relating to their children that are uniquely their own—not just typically Japanese American.

Working with culturally diverse families requires balancing awareness of the family's cultural patterns with awareness of their own cultural patterns and using that awareness to track what is happening within home visits. For example, a home visitor knows her strong preference for children sleeping in their own beds, yet is working with a family in which the toddler sleeps with her parents. As the toddler's mother discusses her child's nighttime sleep patterns, the home visitor monitors her own comments to make certain that she unwittingly does not share her bias.

The tasks of some home visitors include developmental assessments. When home visitors learn that a child has a potential problem, they not only need to gain an accurate evaluation of the child's abilities but they also need to assess the family's perspective on why their child is being referred for services. Parents may disagree on the scope or severity of the concern, or they may not be concerned at all. For example, a home visitor may be very concerned about a 3-year-old's hyperactivity and aggression, but the parents may see these behaviors as favorable because the child is independent and expresses him- or herself—two characteristics that are supported by the family's culture.

Cultural differences also can emerge regarding relationships with service providers. Some cultures provide supernatural explanations for a child's problem, for example, that a fever is caused by God or a malevolent spirit. Furthermore, families and home visitors may differ on what course of action to take. Parents may agree that their child has a problem, but they may not agree that their own behaviors need to be modified. Col and Magnus spoke of three issues to be considered when professionals want to provide intervention for a family of a different culture:

1. Whether the family believes that a problem exists

2. The family beliefs about the cause of the problem

3. What different family members think about the course of action that should be taken[8]

ETHNIC DIFFERENCES

In the United States, ethnic minorities are increasing at such a rate that soon they will be a majority. Ethnicity—belonging to a group that shares specific social and cultural traditions—is a very important aspect that shapes a young child's identity. Ethnicity influences the way a person thinks, feels, and behaves. Membership in an ethnic group gives a person a sense of belonging and continuity. Garbarino clarified:

Ethnicity enables children to form a map of how they perceive themselves and their world, and bestows meaning on their experiences. Ethnicity influences such factors as the child's role in his or her family, how he or she is perceived at school, how he or she is treated by peers, and how he or she is accepted by the community.[9]

Ethnic minorities in the United States include refugees, resident groups, and immigrants. Refugees have fled their home country because of war or religious or racial persecution. These refugees, in addition to adjusting to new language and culture, must deal with any prior traumatizing experiences they have had.

In the United States, minority groups historically have suffered from many barriers: unequal access to economic and political influence, few opportunities in education and employment, and insufficient health services. These conditions often produce alienation and social isolation, providing stress for children and their families. Furthermore, each minority group has its own unique history in the United States. Young children of ethnic minorities need to learn to function in two cultures, the culture of their home and that of the United States in general. Garbarino identified the factors needed for children to successfully live in two cultures simultaneously:

1. *Shared norms, values, and beliefs between the cultures*
2. *Cultural translators, mediators, and models available for the child*
3. *Feedback provided by each culture about the child's behavior*
4. *Similarities in both cultures in conceptualization and problem-solving*
5. *Ability to speak the language of both cultures*
6. *Similarity in the child's physical appearance to the people of the mainstream culture*[10]

In minority families, children often experience conflict between the beliefs of their parents' culture and that of their peers at school. These children's problems can be manifest in depression, behavior problems, and school adjustment problems. Some children from minority groups have difficulty blending two cultures into one identity. For example, some Native American children may go back and forth between their Native American identity and American identity. Some minority parents need a longer time to adapt to their new environment than do their children. Minority parents may also give their children conflicting messages. For example, they may want their children to succeed in school but not be become Americanized.

Home visitors can understand a minority family's transactions with the environment when they consider three types of segregation: 1) residential segregation, which can be a limiting fact because a family's location has a direct and often constraining effect on resources such as health care and employment; 2) economic segregation, continued because of employment discrimination; and 3) social and psychological segregation, when families and children are not given access to important social and emotional resources.[11]

African Americans, Hispanic Americans, East and Southeast Asian Americans, and Native Americans are the four largest minority groups in the United States.[12] Native Americans have suffered immeasurably. Over the years, Native Americans have been uprooted and relocated as their land has been seized. African American children may be at risk because they are more likely to experience persistent poverty. African American parents' goals and behaviors affect the developmental outcome of their children. Fitzgerald and Montanex identified 10 patterns of African American parents:

1. Spirituality or belief in a supreme being or supreme powers, which goes beyond religiosity to focus on the qualities of people rather than material possessions

2. Communication or an interpersonal orientation reflects an emphasis on group over individual goals, people-focused versus task-focused activities

3. Harmony refers to the importance of integrating one's life into a whole, recognizing one's interdependency with the environment, and seeking unity rather than control

4. Expressive communication or orality emphasizes transmitting and receiving information orally, through rhythmic communication and call and response

5. Affect sensitivity to emotional cues reflects the integration of feelings with cognition, and a synthesis of the verbal and nonverbal

6. Rhythmic movement is expressed in gross motor behavior and reflects an interest in flexible yet patterned action

7. Multidimensional perception, or verve, is illustrated in the preference for stimulus variety in learning (e.g., visual, auditory, tactile, motor); both parent and child value experimentation

8. Stylistic expressiveness refers to the valuing of the individual's unique style, flair, or spontaneity in expressing oneself, (e.g., the way one walks, talks, or wears an article of clothing), but this value is emphasized only when it facilitates group goals

9. Time is a social phenomenon that reflects the view that time is spiritual, not material or linear. For example, an event begins when the first person arrives and ends when the last person leaves, rather than at fixed points on the clock.

10. Positivity refers to the desire to see good in all situations no matter how bad they seem on the surface[13]

African American mothers tend to be younger, with a higher percentage of single parenting and a greater likelihood of living with extended families or other adults.

Cynthia worked for many years with African American families in a center-based Head Start program. I interviewed Cynthia after her first year as director of an Even Start program where she made home visits twice a month. Cynthia discussed her home visiting experience with African American families.

I think I have worked with maybe one or two families where a wariness stayed there the whole time, but I don't blame people for that. It's a scary thing to have people come into your home, especially if you have had to deal with social workers and that kind of thing. I am not naive enough to think that I am everybody's best friend. People take from me what they want, and that's okay. So, my relationship with a lot of black families is probably a little different than that with my white families.

Over the years, Cynthia has had many positive relationships with African American parents; however, she knows that not all African American families will accept her, just as not all Hispanic families nor all Caucasian families will accept her. She understands that many people have had problematic relationships with people from public agencies and that opening one's home to strangers is a new and scary experience for some people. At the same time, Cynthia understands the unique contributions that home visiting can offer to both professionals and parents.

This program has taught me so much about working with families in general, and in particular, about working with families of color. I have had a lot of experience with that, but not in the same context. This is the first time I have had the opportunity to visit homes as well as see parents at the center, for we are doing a home-based and a center-based model. Before, I just worked at a center-based program and never saw people's homes and didn't go there all the time and know what's going on with the family as intimately as I do in home visiting.

In visiting homes, Cynthia now has a new and more intimate understanding of the families with whom she works. Although she had many years working with similar families in a center-based program, she did not understand the unique particularities of individual family's daily life until she regularly visited their homes. Cynthia also understands that if she is successful, she must meet each parent where he or she is.

Cynthia acknowledges the wide range of differences among and within cultural groups, and she does not expect every parent to readily accept her. She realistically acknowledges that she will not develop a personal relationship with each parent. Cynthia is sensitive to this reality but does not let it hamper her work. Visiting homes has given her depth in understanding of the complex problems that at-risk families confront daily. Within this understanding, she respects each parent and understands that regardless of the developmental level or complexity of problems, all parents have hopes and dreams and want the best for their child. In turn, parents feel Cynthia's respect and can be open to learning from Cynthia. Latoya and Ann, two mothers participating in the program, described their feelings toward Cynthia.

Latoya: Cynthia cares about everyone. She's helped me have more patience, play more, know how to relate more without yelling and without feeling like I gotta pop them.

Ann: Now I'm more prone to keep busy instead of slouching around the house. It's built my self-esteem, and I have a more positive outlook. I have a different perspective on things. I'm a different person as far as doing frivolous things. Now I read, go to the library. Before, I would rent action-packed movies. Now, I read something I could learn from.

Effective home visitors recognize and respect these differences and strive to work with the family within the framework of a family's beliefs and practices. The effective home visitor knows that what is happening within a home visit can be interpreted in different ways. For example, the home visitor may worry about a shy child while the parent sees this child as a very good, obedient child. When a home visitor recognizes differences, it is helpful first to ask questions to understand better what a specific belief or practice means to a parent. What does "spoiling" her 4-month-old baby mean to a young African American mother? Does this "spoiling" mean something different to a Vietnamese American mother? Being spoiled may be the label that this mother's extended family has given her baby or "spoiling my baby" may be the mother's way of telling the home visitor she thinks her baby cries because he knows she always will pick him up when he cries. Once the home visitor understands and shows respect for this mother's interpretation of the meaning of her baby's behavior, then he or she can explore alternative meanings.

Bilingual Families

When young children learn two languages from birth, they have a special advantage. If infants hear two languages and they keep using the languages as they grow, they will be able to speak both languages fluently, like native speakers. Early childhood is the best time to learn more than one language because young children automatically develop second speech centers. Young children learn two languages easiest if they hear each language from a consistent source, for example, if the mother speaks English and the father speaks Chinese.

Talking to bilingual parents often requires tact because some parents may be embarrassed by their poor English. Home visitors can help bilingual parents recognize that their children's goal is to develop strong communication skills, regardless of the language. Young children learning two languages may need some extra time to reach certain language milestones; as a result, on early language screenings, these children may have a slight language delay in expressive skills, but home visitors can stress that the long-term advantage of being bilingual is worth the short-term delay in expressive skills. Home visitors can encourage parents to speak their native language with their child at home. When parents speak to their child only in English, parent–child interactions may suffer because the parents may speak less to their child.

EXTENDED FAMILIES

In 1990, 3.2 million children in the United States lived in extended families, a 40% increase during 10 years.[14] Home visitors sometimes visit children who live within an extended family that offers them multiple, strong emotional attachments with adults committed to their well-being.[15] Extended families often can buffer parents and their young children from the impact of stress (e.g., availability of child care, pooling of money for food and housing). When home visitors work with several extended families, they recognize that there are considerable differences in the way extended families are organized and relate to each other. Cynthia discussed previously how important it is for home visitors to have the parent decide who is a part of the home visit. When other family members are a part of the visit, they are included in the discussion; however, the focus remains on the parents as primary decision makers for their child. At the same time, home visitors have opportunities to affirm the role of grandmother, aunt, or other extended family member.

Grandparents give to their children and grandchildren in many ways. Often, they help ease the transition from intrauterine life to birth and provide support and nurturance for the baby's parents. Through grandparents' windows into the past, grandchildren can learn about the childhoods of their parents as well as their grandparents and thereby gain an understanding the flow of both constancy and change over time. Grandparents often have more time than parents, so they can become special friends and teachers. They can engage in long talks with older grandchildren on substantive issues such as the meaning of life and religion. Often, grandparents play endless board games with young grandchildren or take them on outings such as to special parks.

More and more grandparents are bringing up their very young grandchildren. Due to teen parenting, these grandparents often are not retired or gray-haired, but in their 30s, 40s, and 50s. Many grandparents have limited resources and educational and experiential backgrounds. Financial, medical, legal, and access difficulties are interconnected. Most grandparents raise their grandchildren without legal custody. Many grandparents have difficulty accessing medical care, especially preventive medical care such as immunizations, for their grandchildren.[16]

Working with young parents in extended families also can be challenging. Some homes may be overcrowded, and it becomes difficult to have both space and time to focus during a visit. Thus, home visitors may choose to have some visits at their offices or a neutral place such as a park or library. Some young parents may be immersed in disagreement, power struggles, or conflict with other family members. Then, when home visitors express child-rearing views different from the beliefs and practices of the extended family, home visitors can be viewed as threatening. The home visitor can listen respectfully; however, the conflict may be beyond the task or expertise of the home visitor. In these difficult situations, home visitors can gain help from administrators, supervisors, and meetings of peers in which they can discuss the issue and gain feedback, interpretations, and suggestions.

POVERTY

In the United States, children younger than 6 years of age have the highest poverty rates of any age group.[17] Families of all social classes have problems; however, low-income family problems are more likely to be multiple and complex because poverty increases the likelihood of the presence of risk factors such as employment problems, inadequate housing, violent neighborhoods, and accompanying social-emotional problems.[18] As Shonkoff and Phillips explained, "Families who occupy different socioeconomic niches because of parental education, income, and occupation have strikingly different capacities to purchase safe housing, nutritious meals, high-quality child care, and other opportunities that can foster health, learning and adaptation."[19]

Poverty among children from minority groups has increased much more than poverty among children who are not from minority groups. Young children are the poorest age group in the United States. The combination of family poverty and neighborhood poverty is a double risk for a substantive number of minority children, including African American children and, to a lesser extent, Hispanic children.[20] The malleability of young children's development and the overwhelming importance of the family suggest that economic conditions in early childhood may be far more important for shaping children's ability, behavior, and achievement than conditions later in childhood.

Poverty affects the healthy development of young children, most commonly through low birth weight, increased infant mortality, damaged early brain development, increased accidents, and increased illnesses such as asthma, upper respiratory infection, tuberculosis, and pediatric acquired immunodeficiency syndrome (AIDS).[21] Poverty interferes with parents' early caregiving relationship; mother–baby attachment; and subsequent externalizing behavior such as hyperactivity, aggression, and impulsivity. It also affects parents' ability to provide a healthy early home learning environment. Crowded household conditions, community disorganization, and violence often accompany poverty and have a negative effect on young children's development.

Exposure to lead in early childhood has a potential negative impact both on early brain development and cognitive development.[22] The National Center for Heath Statistics has reported that young children of low-income families are more than seven times as likely to have elevated blood lead levels than those living in high-income families.[23]

Home visitors working with low-income families have a complex, difficult job requiring great flexibility and sensitivity. They need to believe that, in spite of their difficult circumstances, people with low incomes are worthy of respect and dignity and have hopes and dreams that can be fulfilled. Cynthia described how to look for common ground when working with these families.

I think I use the same approach. It's just that what you use or what things you talk about may be different. But the approach is the same, and that is, I look for a common ground. I look for something to make that first contact with. It might be a hairdo; it might be the clothing they are wearing. "Oh, that is a pretty color; it really suits you." It might be something that decorates the home, and that wouldn't make any difference whether it is a middle-income or low-income home.

For me, the thing that makes the difference is that it has to be genuine, and you really have to like the hairdo or like the knick-knacks on the shelf or it doesn't ring true. From the time you get out of your car you are being assessed and the look on your face makes a big difference in how that person is going to receive you when he or she opens the door. I usually try to find something that I can talk about that is not stuffy so that I can be natural, but not forcing, such as "What a pretty shirt" or "It's a pretty day out"—a comment that will get me going.

Many middle-income homes have different things in them than low-income homes, but it is just the material things that are different—although most families have TVs and a VCR, so that is always a good topic of conversation. "Seen anything good on TV lately?" or "Have you watched any good movies?" People feel comfortable talking about that.

And it doesn't matter what kind of family, what age, race, or income level. The child is the common ground, and there always are lots and lots of things you can say about that child. "Oh, look at all that hair. Look at the way he smiles." How much a family makes or where they live, that shouldn't matter because you are trying to serve that family and help them do the best that they can do.

Cynthia knows that from the moment she steps out of the car, she is communicating with parents. Body gestures, such as her facial expression, communicate as much as words. She also knows that the first step in building a relationship is being genuine. Whatever she says, she honestly believes or feels it. Cynthia begins her interaction on a common ground with parents. She is able to do this because she deeply believes that people are more alike than they are different. She establishes mutuality at the outset in a conversation about some aspect of the parent that she likes. Because the program's purpose is fostering the child's development, there is always a child present. Cynthia also can find something wonderful about each child to talk about with his or her parents. Her primary focus is the child's parents, though, because she understands that it is her relationship with the parents that allows her to promote the parents' relationship with their child.

When home visitors work with low-income families, potential problems may include 1) difficulties regarding the accessibility of families, 2) difficulties in recruitment of families, 3) increased external and personal problems, and 4) safety issues.[24]

Accessibility

Low-income families tend to be very mobile, and often they do not inform their home visitor of their impending move. Thus, home visitors may spend a lot of time tracking down families who have moved. Even when low-income families are not mobile, it may be difficult for a home visitor to have minimal distractions and adequate space to conduct a home visit. Low-income families also often live in impoverished neighborhoods with limited resources, such as parks or libraries, where a visit could be conducted.

A common dilemma is that parents may not keep their appointments; that is, they may not be home on the scheduled time for home visiting. Low-income families who have been exposed to an array of agencies, such as public aid, emergency rooms, and WIC, are accustomed to long periods of waiting and assume that professionals think that their time is of no value. Furthermore, some have never had trusting relationships with adults, so they see no reason for taking a time commitment seriously. As a result, some low-income parents do not take responsibility for being present for their home visiting appointment.

Home visitors who work with these families learn that frequent reminders make home visits more successful. If a parent has a telephone, a call before a home visit can be effective. If parents have no home phone, a reminder via postcard can be helpful. Once home visitors have established a trusting relationship, an impromptu visit is most helpful; that is, the home visitor drops by the home, explains that he or she is are in the area and merely wants to remind the parent of the visit the next day.

Recruitment

Home visiting programs that serve low-income families cannot depend on written brochures, newspaper releases, and word of mouth—strategies that often are adequate for other families. In home visiting programs serving low-income families, staff probably need to be very assertive in recruiting the families. Smith and Well's case study of a program serving low-income urban families described successful strategies.[25] Their suggestions include setting up tables at grocery stores, meeting parents at bus stops, meeting parents at homeless shelters, and networking with public aid and WIC staff so that they give parents the needed information. They also suggest that programs hire individuals who do nothing but recruit families.

Increased External and Personal Problems

Low-income families are disproportionately at risk for having personal, social, emotional, and health problems, as well as external problems such as unemployment, inadequate housing, or inadequate neighborhoods. When families are experiencing multiple problems, they often cannot focus on their parenting or on their young child's needs until basic family needs are addressed. When home visitors first address the concerns foremost in the parents' minds, such as the threat of the heat being turned off, parents can develop trust in their relationship with the home visitor over time and begin to pay greater attention to the needs of their child. In these situations, the home visitor's agenda cannot be the initial focus.

Maintaining one's professional boundaries can be an essential skill when working with families experiencing multiple problems. These families may need services that are beyond the expertise of the home visitor or more comprehensive than those available in the home visiting program. Weiss argued convincingly that home visiting is a "necessary but not sufficient" service for families with multiple, complex problems.[26] When home visiting is a stand-alone program, home visitors need to gain knowledge of available community resources so that they can assist families in seeking additional help.

Given the stressors that accompany poverty, home visitors regularly experience unexpected complications. Flexibility, patience, and a strong commitment to service become requirements when working with families experiencing multiple, complex problems. As with all families, establishing a personal relationship is the first task before other issues can be addressed. It may take more time to develop trust and rapport and for parents to feel their home visitor's genuine concern and caring. It may take persistence, returning again and again, before a parent can feel enough trust to maintain appointments. Home visitors know that most parents want the best for their child, regardless of how their parenting may seem to be compromised. Supervision and team meetings in which home visitors can share their difficulties and successes are important supports for working with families having multiple complex problems.

Safety Issues

Chapter 11 discusses domestic as well as community violence and child maltreatment. Violence is commonplace in the United States, and low-income families in particular are more likely to experience violence. When young children are traumatized by violence, this traumatization leads to significant problems. Garbarino and Ganzel reported that since the 1980s, young children's need for foster care has increased parallel with increases in child maltreatment and the rising use of crack cocaine.[27] Osofsky and Dickson have identified the most significant problems:

- *Children exposed to violence have been referred to services 2 years or more after the incident and tend to have significant learning problems.*
- *Some children referred later are intensely and unpredictably aggressive.*
- *Some late-referred children are withdrawn, showing significant depression.[28]*

Groves, Lieberman, Osofsky, and Fenichel offered the following advice for home visitors working with children who live in violent environments:

- Remember that healing begins with relationships.
- Do what you can to stabilize environments for children and families and to provide safety and security for them.

- Help children by helping their parents.
- Be comfortable with the limits of the home visiting profession.
- Make sure you have good supervision, peer support, and self-care.
- Look at your own attitudes toward violence as you seek to understand and inform the attitudes of others.
- Find ways of involving and supporting all family members when violence is a concern: Blaming is not the answer.
- Have a network of support.[29]

Maintaining personal safety is basic to effective home visiting. Safety concerns differ across communities. In isolated rural areas, inadequate roads may require that the home visitor's car be in good condition for rough use. Inner-city communities with high rates of violence may demand that two home visitors, rather than one, conduct visits. At all times, when visiting in high-crime areas, home visitors need to make certain that another responsible staff member knows their visiting schedule, which includes the family's name, the date, the time of the visit, and their expected time of return. Some home visitors who work in dangerous communities use a two-way radio communication system. Others call their supervisor before and after such a visit. In some programs, each home visitor is given a cell phone. When neighborhoods are potentially dangerous, it is important to know the neighborhood well in order to avoid getting lost. Once families and neighbors become familiar with the home visitor, they can look out for him or her (e.g., watch for his or her car, greet the home visitor outdoors). If parking is questionable, some home visiting programs hire drivers to transport visitors to and from the homes.

If, upon arrival, home visitors discover that they have entered in the middle of a domestic dispute, they should leave. Personal safety is always the first necessity when working with troubled families. Cynthia described her work with families living in chaos.

> More often, what happens is you get to a home and something is going on, either the electricity is going to be shut off or Mom has had a fight with her boyfriend or something unexpectedly has happened to upset the parent. I take the cue from the parent. Generally, they will tell me what is going on. My first response is to say, "Do you want me to stay, or do you want me to come back at a different time?" It is a respect issue. This is not my chaos; this is someone else's chaos. People, generally, when they are in flux like that, don't want someone watching their chaos. So, I respect that, and I'll just say, "Do you want me to come back later?" Sometimes they will say yes, and I will reschedule our appointment. If it is a situation where some-

Table 2.   Safety precautions for home visitors

Make certain your car is in good working condition.

Post a sign in your car that identifies your program.

Call the office before and after a visit that could entail danger.

Make a home visit with a colleague.

In dangerous neighborhoods, make home visits in the morning.

Call the parents just before a home visit so they can watch for you.

Carry a cell phone.

Be respectful and professional.

If a situation does not feel right, do not leave your car. If you are indoors, leave the home immediately.

Be organized with materials that are beside you.

When you leave the home, have your car keys in hand.

one is in danger—if I feel the mother is in danger of hurting herself or the child—then I may not leave without making sure that the mom has a hotline number or some other support. Then, there is the scenario where I will go in and they will want me to stay because they need help or someone to talk to, and then I will stay.

Table 2 lists some safety precautions for home visitors to consider when working in high-crime neighborhoods.

DIFFICULTIES AND DILEMMAS

Some home visitors stumble over their own feet when working with people from cultures other than their own. Some are not aware of their own cultural biases, which they may unwittingly project onto the parents they work with. For example, a home visitor may not be sensitive to his or her bias against young children sleeping with their parents. He or she may not be aware that sleeping with one's parents occurs across many cultures and in many American families. With this bias and lack of awareness, the home visitor may make inappropriate negative comments about this sleeping pattern.

Home visitors who do not understand other cultures may inappropriately interpret a family's values, attitudes, or actions. For example, a home visitor has several middle-class, educated Asian American families in her caseload. She assumes that all of these families should share her cultural biases and patterns because they live in the same city as she does. This assumption may lead her to frown on specific customs that pertain to Asian Americans.

Skilled home visitors are knowledgeable about dominant patterns across different cultures. With this knowledge, the home visitors can be respectful and supportive when encountering everyday patterns that are different from those of his or her own culture. To be knowledgeable about other cultures often entails commitment to independent study beyond field work.

CONCLUSION

This chapter discusses working with families from diverse cultures. People from many cultures, ethnicities, and races live in the United States, so home visitors are likely to encounter families who have a different culture, ethnicity, or race than that of the home visitors. These home visitors must be careful how they interpret a caregiver's actions because the norms, values, attitudes, and behaviors of the caregiver's culture influence the way he or she interacts with the child. Home visitors who do not have knowledge and understanding of diversity may think that what a certain caregiver does is wrong, when in fact it is just different. With knowledge of other cultures, home visitors can distinguish between a behavior or belief that is harmful to the child and one that is simply different from what the home visitor's culture advocates.

This chapter also discusses working with extended families. When home visitors arrive at a home and find grandparents or other extended family members present, they should allow the parents to decide who can remain during a visit.

The chapter concludes with a look at the difficulty of working with families who live in poverty. Socio-economic status is similar to culture in that it may affect beliefs and behaviors. A large proportion of home visiting programs serve low-income families living in high-poverty neighborhoods; however, most home visitors come from a higher SES. Given this disparity, home visitors need to acknowledge the differences between their values and behaviors and those of low-income families. Home visitors working with families living in poverty may also face other difficulties such as accessibility, recruitment, internal and external problems, and safety issues. Home visiting with children at risk is a daunting task. In order to be effective and avoid burnout, these home visitors need regular supervision so that they can process their work and gain feedback and support.

4
Professional Development

The starting point of any process of thinking is something going on, something which just as it stands is incomplete or unfulfilled. Its point, its meaning lies literally in what it is going to be, in how it is going to turn out.

John Dewey (1916, pp. 146–147)

The quality of the relationship between the home visitor and the parent determines the likelihood of the parent's gaining an understanding of child development and effective parenting skills. Previous chapters discuss skills that enable home visitors to be effective in helping parents understand their child's development and develop appropriate parenting approaches. This chapter explores ways to help home visitors improve their understanding and skills. Just as the home visitor enables parents in the practice of parenting, so too do team members, mentors, and supervisors help home visitors in their practice of home visiting.

Home visiting is a craft, and home visitors are artisans in the same sense that musicians and athletes are artisans. As artisans, much of home visitors' craft is learned on the job. Home visiting can be understood only as it evolves in each visitor's practice, which takes place in many unpredictable and unique situations.[1] Much of the home visitor's knowledge is tacit. That is, the knowing is in the action, and thinking and doing are interwoven. Just as the athlete and musician improve their skills by reflecting on what they do with coaches to help them think about how they are playing, how to develop their strengths, and how to recognize their weaknesses, home visitors can benefit from reflection and advice. This chapter explores the kinds of coaching a home visitor needs to improve his or her reflection and practice. In home visiting, peers, mentors, and supervisors can serve as coaches.

The continued professional growth of home visitors is a process parallel to the dynamics of parent development within home visits. As in parenting, professional development is continual and learned on the job. There are no recipes or formulas. Often, the job seems untidy and unpredictable. Like parenting, the home visitor's work includes both feelings and thoughts—emotion and intellect.[2] The relationship between home visitors and their professional peers, mentors, and supervisors is the key to continued growth, and this relationship should be based on mutual respect and collaboration.

Three powerful ways of learning for home visitors are 1) education to gain new knowledge and understanding of how that knowledge can be applied to their practice, 2) reflection on action and 3) learning by doing—practicing over time. Reflection on action means that home visitors stop and think about how they understand their work. They know that each home visit is new and that parents have their own way of thinking and their own goals for their child. With practice, home visitors learn to think about what they are doing while they are doing it. They become more aware of both the uniqueness of each family and common themes across families. As their relationship with a family evolves, they develop a series of expectations of parent, child, and themselves (i.e., their actions and reactions). They become more aware of both successful and problematic approaches they are using, and as they reflect on their experience, home visitors learn to focus in concrete ways on the key struggles of parents and young children.

Home visitors often go into a home where there is a great deal of activity. Reflection on that complex experience allows home visitors to focus on what is important in the moment. They develop expertise in practical, "how to get the job done" parenting skills such as getting young children to sleep, toilet training, and so forth. One of the difficulties involved with clarifying the process is that home visiting is implemented across several disciplines, most commonly social work, education, and nursing. In addition, some community-based home visiting programs hire visitors without related professional training.[3] Because home visiting is an evolving profession, effective professional development for home visitors may involve learning processes that may not be a part of the disciplines in which the home visitor was educated.

This chapter describes education and supervision from a perspective that sees both as environments for relationships and learning. This approach to professional development is fundamentally different from a lot of in-service education, which offers unconnected workshops or courses of instruction. The supervision described here, in which supervisor and supervisee have shared power with mutual expectations and shared evaluation, is very different from a model of supervision based on monitoring and evaluating against a set of standard competencies.

EDUCATION

Across the United States there is a critical shortage of professional education for home visitors. One of the most significant causes of this shortage is the lack of preservice preparation in colleges and universities. Most people's educational experiences consist of didactic teaching: memorizing and rote learning of information, habits, and skills. This chapter promotes an educational approach that is different from traditional teaching and follows the educational style of Rogers, Dewey, and Bruner.[4] This educational approach takes place in a climate of inquiry in which learners actively think about their lived experience and integrate new information in order to discover new meaning in their experience. Because most home visitors begin work with no academic education in home visitation, this discussion focuses on continuing education of home visitors.

The aim of continuing education is to assist home visitors to be reflective practitioners and to recognize the meaning of their actions and experiences. New information can help home visitors look at their actions and relationships in a new way and thereby reconstruct their experiences. This approach is not linear; home visitors' learning is experiential. They take new understanding and apply it to their everyday practice.

Janice explained how discussions with occupational therapists in her program's weekly staff meetings assisted her not just in learning something new but in opening new ways of working with her families.

> Occupational therapists have been very helpful. They can break down motor development in a way you don't see, for example, how a child gets in a sitting position, how they reach for things—the detail that makes a difference in how a child functions. I didn't have a clue about these details until occupational therapists came to staff meetings on a regular basis.
>
> In a program like PAT with a strong focus on language and cognition, we can let motor development happen rather than pay attention to it. Paying attention to motor development makes a difference, especially if visiting a child whose development takes a different twist, for example a [child with low muscle tone or a] child really slow in walking. I have learned what are the very small signs of progress. I can help the parent see these signs and encourage ways to promote the development.

Janice was able to integrate information from occupational therapists directly so that she could see more in a child's movement and provide additional information and guidance to the child's parents. Janice uses this sensitivity to movement often in her work with families. For example, as Erin (age 18 months) watches Janice take toys out of her bag, she backs up and sits on her mother's lap. Janice comments to Erin's mother, "It's interesting to see how she backs up into you. She has a good sense of body space." Janice's education included content (new information from occupational therapists) and reflective action (her application of this information in her work with families.)

Home visitors' work is planned, but not predictable. Each day, teachers go to work in a classroom with a set of textbooks with which to teach specific subjects and with a principal who can help in a crisis. Nurses work in a hospital with a predictable set of work procedures (e.g., distributing medications, filling in medical records, and making rounds) and with physicians who are in charge. In contrast, home visitors carry a small bag with materials they have chosen into homes of young families, each of which is different, with its own patterns and problems. Home visitors also rarely have on-the-job supervision.

Home visitors make minute-by-minute decisions in ever-changing, unique environments. Individual home visitors' personal histories influence how they understand and value their work. At the same time, everyone is inescapably social in the sense that they not only perform actions and see things from their perspective, but also can take the role of another and see themselves from the perspective of another person.[5] What the home visitor does is deeply rooted in learned ways of seeing, thinking, and doing. These ways were learned through relationships with others beginning in infancy. The complexity of self as both an individual and a social being sets up provocative challenges for educating home visitors. Effective in-service education includes a dual process: every individual's way of working needs to be valued and nurtured while the individual's growth remains within a social setting. So the *process* of professional development opportunities is as important as the *content.* Just as the relationship between the home visitor and parent is as important as play activities, so too the relationship between the home visitor and peers, mentors, and supervisors is as important as the education curriculum.

The Structure and Process of Continuing Education

Continuing education is an integral part of a home visitors' professional life when active, reflective learning is a central part of the home visiting program. Administrators of a program can structure this active learning within their team meetings. Cynthia discussed this need.

> The program is a place for growth, not just for our children and our parents, but for ourselves. Everyone needs to know that this is a place for growth. When home visitors are hired, we tell them they are expected to actively learn new knowledge and skills. For this to happen, it takes a leader who is able to forge relationships of respect and support in working together. The art is to know how to help people become active, reflective learners.
>
> Last month, I gave everyone a reading I thought was very helpful because it clearly described effective approaches with families. No one touched it. Then, last week I shared this material in terms of concrete happenings with everyone's families. I made it come alive in the context of peoples' work with their families. There has to be engagement, and people need to learn to reflect on how new knowledge relates directly to work with their families.

Cynthia provides clear administrative expectations of professional development in a community of respect and support in working together.

Program Philosophy and Principles

Effective administrators provide a clear program philosophy and principles to help guide their home visitors. Home visitors work in many different home settings, but key principles and a consistent philosophy guide their minute-by-minute decision making as they relate to families. My conversation about key principles and philosophies with three professionals in three different positions of the PAT program in one school district illustrates this program's overarching principles and philosophy. As Director of Early Education, Margaret has been in charge of her district's home visiting program for 14 years. Janice has been a home visitor for 9 years. After working as a home visitor for 4 years, Cynthia now directs the district's Even Start program.

Margaret: You integrate the principles and philosophy in the totality of your program, coming back to it in a lot of ways, in what you say in all the different contexts of working with the staff. First is empowering the parents, and that's not possible without having rapport with parents and supporting them. And at the core is the home visitor's strong foundation in child development.

Janice: We always are striving to empower parents. In as many subtle ways as possible, I find the strength of the parent and build on that. When I use handouts, I'll say, "You probably are doing this already." If you have a mindset that you'll fix parents, they'll know it. If you go in with the attitude that parents know a lot, and together we'll be working for the benefit of the child, they'll sense the respect you have for them. Respect is essential, and the home visitor must be secure in the basics of child development.

Cynthia: The key is respecting parents and understanding the notion of reciprocity. You are a partner, not doing something for parents, but everyone is learning together. And you must be knowledgeable about what you are talking about. Basic child development is a must, but so are several other disciplines, too, like nutrition and health. And you have to be introspective, for we learn by reflecting on our experience.

I interviewed Margaret, Janice, and Cynthia on separate days in different settings, yet parallel themes that are central to the PAT program emerge through the portrayals of these three professionals.

Team Meetings

To ensure active reflective learning, administrators can structure regularly scheduled team meetings. These meetings can be in an informal setting where home visitors can learn new content and then directly apply that content to their everyday work with families. Whenever content is provided, actively processing the meaning of this content in terms of home visitors' everyday work not only has an impact on their work but also promotes their ability to be reflective.

It takes time for colleagues to know and trust each other so that they can feel safe to both share their own experiences and to respond to what others are saying and doing. Furthermore, not all home visitors are introspective. Some need team meetings to promote this ability. When team meetings become a safe environment in which home visitors can share their work with one another, each person learns about the others' styles and can compare these to his or her own style. Home visitors each have unique styles, personalities, interests, beliefs, biases, and distortions. Exploring differences can increase home visitors' sensitivity to their own way of working and can provoke questions about taken-for-granted practices or beliefs. Any new changes or approaches will be personal and are made to address the home visitor's pattern of knowing, interacting with, and understanding of families being served.

Given the solitary work of home visiting, team meetings can provide opportunities for support and encouragement.[6] Home visitors are bonded together by shared commitments and experience. Janice described the importance of sharing with colleagues.

> Colleagues who do the same kind of work that I do, other home visitors, are important to me because we share similar experiences. So when I run into a problem, I know that I can talk with one of my colleagues, that the conversation will be maintained as confidential. With them, I can sort of brainstorm and process things that I need to work on to help a family. We can share how each of us has dealt with similar situations with different families and what the outcomes have been. In reality, there are few problems that are really unique to a family. That is the nice thing about having a fairly large staff, the sharing among team members. You need to have a way, among your colleagues in a protected environment, that you can work through some of the difficulties that you confront.

Janice described team meetings as an environment for home visitors to reflect on their own actions and those of the families they serve. Together, home visitors can collaborate in solving problems—in expanding notions of what is possible. This mutuality of interest, respect, and support provides encouragement for individuals to take risks and attempt new approaches.

Ernestine, an experienced home visitor, discussed a problem she was having with her team members.

> Ernestine describes her frustration in working with a directive mother, Kamera, who seems only to be interested in promoting the academic learning of her 26-month-old son. Regardless of the play activity or Ernestine's interactions, Kamera focuses on color, shape, or number. Ernestine told the group, "I'm out of control. It seems no matter what I do or say, Kamera remains

directive." Individual home visitors shared similar frustrations and then brainstormed together possible strategies. They suggested that Ernestine could choose only very open-ended activities, such as sensory play with birdseed or sculpting with playdough. In fact, introducing sensory play with birdseed did provide a setting for Kamera to interact in a new way with her son. Over extended additional visits, with Ernestine's support and assistance, Kamera learned to value her son's actions as a 26-month-old and to encourage developmentally appropriate play. Ernestine gave brief reports in team meetings, and together the team explored both the meaning of ongoing happenings and additional possible approaches with this family.

When Ernestine stepped back from her involvement with Kamera and shared her concerns with her peers, she gained new perspectives on what might be possible. As she heard individual home visitors share similar frustrations, she gained support and encouragement. Ernestine had felt out of control during her visits with Kamera. After discussing this visit with her colleagues, she returned feeling hopeful that she had a new possibility of making contact with this mother.

When a team has more than 10–12 members, the group is too large to have mutual, reflective sharing. For a large staff, structuring part of each team meeting into small groups is necessary to ensure this open sharing of practice, exploration of possible meaning of this practice, and brainstorming of possible additional approaches. There always will be some need for total-group presentations or use of videotapes. These total-group activities can be most productive if home visitors can reflect on how the topic relates to their own practice in small groups. Afterward, a total-group wrap-up is an effective closure to such meetings.

Most programs have home visitors of different ages and with different lengths of experience. Increased experience gives greater understanding of the meaning of the home visiting process. Informal team meetings with regular, open sharing allows the more experienced home visitors to share insights and discuss their own changes. They can be models of learning how to learn and can expand the perspectives of the less experienced. When less experienced home visitors feel supported and safe, they can actively question their practice and gain assistance from their experienced colleagues. In this way, a climate of inquiry develops.

Seminars, Workshops, and Conferences

Other structures for learning are seminars, workshops, and conferences sponsored by other organizations and agencies. When home visitors can meet people in related professions and learn from these professionals, their own knowledge and understanding is expanded. This multidisciplinary experience is especially important for home visitors because their work can encompass education, health, and social services. Janice explained why attending conferences has been one of the most influential ways for her to develop new knowledge and skills.

> I like conferences because they give me the opportunity to hear people from other fields, such as a physician or child protection worker. It broadens my perspective. It also is stimulating to meet other conferees who are in related fields, and I get ideas for reading—for I also like to read, to dig into books for new perspectives or depth of understanding.

Janice understands that her work cuts across disciplines. Thus, she actively seeks new learning opportunities from professionals in other related disciplines, with support from her home visiting program, which has funds to support this form of continuing education.

Programs can create an educational structure and process that provides sharing of experience and support, both giving and receiving, so that home visitors can pursue their craft with confidence and enthusiasm. Learning is a continual, fluid, and individual as well as a collaborative process, and it is a natural part of the culture of a home visiting program.

Content of Continued Education

Home visiting is a complex, dynamic process. Home visitors' actions are an interaction of their personal abilities, style, and experience; their professional education; and the requirements of a particular program. In addition, each family is unique; thus, visitors use different approaches with different families. For example, when Erin is 24 months, Janice initiates a game in which Erin makes a parade by matching similar toy vehicles and people (e.g., police car and police officer). Then, Erin matches cards depicting mother and baby animals. That same day, Janice initiates the same vehicle-matching game with Molly, who also is 24 months. Janice knows that Molly is not as intellectually advanced as Erin, so she omits the second, more abstract game.

In examining the continuing education of home visitors, it is important to recognize that knowledge and skill, and the different domains of knowledge, overlap and often are interdependent.[7] For example, home visitors have skill in understanding the vulnerabilities unique to low-income families when they understand how neighborhood, welfare, housing, employment, health, and education can have an impact on a family's functioning. Given this complexity, arranging for the content of home visitors' continued professional development involves the challenge of providing education across disciplines in many areas of knowledge and skill.

Child Development

Regardless of whether home visitors are nurses, social workers, or educators, when they work with families with young children, a solid foundation in child development is the first priority of professional education. As home visitors learn about development in the areas of cognitive and language, as well as biological or physical, sociocultural, and psychological-emotional development, the emphasis needs to be holistic; that is, intertwining all of these developmental realms. For example, when discussing cognitive development, Janice can relate how she needed to provide different activities for Erin than for Molly, children the same age with different abilities. Ernestine can describe how she structured a toddler's play with birdseed so that his mother, who is a concrete learner, could have simple concrete experiences in managing her child's behavior. When in-service sessions combine child development content with process (i.e., home visitors talking about the families they work with), learning becomes more active and reflective. Then, there is a higher probability that home visitors will be able to use this learning in their everyday work with families.

Education to Broaden One's Perspective

Education for home visitors cuts across many disciplines beyond child development: health and nutrition, language and communication, occupational and physical therapy, special education, and social services. Given this complexity, regular scheduling of outside consultants to provide staff in-services can assist home visitors in gaining new tools beyond their personal and professional experience.

In Margaret's program, outside consultants across disciplines regularly lead the weekly staff meetings. A child psychologist who has a family therapy practice leads two sessions each month: one group supervision session for staff to discuss difficulties they are having with specific families and one to share child development or family systems information. Consultants representing other disciplines (e.g., health, nutrition, occupational therapy, pediatrics) and community agencies (e.g., child protection bureau, substance abuse clinic) also lead sessions. Margaret discussed the purpose of these staff meetings.

> We need to bring in people with different lenses, different expertise, to broaden the staff's knowledge—people such as social workers, child psychologists, pediatricians, occupational therapists, people knowledgeable in drug and alcohol abuse [and] children's learning problems, and people representing community agencies. But we also need a balance. Sessions also

need to involve the staff in issues directly related to their tasks, such as parenting skills for helping your baby go to sleep, baby massage, movement and music, even nitty-gritty kinds of things like toy making.

Home visitors gain a deeper, broader, richer understanding of what they do as consultants provide multiple perspectives on the home visiting process. At the same time, in a significant number of meetings, staff can work together to improve their skills in tasks basic to the home visiting process. In these sessions, staff can think aloud about their work and build on their expertise and the expertise of their professional peers. Colleagues become a source of not only new information and insight but also new ways of working with families—expanding ideas of what is possible. The process is interactive and includes self- and collaborative reflection.

To reemphasize the point, beyond child development knowledge, home visitors' best resource is their own experience and active reflection on this experience. Thus, active learning is enhanced with close connections between educational topics and the professional concerns and experiences of home visitors. At the same time, professional education involves home visitors' moving beyond their unique individual experience and perspective and expanding their lens so that they can understand the complexities of their work, take on multiple points of view, and be open to new perspectives. Five areas of knowledge and skill that are useful in helping to be open to new tools beyond one's personal and professional experience are

1. Ecological approach, or an understanding of social systems
2. Culturally diverse families and families at risk
3. Adult development, family systems, and family life cycle
4. Divorced, single-parent, or blended families
5. Networking with community agencies

Ecological Approach, or an Understanding of Social Systems
When using an ecological perspective, home visitors assume that child development moves forward as an interaction of biology and society; that is, how children turn out is a product of both the characteristics of the children and the way the world treats them. Garbarino and Ganzel wrote, "One of the most useful aspects of the ecological approach is its ability to highlight situations in which the actions of people with whom the individual has no direct contact significantly affect development."[8] Each situation contains a set of obligations and beliefs about actions that should take place and can offer both opportunities and constraints for young children's development.

The first law of ecology is that a person can never do just one thing. Individuals and environments influence and depend on each other. Garbarino noted, "The most important characteristic of this ecological perspective is that it both reinforces our inclination to look inside the individual child or parent and encourages us to look beyond the individual to the environment for questions and explanations about individual behavior and development."[9]

Discussion of home visiting often focuses on parent–child relationships and the home visitor's striving to enhance this relationship, but when home visitors take an ecological approach, they also consider young children in their total family environment and the interplay of family with other social systems, such as neighborhood, church, and workplace.[10] They understand that the quality of a family's life is interconnected with the quality of their social environment. Taking an ecological perspective, home visitors look inside to the everyday patterns of parent–child interactions and outside to those social systems and environments that support or constrain these everyday patterns.

There is a give-and-take mutuality between these external social systems and the child and family. For example, the manner in which child care teachers and parents greet each other as the young child arrives influences not only the parent's feeling of trust in this caregiver, but also the caregiver's feeling of support and affirmation. In turn, the child feels secure in the similarity between home and the child care program or feels insecure because of mixed messages or tension between parent and child care staff.

When home visitors take an ecological, social systems approach, they locate each family in its social environment in terms of ethnicity, race, religion, education, and occupation. With this perspective, they are sensitive to a family's access to resources, to personal–social networks, and to potential constraints, all of which influence the family's everyday lifestyle. With this knowledge and sensitivity, home visitors then can individualize their approach so that they communicate respect, support, and affirmation to each family they serve.

Given the individualistic nature of American culture, one cannot assume that every home visitor will have an ecological approach. Staff development sessions can expand perspectives by providing informational sessions on the notions of ecology, social systems, and how home visitors can take an approach that includes the family's environment. Having this understanding, home visitors are sensitive to the messages parents receive from various parts of their environment, including the neighborhood, church, elementary school, workplace, and media. They know that sometimes parents receive mixed or contradictory messages from different parts of their environment. In team meetings, staff members can share how the social environment has an impact on the families they work with, and in this sharing, gain new understanding.

Culturally Diverse Families and At-Risk Families

In paying attention to children's and families' social environments, home visitors develop sensitivities and accompanying skills in recognizing and relating to cultural diversity and the differing individual and social patterns of cultures. They know that relationships and understanding can have different meanings for people of a different race, ethnicity, religion, educational status, or SES. For example, they expect families from different cultures to have different informal networks—people outside the home with whom the family participates in activities. Social networks can be helpful in providing information and support, or they can be stressful. Knowing that some families have fewer support networks helps home visitors to see where they can provide assistance. Knowing that some families may be very close to extended families who give young parents strong child-rearing messages helps home visitors recognize the potential conflicting messages the parents may be receiving from their family and from the home visitor.

A first step in education for working with families from diverse cultures is helping home visitors recognize how their own behavior, attitudes, and values reflect their culture. Then, when relating to families of a different culture, home visitors can be alert to their own biases and keep them from blocking communication with a family. Second, staff in-service can assist home visitors in gaining specific knowledge of the cultures of the families they serve. This is another topic in which consultants who represent different cultures can broaden a program's perspective.

Professional development of home visitors working with at-risk families entails additional content and process. When home visitors work with at-risk families, they encounter an increase both in the personal problems families face (e.g., family conflict, depression, anxiety) and external problems (e.g., inadequate housing, unemployment). Given these problems, it is not unusual for these parents to have difficulty in focusing on their young children's needs. Just as home visitors need to make more visits for at-risk families, so, too, they need additional professional guidance. It is not uncommon for home visitors who work with families with multiple problems to see the needs of young children unmet and to feel frustrated, angry, discouraged, and overwhelmed.

At-risk families are more likely to have group patterns that conflict with the home visitor's traditional purposes. Often, there is no quiet place to meet with parents, or there are repeated interruptions during a home visit. Home visitors may provide a safe target for parents to vent their frustrations and be angry and hostile. Given this work environment, staff meetings that focus on patterns of at-risk, troubled families and adaptations in working with these families provide an invaluable resource for home visitors.

Adult Development, Family Systems, and Family Life Cycle

A third area of continuing knowledge and skill includes adult development, family systems, and family life cycle. Social scientists have developed theories of adult development to aid understanding of individual adults and differences among adults as a group. Developmental theories describe predictable sequences of growth and adaptation throughout life.[11] Changes in development include changes in a complex interwoven fabric of interpersonal behavior, moral and ethical behavior, cognitive complexity, and preoccupations. Different periods in life include different age-related tasks and life issues. For example, middle-class parents in their early twenties are preoccupied with different issues than parents ages 30–40. Younger parents may be just beginning a career. In contrast, 30- to 40-year-olds may be preoccupied with their careers because this period is usually a time of rapid career advancement. Just as home visitors individualize their approach with families of different cultures, so, too, knowledge of adult development helps them relate effectively to differences among parents.

Family systems theory hypothesizes that the behavior of each member of a family is interdependent with every other family member. Each family member has a role that includes what is expected of him or her and how this role fits into the total family structure. A gifted child may have the role of strengthening his parents' feelings of competence and thus feel compelled to succeed in all tasks. Alternatively, a father may have the role of unquestionable control and power and, thus, feel obligated to reward and reprimand each family member.

Family systems theory explains that families go through a developmental process—a family life cycle—that includes shifts in family organization and functioning. It is helpful for home visitors to learn how a family is organized and to understand that this organization is different depending on the life cycle of the family. Family life cycles include issues of marriage, childbirth, separation (e.g., entering child care or school, a mother or father returning to work), school age and adolescence, the empty nest, and retirement. Home visitors most often work with families within the same life cycle; however, these families may be intimately related to extended families in different phases of the family life cycle. Thus, an understanding of the family life cycle can assist home visitors in their ecological approach to families.

Divorced, Single-Parent, and Blended Families

Home visitors can expect to work with divorced, single-parent, or blended families. Professional education can provide understanding of these increasingly common family patterns. Divorce rates in the United States continue to be about 50%.[12] Divorce is a transitional process, not just a legal relationship, and children are an integral part of the process. Every divorce includes a challenge for parents and children to reorganize. Daily routines change, separation issues become dominant, and issues of marital responsibility versus parental responsibility need to be clarified. As parents go through the divorce process, they redefine themselves. In this process, home visitors can assist parents in helping their young children understand these substantive changes and, at the same time, feel secure in their parents' love.

Once a separation is finalized and the young child lives with only one parent, patterns of single parenting emerge. It is important for home visitors to acknowledge that single parents—mothers as well as fathers—can manage the economic, physical, and psychosocial tasks of family life. Home visitors can learn the many strengths of single parenting, such as increased flexibility, children's increased understanding of their parent's work, and increased expectation that every family member contributes to the maintenance of the whole family. Understanding the potential strengths of single parenting assists home visitors in relating to single parents in a respectful, supportive, and affirming manner.

Blended families also involve challenges for parents. Before the unification, each family developed unique daily routines and patterns of family celebrations. Some patterns are been taken for granted by young children and/or their parents. Thus, it can be an unexpected adjustment to encounter different daily routines or different ways of celebrating. Creating new routines and rituals together can be a very important step in a blended family's life. Home visitors can offer support and encouragement to parents experiencing these new challenges.

Networking with Community Agencies

A fourth area of knowledge and skill includes networking with community agencies. As discussed in Chapter 2, home visitors need to know what they can do and what is beyond their expertise. With visits in a family's home, it is not uncommon for parents to initiate discussion of personal difficulties, such as conflicts with their spouse or parent, or external difficulties, such as child care or housing. As a result, familiarity with community resources becomes knowledge on which home visitors often rely. When home visitors work with families with multiple problems, networking with community agencies is a recurrent part of their work. Cynthia described some of her experiences.

One of the successes and also frustrations we have had in our work with different community agencies that serve our families is discovering how difficult it can be to get services. For example, I called a rape crisis line at 10 [o'clock] in the morning because a mom had come in and told us she had been raped by her boyfriend and needed to talk to someone. We had never handled this kind of situation before, so we called the rape crisis line. The machine said to call back at 10:30.

Just the phone systems we have now can be problematic for our families. You call a number and are told to press 1 for this, 2 for this, 3 for this, 4 for this. A lot of people get lost and don't know which button to press. And they'll hang up and won't try. Just the way the system is set up sometimes thwarts people's attempts to get help.

Then, we have situations where counseling is available with a sliding fee. But again, child care and transportation are not available, and most counseling centers do not do home visits. On the other hand, once we work with our local medical clinics, we often can get expedite getting appointments for the kids when we call the clinic and tell them this is one of our families. We have a contact person there. In fact, we have a case now in which the child had been seen at one of the bigger hospitals in town. Because Mom missed two appointments and had no transportation for a 30-mile round trip, the hospital said they would not work with this family anymore. I called our local clinic, who got the family into a different hospital that does provide transportation, and now the child is being served.

Cynthia and her staff know the individuals who work in different community agencies and know how the agencies operate. Thus, they can both help their parents learn how to work within an agency, and when necessary, they can call upon a specific person in an agency to help a parent who is having difficulty using the agency.

That kind of coordination makes a world of difference. We try to put our people into job training and vocational rehabilitation programs. Through networking, knowing someone who works there and [will] take our calls, we can get our parents access. The parent doesn't have to deal with number 1, number 2, and so forth. Once you have a person who knows who you are and knows your program, then you are much more likely to get something done.

The other day, we had a parent who wants to go the community college and was having difficulty getting a transcript. I called my contact at the community college, who went to admissions and was able to troubleshoot for the parent. That's the way things can happen. All too often people get lost in the system and have trouble getting services; they get frustrated and give up.

What we are able to do is walk them through the process and thereby keep their spirits up. "Yes, it's a pain. Yes, it's a bummer. But yes, you can do it. Here's the number. Call now. Here is what you need to say." And the next time our parents know how to do that, will know how to ask that question.

Staff meetings can be a setting for joint exploration of community resources: governmental agencies such as public welfare, WIC, the child protection agency, and mental and physical health agencies, as well as private agencies such as recovery programs, battered women's shelters, and child care. This is an area where outside consultants can broaden the staff's knowledge. In some situations, home visitors may have the knowledge of available community resources but lack the skill in helping parents get to these resources. Skillful approaches to networking with community agencies can be discussed at a staff meeting and often are an important topic for an individual's supervisor (see the Supervision section of this chapter).

Education for Effective Skill Building

Knowledge and skill are mutually interdependent. Team meetings can focus specifically on skill building, especially communication and relationship-building skills—the building blocks of home visiting. When staff meet regularly and discuss their work in small groups, these meetings can become an environment for reflecting together about their hands-on work. The skills discussed in Chapter 2 can be addressed, either by people sharing concretely their experience or by sharing videos of their work. Given the intensity of home visitors' work, these group discussions include some of the following recurrent themes:

- Forming and maintaining relationships of trust and support
- Learning to take the perspective of the parent
- Expressing strong feelings, negative and positive, and having these feelings reflected back
- Understanding the developmental potential of individual children and individual parents
- Understanding the program's limits of responsibility

Working collaboratively to learn and reflect on practice is a slow process. This process is possible when all staff members are committed to support, affirm, and guide one another's personal and professional growth in a climate of openness and inquiry.

Continued Education Across Large Geographical Areas

A significant proportion of the United States is rural; thus, some home visiting programs cover large geographical areas. In these situations, administrators can initiate innovative forms of continued professional education. Use of telephone, telecommunication, and mail are useful avenues of collaboration among home visitors and their mentors. Programs can develop a videotape library as an integral part of ongoing education. Videotapes can illustrate exemplary home visiting and/or can demonstrate and discuss the use of supervision and mentorship processes. A user's guide provides additional assistance. Similarly, technology such as faxing, voice mail, and e-mail systems on the Internet can offer a means of continual collaboration with both peers and mentors. Networks among professionals formed across large distances also provide support and opportunities for continued growth. The Foxfire Teacher Networks provide a model of professionals across geographical distances. Foxfire offers summer workshops for educators, and these workshops evolve into networks—support systems in which Foxfire graduates engage in continued collaboration in the interest of promoting professional development.[13]

SUPERVISION

Home visitors' work is intense and is based on trusting relationships. Forming and maintaining these parent–home visitor relationships involves emotions as well as intellect. Self-knowledge is necessary for professional competence, and the core of continued education is home visitors' active reflection on their experience. This reflection helps them recognize the meaning of their actions and experience. Regular collaborative supervision provides a relationship to promote this continued professional development. A supervisory relationship offers a safe environment for home visitors to discuss their experiences, both successes and failures, and gain feedback from an experienced practitioner. Through reflective supervision, home visitors gain greater understanding of their emotions and actions encountered in their work. Through sharing of stories, home visitors become aware of what they implicitly know and consider the meaning of their work. As they work with their supervisor, they develop a common language and shared vision of their work.

This discussion of supervision is guided by the work of ZERO TO THREE: National Center for Infants, Toddlers and Families.[14] ZERO TO THREE has taken a leadership role in addressing the need of supervision in home visiting and other programs supporting the development of babies, toddlers, and their families. ZERO TO THREE discusses how reflection, collaboration, and regularity are key features of effective supervision.

Effective supervision parallels home visitors' relationship with the families that they serve because it is a relationship of respect, support, collaboration, and mutuality. Ideally, the supervisor's expertise includes having been a front-line worker conducting home visits. Within supervision, home visitors become increasingly skilled in focusing on the nuts and bolts of their experiences; reporting these experiences; and gaining feedback, knowledge, and/or suggestions.

Dan is an outside consultant who provides group supervision for Cynthia's home visiting program. Cynthia described her early work with Dan.

It was my first year doing home visiting. I was working with two small kids, Mom, and Dad. I had completed a developmental screen with each child and was explaining it to their mom and dad. Out of nowhere, when I asked the question, "Is the child learning to help in the house or imitating helping?" Mom commented, "I wish I could get him [the dad] to help," as she looked at her husband. The dad replied, and they began arguing back and forth. Dad walked out of the room, angry. Mom sat there and began crying. I just sat there like a bump on the log. I finally said, "Would you like me to leave?" She replied no, and Dad was within an earshot. Everyone felt uncomfortable. I finished explaining the Denver [Developmental Screening Test] and left as soon as I could.

That week when we met with Dan (the team's supervisor), I explained the situation—how I felt ill at ease and didn't know what to do. Through talking it over, Dan helped me understand that I'm not there to be a marriage counselor or help them talk it through. That's not necessarily what I'm there for. It's obvious they are having marriage difficulty. And they let me see that. Dan's suggestion was when you find yourself in that situation, instead of getting pulled in or doing nothing, you could say, "You both seem to be having difficulty, would you like to talk to someone? Would you like me to recommend someone for you?" Or you can say, "This seems to be a difficult time, would you like me to leave and come back later?" Dan affirmed my response, which was the same as his second suggestion. And when I went back to their home, I suggested someone for them to talk to.

In this visit, Cynthia had responded in an appropriate manner to these parents' fighting. Her response was intuitive. As a new home visitor, she had not thought through issues of maintaining boundaries, and she did not have a clear understanding of the options she had in situations like this. Being able to share this experience with the team and the team supervisor provided Cynthia with a deeper understanding of her work, at the same time affirming her response to these parents.

Within supervision, the focus is primarily on process and on interaction. Supervision offers a setting to feel secure enough to reflect on emotional reactions to one's practice.[15] The setting is safe enough to expose one's insecurities, mistakes, and questions. In turn, the supervisor reflects back the home visitors' thoughts and feelings and offers support. Collaboratively, the home visitor and supervisor interpret and gain understanding both of troublesome aspects of work and the successes. In these experiences, home visitors can gain improved understanding of their thoughts, feelings, and actions, as well as support, guidance, and encouragement to move forward in their work. Cynthia describes a supervisor who helped her better understand herself and her experiences at work.

> One of the people who influenced my work life was Lee Samuels. Lee was my supervisor when I worked for the Head Start program in Oregon. Lee was extremely bright. What Lee did for me was to help me look at myself and look at my strengths and my weaknesses and learn to understand myself better. He was able to do that in a supervisory role. He's probably the only supervisor I ever had who would sit me down on a regular basis and process what was going on in the program, what was happening, why it was happening, and how we could take it somewhere else. Lee helped me look at my own personality traits, where they were effective and where they weren't.
>
> Lee helped me realize I don't have to have all the answers. Performance has been very important in my family, and I've always felt like I have to know everything. He helped me realize I don't—that true power lies in knowing what you don't know, in being able to admit it, and then seeking help.
>
> Lee taught me a lot about being a supervisor, how to help people grow. He was never afraid of his female side. In that respect he taught me something about men, too. He would talk to me about being a man, and I never had a man do that. If I'd be upset with my husband or something, Lee would say, "Well, Cynthia, this is the way men look at it." That really helped me, too, on a personal note. No one had ever done that for me.

For Cynthia, Lee helped her reflect on her personal style and her work experiences. Their relationship had the same kind of mutuality that effective home visitors have with the parents with whom they work. Just as Cynthia shared her perspectives, so, too, Lee shared his.

When home visitors work with families with multiple problems, supervision is even more important. Home visitors always encounter two forces at work: the external and the internal. External forces can be awesome and out of control, especially while working with families with multiple problems. Working with such families sparks powerful feelings in the home visitor, feelings he or she needs need to acknowledge and control. Some of the feelings are problematic, such as the sense of futility, vulnerability, and hopelessness. At these times, home visitors need to be self-aware. Self-monitoring becomes essential, as does support, affirmation, and guidance from peers and supervisors.

Introducing the topic of supervision may spark multiple dilemmas. The term *supervision* is understood differently in different disciplines. For some disciplines, supervision means overseeing, monitoring, and evaluating. This discussion of supervision uses an alternative, process-oriented approach. A further problem is the many structural barriers within home visiting programs, such as limited or no funding resources to have individuals providing one-to-one supervision for all staff members. Notwithstanding these dilemmas, for all program administrators, the first step in moving toward a supervision model is awareness of the need. Once administrators understand supervision, they can work toward lessening or removing structural barriers.

Once administrators are committed to a supervision model, they can adapt the structure of their program to provide features of this model. Commitment is the first step because demands of direct service can obscure supervision needs. As previously discussed, self- and collaborative reflection can be central features in the shared culture of staff meetings, a culture that is valued and protected by administrators. Time, structure, and clear expectations make the occurrence for these processes possible. Sharing successes and problems of work with families can be incorporated into staff meetings as a framework for staff to share their work and gain feedback and suggestions for their practice. As previously discussed, small-group meetings of staff are a safe environment in which peers can share and reflect on one another's home visiting experiences. Peer supervision also can be a powerful force for improved self- and collaborative reflection. Home visitors can attend one another's sessions, take written notes or videotape these sessions, and then meet to reflect collaboratively on both the happenings and the home visitor's thoughts and feelings. Often, home visitors learn as much from observing their peers as from being observed. Outside consultants can provide supervisory expertise to support and guide this type of collaborative reflection.

One example of supervision at work is an Early Head Start (EHS) program in a rural community in Missouri. This program is run by the town's mental health center. The EHS coordinator has a master's degree in psychology and worked as a psychotherapist for children before her current position. The EHS program contracts child care with existing family and center-based child care programs at the mental health center. In addition, the EHS program has two child care classrooms, each with two teachers and six children. The program also has six home visitors. Each week, the EHS coordinator has 1 hour of reflective supervision with each home visitor and teacher. The coordinator believes that this reflective supervision has helped keep staff turnover very low.

PEER MENTORING AND SUPERVISION

The typical home visiting program does not offer the kind of supervision that could help home visitors to be self-reflective. Peer mentoring and supervision can fill this void. Professional development of home visitors is optimal if it focuses on both content and process, incorporating content areas such as child development, parenting practices, at-risk factors, family systems theory, and potential community resources. Many home visiting programs have regular staff meetings in which topics are discussed, often with the help of an outside professional.

Although changes in parents and children are relationship based, discussion on this process often does not occur in meetings. Home visitors learn on their own to reflect on the process area of establishing and maintaining a positive, facilitative relationship with parents and their children. The positive relationship between the home visitor and parents makes it possible for parents to learn about child development as well as to improve their parenting skills. Parents usually do not care about the home visitor's knowledge until they realize that the home visitor cares for them. Home visitors can improve how well they do their work when they understand both content and process—what they bring to the parent and how they bring it.

One Program and How it Worked

One example of effective peer mentoring and supervision is a program in a large, multicultural district with 30 home visitors. The 5-year project of peer mentoring and supervision had several dimensions. As in most home visiting programs, no home visitors had academic courses on home visiting or any academic training or experience in reflective supervision. The home visitors were divided into teams of five or six, and each team leader videotaped the team members once a year. After a team member viewed her video, she met with the team leader to discuss it. Teams met twice a month: once a month to meet with a child and family therapist to talk about their work with high-risk families or difficulties they or their families were experiencing, and once a month to share one video of a team member's home visit and to discuss it. Early in the program, team members found that in order for this process to be effective, they needed to trust each other. All but four home visitors had worked together for several years and knew each other well. Often, they had used the staff room to complete their paperwork, and during this time, individuals had chatted informally with each other. Despite their close relationship before the project, they needed to develop a deeper level of trust.

Using Videotapes

Once home visitors became comfortable with being videotaped, they usually thought the videotapes were engaging. Often, the videotapes helped home visitors see when things were going very well. Usually, the home visitor could identify when a difficulty appeared in the process. Reviewing the videotape provided time to reflect subjectively not only on what the home visitor was experiencing, but also on what the parent and child were experiencing. For some home visitors, reflecting this way on subjective experiences was new.

During the first 2 or 3 years, the project progressed very slowly. Although the home visitors knew that videotaping was part of their job, most resisted being videotaped. Also, many families were not willing to be videotaped during a home visit. The few brave souls who shared their videos made the meetings very successful. Team members provided feedback, suggestions, and alternative approaches. For example, a home visitor's video showed the home visitor giving developmental information to the parent, but she did not give an appropriate developmental interpretation of either child or parent action that she had observed. When the parent and toddler, Susie, repeated "Mommy" and "Susie" to each other, the home visitor could have told that parent that this turn taking helps Susie understand that turn taking is a component of all conversation. Or, when the toddler walked backward into her mother's lap, the home visitor could have commented that the child's action indicated her increased sense of body in space. The home visitors who shared their tapes thought that comments from their peers were constructive. They did not feel that their colleagues were cutting them down. Slowly, more and more home visitors volunteered to share their tapes.

Learning to Give Descriptive Affirmation

Initially, all feedback was positive praise. With time and experience, though, individuals learned new skills in peer mentoring and supervision. They learned to ask open-ended questions regarding the home visitor's intentions and expectations of the visit. The meetings became contexts to discuss difficulties, for example, work with teen parents, parents with developmental disabilities, or parents who often are not home at the agreed-on time of a visit. By the fourth and fifth year of this program, most home visitors developed an increased ability to be self-reflective. They also developed new home visiting skills such as descriptively affirming parents and children rather than using global evaluative comments such as "good" or "nice." When descriptively affirming a child or parent, the home visitor concretely described observations of parent or child behavior and thereby helped the parent or child recognize his or her successes.

Team Leader Meetings

To assist team leaders, a psychologist with experience and knowledge of reflective supervision met monthly with team leaders and the coordinator of home visitors. In these monthly meetings, team leaders shared what had happened in their team meetings. The team leaders' meeting became a parallel process for team meetings. When team leaders shared at their team leaders' meeting, they received feedback, support, and suggestions for new strategies to be used in forthcoming team meetings. Not surprising, different teams had different team processes; yet, across teams, salient issues emerged, such as strategies needed to keep team members on task, and leaders learned to ask open-ended questions. Sometimes, team leaders discussed a difficulty they were experiencing such as being distracted at meetings when team members chatted or feeling stifled when one home visitor was negative. Topics extended beyond the team meetings and included all aspects of the program as well as experiences and possibilities of staff meetings. Individual team leaders shared that these meetings were very important, both to help them develop leadership skills and to give them needed structure.

Training New Home Visitors

Home visiting is daunting, and new home visitors need a good introduction to the job. Within teams, members took responsibility for giving suggestions to new home visitors; and in time, new home visitors used team meetings as a context to ask experienced home visitors specific questions. Each team had different strategies for using the effective approaches previously described in this chapter; however, a consistent theme was the home visitor's increased skill in giving descriptive affirmation as an alternative to global evaluative comments.

In the project's fourth year, two home visitors were chosen to mentor the first and second year home visitors. For their first 6 weeks, new home visitors observed their mentors and other experienced home visitors conduct home visits, which gave them a new perspective of important issues to focus on during home visits. After the first 6 weeks, all new home visitors met with their mentors monthly. They spoke with other new home visitors during weekly phone conversations and met the other new home visitors twice monthly after staff meetings. Given the close one-to-one relationships new home visitors developed, meetings often became a time to discuss the dilemmas of being a new home visitor, for example, managing the required paperwork or balancing work time with personal needs.

At mid-year, each new home visitor's mentor visited her on the job, took written notes of this visit, shared the notes with the new home visitor, and met with the home visitor to talk about the visit. This new aspect of the program revealed that home visitors initially do not understand what they should be doing and that they experience a lot of anxiety about being knowledgeable. Thus, they spend unnecessary hours preparing for each home visit. Mentors explain that the most important skill is developing a relationship with the family, and new home visitors should focus on this.

Creating a Videotape Library

After the third and fourth year of the program, two videotapes were created of exemplary home visiting practice. The first video had one example of a home visit that illustrated each of 16 effective approaches. Following suggestions by the home visitors, a second video was made that gave two or three examples of the four approaches that team members thought were the most salient, and for some, the most difficult: providing developmental information about the child, giving suggestions within context, giving developmental interpretation of observed child and adult action, and promoting active involvement of the parents during the home visit. These videos of exemplary practice were used during the first team meeting each year and whenever the team leader thought appropriate.

Evaluating the Program's Success

By the fourth year, the project of peer mentoring and supervision had become a taken-for-granted part of each home visitor's work. During the fourth and fifth years, team meetings focused on one of the difficult approaches: first on promoting parents' active involvement with their child, and second, on promoting the parent's active involvement during the home visit. In addition, team leaders requested that each home visitor choose one approach and document the ways she used this approach throughout the program year.

A qualitative formative evaluation was implemented each year, and home visitors also completed an evaluation at the end of the year.

For the formative evaluation, verbatim written notes on each team leader meeting were given to all team leaders. Thus, as the program progressed, there was data to use to evaluate the program and to make needed changes. At the end of the fourth and fifth program years, about 80% of home visitors evaluated their experience in this project as being very helpful. They not only thought that they had developed new home visiting skills and insights, but they also spoke of their increased skill in giving their peers feedback, support, and suggestions. Benefits of the program included personal development such as increased flexibility, ability to listen, and ability to be self-reflective. Professional development had encompassed personal development—the intertwining of the personal and the professional.

In contrast, negative comments most often involved the high demands of this part-time position. Each case load included high-risk families, each visit included paperwork, and the new neuroscience curriculum meant more preparation time.

Before this project began, one coordinator was responsible for all the observations of home visits as well as all the mentoring and supervision. The project developed three new tiers of leadership: first, home visitors with skills in peer mentoring and supervision; second, the team leaders who videotaped visits, mentored, and supervised; and third, mentors to work with new home visitors.

DIFFICULTIES AND DILEMMAS

The professional development discussed in this chapter may seem new and may offer challenges to both home visitors and their administrators. Some home visitors may have difficulty with the professional development principles and suggested approaches discussed in this chapter. They may not be introspective, or they may not have had prior experiences that promote self-knowledge. Individuals may have a very private personal and professional life and may be offended with the expectation that they openly share their home visiting experiences with others. If home visitors' prior professional experiences have involved hierarchical communicating and relating, promoting partnerships with parents characterized by mutuality may be frightening. Change can be frightening for everyone. Change includes unpredictability and accompanying uncertainty. Each person enters a field with a distinct personal and professional biography. When an individual's biography is very different from the demands of the current position, uncertainty can be expected. By recognizing these obstacles when administrators change the form of professional development, they can provide time and support for home visitors to adapt to change.

Administrators also have professional development needs, but their needs may not be addressed by program policy, structure, and finance. In many programs, administrators work independently and may feel the same kind of isolation as do home visitors. They may have been promoted from direct service and may not have the benefit of preservice education directly related to their new role. As a result, administrators often have to create innovative ways of ensuring their own professional growth. Seminars at national conferences such as the ZERO TO THREE Training Institutes can offer a setting for shared learning and gaining new insights, similar to good continued education of home visitors. The administrators within a geographical region can meet regularly. These meetings can provide the kind of peer supervision and guidance discussed in this chapter. An outside consultant with supervision expertise can assist in facilitating these regional meetings and can help expand members' notions of what is possible. The Erikson Institute, for example, has taken leadership in offering a nine-session supervision seminar for administrators and supervisors of programs serving babies, toddlers, and their families in the Chicago area.[16] Development of videotapes on supervision can be an invaluable resource, especially for those living in rural areas. When programs cover large distances, telecommunication and the Internet can offer professional support, information, encouragement, and guidance.

CONCLUSION

This chapter discusses how home visitors, like artisans, learn best through practice over time. This learning through practice is possible if home visitors reflect on their practice, and in this reflection, gain new understanding of the meaning and purpose of their practice. The skills of reflection on practice can be promoted when a program's staff development is interactive. Team meetings can provide a setting in which home visitors tell stories to one another in a climate of mutual inquiry. They can share successes (e.g., a directive mother now engages in spontaneous play), express frustration (e.g., repeatedly, the family is not home at the scheduled time), share dilemmas (e.g., experiencing conflicting concerns between grandmother and teen mother), and sometimes share failures (e.g., a family's withdrawal from the program). When team meetings are small enough to develop relationships of trust, these home visitors' stories can be the springboard for them to practice reflection and gain support, feedback, encouragement, and new ideas. Learning from one another is the given expectation. Just as the personal relationship between home visitor and parent can strengthen a parent's role, so too, when home visitors work together with shared goals and common bonds, the experience can be strengthening, deepening the home visitor's understanding and enabling him or her to move forward with renewed commitment.

A solid foundation in child development is the first step in home visitors' continued education. Home visitors' work cuts across disciplines beyond child development; thus, staff meetings can be the setting for outside consultants to broaden the home visitor's knowledge base. When process is intertwined with content, that is, when home visitors can talk together about how their work relates to this content, then they can apply this new learning to their everyday work.

In addition, regular collaborative supervision gives home visitors a trusting relationship in which to discuss their work and gain feedback and guidance from an experienced practitioner. Supervision offers a safe setting to reflect on one's emotional reactions and to expose mistakes, insecurities, and questions. Together, supervisors and home visitors reflect on and interpret both the difficulties and the successes. Supervision is an especially important resource for those who work with families with multiple problems. There are indeed many structural barriers with home visiting programs that may make individual supervision impossible. Given this reality, administrators can adapt their program structure to provide features of the supervision model.

In sum, professional development is a lifelong process in which home visitors actively reflect on their practice, individually and with peers. Program participants meet together in a climate of inquiry. Team meetings are a place to share stories, grow, and learn and to give and accept feedback, new perspectives, and new strategies. This mutual, respectful collaboration cuts into the individualistic nature of home visitors' everyday work and provides support, encouragement, and guidance to return to the field.

II

Promoting Healthy Parent and Child Development

5

Developing a
ſense of ſelf

The Foundation of ſocial and Emotional Development

"I do like a mother's love," said Tottles, hitting Nibs with a pillow. "Do you like a mother's love, Nibs?"

"I do just," said Nibs, hitting back.

"You see," Wendy said complacently, "our heroine knew that the mother would always leave the window open for her children to fly back by; so they stayed away for years and had a lovely time."

J.M. Barrie, *Peter Pan* (1911, p. 128)

The concept of "self" or "sense of self" is an elusive one. This chapter uses the terms *self* and *sense of self* to reflect the perspective of current infant research and theory.[1] People demonstrate a sense of self when they say at a department store, "This jacket looks like me." As they become self-aware, people get embarrassed when they make a faux pas. Initially, infants have no awareness of self, but the components of sense of self are observable; they are inner experiences inferable through observed infant behavior. Sense of self is an inclusive concept that comprises social and emotional development and influences all other developmental areas, such as physical and sensorimotor, language, communication, and cognition.

The sense of self appears to develop within a paradox: A person develops an individual sense of self only within interactions with others. The sense of selfhood is a social achievement and is learned from living with others. Babies and young children develop a sense of self within parents' taken-for-granted day-to-day child-rearing interactions. These child-rearing interactions are mutually created; that is, parents shape their infant's actions at the same time that babies shape their parents' actions. This sense of self begins at the moment of birth and remains throughout life.

The infant's emerging sense of self is the organization of feelings, actions, and expectations underlying behavior.[2] The sense of one's self is extremely complex, but it is the core of what it means to be human. Adults can talk about their inner lives, but the components of the infant's sense of self are inner experiences inferable only through observed behavior. For example, when a 3-month-old engages in social smiles and coos at others, we can infer an emerging sense of self in relation to others—a social self. Young babies experience a sense of self long before they experience self-awareness. Explaining sense of self is difficult because the word seems so abstract and unobservable. Yet, the developing sense of self is the scaffolding, anchor, and foundation of development.

Since the mid-1980s, infant research using film and videotaping of newborns, young babies, and their parents has revolutionized our understanding of the infant's developing sense of self. For example, infant researchers now know that babies are born with specific emotions and abilities to relate socially. Changes in sense of self do not happen because of changes in the infant alone; rather, they are the result of the infant's physiological and mental capabilities *and* their experience with significant others. From the beginning, the newborn experiences both self and other. As Winnicott stated, "There is no such thing as a baby."[3] That is, there is no such thing as a baby without its parent. The capacity to experience oneself only occurs as the infant relates to another.

Given their drive to explore and master their environment, young children are active participants in their own development. Development is shaped by a dynamic interaction between biology and experience, between nature and nurture. The amount of change in the child's first 3 years has no parallel in the life cycle; and in no developmental areas is this change so dramatic as in the sense of self.

In what context does the sense of self develop? Social-emotional development encompasses developing sense of self and is intertwined with all other developmental areas. The baby and young child's sense of self as well as social-emotional development takes place in developmental leaps.[4]

Emde and Robinson identified five basic motives in early development. The first is activity. Babies are active, like to explore, and are eager to master their everyday world. Second is self-regulation; babies have an inborn propensity to regulate their behavior as well as their bodily processes. Third is social-fittedness; babies are motivated and programmed to initiate, maintain, and end social interactions. Fourth is affective monitoring, or the baby's ability to guide experience based on what is pleasurable or not. Finally is cognitive assimilation, or the impulse to explore the environment and see things that are new.[5]

Every few months, significant changes occur in the baby and young child's sense of self. Major shifts in the infant's social experiences result from these gains; in turn, these shifts impact the infant's sense of self. The following discussion tracks these developmental changes, which encompass the behavior of infants and young children and their parents because changes in the child's sense of self are intertwined with their relations with their parents. As the chapter tracks the young child's developing sense of self in relation to significant people in the child's life, it explores how home visitors can support, affirm, and promote parents' understanding and relationships with their infants and young children.[6]

NEUROPHYSIOLOGY

The central nervous system controls the complex processes that regulate both signals from within the body and signals from the environment. Since the early 1990s, neurobiological research has helped us explain the connection between psychosocial and neurological aspects of development. Neuroscientists now are able to use new technology to look at the brain and to watch it work. Through neuroimaging, researchers can measure chemical functions within the brain, such as glucose utilization, cerebral blood flow, oxygen utilization, and protein synthesis.[7] This research indicates that emotional development and emotional regulation parallel brain development. Changes in the brain trigger changes in babies' behavior and social-emotional development. In turn, the babies' experiences, especially everyday moment-to-moment caregiving interactions, influence brain structure and chemistry.

During the first 3 years of life, children learn more than they will in any other period in their lives. Beginning 3 weeks after conception and continuing throughout pregnancy, the baby produces hundreds of millions of brain cells. The brain is not finished developing when the baby is born. The majority of connections between the cells are made during the first months and years of the child's life. These connections determine how a child functions.

Scientists once thought that babies' genes alone determined their intellectual potential and how they behaved. Neuroscientists now know that the combination of genetic and environmental influences ultimately determine babies' social, emotional, and intellectual development.[8] Babies' environments include everything from foods and substances pregnant mothers eat; to people, places, toys, and books; to language; and most important, to interactions with their parents. Not only does brain development have an impact on emotions, but also babies' early experiences, especially their interactions with their parents, actually cause physical changes in the brain.[9] Repeated positive caregiving experiences make a decisive impact on the architecture of the brain. Neglect of a baby's need for love and stimulation can impact brain development and cause lifelong problems. Damaged brain cells cannot be repaired or replaced. Neuroimaging reveals significantly less density in the brain cells of neglected or traumatized babies.

The brain is an interconnected network of billions of cells. The term *brain development* refers to neurochemical and structural changes in the brain. The basic units of the brain are very complex cells called neurons. Neurons have characteristics that allow them to receive and send electrical and chemical signals to other cells. Each neuron is made up of the cell body, the axon, and dendrites, which are like tree branches that extend from the neuron's cell body and are the neuron's receivers. Neurons work by sending information in the form of electrical signals throughout the body. Experience activates neurons. Researchers note that neurons are genetically programmed to communicate with each other and wait for stimulation to enable them to adjust their connections.

The brain is remarkably plastic, and in the early years, children's brains form twice as many connections as they eventually will need. A single neuron can have many dendrites, and babies' experiences determine the number of dendrites that will form. Infancy and toddlerhood is a critical time of accelerated and continuing brain growth that is dependent on environmental influences, especially child-rearing interactions. At 6 months of age, the infant's brain is 50% of its adult size; at 3 years, the child's brain is 80% of its adult size. This growth is primarily because of the growth in number and density of dendrites. At 10 months the cerebral cortex, the part of the brain responsible for problem solving and complex thinking processes, develops, and receptive language emerges. Between 10 and 12 months, the baby's prefrontal cortex, which makes emotional regulation and focused attention possible, grows.[10]

Neuroscientists believe there are sensitive periods of time during brain development when neurons can create connections most easily and efficiently. Sensitive period means that having a certain kind of experience at one time in development can have a profoundly different influence on future behavior than having that same experience at any other time in development. (Scientists speak of _sensitive periods_, though the term _critical periods_ is often used in the early childhood literature.) Given the brain's plasticity, there are times when negative experiences or the absence of stimulation can have serious and permanent effects. Each of the brain's abilities—vision, hearing, language, intellect, motor, social-emotional development—has its own sensitive period. Some brain systems are subject to sensitive period constraints; others are not. There are different sensitive periods for different brain systems, such as vision and language processing. For instance, the grammatical processing subsystem is more sensitive to early experience than is the semantic processing subsystem. Even so, individual differences in biological and environmental factors can blur the effects of sensitive periods on individual children.

Emotional Regulation

Emotional regulation is part of social-emotional development. It is babies' ability to modify emotional reactions to accomplish their goals and to adapt to environmental demands. Adequate adaptation requires both reaction and regulation. Babies often are good at reaction but need help with regulation. Initially, the parent and child accomplish emotional regulation together, but accomplishing this regulation is not always easy. Parents need to be able to read and understand their babies' needs and have the knowledge and resources to respond in helpful ways. In order to help the baby maintain a calm and alert state, she cries, and her mother comforts her. The baby smiles, and his mother talks to him. Early regulation is deeply embedded in the baby's relations with others.

The key to emotional regulation is the baby's emotional security. Emotional security emerges from a regular schedule of daily activities, the presence of a parent, the baby's attachment to his or her parent, and the home's emotional climate. Emotional regulation develops as mothers and their babies engage in a contingent cycle of signals and responses. Mothers' sensitivity is closely linked to her baby's developing emotional regulation. Research also documents that fathers' sensitivity during play is linked to their baby's emotional regulation.[11]

Beginning in the third month of life, babies develop effective communication and emotional regulation within the context of their repeated interactions with their parents. Parents' behavior can stimulate and confirm their baby's emotions and guide the baby's emotional regulation. Babies are quite skilled at tailoring their behavior to fit their caregiving environment and to optimize the likelihood that their parent will remain nearby.[12] For example, if they become overstimulated during an interaction, babies can avert their gaze and thereby lower the intensity of the stimulation.

THE BODY SELF: BIRTH TO 6 MONTHS

Parents' interactions with their newborns primarily center around physiological regulation. As parents hold, caress, rock, and talk to their newborn, they learn to adjust their behavior to their baby's behavior; for example, parents gently rock their baby after the baby begins to fuss or talk to their baby during feeding. In the same way that the baby's behavior triggers a response from the parent, parents' behavior triggers a response from the baby. For example, the baby becomes quiet as a parent rocks him or her, or the baby looks intently into the eyes of a talking parent while nursing. A pattern of mutually influencing each other begins and continues in their everyday interactions. Some babies may have sensory systems that are over- or underreactive, and thus these babies may not readily respond to parents' efforts or may be fussy. In turn, some parents may themselves have shortcomings in their ability to be responsive to their babies. The Difficulties and Dilemmas section of this chapter discusses these problems further.

Parents of newborns experience both delight and uneasiness. Their uneasiness arises from the awesomeness of their task as a parent. Home visitors can help parents feel more at ease by providing helpful developmental information so that parents can have *predictable expectations* of their newborn. Home visitors can explain to parents of newborns that an infant has a built-in cycle of six states of consciousness: deep sleep, light sleep, semi-alert, wide awake alert, fussing, and crying. During deep sleep, babies can shut out most environmental noise. During light REM sleep, babies are more vulnerable to being awakened. Newborns typically sleep 16–17 hours each day. During their visits, home visitors can describe the baby's different states of arousal. Knowing that the infant experiences this predictable cycle allows parents to be more in control of their caregiving. One parent's comments about her home visitor are illustrative.

> I tell people that don't know anything about the program that home visitors will give you ideas of what to look for, what to expect next in the development of the child, and things you can do that can help that development to go along. And I just tell them that we wouldn't be without it. . . .We waited a long time before having children, and not knowing what to do after having the baby. . . .I guess I was kinda iffy about some things and not knowing how to do other things.

Newborns show preferences for familiar sights, sounds, and odors. They especially prefer the familiar voice and face of their mother. They can turn their heads to the sound of their mother's voice. Newborns even prefer listening to melodies sung by their mother and stories they heard while they were in the womb.[13] This preferential attitude toward the mother plays an important part in the formation of the mother–child bond. These preferences can help mothers bond to their babies. The way parents hold their baby influences the baby's sense of security and ability to focus calmly, and home visitors can encourage parents to vary how they hold their baby to learn which helps to relax the baby most. For most very young babies, swaddling gently but firmly the arms and legs in a blanket wrapped around their bodies is soothing.

Babies demonstrate interest in their surroundings through facial expressions, body movements, and eye gaze. They find parents' faces fascinating. Babies have both a physical/cognitive reaction and an emotional reaction to each experience. They experience basic emotions of pleasure, comfort, and distress. Young babies can focus at a distance of about 8–10 inches, which is why the nursing position is ideal for mutual gazing and interaction. Between periods of fussing, sleeping, and eating, babies develop longer periods of quiet alertness when parents can interact with them. These periods of mutual attentiveness and interaction deepen the parent–baby bond.

Self-Calming

The newborn's first task is to achieve calmness (i.e., to be regulated inside) and be interested in the surrounding world. One of parents' first areas of guidance is assisting their new baby to self-calm.[14] When babies can self-calm, they can stop crying or fussing and settle down without help from anyone else. Self-calming is the first form of independence and self-control that a baby learns. Usually, by age 8–10 weeks babies learn to calm themselves. Sammons identified ways in which babies self-calm: by sucking; by moving their hands, arms, or legs; by taking a certain body position; or by using their vision.[15] Self-calming is a mutual achievement of parent and baby and is achieved through their communication. Parents learn the meaning of different cries, for example, learning when they can let their baby calm herself and thereby put herself back to sleep, as opposed to when their baby needs to be fed. Parents also learn what type of rhythm most attracts their young baby. Research indicates that babies may show early individual differences in both self-calming and in attention, perhaps in response to emotional parts of their environment. Soothing abilities and attention may be linked to later learning of complex tasks. Discussing self-calming during home visitors' first visit after a baby's birth can be very helpful because many parents are not aware of the occurrence or the importance of self-calming.

Early child development theorists and researchers discuss affect and emotion interchangeably. When discussing emotional regulation, the parent has a central role in helping the young baby regulate. Affect regulation designates a parent's empathic response to the baby's signal. For example, the baby cries, and the father picks her up, rocks her, and sings to her and in this manner helps her to maintain a calm, alert state. Daily child-rearing interactions such as holding, hugging, stroking, singing, and talking softly are ways that parents provide babies with comfort, love, and security. Dejonna illustrates this responsiveness to her 11-week-old daughter, Diamond.

> As Diamond sits in the swing, she begins to fuss. Dejonna picks her up, holds her snuggly as she rocks back and forth, and softly sings. Diamond immediately stops fussing and reaches for Dejonna's face. After a few moments, Dejonna returns Diamond to the swing.

A baby's healthy social-emotional development depends on the baby's parents' ability to see meaning in the baby's behavior and respond appropriately. Home visitors can help parents understand the meaning of their baby's gestures and movements. Parents who successfully read their baby's cues and respond appropriately feel confident and enjoy their parenting.

Some parents are not responsive to their baby's signals of distress. Crittenden identified four reasons for parents' lack of appropriate response.[16] First, parents appear to be unaware of their baby's signals. Second, parents recognize the signals but misinterpret them. Third, parents interpret the signals correctly but do not know how to respond appropriately, and fourth, parents understand how to respond but for various reasons, such as being depressed, do not respond appropriately. Home visitors can assist parents in learning how to respond to their baby's distress. For example, they can explain to parents the different ways of soothing a young baby.

Pruett's research indicates that babies whose fathers participate in bathing, feeding, diapering, and dressing are more socially responsive and scored higher on the Bayley Scales of Infant Development than did babies who did not receive regular care from their fathers.[17] Even when they do the same activities as mothers do, fathers interact differently with their babies than do mothers and thus expand the baby's range of potential emotions. When fathers share in caregiving, they also provide emotional and physical support for the mother.

Temperament

Home visitors also can help parents understand the wide differences in baby's responsiveness to people and the environment, in the baby's activity level, and in how quickly the baby becomes upset. These differences reflect inborn patterns termed *temperament*.[18] Temperament is biologically based and is influenced in part by genetic factors. Temperament differences are seen in movement, ease of soothing, degree of alertness, and manner of sleeping. The baby's temperament affects the way he or she responds to his or her parents. In turn, parents need to learn to adapt their responses to their baby's unique temperament. Karyn's discussion with Janice is illustrative.

Karyn: One day he screamed all day. I called the pediatrician, and he said to put him on the dryer and turn it on. I let go and got angry; and then he said to bring in the baby. He said that Greg was okay and [that] he is going to be a difficult baby.

Janice: He still cries, but now you feel better because you know it is not a health problem. [Karyn nods yes.] There's so much learning that goes on. The baby needs to learn your signals; you need to learn his signals. And the baby needs to learn your husband's signals, and he needs to learn those of the baby. You don't know each other very well yet. It's really tricky.

Karyn: He's jumpy—like when the nipple on his bottle makes a sound, he jumps. Even when he's sleeping, he's jumpy.

Janice: Swaddling—wrapping him snuggly in his blanket and cuddling him—
           often helps, keeping him closed in. My third baby was colicky. Even
           when it's the third baby, it's tough when they cry a lot. Have you tried
           massage?

Karyn: No.

Janice: Try rubbing his shoulders. Babies carry tension in their shoulders, like we
           do. And put him on his back, stretch and bend his legs one at a time,
           and massage them, and rub his tummy.

Janice's comments that the pediatrician's suggestion of calming Greg by using the hum and vibration of the dryer is the physician's way of telling Karyn in everyday language that her baby's temperament is *difficult*—that Greg is difficult to soothe and comfort. By rephrasing Karyn's description, Janice let her know that she understands her feelings. She supported Karyn by sharing her own parenting experiences. She used everyday language to provide developmental information regarding the mutuality of parent–baby relationships, and she provided a suggestion directly related to Karyn's concerns. In this conversation, no doubt Karyn felt understood and affirmed.

Newborns are predesigned to seek stimulation, to selectively respond to their environment, and to participate in social interaction. Newborns have some voluntary muscle control and can turn their heads, suck, and look. They choose to look at faces, suck to soothe themselves, and turn away from unpleasant sounds or sights. These behaviors indicate that the newborn is capable of purposeful actions.[19]

The newborn's sense of being is integrated. Different experiences can be joined if they share the same quality of feeling.[20] A mother may comfort her baby in different ways, such as speaking quietly, stroking softly, or holding the baby while walking calmly. The baby experiences these different occurrences as the same form of comfort. A sense of organization thus is created.

Emotions are the organizing basis for guiding young babies' behavior.[21] Initially, very young babies have little ability to manage their feelings and are dependent on their parents for this regulation. As they interact with their young babies, parents respond empathically and help their baby avoid too much excitement or discomfort. Infant theorists term regulation of babies' feelings *affect regulation*.[22] Brazelton and Cramer explained how parents regulate their infants' behavior.

A mother will lean over her baby, reach for a flailing extremity, hold the baby by the buttocks, enclose him or her in an envelope made up of her intense gaze and her soft vocalization. Out of this cluster of five behaviors, she will heighten one of them, her voice, to elicit a response. As her voice increases gently, the infant responds with a cluster of behaviors—relaxation of the whole body, softening of facial features, intense looking at her, then a soft "coo." The mother's clustering of behaviors around each vocalization is as important in producing the response as her voice alone. A baby must be "contained" in order to attend to her. The mother also must learn her baby's system of clusters.[23]

When babies are about 3 months, a developmental leap brings new behaviors that promote sociability. Cycles of wakefulness are extended, babies become more focused, eye-to-eye contact is extended, and the infant enjoys frequent spontaneous social vocalizing and social smiling. Young babies have excellent motor memories. Memory allows young babies to have a sense of continuity with their previous experiences. For example, babies have memories of past interactions with their parents that provide them with expectations guiding their behavior.[24] These memories are nonverbal, consist of internal experiences, and provide a guide for their present experiences. They include a wide array of social behavior between infant and caregiver, for example, simple interactive games that all parents invent with their babies. Specific emotions emerge, joy becomes differentiated from contentment and sadness, and later, anger becomes differentiated from general distress. By 3–4 months, babies' vision approaches 20/20.

Bonding and Attachment

Young babies develop the qualities of sense of self within everyday, taken-for-granted child-rearing relationships. Infant theorists use the terms *bonding* and *attachment* to explain this relationship.[25] Most mothers and fathers form a strong initial bond with their infant at birth or in the hours and days immediately following. A variety of parent behaviors are automatic and seem to be specieswide, for example, exaggerated greeting responses, body-touching games, and imitation of the infant's facial and vocal expressions. Home visitors must understand that not all parents have positive feelings after their infant's birth, and not all parents quickly bond to their infant. When parents do not immediately feel bonded, they think that something is wrong with them, and they may feel guilty. Home visitors can assist these parents in recognizing that, in reality, this new infant brings a giant change in the parents' lives, that their ambivalent feelings are a normal part of being a parent, and that it may take time to learn how to feel comfortable in their new role as parent. Furthermore, some parents experience difficulty bonding with their second child—feelings that surprise and trouble them.

Again, the home visitor can assist the parents in understanding that their feelings are normal.

As the infant spontaneously smiles and coos or fusses and cries, these behaviors become signals for his or her parents to respond.[26] Home visitors can help parents recognize these early forms of communication and understand how these parents' responsiveness fosters their babies' sense of connectedness and security. Janice's observations of Natalie's responses to her baby, Jene (age 3 ½ months), are illustrative.

> Janice puts Jene on an infant blanket and gives her a three-ringed rattle. Jene begins to fuss once again. Her mother, Natalie, picks her up and softly bounces her and rubs her back. Janice uses the baby's voice to affirm Natalie's responsiveness, "I know how to communicate with my mommy, and she understands me."
>
> Natalie prepares a bottle for Jene and holds her in her lap as she continues to chat with Janice. Jene falls asleep. Janice affirms Natalie's parenting skills by saying, "It's important to pay attention to a baby's signals. We could have continued on the floor, but we followed Jene's signals. She became fussy. Kids at all ages need to know that adults respect their feelings. 'It's time for Mommy to pick me up.'"

Janice supports and affirms Natalie's responsiveness to her infant's signals. She helps this young mother understand that her responsiveness is communicating respect to even such a small infant.

By age 3 months, babies favor those who regularly care for them. Attachment can be defined as the development of an affectionate relationship between a baby and the baby's parents that will endure over time.[27] Both the baby's temperament and the mother's behavior contribute to the developing attachment relationship. By age 5 months, babies' everyday experience and their development of an internal working model of their attachment figures allow them to have firm attachments. Not all babies have just one attachment figure. Babies show strong attachments to both parents or to parents and another caregiver, such as their child care teacher. Between 6 and 12 months of age, babies develop attachment to their primary parents. Emotional availability, nurturance, warmth, and provision of comfort are the most salient parent behaviors that promote attachment. The securely attached baby will gain emotional regulation and seek comfort from the attachment figure for distress.[28]

Parents and their babies develop a natural pattern of attachment behaviors. Babies signal their needs by crying or smiling, and their parent responds, so the two-person dance begins.[29] Essential for a healthy attachment to form is the opportunity to develop real mutuality—partners smoothly following one another's lead. As home visitors observe attachment behaviors, they can help parents recognize the significance of these behaviors, as illustrated by the following example.

> Maggie (age 9 months) has awakened from her nap, and her mother, Tracy, has just brought her into the living room. Maggie smiles as Janice softly says, "I'm so glad to see you." Maggie then begins crying as she nestles her head in her mother's shoulder. Janice says, "It's so typical of babies this age to switch emotions. Two things are happening: First, they can be happy then sad, and vice versa so quickly, and more importantly, Maggie knows the difference between Mom and other people."
>
> Tracy responds, "That's true even between Mom and Gramma."
>
> "You're so wise to comfort her when she feels that way," Janice says. "She knows Mom is here." Maggie now is smiling at Janice. "And with Mom here, it's okay to smile at others. It's also nice to be having people in your own home. There is security here and a gradual way for Maggie to deal with a couple of new people."

Janice's observations of Maggie's behavior and Tracy's appropriate response supports and affirms Tracy. Maggie is learning that her actions can trigger a response from her mother. As she observes, Janice interprets the developmental significance of Maggie's behavior and gives Tracy a simple suggestion to invite people to her home with whom Maggie can learn to interact.

Secure Attachment

Once an attachment develops, it can be secure or insecure. Securely attached babies feel connected and trust that their parents will be available, responsive, and loving. Babies' attachment figures give them confidence that they are not alone in coping with challenges. In addition, by responding quickly and appropriately to a baby's signals, the attachment figure strengthens the baby's sense of competence and efficacy. A secure attachment helps to structure the baby's brain so that the baby can handle stress better and can relate positively to other people. Thompson discussed how attachment is an important influence beyond infancy.

Secure or insecure attachment is important not only as an indicator of the early parent–child relationship, but it is believed to influence emergent self-representation, social skills and dispositions, personality development, and self-regulation. The influences of attachment security increasingly characterize the child, not just the relationship with the parent.[30]

Home visitors can help parents develop a healthy attachment to their baby when they observe and discuss the baby's actions, the parents' responses, and discuss the importance of secure attachment.

With repeated everyday child-rearing interactions, babies develop an attachment and an internal working model of their relationship with their parents. Babies' internal working models are a representation, a memory of their interactions with parents. Internal working models permit babies to form expectations. For example, "When Mommy puts me on the diaper-changing table, she will sing, talk softly, or tickle me." When most of babies' interactions consist of experiences of comfort, warmth, and pleasure, they develop an inner understanding that close relationships are trustworthy and nurturing.

Insecure Attachment

Though all babies become attached to their primary caregivers, some babies are not securely attached. These babies, whose cries often are ignored, learn that the parents they depend on are unreliable. They avoid or resist contact with a parent after separation or express anger or distress upon reunion. Because these babies have psychologically unavailable parents, they develop models of relationships as empty and unfulfilling. These negative internal models of relationships with significant others shape both their expectations and behaviors. For example, many preschoolers who had psychologically unavailable mothers become aggressive, impulsive, and hyperactive.[31]

Mutuality is central to the attachment behaviors of babies and their parents. A baby smiles and coos, and the mother returns the smile as she talks softly to the baby. Research demonstrates intergenerational influences in attachment: a significant agreement between mothers and their babies' patterns of attachment, and between mothers' patterns of attachment as well as those of their own mothers' attachment patterns.[32]

Crandell, Fitzgerald, and Whipple studied the relationship between mothers' attachment relationships in childhood with their interactions with their own preschoolers.[33] The quality of mothers' childhood attachment relationships was significantly related to their affect and manner of relating to their children during a play sequence. Secure mothers and their children engaged in more fluid, synchronous processes of give-and-take than did insecure mothers and their children.

Babies and young children draw social maps of their everyday world. Attachment is the baby's first social map, and it encompasses how the baby understands his or her everyday social environment. When babies are insecurely attached, they are what Garbarino and Bedard termed "psychologically homeless; and the social map begins to emerge without appropriate boundaries, allies, and orientation to emotional north, south, east and west."[34] Nevertheless, even those babies and young children who have insecure attachments derive important emotional support from the presence of their parents.

Changing Nature of Attachment

Secure or insecure attachments may change during the early years of life. A baby who begins with an insecure relationship may later develop a secure attachment to the same parent. Or the birth of another baby or a period of high family stress may alter a young child's attachment.[35]

Specific attachment patterns result from the interaction of characteristics of the young child, capacities of the child's parent, and the broader context of their relationship. For example, children with Down syndrome, premature babies, very young babies who continue to react to stimuli that other babies have tuned out, and babies who become disorganized when experiencing stress are likely to develop insecure attachments. It may be harder for some parents to provide sensitive care to these children. When a parent can maintain a high degree of sensitivity, psychological availability, and responsiveness, even babies with difficult temperaments can develop secure attachments. A parent's depression, economic difficulty, or marital conflict can interfere with the sensitive and responsive caregiving needed for secure attachment.

Babies may form one type of attachment with one parent that is different from the attachment formed with another parent or caregiver. For example, a baby may have a secure attachment with her mother but an insecure attachment with her child care provider. The baby's secure attachment with his or her mother may temper the baby's insecure attachment with the caregiver, and vice versa. For example, in one project, child care providers cared 5 days per week for babies and young children who were at risk. These children developed secure attachments with their child care providers despite their insecure attachments with their parents.

Many children develop secure attachments with more than one adult. Attachment relationships may vary with different adults so that a young child may have an insecure attachment to one parent and a secure attachment with another. Spending time in child care does not undermine young children's relationship with their parents. Unfortunately, as a result of the consistent high turnover in child care providers in the United States, young children are more often insecurely than securely attached to their child care providers.[36]

Early attachments are important for substantive effects of aspects of a child's development beyond the parent–child relationship. They foster exploratory behavior and have an enduring influence on young children's social-emotional development, such as conscience development, moral values, empathy, and understanding and experiencing friendship. Securely attached young children have an easier time than insecurely attached in developing positive relationships with peers, teachers, and others in their lives. Secure attachment also seems to buffer young children to prevent high elevations in stress hormones.[37]

In addition to developing attachment relationships, babies develop an inner sense of themselves within these relationships. Babies who are loved see themselves as lovable and worthy of attention. As significant adults respond to them, they develop a sense of competence and confidence. When babies' cries are ignored or met with harshness, babies develop a sense of self as unworthy. Two different worlds are created for those babies who are securely attached and those who are insecurely attached.

Greenspan and Lewis identified ways in which babies around 5 months of age typically participate in a loving relationship.

- They respond to smiles with big smiles of their own.
- They initiate interactions with loving looks and smiles.
- They make sounds and/or move their mouths, arms, legs, or bodies in rhythm with caregivers as caregivers move in rhythm with them.
- They relax or act comforted when caregivers hold or rock them.
- They coo when they are held, touched, looked at, or spoken to.
- They look at the caregiver's face with rapt interest.
- They anticipate with curiosity and excitement the reappearance of the caregiver's face or voice.
- They look uneasy or sad when the caregiver withdraws in the midst of playing with them.
- They become angry (with a furrowed brow or piercing cry) when they are frustrated by something a caregiver is doing.
- They recover from distress, with a caregiver's help, within 15 minutes.[38]

Babies' emotional interactions with significant others are the source of their intelligence, morality, and self-esteem. Joyful parent–baby interactions spark brain growth in areas that focus on emotional expression, which in turn helps babies' ability to interact lovingly. Daily positive child-rearing interactions are babies' first lessons in understanding that they can make something happen.

Social Development

As early as 2 months of age, babies are interested in one another. Beginning with the parent and baby gazing intently at each other, simple playful interactions develop. As the 3-month-old smiles, the parent smiles and talks softly; with time, the baby becomes familiar with the emotional language of his or her significant others and the emotional messages conveyed by the tone of voice and body movements. In another month or so, the baby laughs and soon will enjoy Peekaboo. In addition to smiles, movements, speech, and intonation can keep a baby engaged. Babies also enjoy the companionship of other babies and toddlers. They will stare avidly at one another and, at around 6 months of age, will try to get the attention of another baby by smiling or babbling.

THE AUTONOMOUS SELF: 7–18 MONTHS

New Forms of Experiencing Connectedness

Between the ages of 7 and 9 months, babies have a history, a memory of relating to their parents, and increased experience in communicating by facial expression, body movements, and posture.[39] Infant specialist Robert Emde described the developmental leap in this period as "the onset of focused attachment."[40] A new form of experiencing connectedness emerges. Babies are two-way communicators who can initiate and respond to social gestures. They enjoy simple interactive games such as Pat-a-cake and Peekaboo—giving evidence of *shared joint attention*. Babies begin pointing and can follow their parents' pointing. By 9 months, babies will make requests by pointing at a bottle or pointing to go outdoors. Developmentalists say the baby is giving evidence of *shared intention*.

Babies have both a physical/cognitive reaction and an emotional reaction to each experience. By age 9 months, babies begin crawling about to explore their surroundings. In order to resolve uncertainty, babies will pause and look from their desired goal to their parent in order to gain assurance from their parent, providing evidence that the babies can understand the parent's expression of feeling. This two-way communication helps the child become empathic and eventually distinguish right from wrong. These new skills allow babies to begin to understand that their inner experiences are shared with someone else. They can carry an image of Mommy or Daddy inside their head, even when Mommy and Daddy are out of sight, termed *object permanence*. These social skills are the first steps in a process that helps toddlers learn to become more cooperative. Both emotional abilities and intelligence are part of the same pattern of growth.[41]

In the first half of their second year, toddlers become problem solvers. They move in order to get what they want, and they know that they can enlist their parents to help them get what they want. They have begun to figure out how the physical world works. They discover that doors open and close and are used to go in and out. If they can't see something, they can climb on furniture to see. If they press the button, the television turns on.

Life's basic emotional themes such as dependency, assertiveness, negotiating closeness, anger, curiosity, the need to explore, pleasure, dealing with limit setting, and frustration are emerging.[42] Babies have learned patterns of behavior to express these emotions. Home visitors can help parents assist their toddlers in communicating these new emotions and help the parents respect these emotions and respond appropriately to them.

Parents' Responsiveness

In their interactions with their baby, parents often understand the feelings behind their baby's behavior and respond in a way that matches their baby's feeling. Parents' behavior is *not* a strict behavioral imitation. Often, the match is a similar expression by a different action; for example, the baby's stretching movement is matched by the parents' stretching voice tone and tempo. As parents reflect their baby's feelings, the baby feels connected and gains understanding of his or her own feelings, and thus his or her own sense of self. Stern described how babies and their parents share feeling states as follows:

A 9-month-old girl becomes very excited about a toy and reaches for it. As she grabs it, she lets out a exuberant "aaaah!" and looks at her mother. Her mother looks back, squinches up her shoulders, and performs a terrific shimmy of her upper body—like a go-go dancer. The shimmy lasts only about as long as her daughter's "aaaah!" but is equally excited, joyful, and intense.[43]

As parents' behavior reflects the same quality of feeling, young babies experience their parents' empathic responsiveness and communication. When parents label and discuss emotional experiences, they help their toddlers to give meaning to these experiences. When parents frequently discuss emotions, such as, "Demetrius was really sad when he couldn't have more cookies, wasn't he?" or, "Do you miss Sissy now that she's gone to school?" their young children have a clearer understanding of emotion. Whereas initially caregivers might have intervened to soothe an unhappy baby, now they may coach their toddlers to develop strategies to learn to take turns, to deal with a frustrating task, or to comfort a friend.

Trust

As babies become mobile, they actively explore the world around them. When they are securely attached, babies use their parents as a safe base from which to explore. Erikson described babies' first developmental task as achieving basic trust as opposed to mistrust.[44] A trusting baby sees the world as a good, stable place. Trust emerges when babies have their needs met, including the physical needs of nourishment, sleep, and warmth and the psychological needs of cuddling, talk, and play. When babies experience consistency in having their needs met, they gain self-confidence because they can give cues to let someone know what they need and they can influence others.

Home visitors can help parents recognize what their baby is learning when they respond to their baby.

> Greg (age 9 months) begins to cry. His mother, Karyn, picks him up, and he stops crying. Janice speaks as if she were Greg to affirm Karyn's responsiveness, "That's so reassuring to me. Mom really understands what I mean, and she is helping me."

As Karyn spontaneously interacts with Greg, Janice helps her understand how important her actions are for her young baby's understanding of self and the world around him. As Karyn consistently responds to her son's behavior, he develops an understanding that he influences her, and through these experiences, he develops a sense of personal control.[45] That is, when the baby succeeds in gaining a positive response from his or her parent, he or she gains a sense of effectiveness.

When home visitors sense that a parent is not responding to the baby, they can model spontaneous gestural and verbal responses to the baby. In these interactions with the baby, the home visitor can help the parent see the baby's pleasure in the interaction and understand the developmental importance of this process. Some home visitors may be working with parents whose own concerns prevent them from tuning in to their baby. The Difficulties and Dilemmas section of this chapter discusses this issue further.

"Loveys"

Often an object connected to their parents' warmth and love can provide security for young babies and toddlers, especially during transition times, such as from waking to sleeping.[46] Such objects, sometimes called *loveys,* allow young children to comfort themselves in the same manner as thumb sucking comforts them. A single beloved object taken to bed may become part of a young toddler's self-comforting routine. Mia's "aw" is illustrative.

> Mia (age 17 months) asks her mother, Tracy, "Where is aw?" Tracy explains to Janice that "aw" is Mia's name for her special pillow. Tracy explains that the pillow was a fancy pillow that she had received as a shower present. She and her husband would say "aw" as they would put Mia to bed. One night, she asked for her "aw," and ever since, it has been her special pillow. Janice says, "*Aw* has a real warm sound. The message is comfort and security."

Loveys are a typical part of development and provide an important way for young children to comfort themselves. Home visitors can help parents understand how loveys play an important role in young children's learning to comfort themselves.

Stranger Anxiety

A sign of strong attachment occurs around 8 months of age when babies protest being separated from their parents and show fear of strangers and strange places. The intensity of these fearful reactions varies widely from one baby to another. This pattern often is referred to as stranger anxiety. There seems to be no clear basis for this typical fearful pattern. It seems to occur as babies become more aware of new places and of new people. After about a month or so, most babies learn how to handle new experiences.

Because stranger anxiety is quite predictable around 8 months, home visitors can give parents needed information so that parents can expect this first sign of fear in their infant and know that their infant's behavior is normal. When visiting babies during this phase, home visitors can respect the baby's fear and help the family feel at ease.

> Janice arrives at Tracy's home. Maggie (age 8 months) is crawling about the living room. When Janice begins to speak, Maggie stops crawling and begins to cry. Her mother picks her up as Janice comments, "Someone strange is in my house."
>
> Janice then sits on the rug several feet from Maggie and her mother, and says, "I'll stay away and won't rush her. When Janice and Carol come, Maggie is not sure yet. We are not Mia [her sister], Mommy, or Daddy. She knows she loves Mia, Mommy, and Daddy. She's not sure of these new people and needs some time to get used to them."

As Janice speaks, Tracy returns Maggie to the floor. However, Maggie begins crying again. As soon as Tracy picks her up and holds her, Maggie stops crying. Janice comments, "That's so wonderful, the way you just pick her up and love her when she is unhappy. She can feel secure knowing you are there." Maggie coos as she nestles in her mother's arms.

In a prior visit, Janice had discussed stranger anxiety with Tracy. As Maggie expressed fear of Janice, Janice respected Maggie's discomfort and moved away from her. As she observes Maggie, Janice interprets to Tracy the meaning of Maggie's fear response. As Tracy comforts her infant, Janice affirms her responsiveness.

Independence and Autonomy

Developing independence and autonomy is an integral part of the healthy development of sense of self and begins at birth. A newborn gives evidence of purposeful action when she sucks her fist and calms herself. As mentioned previously, this self-calming is the newborn's first achievement of independence. Babies ages 5 and 6 months both initiate and turn away from interactions with their parent—another sign of autonomy. Toddlers, however, want to be in charge and make things happen. They begin to connect their arm and hand movements with the sounds and sights that follow—beginning to understand cause and effect. Similarly, they know that they can elicit a smile, hug, or kiss by their own smile. Once infants and toddlers become mobile, this mobility sparks new explorations and feelings of independence and autonomy, accompanied by feelings of ambivalence. By 8 or 9 months, babies can sequence at least two movements as they go after something they desire. This new skills is motor planning or motor sequencing. As they play, toddlers occasionally "check in" with their parents by making eye contact, or saying something to them, often from a distance. Psychological rather than physical contact can provide the needed security. Toddlers are learning to regulate their own arousal levels, another strand of emotional regulation.

These toddlers are testing new feelings of separateness, yet they continue to be pulled toward their parents. Dependence and independence are a part of toddlers' daily explorations. Within a few moments, the toddler will push away Mommy and cling to her. "No" becomes a favorite word, though often the toddler will desire that which is negated. As toddlers test both their parents' limits and their own growing independent actions, this negativism is a natural phase of the developing sense of self.

Not only are toddlers more mobile, but their plane of vision has changed so that they can view things from a new vantage point, which provides pleasures, challenges, and frustrations. With supportive parents, toddlers now can learn to remain organized in the face of frustration. Toddlers' ability to stay organized emotionally long enough to solve frustrations or problems (e.g., to rebuild a block tower which has fallen) enhances their sense of self-worth and competence.

Parents need to give their toddlers simple, clear limits because limits help toddlers organize their behavior and feel in control. Even when parents firmly set limits, toddlers sometimes protest and have a tantrum; they yell, and their limbs swing out in rage. Home visitors can help parents understand that tantrums are a normal part of toddlerhood. They can let a tantrum run its course and then hug the child and softly talk about the child's frustration.

Home visitors can encourage parents to allow their toddlers to try to master new challenges and frustrations. They can explain to parents the changing behaviors that they can expect in the coming weeks and months. When parents understand that their toddler's sudden refusal to cooperate in dressing is a normal developmental phase, they can develop accepting responses while setting clear boundaries. During her visit with Karyn and Don, Janice discussed changes they can expect in their son's behavior.

> This is about the age that it will seem as if Greg [age 14 months] is saying "Oh yeah, I'll show off my autonomy." He'll test your creativity. [Age] 14–24 months is one of the most difficult times with little guys. Another challenge—he's not going to want to do something you want him to do. This is something that is going on inside him, not like walking. He's testing, not in a nasty way. It is legitimate testing. It'll be important to prioritize what you never are going to let him do. He'll find all kinds of ways to say "no" before he can say the word. He will tell you with his body. It's called negativism. It's one of those things it's nice to know it's coming. There is nothing wrong with my child.

Home visitors have the opportunity to normalize a toddler's negativism and strivings for independence and to help parents see these behaviors as central to the developing sense of self.

Emotional Regulation

Emotional regulation is the foundation of early childhood development. Emotional regulation entails expressing emotions effectively in relationships in many different settings. By around 8 months of age, the frontal cortex has increased metabolic activity.[47] The frontal cortex is linked with the ability to regulate and express emotion as well as to think and to play. The baby's generalized distress now changes to expressions of anger, fear, and disgust.[48] Now, babies experience different emotions in different contexts.

By the middle of the second year, toddlers can make efforts to avoid emotionally arousing situations, can engage in self-reassuring talk, and can change goals that have been frustrated.[49] With appropriate caregiving, toddlers are more able to experience a wide range of emotions. They can learn to tolerate more intense feelings without falling apart and are able to recover from strong emotions. They learn to seek help when needed. Whereas initially parents may use distractions to regulate a baby's emotions, they may not have to do this for toddlers because toddlers can use distraction for themselves.

Young children who learn to regulate their emotions have an easier time with frustrations and have a happier time relating to others. Parents can help toddlers learn to tolerate frustration by not giving in to their demands right away. Not surprisingly, positive relationships with peers are closely related to positive emotional regulation. How a child responds emotionally to an event sometimes is governed by how the event is construed. As toddlers' cognitive and language skills develop, parents' verbal interpretations, especially of distressing situations, are very important. They provide toddlers with tools with which they can learn to reframe situations for themselves. For example, a toddler begins to cry when a very large dog barks loudly. The toddler's mother says, "Oh, the dog scared you. But he's just barking loudly because he saw that cat climb up the tree over there."

Parents can help toddlers regulate their emotions when they select and control the toddler's environment, for example, avoid placing them in stressful or intensely arousing situations. Often, toddlers experience separation from their parents as stressful. Sensitive parents try to ease their child's distress by letting the child take a favorite toy to a new environment or familiarizing the child with the new caregiver and environment.

Emotional development includes learning to regulate emotional expression as well as regulating the emotions themselves. Parents can let young children know that their feelings are valued and that they can express their emotions openly. At the same time, some expressions may be off limits, such as yelling or screaming when upset. The more parents talk about young children's feelings, the quicker children will learn to self-reflect that they are angry, sad, and so forth. Self-reflection enhances skill in regulating emotional expression.

Parent–Child Play

Initially, everyday interactions between infant and parent are the setting for the infant's developing sense of self. As babies grow older, parents' focus on their babies' physiological regulation decreases. Now that their baby can experience new forms of shared experiences, parents' engagement in interactive games enhances their baby's developing sense of self.[50] From the beginning, parents and their babies engage in playful games: making faces, changing voice tone, playing chase, tickling, rolling balls, and so forth. As the baby matures, these games are extended from gestures to simple play sequences. In these games, babies experience warmth, shared attention, shared feelings, pleasure, and connectedness; they have a sense of being understood and valued. They learn turn-taking, the essence of conversation.

Feldman and Greenbaum conducted research on the relationship of mothers' play with their babies to the toddlers' symbolic competence.[51] Mothers and their babies were observed playing together when the babies were 3 and 9 months old. Interactions were assessed for the babies' affect and the mothers' affect attunement as well as the synchrony between mothers and their babies. At 2 years, researchers evaluated symbolic play, verbal IQ score, and the children's use of internal state words. Mothers' attunement and synchrony was significantly related to their toddlers' play and internal state talk.

During their visits, home visitors can affirm parents' playful interactions with their young children.

Janice has just arrived at Karyn and Don's home. As Janice, Karyn, and Don chat, Greg (age 13 months) walks about the room with a small car in hand. He then goes to his father, who hugs him warmly and asks him, "Where is your nose?" Don and Greg then play a brief game of Greg identifying and then touching his own as well as his father's nose and eyes. Greg goes to his mother, who says, "Teeth." Greg replies, "Teeth" as he touches his mother's teeth, then chuckles. He then returns to his father, who hugs and kisses him.

Janice quietly comments, "You are giving your daddy lots of love, and he's going to soak it up, too." When hearing Janice, Greg walks toward her for a moment, then, chuckling, returns to his father and then his mother as he babbles with sentence intonation.

Since Greg's birth, Don has been very engrossed in parenting. Unless he is on vacation, Don usually is at work during Janice's home visits; however, Karyn often discusses with Janice her husband's evening play experiences and sometimes has specific questions from Don, such as suggestions for new play activities. Janice affirms Don's hugging and kissing as important ways of communicating love. Home visitors have innumerable opportunities to reinforce the importance of parents' showing love through physical intimacy, for example, holding, hugging, kissing, massaging, and rocking.

As toddlers spend endless hours playing, they are learning to see patterns. I build a tower, and I know how to knock it down. If I push the car fast, it will roll across the room. As parents play with their toddler, they can show how to rock the dolly gently and to pat the kitty gently. Through these extended interactions, toddlers learn about caring and develop a moral sense of right and wrong. When toddlers become angry or aggressive, the way parents respond teaches them how the family views anger and aggression. Young children can learn acceptable angry feelings and how to express anger acceptably.

During their visits, home visitors can initiate simple play sequences with babies and toddlers and invite parents to enter into this play. As they engage in interactive games, home visitors model healthy baby–adult interactions. As parents play with their child, the home visitor can help parents understand the developmental significance of these experiences. (See Chapter 8 for a more detailed discussion of play, learning, and development.)

THE SOCIAL SELF: 19 MONTHS TO 3 YEARS

At about 18–24 months, toddlers can speak in two-word sentences such as "baby cry" and "me up." Now, toddlers have the ability to refer to themselves as external, objective people (e.g., using verbal labels to refer to themselves, recognizing themselves in the mirror). Increased language means increased shared experience and a sense of togetherness between toddlers and their parents.[52] Independence, autonomy, and negativism continue. Erikson spoke of autonomy as the second developmental task, which, if not achieved, leads to shame and doubt.[53] As memory grows, pretend-play sequences are expanded (e.g., washing the doll's hair, then feeding her). With multiple word statements, extended pretend-play, and declarations of autonomy, toddlers have reached another developmental leap.

Emotions entail thinking as well as feeling. For example, research on theory of mind centers on young children's ability to infer what other people are thinking, intending, believing, or feeling. Even 2-year-olds can understand that people have inner experiences of feeling and desiring, and they will feel good if kissed and hugged.[54] Young children can develop a rich inner life only if they have relationships from which they can derive their inner images. These experiences include images of warmth, security, dependence, love, anger, and protest.

Parental Regulation

Parental regulation, including physical, behavioral, and emotional regulation, continues to be central to toddlers' developing sense of self. In early infancy, much of parenting involves physiological regulation such as regulation of feeding and sleeping. As toddlers struggle with feelings of independence and negativism, parenting involves increased emotional and behavioral regulation, regulating intense feelings and new behaviors that accompany the young child's exploration of self and others. Regulation involves not only clear limit setting but also clear behavior expectations and recognition, support, and verbalization of toddlers' feelings.

Encouragement

As toddlers take initiative, parents have many opportunities to encourage their child's new strivings. As toddlers try to put on their own shoes and socks, open the door, and climb into their car seats, parents can positively acknowledge their child's effort (e.g., "You put on your shoes all by yourself.") Encouragement helps children recognize their accomplishments and know that they are valued. "Mom wants me to try to dress myself; in fact, I can do it." Encouragement requires specific feedback, describing the child's specific action. Home visitors can assist parents in recognizing that encouragement helps their child recognize success, feel a sense of mastery, know that he or she is valued, and continue to be motivated to take initiative. In contrast, global, evaluative comments, such as "good," "nice," and "good job," invite the child to focus on pleasing adults rather than recognizing the value of the behavior for which the global praise was given.

During the following home visit, Cynthia helps Sally understand how her responses to her son, Willy, can support and encourage his play. This is important for Sally to learn because she often tells Cynthia that Willy seems to always be running about and getting in trouble.

Willy (age 19 months) has dumped out the small, colored wooden blocks onto the rug. Willy hands two blocks to his mother, Sally, as Cynthia says to Sally, "He's inviting you to play."

Sally says, "I guess so." She then taps the two blocks together, as does Willy; they both chuckle.

Cynthia remarks, "You brought him right around. He also likes when you imitate him. It lets him know you like what he is doing." As Cynthia speaks, Sally softly hugs her son. Sally and Cynthia then briefly chat about Willy's pattern of throwing things. As the adults chat, Willy begins stacking the blocks. Cynthia says to Willy, "You put them on top of each other. Yeah!"

Sally repeats, "Yeah." Sally evens the blocks on her son's tower as she says to Cynthia, "He gets so discouraged when they fall."

Cynthia says, "And you're helping him so that he doesn't get discouraged."

Sally rolls a block, and her son imitates her. Cynthia affirms, "That was neat. You showed him the roll, and that roll is a way to move the block, not throwing it." Willy then puts a block in his mouth and makes a humming sound. Cynthia puts a block in her mouth and imitates his sound. Willy smiles and continues the game. Cynthia explains, "When I imitate his actions, I am telling Willy that what he does is wonderful."

Cynthia understands that Sally is a concrete learner. She describes what Willy is doing and, in this way, encourages him and models for Sally. Likewise, she describes to Sally what Sally is doing and how her actions are encouraging her son's involvement.

Gender Identity

By age 2, most children can name their gender correctly. By 2½–3 years, most toddlers know whether other people are men or women and boys or girls. This ability to label one's own and others' gender correctly is termed *gender identity*. Accurate labeling does not mean that young children have complete understand of gender. Until children are 5 or 6 years old, they do not understand that people stay the same gender, even when they wear different clothes.

Sex-Role Identity

Toddlers also are developing sex-role identity. Sex roles are socially defined behaviors, attitudes, rights, and duties associated with being male or female. Sex-role behavior is behavior that corresponds to the culturally defined sex role. Traditional sex-role behaviors include mothers cooking and doing child care and fathers working and cutting lawns. Sex-role stereotyping involves rigidly defining sex-role categories. As more mothers of very young children work outside the home and as more fathers share in household and child-rearing tasks, sex role expectations are changing. Nevertheless, remnants of sex-role stereotyping continue, for example, thinking of men as independent, aggressive, logical, and assertive, and women as dependent, gentle, and emotional.

Parents want their children to develop to their fullest potential. Increasingly, occupations are open to both women and men, and more partners in a marriage both work full-time. With these societal changes, young children can develop the behaviors, attitudes, and values that allow them to be active participants both in the workplace and within the home. Boys can learn to express their feelings and develop caregiving skills, and girls can develop assertive and problem solving skills. For children to develop to their fullest potential and take advantage of the full range of available options, it is essential for them to know that men and women perform a wide variety of jobs, and each gender is able to express a full range of abilities and emotions.

Home visitors can help parents understand that they are their children's primary models for learning what it is to be male and female. When young children's fathers cook or change diapers, or mothers replace electrical fuses or put oil in the car, these actions counterbalance our traditional cultural sex-role stereotypes. Parents also send messages to their children about how boys and girls should act by the toys they purchase for their children and by the kind of behavior they allow, encourage, or punish. Parents can provide a range of experiences for both their sons and daughters. Boys can be integrated into household tasks such as cooking and folding laundry; girls can assist in raking the lawn and assembling a toy. Both sexes can enjoy blocks, connecting toys, vehicles, dress-up clothing, dishes, and dolls.

Most parents don't think about sex-role stereotyping as part of their child's everyday experiences; however, television programs for children and commercials frequently reflect sex-role stereotyping. Males outnumber females. Women tend to be portrayed in submissive, passive roles. Like television, children's books often reflect sex-role stereotypes, (e.g., main characters usually are active boys, girls are onlookers.) More nonsexist picture books are available than previously. Home visitors can help parents recognize this sex-role stereotyping and sensitively discuss the stereotyping issues.

Topics like sex-role behaviors are value laden and become sensitive subjects in times of societal change. Home visitors always must be respectful of parents' values and must recognize that some parents value sex-role stereotyping. There are times when a home visitor's information violates explicit values parents hold, and as guests, home visitors may choose to refrain from sharing information in respect for parents' values. On other occasions, home visitors may provide information, but they always must honor the parent as decision maker.

Body Image

Toddlers love their body and its parts. They love to run around naked and are proud of what their body produces. Feces, urine, mucus, and gas are all seen as accomplishments. As toddlers move and explore their everyday environment, they develop new understanding of their bodies. Young children's emerging interest in their body strengthens their sense of self. Toddlers love to play games identifying parts of their body, dance to music, scoot about on four-wheeled toddler toys, play chase, and catch and throw balls. As they move, they gain an understanding of *my body in space* and *my body in movement*. This knowing in movement is termed *kinesthetic understanding*.

Knowledge of one's body begins at birth. The young baby's mouth is very sensitive and is the first body part used for exploration. Much of the young babies' body awareness occurs within their parents' caregiving—soothing, stroking, holding, rocking, and so forth. Parents continue to be central to their toddler's growing sense of body image because parents provide the indoor and outdoor space for movement, toys, and games and participate as play partners.

Sexual Learning

Closely related to body image is sexual learning. Babies learn about sexuality each time their parents bathe, dress, and diaper them. In these everyday interactions, parents communicate to their child their own attitudes toward their baby's body. For babies and toddlers to feel positive about their body and sexuality, it is important for bath time, dressing and undressing, diapering, and toileting to be pleasurable times.

During the first and second years, babies' experiences such as rubbing their genitals and taking pleasure in skin contact with others are close to later sensual pleasure. Stanley Greenspan observed, "The capacity for intimacy and the interest and pleasure derived from the company of others are the earliest phenomena that indicate real desire."[55] The desire for closeness with others continues throughout everyone's life. Babies and toddlers are very curious; thus, they want to explore each part of their body from all angles. All babies touch their genital area and discover that this touching is pleasurable. Because the nerve endings of genitalia are quite sensitive, children naturally experience a pleasant sensation. This masturbation is widely accepted as natural and healthy. Toddlers investigate their genital area with the same curiosity that they poke at their nose or ears. Some parents, however, may not realize that the feeling the children have in their genitals is not the same as the intensely excited feeling adults experience in sexual stimulation. Very young children are most likely to fondle their genitals when they are tired, going to sleep, or listening to a story—not when they are excited or are learning about sexual reproduction. Home visitors can help parents understand that masturbation is normal and will pass with time.

Home visitors can help parents understand their children's sexuality and sexual exploration. Parents cannot prevent these explorations. Home visitors can help parents understand that they can be most effective when they adopt a relaxed attitude and accept the fact that their toddler will outgrow these explorations. If they are uncomfortable with their child's genital play, parents can distract their child with another activity. When parents criticize, punish, frown, or pull their toddlers hand away from genitals, their child learns that their genitalia and feelings coming from them are bad and wrong. Similar to the topic of sex-role behavior, the topic of sexuality is value-laden. Home visitors always need to be sensitive to and respectful of parents' values when approaching these value-laden topics.

Play

From birth, babies explore their everyday world and create new meaning from their experiences. From early infancy, the child participates in shared imaginative family games, musical interactions, and stories. During the second year, toddlers enjoy imaginative pretend play, both alone and with parents. A child's pretend play initially develops through imitation. In pretend play, they try out new roles (e.g., Mommy) and create scenarios (e.g., going to work). They act out simple everyday experiences (e.g., washing their doll's hair, feeding and putting their doll to bed, giving their parents a cup of coffee). In this play, toddlers express their feelings, think about their experiences, and try out behaviors that they have seen others exhibit. In this acting out, toddlers are in control and gain mastery over their feelings (e.g., about having their hair washed). As they pretend to be Mommy or Daddy, they explore a wide range of themes and feelings. When parents join in this pretend play, they can affirm their toddler's behavior, share in his or her enjoyment, and have opportunities to extend the play. Home visitors can help parents understand the importance of pretend play, how it develops, and how important it is for them to join their young child in pretend play. Greenspan and Lewis identify common themes of toddlers' pretend play: closeness or dependence, pleasure and fun, assertiveness and exploration, cautious or fearful behavior, anger, limit setting, and recovering from distress.[56]

When parents are play partners with their child, the child can take the lead, a role that the child rarely has in everyday situations. In playing with their child, parents enter into the emotional tone of their child. Playing together is a time of extended conversation. Often, parents can clarify and extend the child's play. As they play, the child feels a deep sense of connectedness and affirmation.

Social Development

One of the major developmental tasks of early childhood is establishing relationships with other children. How well parents structure play environments for toddlers influences how well they can play together. For example, if toys are readily accessible and invite collaborative play (e.g., blocks rather than puzzles) toddlers are more likely to get along. Toddlers play best with other toddlers they often play with often. As they relate to peers, children evaluate their self-worth and competence. Patterns of peer interaction in early childhood predict whether children will be competent socially in middle childhood and adolescence.[57] At around 30 months, toddlers can talk about feelings (e.g., happy, mad) and other internal states (e.g., want, hurt) of self and other.[58] This ability reflects the toddler's emergent understanding of self and other that is the foundation of learning social skills.

Getting along with peers is one of the core developmental tasks of young children. Secure attachments with parents in infancy promote social competence. Experiences during a child's second and third year of life seem to be pivotal to the development of cooperation and consideration toward others.[59] As toddlers develop motor and language skills, they enjoy playing with other young children; in this play, important social skills emerge.[60] These social skills are significant new aspects of the young child's sense of self. As they play, toddlers learn from other children's actions and get feedback on their own actions. Very young children usually play side-by-side in what is called *parallel play*, during which they learn through imitating each other. Parents play an important role in helping their young child learn to share, take turns, and take the perspective of their young friend.

Beginning early in the second year, toddlers comfort others when they are upset, and as they get older, they develop new ways to express empathy. Not surprising, toddlers' ability to be empathic is associated with how empathic parents have been with them. For example, if siblings are fighting, do their parents talk about each child's feelings and intentions so that the children feel heard? Now, children can reflect on their own ideas and feelings. They may think of an alternative solution to a dilemma or step back from their feelings and choose not to act. Rather than hit a child, they can tell the child, "I'm mad at you."

Increasingly the child has a true moral consciousness. Toddlers learn to anticipate consequences of their actions. Rules are being internalized; this is the age of conscience development. At first, the sense of right and wrong is very concrete; for example, "If I hit my brother, he'll cry." With time, toddlers are able to think of how another person is going to feel when they act. The child wants to do nice things for others to receive a positive reaction in return. When children choose to do nice things, they are assured of good consequences. A child's inner voice has two components: first, the inner voice that guides the child in a positive way, and second, the inner voice that can be critical.

This is a time when many parents form playgroups for their young children in their homes. Many community organizations have programs for parents and their toddlers to come together for play (e.g., churches, YMCAs, community centers, some public schools). Home visitors can assist parents in thinking through possible ways of providing peer play for their young child. Often parents seek their home visitor's advice regarding this issue. Shelly's conversation with Janice is illustrative.

Shelly: Is it important for Erin [age 24 months] to be with children her own age, or is it okay for her to be with older children, like her cousins?

Janice: Erin could handle preschool, but it's not essential. The way you get a child ready for being 3 [years old] is by giving her what she needs at age 2. Most important is the child's secure attachment to her parents. Whenever Erin goes to school, she will be fine because she is securely attached to you and to Rob. You know how to teach her. You're doing a wonderful job. You don't need to force her to go to school. Some children need preschool, either because they don't have exposure with other children or because their parents are not teaching [them well]. But you and Rob are excellent teachers, and from what we've discussed in other visits, Erin and her older cousins have great fun together.

Erin plays frequently with her older cousins, and Janice reassures Shelly that this play is wonderful. When families live in areas containing neither neighborhood children nor relatives with young children, Janice informs the parents of the school district's weekly playtime for parents and their 2-year-olds. She also tells parents how some parents form playgroups within their home with parents whom they meet at the home visiting group meetings.

When young children play together, conflicts are inevitable. Conflicts with parents also are inevitable when children say "no" to a parent's request or parents say "no" to a child's request. Parents can help their children learn to manage disputes by teaching them empathy and skills for negotiating and resolving conflicts. Parents can give explanations for rules, which will help their children internalize these rules. Parents can talk about their own and their children's feelings that emerged within the conflict, and this discussion can help the child understand caring. Within these repeated conflicts, young children learn acceptable ways to be assertive or to ask for help. Conflict and aggression increase as toddlers between 2 and 3 years of age try to play together. Often, this conflict is benign. Researchers observing conflict between toddlers during preschool play found that most play dissolved.[61] Close friends, however, are more likely to stick it out, negotiate, and continue to play.

THE NARRATIVE SELF: 3–5 YEARS

Young children experience another developmental leap at around 3 years old, when they begin telling stories.[62] Usually these stories are autobiographical. Stories for 3-year-olds are typically family-centered. Children replay experiences for themselves that occurred in the past. Stories for 4- and 5-year-olds also include cultural information never experienced, such as television characters, wolves, and giants. With their new verbal skills and mental abilities of representation, young children see connections concerning time (e.g., what I'm doing now, what I did before lunch) and connections in terms of space (e.g., what is next to me, what is in my yard). With this new ability, young children are gaining skills in self-reflection and delight in a new form of shared experience with their parents. Because of their age, young children do not always take the viewpoint of the listener; thus, stories may have significant omissions.[63]

Now, the past, present, and future are starting to make sense. When the child wants to go outside and her mother says, "Give me 15 minutes and we'll go," the child knows that she will be able to go outdoors soon. Children this age also understand the concepts of near and far spaces. They know the difference between going to the store and going to the doctor's office. They can create connections between their ideas and the ideas of another person. Children love to ask questions and can answer *who, what, where, when, how,* and *why* questions; however, they learn to answer *what* and *where* questions before *why* ones. *Why* questions are more difficult to answer because they require children to examine the roots of their own feelings or wishes. In addition, children this age can logically link ideas with "if," "but," and "because." Their emotional thinking expands, and they can describe a wide range of feelings in words, not just actions. They can feel and express a wide range of feelings, such as pleasure, excitement, anger, assertiveness, fear, closeness, dependency, and surprise.

At this age, children can link two ideas together. For example, they can think, "If I pick up my toys, Mommy will be happy." They can anticipate events in the future, for example, going to the ice cream store after a nap or going to the circus on the weekend. Children are beginning to get a sense of their unique features or skills. "I can bounce the basketball really well." "I know a lot of stories and can tell them to my baby brother."

Home visitors can help parents recognize these many changes in their preschoolers. They can encourage parents to be play partners and to have lengthy conversations with their child. When parents understand the meaning of their role as a play partner or a conversational partner with their child, they are more likely to find time to engage in these experiences with their child.

Once parents and children have developed a personal relationship with their home visitor, both children and parents love to report family experiences. These reports are good opportunities for young children to practice their skill in telling stories, as illustrated by the following example.

> Erin (age 35 months) tells Janice, "My daddy comes home, but he has to work at the firehouse now."
>
> Janice asks, "What does he do at the firehouse?"
>
> Erin responds, "He goes out on fire calls. Sometimes he has some parties—when it's dark out." The home visit is in January, and 2 weeks earlier, the fire officers had a holiday party for their families.
>
> Shelly suggests to her daughter that she tell Janice what happened last night when the fire officers were done with their fire. Erin replies, "Honk-honk-honk." Shelly explains that, before returning to the firehouse, the three fire trucks had passed by their house. All three stopped and honked for Erin and Shelly, who were standing at the window. As Shelly is talking, Erin runs into the bedroom and returns with a small walkie-talkie, called a scanner. Erin tells Janice, "That's where my daddy talks."

Shelly and her daughter regularly report family happenings to Janice. Erin's comments contain omissions because she is not always skilled in taking the listener's perspective (e.g., not understanding that Janice does not know that the fire officers have holiday parties for their families at the firehouse). As Erin tells her story, both her mother and Janice ask questions to assist her ability to add details. As she tells these stories, Erin experiences self-reflection, shared reflection, and enjoyment, and her language and thinking skills are strengthened. These stories are a vivid example of sense of self being socially created because, in her telling, Erin gains an increased sense of connectedness.

Young children often are egocentric (i.e., unable to take another person's perspective). Other times, they can be sociocentric (i.e., able to take another person's perspective).[64] Research provides evidence that very young children often adjust their conversations when speaking to children younger than themselves. For example, 3-year-olds use shorter and simpler phrases when speaking to their 12- or 18-month-old siblings.

Social Development

Babies' and young children's sense of self is based on relationships. As children reach 3 years, their relationships expand beyond their immediate family. Preschool children's social skills expand dramatically. Opportunities to play with peers are important to their developing sense of self. Until this point, young children primarily have been relating to parents and siblings. Playing with peers is a young child's first relationship with equals. In this play, young children experience a variety of roles, that is, leading as well as following. They receive feedback, model other children's actions, try out aggression and experience conflict, learn joint problem solving, and learn giving and taking among equals.

Because peer play is a new experience, difficulties inevitably emerge. Parents need to assist their young child in learning to negotiate (e.g., to use words instead of hitting, to take turns). Home visitors can help parents understand this developing process.

As Erin (age 37 months) completes a puzzle, Shelly softly tells Janice that recently when Erin's friend, Kathy, aggravated Erin, Erin pushed her. Shelly states that she is surprised to see her daughter be aggressive.

Janice responds, "You can help Erin learn how to deal with problems by herself. You can suggest that she use words such as 'stop that.' She needs to know that she cannot push, but that there is a way that she can deal with the situation. When children this age get together, they are going to have problems. Frame it in a positive way. Tell Erin that if there is trouble, make sure that you talk about it; however, children this young are not good at negotiating. She also needs to know it's okay to ask for help from you."

Until she was 3, Erin played only with her older cousins. Now, Shelly has begun to provide same-age playmates for her daughter, who is her first and only child. Janice helps Shelly understand that Erin's difficulties are normal and that Shelly can assist her daughter in learning basic social skills.

Sex Play
Children ages 3–5 years express their curiosity about body differences and functions in their exploratory sex play with peers. Sex play most often includes examining one another's bodies and occurs as children engage in simple role-play themes of family or doctor. Usually, parents can redirect their child's sex play. When sex play seems to stem from children's unanswered questions about body differences, then parents simply can discuss these differences or read an appropriate book about the human body to their child.

Pro-social Behavior
Many preschoolers develop special friends. Friends usually have more sustained and more complex play than peer play. Now children can play in small groups and effortlessly move from one peer to another as they play. Some children develop imaginary friends. Children this age have new opportunities in pro-social behaviors.[65] Pro-social behaviors include sharing, helping, and cooperative behaviors. These behaviors expand young children's understanding of self in relation to others. Home visitors can assist parents in providing opportunities for their young child to assist in family tasks and thereby experience being a valued and responsible member of the family. Young children can assist in

household tasks such as cooking, setting and clearing tables, folding laundry, raking leaves, washing cars, and dusting. As the family eats a meal in which a young child assists, the child feels a sense of pride and accomplishment. Repeated family tasks help a young child develop a sense of social responsibility and an ability to respond to others.

As young children play with each other, much of their play offers opportunities of not only shared enjoyment, but also developing skills in sharing and cooperation. As more mothers of young children are employed outside of their home, larger numbers of children experience social interaction with peers in child care programs for longer periods of time. Observations of young children in child care programs provide vivid examples of spontaneous groups of children involved in prosocial behavior. This observation from a child care center is illustrative.

Lucretia, Demetrius, and Jerry (all 4 years old) have covered most of the rug area in the block center with train tracks that they have snapped together. Over the tracks, they build bridges with blocks. Each of the three children then pushes a railcar about their track. Twice they knock down the blocks structures and rebuild them.

These children have used train tracks and blocks to cooperatively build structures for moving their vehicles about. Their play includes give-and-take decision making and shared enjoyment.

Four girls, each with a Hula-Hoop, have formed a circle. Emma seems to be the leader, for she counts, "1, 2, 3, 4, 5, go!" and then the children twirl their hoops. Emma directs the children where to stand. "Lea, you may go over there. No, Cherise over there."

Five girls (3 and 4 years old) are sitting in a circle outdoors. The children are playing Doggie, Doggie, Where Is Your Bone? Josie is the leader and tells the other girls, "Now lay in the middle" for a turn to be the dog. After about 6 minutes, Suzy suggests, "Let's play Duck, Duck, Goose," and everyone does so, with Josie again leading.

Jerome beats a rhythm with the palm of his hand of the bottom of a cylindrical container as four children clap and stomp their feet. Occasionally, Jerome calls out "Stop!" and the children stop. Then, when Jerome says okay, the children again begin clapping and stomping to the rhythm.

In these vignettes, the children spontaneously begin a play sequence together. Emma, Josie, and Jerome are developing leadership skills. All of the children share in an activity in which they experience feelings of connectedness and delight.

Self-Esteem

Central to a young child's sense of self is judgment of self-worth, often termed *self-esteem*. Self-esteem is the evaluative part of the child's sense of self. Feelings of competence and self-esteem develop when young children experience repeated success in their activities.[66] There also seems to be a close relationship between children's cooperative interaction, pro-social behavior, and positive feelings about self.

Home visitors can encourage parents to provide a wide variety of play activities in which their child can experience mastery and success. Parents' everyday child-rearing interactions also communicate messages to their child that the child is valued and of worth. As discussed previously, parents' responsiveness helps their baby develop self-confidence that he or she can influence others—have a sense of personal control. Similarly, parental encouragement through positive descriptions of their children's behavior and achievements helps children recognize their success, develop positive self-esteem, and continue to take initiative (e.g., "You carried your milk so carefully; none spilled," or "You used so many colors in your painting; it looks like a happy picture!")

Play

Preschoolers use their imagination in pretend play and acting out imaginative characters, superhero characters, or other characters they have not experienced. They substitute symbols for real objects as they role-play. With their peers, they cooperate and learn about how their peers view the world and how their peers judge their actions. Their pretend play includes joint decision making (e.g., who will play which role), cooperative activities (e.g., cooking and setting the table), potential disputes (e.g., deciding what specifically to role play), and lots of shared enjoyment. Increasingly, the child develops a sense of self in relation to others, a social self. When parents join their child in pretend play, the child feels a deep sense of connectedness. Often, the parent clarifies the play sequence or extends it. The parent enters into the emotional tone of the child so that the child feels affirmed.

CHILD BEHAVIOR
REPRESENTING THE SPECTRUM OF AUTISM

Young children who are unable to relate to other people, most specifically, unable to maintain eye contact and communicate verbally may have symptoms of autism spectrum disorder. Children with pervasive developmental disorder have some of the patterns of autism but not all. Children with Asperger's syndrome are not as withdrawn as children with autism and have excellent speech and good intellectual skills, but they have a paucity of nonverbal communication, poor empathy, and atypical communication patterns.

Young children with autism exhibit stereotyped behaviors such as hand flapping or toe walking and seem to prefer activities involving objects more than activities involving social interaction. As a result, these children tend to be significantly more delayed in social skills and social behavior than typically developing children. As profiled in psychological testing, children with autism have significant difficulties with abstract reasoning, verbal concept formation, and skills requiring social understanding. In contrast, they may be skilled in rote learning and memory skills and visual-spatial problem solving.[67] Children with autism do not exhibit theory of mind (capacity to understand others' thoughts and feelings) and thus lack reciprocity in communication and empathy. Most children with autism have substantive regulation disorder, especially high sensitivity to touch. Children with autism tend to do well with special education that is highly structured and oriented around the individual needs of each child. Their education should include speech and language therapy as well as occupational therapy.

DIFFICULTIES AND DILEMMAS

As discussed previously, the behavior of babies signals their parents to respond; in turn, parents' response invites further baby behavior. Parent–child interaction is mutual and resembles a dance; that is, parents and children learn to respond to each other in the same rhythm. It is within these everyday "dances" that the baby develops a sense of self. Sometimes, problems of the parent, baby, or surrounding environment can impair healthy development of these mutual interaction patterns, with accompanying difficulties in development of self. If home visitors are keen observers, they can recognize when difficulties are emerging. This section addresses three types of difficulties home visitors will encounter that may be beyond their expertise:

1. Babies' biologically based (i.e., regulation) disorders
2. Sensory overload in babies
3. Lack of parental attunement and responsiveness

Regulation Disorders

Home visitors also need to be alert to biologically based problems within the baby. Stanley Greenspan has made a major contribution to baby studies in his discussions of biologically based difficulties in infancy, which he terms *regulation disorders*.[68] Some babies' sensory systems are over- or underreactive, causing sensitivities in vision, in touch, in sight, in hearing, or in movement (kinesthetics). Some babies have motor tone problems; for example, they feel very loose and have difficulty holding up their heads. Motor tone is the balance between flexor and extensor muscles. If a young baby's motor tone is low, holding his or her head up may require too much work. Babies with high or low motor tone may have difficulty sequencing their actions. Parents will need to provide a lot of tactile stimulation and muscle exercise for a baby who is are underreactive. Parents with an overreactive baby will have to soften voices and other noises.

A baby with these regulation disorders may be very fussy. In turn, parents may have difficulties soothing their baby and may feel they have failed because they cannot engage in smooth give-and-take exchanges. Problematic baby–parent exchanges escalate the baby's difficulties. Often, parents need assistance in adjusting their interaction style to meet their baby's learning style and sensitivities (e.g., varying their voice pitch for a baby with an underreactive auditory system). Evaluation by an occupational therapist may identify specific regulation difficulties. Sensory integration often is a treatment for these difficulties. Study of regulation disorders began in the late 1980s, and many practitioners are not aware of these subtle difficulties in infancy. If home visitors can strive to be sensitive to babies' sensory reactions and motor tone, they can screen for these difficulties at a very young age. Once again, identification of such difficulties warrants a community referral. Often, the first referral is an occupational therapist.

At birth, babies' brains and central nervous systems are immature. The way babies' brains process sensory information forms the foundation for their attention and self-regulation. Most young babies are able to process information from only one sense at a time. When babies are given too much stimulation, they can be unable to easily accept input from their senses. Too many signals at one time impede the smooth transmission of signals to the baby's brain.

Home visitors can help parents learn to read their baby's cues so that they can detect sensory overload. As parents respond to their baby's facial expressions, sounds, and body movements, they can be alert to signals of overstimulation. Indications of sensory overload may include:

- Excessive irritability
- Difficulty in becoming calm
- Continuous cry

- Tense body
- Sleeping more often than is necessary

Personal Problems of Parents

Beyond simply conversing with the parents, home visitors also interact with the child and observe parent–child interaction. Some parents may be able to appropriately talk with the home visitor, yet have serious shortcomings as they interact with their baby. If a home visitor observes a repeated lack in parental attunement and responsiveness to the baby, the home visitor is observing serious parenting problems, which can lead to the baby defending him- or herself by becoming apathetic and unresponsive. Fraiberg explained that unresolved conflicts from the parenting of one's own childhood can be transferred from that old relationship to the new parenting relationship.[69] It is as if one's baby evokes these unresolved (often not remembered) conflicts, which Fraiberg termed *ghosts in the nursery*. Signs of this problem include the baby not responding to the home visitor's attempts to engage the baby and the baby showing little emotional expression (e.g., not smiling, not frowning). When parent–child interactions indicate potential ghosts in the nursery, home visitors need to assist the family in seeking therapeutic resources in the community.

CONCLUSION

Astonishingly, beginning at birth, the newborn is capable of purposeful action and of expressing feelings and relating to the caregiver. These behaviors point to the newborn's sense of self, the inner organization underlying the newborn's observable behavior. This sense of self develops only within the baby's interactions with his or her parents, interactions that are mutually created, with each partner influencing the other's behavior. With time, emerging patterns of behavior point to the developing sense of self. As the baby develops new behaviors, the infant's parents develop new understanding and new strategies for parenting their child. Table 1 portrays the baby's developing sense of self and parent behavior that promotes this development. Once a parenting behavior is initiated, it continues to be an important part of the parent–child relationship. For example, parents' responsiveness and physical affection given to a very young baby continue to be needed parenting strategies throughout the young child's development.

Babies are embedded within and dependent on their caregiving contexts. This chapter stresses how the relationship between child and parent is the foundation of this developing sense of self. In like man-

Table 1. The child's developing sense of self and the parenting behavior that promotes development

Infants' and young children's developing sense of self	Parenting: Understanding and behavior
Birth–6 months	
Cycle of six states of consciousness	Mutuality in infant–parent interaction
Self-calming	Predictable expectations regarding
Individual differences—temperament	development
Qualities of sense of self	Physiological regulation
Capable of purposeful action	Assisting infant to self-calm
Experiencing unity	Adapting to infant's temperament
Experiencing feelings	Regulation of feelings
Memory and expectations	Empathic responsiveness
Attachment behavior	Physical affection
	Bonding and attachment
7–18 months	
Intersubjective relatedness	Respect and responsiveness to stranger
Shared attention	anxiety
Shared intention	Accepting child's lovey
Shared feeling states	Expanding child's language
Trust	Boundaries of acceptable behavior
Sense of personal control	Engagement in interactive games
Loveys	Play with child
Stranger anxiety	
Emergence of words	
Independence, autonomy, negativism	
Emergence of pretend play	
19 months–3 years	
Multiple-word sentences	Behavioral expectations and limit setting
Extended pretend play	Verbalization of child's feelings
Experiencing mastery and competence	Encouragement
Gender identity	Modeling and provisioning for sex-role
Sex-role identity	understanding and identity
Body image	Assisting in child's sexual learning
Sexual learning	Provisions of play
Play with other children	Play with child
Emergence of social skills	
3–5 years	
Telling stories	Providing for peer play
Egocentrism and sociocentrism	Extending conversations
Peer relationships	Providing family responsibilities
Prosocial behaviors	Play with child
Self-esteem	

ner, the home visitor's relationship with parents is at the core of the home visitor's ability to assist understanding and promote the parenting skills of the mothers and fathers with whom the home visitor spends time. Home visitors' interactions with parents affirm and support parents as well as provide observation and interpretation of child and parent actions. In the same sense that the parent–child relationship is formed by everyday child-rearing interactions, the home visitor's interactions—supporting, affirming, and guiding—are the core of the home visitor–parent relationship.

The next six chapters discuss how home visitors can promote healthy parent and child development. Shonkoff and Phillips identified two profound changes since 1970 that have substantively altered service delivery to young children and their families, child-rearing practices, and early childhood policy. First, research in the neurobiological, behavioral, and social science fields has increased dramatically and given major advances in our understanding of what conditions influence whether very young children's development is fostered or hindered. Shonkoff and Phillips identified the gains in understanding:

1. *The importance of early life experiences, as well as the inseparable and highly interactive influences of genetics and environment on the development of the brain and the unfolding of human behavior*

2. *The central role of early relationships as a source of either support and adaptation or risk and dysfunction*

3. *The powerful capabilities, complex emotions, and essential social skills that develop during the earliest months and years of life*

4. *The capacity to increase the odds of favorable developmental outcomes through planned interventions*[70]

The second change is that the capacity to constructively use this scientific knowledge has been constrained by substantive transformations in the social and economic circumstances of the United States. Shonkoff and Phillips identified these transformations:

1. *Marked changes in the nature, schedule, and amount of work engaged in by parents of young children and greater difficulty balancing workplace and family responsibilities for parents at all income levels*

2. *Continuing high levels of economic hardship among families with young children, despite overall increases in maternal education, increased rates of parent employment, and a strong economy*

3. *Increasing cultural diversity and the persistence of significant racial and ethnic disparities in health and developmental outcomes*

4. *Growing numbers of young children spending considerable time in child care settings of highly variable quality, starting in infancy*

5. *Continuing high levels of serious family problems and adverse community conditions that are detrimental to children*[71]

Given the explosion of new scientific knowledge, home visitors need to be active learners by reading and attending seminars to learn about the latest findings in neurobiology, child development, cultural diversity, and early intervention. All babies are able to have feelings, participate in relationships, and learn. Taken-for-granted everyday interactions between parent and baby nurture or inhibit the child's development. Young children thrive in a context of nurturing, responsive, and secure caregiving interactions. Home visitors have the opportunity to actively promote these caregiving interactions and thereby substantively promote the development of both child and parent.

6

Guidance and Discipline

The widow she cried over me, and called me a poor lost lamb, and she called me a lot of other names, too, but she never meant no harm by it. She put me in them new clothes again, and I couldn't do nothing but sweat and sweat, and feel all cramped up. Well, then, the old thing commenced again. The widow rung a bell for supper, and you had to come to time. When you got to the table you couldn't go right to eating, but you had to wait for the widow to tuck down her head and grumble a little over the victuals, though there wasn't really anything the matter with them. That is, nothing only every-thing was cooked by itself....Pretty soon I wanted to smoke, and asked the widow to let me. But she wouldn't. She said it was a mean practice and wasn't clean, and I must try to not do it any more.

Mark Twain, *The Adventures of Huckleberry Finn* (1855/1947, p. 2)

Discipline topics are the focus of more parent meetings than any other child-rearing topic regardless of SES or geographic area. With the changing nature of American society, parents' ambivalence in directing and setting limits for their children is understandable. Parents often are uncertain about religious values and male and female roles. They may not have a predictable income source or live in homogeneous neighborhoods. Parents and school staff often do not live in the same communities; as a result, many parents are not sure if they share the same values and attitudes that their children experience at school. With increased mobility, many new parents live far from their extended families and from the support and guidance extended families provide. In single-parent families and families in which both parents work outside the home, parents have little time to develop informal social support systems to draw on for assistance. As they experience these societal changes, parents often feel uncertain when guiding, teaching, and setting boundaries for their young children.

Everyday guidance and discipline of babies and very young children has crucial significance. Physiological traits alone do not define a baby's potential. Research since the late 1980s has shown that a baby's inclination toward boldness or timidity stems from a complex interplay of biological and environmental factors.[1] What children experience from moment to moment, especially in their early years, is just as important as their genetic heritage.[2] Patterns established by the caregiver can alter children's innate tendencies. A soft-spoken caregiver who minimizes auditory and tactile stimulation, for example, can lessen a baby's irritability that is caused by her sensitivity to sound and touch.

Social interaction also affects the physiology of the brain, and the physiology of the brain determines the possibilities of babies' and young children's interactions with caregivers. The quality of everyday caregiver interaction shapes and strengthens babies' and young children's growing experience of both inner and outer reality. Nature and nurture—biology and experience—are continuously interacting. As Greenspan explained, "Consciousness develops from this continuous interaction in which biology organizes experience and experience organizes biology."[3]

Parents may have good intentions about discipline, but they may not have all of the information they need to be successful. For example, they may be strongly motivated to parent differently from their own parents but may still choose inappropriate parenting methods because they don't understand young children and developmental principles. A young father whose own father was unavailable may strive to be his son's best pal and thus avoid limit setting. A mother whose own mother was harsh and critical may worry that she will harm her daughter's self-esteem if she is firm and gives consequences for misbehavior.

Anger and violence also lead to ambivalence about discipline. Violence is deeply embedded in our culture and is the dominant theme in children's television cartoons, political rhetoric about crime and foreign policy, and the everyday lives of many families. There are two parts to the issue of anger and violence in parenting that lead to parents' ambivalence. First, parents don't know what to do and sometimes are frightened when their children are angry and violent. Second, they don't know what to do with their own anger and violence, often expressed in impulsive physical punishment. Although parents hear about nonpunitive, rational means of disciplining their children, many have no experience with this sort of discipline from their own childhood. Parents may need the home visitor's help in dealing with their confusion about discipline.

This chapter presents three themes:

1. *Parental discipline*: Teaching appropriate cultural and familial norms and setting limits

2. *Parental guidance*: Providing experience and assistance to enable development of understanding and abilities

3. *Child development*: Young children's development of autonomy, self-confidence, competence, and control

Child development is the goal of parental guidance and discipline.

GUIDANCE AND DISCIPLINE DEFINED

Discipline is a form of teaching that is defined as "training that corrects, models, or perfects the mental faculties or moral character" and "a control gained by enforcing obedience or order."[4] Early education literature on obedience and discipline often has emphasized that the goal is to help young children develop self-control. In other words, according to much of the early education literature on discipline, young children adopt their parents' and caregivers' rules of behavior as their own.

This book proposes an additional goal of discipline: teaching the child emotional self-regulation. *Emotional self-regulation* is the ability to respond emotionally and to adapt one's emotional experience to moment-to-moment situational demands. Each stage and age makes its own demands, builds on earlier achievements, and requires new adaptive behaviors to respond to the environment appropriately. Thompson and Calkins identified a range of developmental tasks that are a part of the regulation of emotion.

Although strategies of emotional self-regulation originate in the young baby's simple efforts to cope with distress through self-soothing, they quickly become integrated into a network of behavioral strategies by which children (and adults) seek to maintain personal well-being, manage their relations with others, behave consistently with their self-image, manage the self-presentation to the social world, and achieve a variety of other goals.[5]

This chapter discusses how emotional self-regulation develops within the relationships of babies and young children with their parents and caregivers. Structuring and limiting young children's everyday experiences by caring adults is essential in helping them control feelings such as anger, greed, and envy, which are as basic to being human as are empathy, love, and compassion. If young children experience being cared for in a loving and consistent fashion, they can learn to care for others.

Parents are the mediators between society and their child. A primary task of parenting is to teach appropriate behaviors, attitudes, and values that will allow the child to manage self-control and relate well with other people. Two primary purposes of discipline are readily apparent: "First, to stop children from doing something dangerous, hurtful or annoying to themselves and to others, that is to *control children*; and second, to impart values—that is, to *teach children*."[6] Parents are most effective when they have both short- and long-term goals as they discipline their children. Obedience is the short-term goal, and self-control is the long-term goal of discipline. The ultimate goal in discipline is the *child's* self-control. Initially, the young child obeys. Over time, this obedience becomes internalized; that is, parents' rules become a part of the child's conscience and natural way of acting and relating to others.[7]

Brazelton described three stages of self-control, or self-discipline: "1) trying out the limits by exploration, 2) teasing to evoke from others a clear sense of what is okay and what isn't, and 3) internalizing these previously unknown boundaries."[8] First, a crawling baby is fascinating by the many electrical cords and goes to the electrical outlet. Her parent reacts strongly and negatively to impress upon her that electrical outlets are off limits. Second, once the baby knows her parents will react, she will look to make certain her parent is watching before she reaches to touch the outlet. She is eager to hear her parent forbid her to touch and thereby is reassured. Third, after several months, when she comes to the outlet, she'll shout "No!" to herself. Now, the limit is a part of herself—she has internalized it.

Guidance is closely related to discipline. To *guide* is "to assist (a person) to travel through, to reach a destination in, an area in which he does not know the way, as by accompanying him or giving him directions."[9] Babies, toddlers, and preschoolers are new to this Earth, with a very small amount of experience and much to learn. Parental guidance is an essential task in helping these very young children learn how to get along with others and to feel accepted and loved and thereby accept and love themselves.[10] Whether the activity is feeding, dressing, playing, or disciplining, guidance is embedded in parents everyday interactions with their young children.

A DEVELOPMENTAL APPROACH

This chapter follows a developmental approach in discussing guidance and discipline. This developmental approach assumes that as new developmental accomplishments are achieved, babies and young children need new strategies of parental guidance and discipline to nurture their development. For example, helping the baby to learn how to self-calm is one of the earliest responsibilities of parenting. Once the baby begins to crawl, setting limits becomes a priority. As the young child develops symbolic skills in thinking and speaking, problem-solving skills are a major component of guidance and discipline. Although the need for a specific parenting strategy may emerge at a specific developmental phase, parents need to continue using these strategies as their children develop. For example, children of all ages require assistance in self-calming (though the skill may be termed *frustration tolerance* once the child is a preschooler). Similarly, both children and youth need clear, consistent limits and problem-solving skills—limits so they know the boundaries of safe and acceptable behavior and problem-solving skills to resolve their difficulties with other people.

GUIDANCE AND DISCIPLINE IN
EARLY INFANCY: BIRTH TO 8 MONTHS

The important events that help or hurt development are the split second, ordinary, daily, repetitive, nonverbal events that occur between baby and caregiver. Stern called these interactions *microevents*, or "relatively small and short-lived events, such as what the mother does with her eyes and face at the moment when the baby's smile at her increases in amplitude."[11]

During the first few months of a baby's life, much of what goes on between baby and caregiver includes helping the baby achieve physiological and emotional regulation. Sleeping and eating are two primary tasks of the baby. During the babies' first 3–4 months, the brain has not matured enough to allow for regularity in sleep. By age 3–4 months, however, babies may take two to three regular naps throughout the day. By 6 months, most babies need a morning and afternoon nap, for a total of 2–4 hours. Research has shown that sleep, emotion, and attention are all linked.[12] Naps are very important for optimal learning when babies are awake. Babies who are good sleepers are able to maintain focus and learn. During their first 3–4 months, colicky babies often have irregular sleep patterns and can cry inconsolably. Like adults, babies who have are not getting enough sleep tend to be quite irritable.

Beginning at the birth of a baby, a positive climate within the home sets the stage for positive parental guidance and discipline. Routines and schedules are central components of a positive home environment. Babies thrive on safe, predictable routines: periods of soft cuddling prior to sleeping, parents' soft talking during feeding and diaper changing, and parents' responses to crying. During a baby's first 6–8 weeks, the baby's patterns of sleeping and feeding are not very predictable. After the first 6–8 weeks, parents can begin to adapt their baby's waking and bedtime feeding to their desired schedule.

Balancing the Needs of Babies and Their Parents

Parents of very young babies find they need to structure their own lives to ensure enough sleep, healthy food, time off, and time with friends and family that is not centered on their child. Then, they will be able to interact with their baby with patience and understanding. When home visitors work with parents of very young babies, they can ensure that parents are taking care of themselves. Janice's first home visit after Greg's birth is illustrative. Janice's initially inquired about Greg's delivery and his mother Karyn's social support during the first few weeks. In her conversation with Karyn, Janice ensures that Karyn also is caring for herself. This is especially important, for Greg (age 5 weeks) has been very colicky.

Janice: My third son was colicky. Even when it's the third baby, it's tough.

Karyn: I did get out for 45 minutes to go shopping last night.

Janice: You need to do that for yourself. It's normal. Also, you are having changes in your hormones.

Karyn: It's a more difficult adjustment—not working. It's hard, not getting that feedback that I got when working.

Janice: And your husband wants attention.

Karyn: I told him, "At least you get feedback at work."

Janice: Nobody says, "You're doing a good job." I can tell—you are doing a good job. Have you talked with your sister-in-law?

Karyn: Yes, a little, but it's different for her. She has a good baby, and she is breastfeeding.

Janice then tells Karyn about a forthcoming group meeting for mothers and their new babies. She suggests that the group meeting can help Karyn meet people with common experience who can support each other.

Janice: When you have a baby who cries, no one knows what you're feeling. I know that's how I felt with my third one. I remember calling the doctor and asking if I was doing something wrong. He was wonderful, told me to call him back in a week, and he offered to give me something to help me with my hormones. The information helped me to settle down. Yet, I still didn't want to hear [my baby] cry anymore.

In this first visit after Greg's birth, Janice listens empathically to Karyn's comments regarding Greg's colic and her missing feedback. Not only does Janice listen to Karyn, but she addresses Karyn's need for support. With some parents, home visitors can suggest the parents visit their physician for additional help. Janice also shares her own parenting experiencing with a colicky newborn. In this sharing, Janice strives to build a sense of connectedness with parents. Just as they share the intimacies of their life, she lets them know that she is a person with similar thoughts and feelings. Chapter 1 discusses this pattern of sharing by parent educators more fully.

Temperament

Temperament is the inborn characteristic ways a baby reacts to others and the environment, including activity rate, rhythmicity, adaptability to new experiences, response intensity, and general mood. Babies' temperaments not only affect the way they respond but also the way others respond them. Babies express three distinctive temperaments: easy, difficult, and slow to warm up.[13]

Different baby temperaments call for different parent responses. A need exists for a "goodness of fit" between a baby's temperament and his or her parents in order for healthy baby and child development to occur. Goodness of fit "exists when the demands and expectations of the parents and other people important to the child's life are compatible with the child's temperament, abilities, and other characteristics."[14]

Parenting a baby labeled as difficult can be very challenging. Difficult babies are slow to develop regular sleeping and eating cycles. They respond vigorously and negatively to new things. They cry more often. Temperament patterns can persist through preschool years and, occasionally, through adulthood. At the same time, temperament is not fixed, but can be adapted by the baby's and young child's relationships and experiences.

How parents react to their difficult baby depends on their own characteristics, expectations, and history of childhood parenting. Parents who are easygoing can adapt to a difficult baby more readily than parents who are intense and somewhat inflexible. Different styles between parents and babies do not automatically lead to problems. When problems do persist, developmental guidance can assist parents. For example, home visitors can clarify innate temperament differences for parents. This clarification assists parents in understanding their new baby and in helping them have appropriate expectations.

Essential to parental guidance is availability—not only physical, but especially *emotional* availability. When parents are emotionally available, they can respond empathically to their baby; thus, an ebb and flow of interactions involving mutual feedback develops. Brazelton and Cramer explained:

In periods of attention, infants can begin to signal their mothers with smiles or frowns, with vocalizations, with motor displays such as leaning forward, reaching, arching the head coyly, and so on. Mothers respond contingently when they can read the messages conveyed in these signals. As a mother responds, she learns from the success or failure of each of her own responses, as measured by the baby's behavior. In this way, she refines the contingency of her responses and develops a repertoire of "what works" and "what doesn't."[15]

Along with emotional availability is the need for parents to respond to their babies' cues. That is, babies' behaviors such as vocalizations, smiles, and frowns signal their parents to respond. In turn, parents' responses to their babies invite further baby forms of communication; then, mutual communication and shared enjoyment takes place.

Beginning in their first visit, home visitors keenly observe how a parent and his or her baby interact. Does the parent *respond* to the baby's vocalization (e.g., grimace, smile), and is the response a good *match* to the feeling state being expressed (e.g., pleasure, curiosity, discomfort)? The match does not have to be a mirror of the baby's behavior; rather, the match needs to speak to the baby's feeling. When the parent coos or cuddles the baby, does the baby respond with a similar emotional expression? Home visitors themselves can observe the baby's

behavior and model for the parent's responsiveness and reciprocal communication. In this way, they can promote parents' skill. This responsiveness and mutuality is the foundation for healthy attachment that
gives babies a sense of trust, both in having their needs met and trust
in their ability to signal their parents' responsiveness.

GUIDANCE AND DISCIPLINE: 8–17 MONTHS

As babies begin to move, their behavior is no longer predictable and
new parenting challenges emerge. Babies' mobility means the ability to
leave their parents and discover their own independence. This new independence may cause the baby to feel overwhelmed and to seek renewed dependence. Babies need to trust that their parents are available because this availability provides the security for the child to leave
the parent. At around 10 months, when confronting something new or
uncertain, babies first look at their parents' faces to check for the parents' expression to know whether this new situation or object is going
to be fearful or pleasant. Psychologists call this checking with the parent *social referencing*.[16] The parent provides security for the baby to continue to explore.

With the child's mobility, consistent discipline becomes a necessary part of parents' love of their child. Given today's parental ambivalence regarding discipline, this is the time that home visitors need to
help parents understand their child's need for *learning limits*. Such
learning is dependent on parental discipline and guidance. Between
ages 8 and 17 months, toddlers do not have the developmental skills to
learn self-control; thus parents' *external control* of discipline and the
child's increasing *obedience* becomes very important.

During this phase of baby and toddler development, issues of control surface and often dominate parent–child interaction. Home visitors can assist parents in learning how to distract their toddlers, which is
an effective guidance strategy for children this age. Providing a substitute or alternative activity can refocus the toddler's attention and prevent angry outbursts. Instead of saying, "Don't grab your brother's
block," the parent can hand the toddler another toy.

This developmental period often includes a tug and pull between
parents and their toddlers. Daily tasks such as diapering, feeding, and
dressing can become times of struggle (e.g., the baby's constant
movement during diapering and dressing). Central to learning independence is the inevitable "no" response to parental requests. With
walking, toddlers want to explore their newly discovered "walking
world" nonstop, with no understanding of the danger of electrical
cords, hot stoves, stairs, heights, and so forth. They initially resist their

parents' limits. With the onset of words comes demands. These new strides entail ambivalence, which the baby expresses in sending contradictory messages; for example, she does and she doesn't want to sit on Mom's lap.

Between 6 and 12 months of age, babies are able to maintain a regular eating and sleeping schedule. Once babies have learned new motor skills like crawling and climbing, however, the surge in development may disrupt their nap schedule, and they may be more resistant to being put in their crib. During these times of developmental growth, a calming activity such as reading or singing can assist babies in settling down. Most important is regularity and firmness. It helps to always remember that learning to fall asleep is an important skill for babies to master. It is very important for caregivers to avoid putting babies to sleep in their arms because then the baby will have a harder time learning how to go to sleep on his or her own.

Once babies are 12 months old, they can eat together with other babies in child care, and eating becomes a dual activity—mealtime plus social time. Now babies are able to eat solid food, and as soon as they develop their pincer grasp (around age 8–10 months), they like to feed themselves with their hands. Exploring food becomes as important as eating it. Eating is an activity in which babies can begin to exercise autonomy. Learning to play with a cup and handle it themselves is exciting for babies. Once caregivers realize this, they can allow time for babies to explore their new skills and avoid making mealtimes into a battleground. By 12 months of age, babies should be able to eat finger foods (e.g., cheese and bread cut into small pieces) on their own, and by 16 months, they should be able to master a small spoon or fork. Feeding oneself is a sign of growing independence. Admittedly, eating becomes more messy and parents' clean-up task more demanding, but parents can learn to accept the increased mess if they recognize that their child is learning self-help skills.

As the child becomes mobile, discussion of safety becomes part of home visiting. Observation and supervision by parents are preconditions of safety. When observing, parents can anticipate potential safety hazards and redirect their children's action. The following interaction between Jean and her 17-month-old son is illustrative.

Jean is folding laundry on the couch as Ricky rides his wooden horse about the living room. Ricky gets off his horse and climbs on its back to stand.

Jean asks, "Ricky, is that safe?" Ricky does not say anything or get off his toy horse. Jean says, "You better get down, Ricky. The horsey might fall over, and you would bump your head on the chair."

Ricky gets off the horse and knocks the toy over so that it is lying on its side. Jean asks, "Is the horsey okay? Did the horsey get hurt?"

Ricky says, "Check and see."

Jean responds, "Check and see if he's okay."

Ricky says, "Horsey ouch."

Jean says, "The horsey has an ouchy. Maybe you'll need to get the doctor's kit."

Toddlers like Ricky constantly explore and experiment; yet, they do not have the capacity to judge potentially dangerous situations. By being a careful observer, Jean was able to anticipate potential problems, an important guidance skill. When Ricky stood on his horse, Jean positively redirected his potentially dangerous action with an explanation that he could understand. Jean then used Ricky's action (i.e., knocking over his horse) to initiate an alternative activity—role-playing that the horse was injured. Once babies begin moving, childproofing the house becomes very important. Table 1 provides a checklist for home safety that can be helpful for parents.

Another normal part of a toddler's exploration that emerges at around age 1 year is biting, hair pulling, scratching, and hitting. The toddler initially does not understand that these actions hurt the other person. Parents should respond calmly but firmly, telling their toddler they may not do that, and stop them until the toddlers can stop themselves. If a parent becomes horrified and overreacts, this overreaction sets the pattern rather than removes it. Biting is especially frightening for parents. Home visitors can help parents recognize that they need to help their toddler understand that under no circumstances do they allow biting. Substitutions such as dolls or teething toys can be given for the child to bite when needing to release feelings of anger and frustration. When biting, toddlers do not mean to hurt and are frightened afterward—especially if the victim is another small child who now is screaming. Parental response should include a firm limit and reassurance that they will help their child overcome the incident and that they love the child. Janice discussed biting.

Parents need to understand that kids bite because it works. Biting is done out of frustration. Usually, biting is to get someone's attention, or a way to get a toy. Children bite because they don't have other tools to get what they want. Biting needs to be approached in stages. A baby explores with her mouth through biting. A toddler bites to get what he wants, for he can't talk very well. When an older child bites, the biting often represents a larger problem.

Table 1.   Home safety checklist for parents

Is your home poison-proof? (This includes house plants)

Is the bathroom safety-proofed? (Keep bathroom door closed.)

Are all sharp objects (e.g., knives, pins, scissors) out of the baby's reach?

Are all small objects (e.g., buttons, beads, hairpins) out of the baby's reach?

Are electrical plugs covered?

Are your child's crib and room area safe?

Have you removed easily overturned lamps and tables, electrical cords, and sharp-edged furniture?

Are stairways gated at the top and gated two or three steps from the bottom?

Are plastic bags and soft pillows kept out of your child's reach?

Are long cords out of the child's reach and away from the crib?

Are there guards in front of open heaters, fireplaces, furnaces, and so forth?

Are hot liquids, curling irons, toasters, coffee pots out of the baby's reach?

Are the baby's toys safe?

Are all kitchen cabinets (within the baby's reach) free from harmful items or safety locked?

When in an automobile, does your child always ride in the back seat in a child safety seat?

Are guests' purses (which may contain medications) always put out of the child's reach?

Is there any chipping or flaking paint in a home built before 1978?

From Parents as Teachers National Center. (1999). *Born to Learn Curriculum Prenatal to 3 Years* (p. 363). St. Louis, MO: Author; adapted by permission.

As babies become mobile, a primary task of the home visitor is to help parents recognize that, as soon as their baby begins to move about, parents must set limits (see Table 2), and then help their children follow them. Safety is parents' first guide, and distraction is their most effective strategy. As mobility increases, accompanied by independence and determination, setting limits becomes much more difficult, and at this time, home visitors can give parents needed support and guidance.

Clear limits help young children know what is expected of them. Behavioral expectations make children feel secure. When very young children are tired, very hungry, or overwhelmed with stimulation, they

Table 2. Positive guidelines for setting limits for toddlers

Choose the most important issues, and limit the number of rules so they can be enforced consistently.

Rules should be reasonable for the child's age and developmental level of understanding.

Tell the toddler in a positive manner what you want him or her to do. Rather than stating rules in the negative (e.g., no running), offer a positive alternative (e.g., please walk).

All adults need to consistently enforce the rules at all times and in all places.

State rules in a simple, brief, specific manner, and be sure the toddler understands.

Focus on the behavior. Avoid labeling the child negatively (e.g., "bad," "naughty," "dumb"). Instead say, "It hurts him when you bite."

Talk in a calm but firm manner. Avoid shouting.

are most likely to lose control and need parental limit setting. Parents can offer an alternative activity and divert children of this age. Some parents have difficulty being consistent in their limit setting. Open discussions with home visitors can give these parents the courage to persist, even when they feel unsure of themselves.

GUIDANCE AND DISCIPLINE: 18 MONTHS TO 3 YEARS

Throughout their waking hours, toddlers continue to use exploration as their primary way of relating to the world. The toddler wavers between bold demands of independence and autonomy and intense periods of clinging and dependency. Toddlers insist on doing tasks without help, such as dressing or getting in the car seat, even when they do not have the necessary skills to do them alone. As toddlers struggle with independence, they frequently respond to their parents with intense negativism. It is as if they are testing both their parents and their own newly discovered independence.

As toddlers explore their everyday home environment from their new vertical, mobile perspective, it is natural for them to be absorbed with feelings of independence and autonomy. Toddlers explore without stopping to remember limits. An adult blocking and thereby frustrating a toddler's exploration most likely will lead to an angry, aggressive outburst from the toddler. Home visitors can help parents understand that negativism is a normal phase of development and should be expected as their toddler navigates between striving for independence, parental obstacles, feelings of dependency, and fears of separation. If parents overreact to their toddler's exploratory or negative behavior, they may be reinforcing, that is, strengthening this behavior, because negative attention is better than no attention at all. Negative behavior that at first is merely exploratory (e.g., testing new limits) can become energized to continue if parents overreact. Often, a toddler's "no" does not even signal a negative intention; rather, it is voiced as a declaration of independence. Many times it can be ignored. Sally's response to Jeff (age 27 months), for whom she provides child care, is illustrative.

> Jeff and Suzy (age 4 years) have just finished eating breakfast. As the children get up from their chairs, Sally says to them, "Let's brush our teeth before we go outdoors."
> Jeff replies emphatically, "No, no, no, no!"
> Sally replies in a singing voice, "No, no, no, no."
> They enter the bathroom, and Jeff sits on Sally's lap as he watches Suzy brush her teeth.
> Sally says, "Let's watch Suzy. While we wait, let's squeeze a little [toothpaste] on your brush." Jeff initially is restless, but as Sally continues speaking softly, he calms down.
> Sally continues, "Now let's get it wet." Then, Jeff takes the toothbrush and puts it in his mouth. Suzy finishes and leaves the bathroom. Jeff immediately goes to the stool in front of the sink and begins brushing his teeth.

Sally consistently expects Jeff to brush his teeth after eating and merely ignores Jeff's negativism. Jeff seems rebellious as he frequently says "no," as he tests Sally's limits and asserts his independence. Understanding toddlers' struggle for independence and their frustration with limits, Sally maintains her consistent expectations. Jeff follows through without resistance. Unlike Jeff, some toddlers do not obey; instead, they may have a temper tantrum.

Temper Tantrums

In this period of ambivalent struggle for independence, toddlers' inner turmoil sometimes erupts into a temper tantrum. Frustrated from not being able to do or get what they want, toddlers may roll on the floor, kicking and screaming. When having a tantrum, toddlers are out of control, which can be very frightening for them and difficult for their parents to understand and tolerate. Home visitors can help parents understand that tantrums are another normal part of development, and that, even when he or she is having a tantrum, their toddler *must* accept their limits. Home visitors can help parents understand that they need to respond to their child's feelings and explain the reason for the tantrum. That is, parents should give their child the words to name how he or she is feeling and at the same time let the child know that they understand what their child wants, but that now is not the time (e.g., "I know you are angry because you want to go outdoors, but you must take a nap before we go outdoors.")

Different children respond differently to parents' assistance in calming down. Some children need a time alone in a quiet room. Others need a parent's soft cuddling. All children need to understand that their parents understand how awful they feel. But a tantrum is not the way to get what is wanted. Once a tantrum has ended, parents can reassure their toddler of their love with a warm hug. As toddlers approach 3 years of age, if their parents have given them consistent limits, they most likely have achieved inner controls and tantrums have disappeared.

Parents can be embarrassed when their child has tantrums and may think something is wrong with their child or that something is wrong with the way they are handling their child. They can think that their child's tantrum reflects that they are not good parents, so they may respond to the tantrum with their own anger and violence. Home visitors can normalize tantrums and help parents understand ways to handle them. Janice explained her approach.

If you say, "Does Joey have temper tantrums?" often parents will be defensive because they might be embarrassed about tantrums. But I still want to talk about tantrums at the appropriate age. Rather, I say, "How is Joey handling his temper?" I want parents to view it as normal and as temporary, and I want them to realize the importance of dealing with the emotion. For example, the child really does feel crazy, and parents need to be supportive: "I know you are mad." And that is different than giving in on the issue: "I'll give you a cookie so you stop crying." I want them to know they can support the child and still maintain their firm limits.

Learning Rules

Young children learn rules and expectations unconsciously in the course of their everyday lives with family members. These rules are learned in the same manner that toddlers learn rules of grammar, what David Reiss has termed *practicing knowledge*.[17] When parents take time to have extended play with their toddlers, this play gives the toddler a web of important meanings. The toddler feels affirmed and connected, especially when a parent enters into the toddler's emotional tone of play.

When toddlers have lengthy interactions with caring, nurturing adults, they not only learn how to regulate their own behavior, but also they begin to do so in terms of the perceived needs of others. Parents communicate moral concepts about caring and compassion each time they show their toddler how to pet a dog, rock their baby doll, or pat their baby sibling.

Toddlers learn about how to care by the way that their parents respond to them, for example when they fall or are sad, and over time, how toddlers respond to their parents, for example, giving them spontaneous hugs. Toddlers are quick to learn the "ssssh" gesture. Around 18 months of age, toddlers are able to be empathic and express altruistic behavior, for example, patting the head of a baby sibling who is crying.

Misbehavior

There are times when no matter what strategy a parent uses, the child refuses to cooperate. Toddlers' struggles can be very difficult for their parents. With growth in mobility and more mature cognitive functioning, toddlers begin to understand themselves as separate from their mothers. Ambivalence and conflict emerge when toddlers desire both to be separate from their mothers yet want them to satisfy their wishes. At the same time, the toddler is a central part of his or her mother's own identity, and as the toddler struggles with independence, the mother is struggling with her own identification and separation from the child.[18]

When toddlers misbehave, parents can use *time-out* to allow both their child and themselves to calm down. Time-out can be an effective way to help an out-of-control child to become calm. In time-out, parents remove their child from all attention for a short period until the child feels he or she can manage. Tracy's response to Mia provides an example of using time-out.

Mia (age 34 months) begins moving her doll's bed across the living room floor. Her sister, Maggie (age 18 months), tries to assist, but Mia pushes her away. Finally, Mia pushes Maggie so hard that she tumbles down. Tracy then tells Mia that she needs to go to her room if she can't manage her behavior.

Mia shouts, "No."

Tracy then carries Mia, who cries loudly, into her bedroom. When Tracy returns, she tells Janice, "She goes crazy in her room, and then suddenly she comes out when she's all done crying. I tell her to stay in there until she's done crying."

Janice replies, "It's good that you have followed through. You handled that situation so well. I hope that everyone could do it that well." Mia then returns to the room and sits on her mother's lap.

Tracy comments that usually she might have left Mia in her bedroom a while longer.

Janice says, "The amount of time isn't the important thing. She just needs to have time-out so that she can gain control. You let her come out when she's feeling better; then, you can explain to her what's happened. Sometimes when she is screaming, she can't even hear you. She has to first get it all out. Once it is all out, then she'll be fine. It's important that she knows you understand how she feels, but she still cannot push her sister."

Time-out need not be a punishment; rather it is parents' strategy to help their child calm down. Once the child has calmed down, the parent can talk about feelings to the child. When a child misbehaves but is not out of control, time-out is not an appropriate parent response. Parents can give consequences that relate to the child's misbehavior. For example, if a child refuses to eat any dinner, the parent can inform the child that there will be no more food until breakfast. Children's misbehavior can be a learning situation. With young children, it often is enough for parents to stop the inappropriate behavior and offer an alternative behavior. For example, a parent can suggest to her 3-year-old son that he give his 2-year-old sister a toy to trade, rather than grabbing his sister's toy. What many parents find difficult is their need to be consistent and follow through once they address their child's misbehavior. For example, if a parent warns his 3-year-old that she must stay in the grocery cart or they will leave, the parent must leave when his daughter gets out of the cart, even when this decision is very inconvenient for the parent.

Toddlers gain security in knowing their parents control them. When rules are broken, toddlers need to know there will be a consequence—a parental response. Consequences can be natural or a logical follow-up of the misbehavior. When playing at dinner, Suzy spills her milk. Suzy then is responsible for cleaning up her milk—a *natural* consequence. Suzy whines throughout her friend's birthday party. Because Suzy cannot manage her behavior, her mother takes her home from the party—a *logical* consequence. Often, there is no appropriate natural consequence for misbehavior. For example, if a toddler bites, it is not appropriate for his parent to bite him or her. In these situations, parents need to acknowledge their child's angry feelings but let their child know that his or her behavior is not allowed. Parents should provide an alternative, for example, vigorously punching playdough.

A calm home atmosphere with predictable routines, uninterrupted periods for play, and time for parent–child shared experiences nurture young children's development of self-control. As home visitors help parents understand what to expect of their toddlers and how to positively nurture their development, they can emphasize preventive discipline, that is, parenting that prevents the occurrence of misbehavior and prevents parent–child battles. Giving clear behavioral expectations assists young children in controlling their behavior and prevents misbehavior. When changes will occur in routines, children can be told in advance so they can be ready for these changes. Anticipating potential problems and providing alternatives can avoid struggles. For example, when a mother knows her son will become overstimulated if she takes him grocery shopping with her, she can choose to take him on errands that do not invite overstimulation, such as to the gas station or cleaners. When single parents do not have a ready support system, completing errands without their child may demand careful planning, for example, doing an errand before picking up their child from child care or swapping child care with a friend so that each can shop alone.

Giving limited choices respects the child's emerging abilities and encourages independence and autonomy. In the following example, as Mia (age 26 months) and Maggie (age 8 months) are playing, Tracy and Janice discuss preventive discipline strategies.

Mia has just tossed a wooden square across the floor. Her mother tells her, "Don't throw; it may hurt Maggie."

Mia then returns to the shape-sorter truck and places a green triangular shape in the appropriate space. As Mia is playing, Janice comments to Tracy, "When Mia gets ready to throw, it is good to head her off at the pass. That is, tell her what she can do—before she gets herself into trouble."

A few moments later, Tracy gives Mia a cracker to eat. As Mia sits on her mother's lap, eating her cracker, Tracy says to her, "Crackers all over. We'll need to vacuum."

Mia says, "I'll help."

Janice responds, "It's important for children to realize consequences of what they do—not punishment. If I spill something, I'll help clean it up."

Tracy says, "She's driving me nuts—getting her dressed in the morning. I give her choices, but she'll want something else."

"You need to choose your battles—what matters," Janice explains. "Possibly you could take turns. Yesterday, it was your turn [to choose the clothing]. Two-year-olds are beginning to understand taking turns. I'm not saying it'll be a lot easier, but it also can help her understand turns."

"She wants to do everything herself," Tracy adds.

"And it's frustrating for you," Janice acknowledges. "You are wise to give her limited choices, even if she chooses a third. Limited choices, instead of, for example, 'What do you want for breakfast?' It's important if a choice is offered, you can let her have what she chooses. When we give children choices, we are nurturing their decision-making process. Psychologists talk about it as autonomy. There is an underlying developmental issue in giving choices. Just remember, it's not part of her personality but part of her development!"

In this conversation, Janice achieves a healthy balance as she affirms Tracy's parenting actions, interprets the developmental meaning of the 2-year-old's actions, and gives suggestions related to Tracy's ongoing parenting dilemmas.

When young children misbehave and are in conflict with their caregivers, caregivers can help them learn how to manage experiences of disagreement and provide a foundation for the growth of empathy. For example, when caregivers discuss their child's feelings, for example, "I know you are mad that you cannot have that cookie you took," young children learn first to recognize their feelings, and second, that their caregivers care about them. When caregivers give explanations for rules, young children can more readily make them their own, a part of their conscience formation. Having disagreements often involves experience in negotiation, for example, "No, now is not the time for cookies, but I promise you may have them after lunch." Toddlerhood is the time that children's cognitive skills are developing so that they can understand their caregivers' rules and apply them to their own behavior, and with time, internalize them.

Fears

As the sense of self and sense of outside world expand, fears of such things as strange places, loud noises, Halloween masks, or specific animals may develop. Home visitors can help parents understand that all young children sometimes are fearful. Janice's response to one parent's concern about her daughter's fear illustrates how a home visitor can assist parents in this area.

As Erin (age 30 months) plays, her mother, Shelly, softly tells Janice, "Erin seems to be afraid of men. At the grocery, an elderly man talked to Erin, took her arm, and playfully said, 'Why don't you come home with me?' I thought he was being playful, but Erin seemed frightened."

Janice says, "Fears are quite typical for children Erin's age."

Shelly continues, "I told Erin, 'Did he scare you? He didn't mean to.'

And I left it at that. Later, I told her that if a stranger touches you, you need to get me. But then my brother-in-law, who Erin knows real well, walked into our home, and Erin cried."

Janice explains, "This is very typical. Don't try to talk her out of it. Tell her to come to you, just as you did. Let her know that you'll keep her safe. Don't discount her feelings. She really is afraid. It's her age, and it's a piece of development. It's very important never to belittle her feelings."

"I have a tendency to say, 'Don't be wimpy,'" Shelly admits.

Janice says, "Her fears are very real, and at this age, fantasy and reality are not separate."

As Shelly describes her daughter's fears, Janice helps Shelly understand that fears are a normal part of development and that parents need to respect their child's fears. Within the context of a parent's concern, Janice is able to provide developmental information (i.e., "Fears are real at this age") and suggestions (i.e., "Let her know you'll keep her safe").

Home visitors can help parents understand that they cannot eliminate their young children's fears, but they can help them understand and learn how to deal with their fear. For example, parents can respect their son's fear of monsters by explaining that monsters are make-believe, by reminding the child that mom and dad are in a nearby room, and by adding a nightlight to his room. It is helpful for parents to know that fears are a normal phase that will pass if the parents do not overreact. Parents' overreaction can validate and reinforce young children's fears. As a child's world expands, he or she experiences new fears (e.g., loud noise of fire engines, unpredictability of a neighbor's dog). When parents recognize what their young child fears, they often can prepare their child and let their child know that they are present to protect him or her. Similarly, parents can limit television viewing and be with their child during potentially scary programs. Young children sometimes have nightmares, which are frightening but also a normal phase of development. Home visitors can help parents understand that they can calmly and quietly awaken their child and offer comfort, which usually allows the child to return to sleep. Nightmares most often occur following stressful days.

GUIDANCE AND DISCIPLINE: 3–5 YEARS

Negativism, tantrums, and recurrent parent–child struggles diminish as the child turns 3, and the calmness of early infancy reappears. Given their verbal and intellectual ability, 3-year-olds delight in shared experiences with others. Dinners with 3-year-olds can be enjoyable shared family experiences. Feelings now have words. Children can carry on internal dialogues, plan their play, use words as substitutes for objects or people in role-play, and begin to control their own behavior. Three-year-olds can tell a story with a dramatic story line, and a beginning, middle, and end.[19] Their stories usually are autobiographical.

Beginning at age 3 years, preschoolers have expanded experiences with others their own age. In these experiences, they learn new patterns of behavior from their peers and try out their own actions. Conflict and emerging aggression is common, especially when the preschooler is frustrated by his or her peers. At the same time, preschoolers develop skills in sharing, turn taking, and cooperative play.

Simple Explanations and Alternative Action

With the child's increased verbal skills and beginning reasoning skills, parents can give simple explanations with suggested alternative action as they redirect their child, for example, "Throwing your ball in the house will break the lamps. Let's go outdoors to throw." In other words, parents should give reasons for their limits. Reasons help children develop standards of right and wrong. Parents can verbalize children's feelings and thereby help their child recognize their feeling, a first step in controlling one's feelings. When a child grabs her sister's doll, the mother can say, "I know you're angry because you want the doll." Parents also can help their child know they will help solve the problem: "When Lucretia is finished, I'll make sure you get the doll." Now that children can think about ideas and understand consequences of their behavior (e.g., "If I kick my brother, Daddy will catch me and punish me"), they are developing a true moral consciousness. With time, children learn to think about the consequences in terms of how another person will feel, for example, "If I hit Sammy, he'll be mad at me."

Now that young children have a sense of causality, they sometimes want to be nice to others so that others will be nice to them. For example, "I think I'll climb on Mommy's lap and give her a big hug." The child knows that Mommy then will give a return hug and kiss. The child's sense of right and wrong no longer focuses on not doing bad things. Doing nice things leads to simple rewards.

Sexual Curiosity, Increased Aggression, and Misbehavior

Parenting 4- and 5-year-olds entails some new challenges. As the sense of self and sense of outside world expand, sexual curiosity and increased aggression emerge. Four- and five-year-olds are fascinated by aggressive television superheroes, ghosts, and monsters. Given the high proportion of violence on children's television programming, preschoolers benefit from having their television viewing limited and monitored by their parents. Home visitors experience a dilemma when approaching this topic with parents who have their television on all the time and whose children often watch television alone. In these situations, home visitors need to remember that it is not their role to change family patterns but to support families and provide developmental information.

Whining, stuttering, lying, stealing, and swearing emerge at 4 and 5 years. These behaviors often are exploratory and temporary. When parents overreact, their child's behavior may become habitual. Four- and five-year-olds have some skills in cooperative play, but possessiveness, conflict, lack of sharing, and name calling also characterize their peer play.

As young children get older, parents begin to rely more on explanations, compromise, or other nonassertive negotiating strategies. Preschoolers tend to follow behavioral standards more readily, but they also can be quick to assert their own opinion. For example, they may think any food that is mixed together is "yukky" and therefore not eat stew or spaghetti. In healthy, positive parent–child relationships, preschoolers' cooperation is not a matter of compliance but rather a combination of the child's ability to understand, accept, and want to cooperate.[20] Caregivers who consistently give clear explanations as well as talk about feelings and intentions, especially in disputes, are promoting healthy conscience development. Children learn the predictable consequences of their misbehavior, and these consequences help them remember the rules. They learn why some actions are not appropriate, how some actions can be harmful, and how some of their actions affect other people.

Conscience can develop in situations other than misbehavior. When parents and their young children talk often about what they are doing or have been doing, these conversations often contain implicit moral lessons. For example, at dinner, a father described how his secretary needed to leave work early each day to relieve her sister and take care of her elderly mother who is very ill. His young daughter learned that he was understanding of his secretary's personal life.

Anger

Anger is a feeling that people experience when a goal is blocked and they become frustrated. A key function of anger is to provide the energy and motivation that help to eliminate barriers that block intention. Typical stresses of preschoolers that lead to anger include conflict over possessions; physical assault or verbal exchanges by an adult or child, such as teasing or taunting; rejection; and issues of compliance.[21]

Young children can learn to express their anger in a way that helps them either to reevaluate the intention that is blocked or to find constructive ways of eliminating the block. Home visitors can help parents realize that they can play a pivotal role in helping their children recognize their anger. Talking about feelings helps young children recognize and understand their feelings. When parents see an angry child, they can talk about the child's feelings (e.g., "I see that you are very angry because you cannot go outside now"). Expressing the child's emotion in words is an important first step toward enabling the child to recognize and understand the emotion. Once parents have helped their child recognize his or her anger, they can encourage the child to label it verbally (e.g., "I'm mad that you took my truck"). In situations with peers or siblings, parents and children can discuss what makes them mad and how they can express anger. Then, they can find a solution that allows everyone to get what they want without blocking what another person wants.

Home visitors can suggest to parents that reading children's books about anger also assists young children in understanding this feeling. Some suggestions include *I Was So Mad*[22] and *That Bothered Kate*.[23] The home visitor may end up helping the parents manage their own anger better in the process of teaching their child.

Conscience

It is well known that behavioral difficulties often emerge as a part of normal, age-specific challenges. Four- and five-year-olds may delight in imitating aggressive models on television and videotapes. Misbehavior becomes problematic when the behavior is repeated across situations, with different people, and at different times. In other words, the behavior consistently erupts.

Once preschoolers understand consequences and internalize rules, they develop a moral consciousness, or conscience. Now, they have learned to anticipate the consequences of their actions. "If I hit my brother, he'll cry, and I'll be sent to my room." At first, consequences are concrete: Specific behaviors lead to specific consequences. As they get older, children learn also that consequences include how another person will feel after a given behavior. Preschoolers who live in emotionally healthy families expect pleasant consequences when they do nice things and will do nice things in order to receive positive reactions. They have learned to anticipate their parents' warm hugs or nodding smiles. It is as if they have a little mother or father in their mind. Now, parents' warnings or warm expressions are experienced as the child's own inner voice. Greenspan and Lewis explained that this inner voice has two components, "the inner presence that guides you in a positive way, eventually with ideals and values, and another presence that can be critical or make you feel guilty or bad."[24]

Children at this age have triangular thinking, which helps them set their own limits. A girl may stop hitting a playmate because she now can consider how the other child or her father might feel about the action. She knows that her playmate would get upset if hit, and her father would disapprove. Once the child has internalized her parent's approval, she may stop hitting playmates. A preschooler who receives lots of nurturance and lots of love from his or her parents can learn to tolerate disappointment without misbehaving.

Aggression

In the 1990s, early educators across America reported an increasing number of hyperactive, impulsive, and aggressive young children in their classrooms.[25] Aggressive behavior can be defined as behavior directed toward another person with the intent to hurt or frighten.[26] Aggressive disorders can begin before age 3. Children younger than 3 years old have limited ability to understand the impact of their aggressive behavior. Longitudinal research indicates that aggression that begins in early childhood shows moderate to strong continuity over time.

Factors influencing young children's aggression include maternal unresponsiveness and poor attachment, marital conflict, and multiple familial stressors.[27] These behaviors can also be triggered by anxiety found in young children who are experiencing consistent violence, maltreatment, or domestic violence; who are given no behavioral limits or consequences; or who have minimal shared time with their parents. Inconsistent limits and lack of routines or consequences can generate a great deal of anxiety in children, and this anxiety most often is expressed in aggression, impulsivity, and hyperactivity.

Hyperactivity, impulsivity, and aggression are also typical behaviors of children with attention-deficit/hyperactivity disorder (ADHD), a disability rooted in brain dysfunction. Karr-Morse and Wiley identified five basic behavior problems that are part of ADHD:

- Lack of planning and thinking before action
- Inability to select what is important from what is not important
- Easy distractibility

- Inability to maintain attention
- Difficulty in self-monitoring how one is doing in a task[28]

Children of every ethnicity and social class suffer from ADHD. Darryl lived in a two-parent, upper middle–income family. The following vignette illustrates Darryl's experience with ADHD.

Four-year-old Darryl has attended a child care center since he was 8 weeks old. His teachers report that he is continually hyperactive and impulsive. The only time he remains at a task is during sensory play (e.g., playing with water or playdough). Teachers have difficulty helping Darryl follow directions and redirections. When they speak to him, it seems as if he doesn't hear them. He is, however, rarely aggressive.

Darryl's parents, Barb and Jesse, were 18 years old when their first child, Andy, was born. A year later, they had a daughter, Amy, and 10 years later, Darryl was born. Both parents are successful professionals who work long hours at demanding jobs. Jesse is an engineer, and Barb works at a large travel agency. When Darryl's teachers expressed their concern about Darryl, his parents joined in a parenting group that included three other parents and lasted 8 weeks.

Barb told the group that her corporation once had 400 employees but downsized to only 25. With the decrease in employees, Barb's job became exhausting and stressful. In addition, Darryl's siblings were involved in after-school activities, and each night Barb had to drive them back and forth to acting school, soccer, swim practice, and so forth. Therefore, Darryl's family did not eat dinner together because their schedule was almost never consistent. They had no family routines. Barb said that she spent far more time with her first two children when they were Darryl's age because she was working part time. Also, both children are more even-tempered than Darryl.

At home, Darryl spent most of his time watching videotapes and television. His parents noted that he rarely followed their directions or redirections. They were not with Darryl very much, and their life is so hectic that they never slowed down to focus on his hyperactivity or impulsivity.

Barb decided to take a month's leave of absence so that she could spend more time with her son. Rather than return to work after this month, she took another position with less stress. The family began eating meals together, and Barb and Jesse developed rules and consequences for Darryl's misbehavior.

When Darryl was in kindergarten, Barb reported that Darryl seemed better able to focus on tasks, but that he continues to be quite impulsive.

> When his kindergarten teacher shared her concerns with Barb and Jesse,
> they arranged for Darryl to attend weekly play therapy with a child psychol-
> ogist. Barb reported that his therapy has triggered significant change in Dar-
> ryl's ability to manage and further changes in the family's interactions with
> Darryl.

Not all children with ADHD have the luxuries of Darryl and his
parents. Once home visitors suspect a child has ADHD, however, they
can offer support, guidance, and referrals to community agencies.

The "Impossible" Child

Some children, termed *impossible* by Garbarino and Bedard,[29] become
explosively angry when they cannot handle their environment. These
children seem to be delayed in developing skills critical to tolerating
frustration and becoming flexible. Some parents are better equipped to
help these children get along with others. Without early intervention,
however, these children are likely to have serious problems as they get
older and their behavior becomes more and more problematic. Some
children refuse to listen to parents or teachers, others do not pay attention at school, and others turn to chronic aggression. Young children who are not only impossible but also live in deprived environments may end up in psychiatric facilities or juvenile prisons.

Young children can be impossible for many reasons. They may
have genetic abnormalities or a temperament that is quick to become
angry. Although some young children are more biologically vulnerable
than others, this predisposition depends to a large degree on the young
children's experiences. Impossible children may have been emotionally or physically hurt at an early age, neglected, or abused. They may
live in an environment with unhealthy habits of interaction and little
response to the children's needs.

This phenomenon is more prevalent now than in past years. Garbarino and Bedard provided four reasons why. First, a greater number
of seriously premature infants survive today than in the past, and some
of these babies face the added complication of maternal cocaine or alcohol abuse. Second, more and more children live in single-parent
families in which one adult is responsible for child rearing. This parent often does not have the social supports that promote effective
parenting. Third, the fast pace of modern life does not allow the time
that child rearing takes. Parents spend less time with their children,
and the less time a caregiver spends with a child, the less likely the
child will respond to the caregiver's requests. Parents then have to seek
outside assistance in dealing with their children. Finally, parents face

multiple demands, and child rearing may not be their priority. They may leave the task of child rearing to other people or it may be neglected altogether.

If an impossible child lives in a violent environment, anger will become a dominant theme. Fortunately, if the child's caregivers teach him or her socially acceptable behavior and communication skills, the anger may become immersed in healthy emotions.

Problem Solving

The ability to solve problems is a powerful skill in maintaining self-regulation and can be a guiding principle of discipline for preschoolers. Preschoolers have the verbal and cognitive skills needed to participate in solving misbehavior problems. When parents include their child in this process, they show that they respect and value their child's perspective. Children can be encouraged to think of alternative solutions to grabbing, hitting, racing in the house, and so forth. Home visitors can assist parents in understanding that, when solving problems, their children can develop a sense of responsibility for their actions. Young children may need their parents' assistance to think of alternatives.

Just as parents strive toward nurturing problem-solving skills in their young children, so, too, home visitors can strive to approach parents' discipline questions as opportunities to solve problems jointly with them. If a parent's question about discipline can be solved jointly, then the parent can own the solution. Janice uses this approach when Le-Toya, the mother of Suzy (age 38 months), expresses a concern.

LeToya: We've had problems with Suzy sleeping in her bed, going to sleep. Last night, she lay in her bed and screamed for an hour.

Janice: Do you have a routine?

LeToya: We read a story and get a drink of water before bed. She wants a light on.

Janice: Was there anything different yesterday? What about her food?

LeToya: We had roast, potatoes, and carrots, and she loves roast. Last night, we ate later than usual—8 o'clock.

Janice: When do you usually eat?

LeToya: About 6:00, but last night we ran errands before dinner.

Janice: Children this age have no sense of clock time, rather a sense of event time. It sounds like you've figured it out—having such an unusually late dinner. She probably knows that after dinner, she gets to play. Maybe not having playtime had something to do with it. Small children are hooked on routines. I would encourage you to stick to routines, of having the same thing happen in the same order every night. Then, she'll know that falling asleep is the last step in what is supposed to happen.

Janice strives to support and empower parents, and at the same time, offer developmentally appropriate strategies. She asks parents what they have tried and does not hesitate to probe the situation so that she can understand what is going on in the family. She explained:

You want to get all the alternatives on the table. And in the discussion, you can intersperse your own ideas, but you want the parent to come up with the solution. I try not to make many suggestions. Rather, I try to point out strong points of the parent and build on that. They are more likely to use these comments of mine than a suggestion. If I were to give a lot of suggestions, I doubt if they would be remembered. But also, our primary task is empowerment. I have learned that parents respond much better if an idea is coming from them rather than from me. For example, when figuring out a problem, I search for a way to say, "That's probably it; you figured it out." I might highlight something on a handout, or I might frame a suggestion as "Some parents have found it helps if . . . "

Beyond discussions with parents, home visitors can model effective guidance and discipline as they engage in activities with young children. In her interactions, Janice is a skillful model. She frequently anticipates problems and redirects children with alternative actions. If a child does misbehave, she positively redirects the child with a simple explanation. When a child is frustrated or angry, Janice verbalizes the child's feelings and thereby helps the child recognize and accept his or her feelings. Throughout her interactions, she frequently describes the child's actions and thereby affirms the child.

DIFFICULTIES AND DILEMMAS

Methods of Discipline

Parents most often raise their children in the manner in which they were parented as young children. Our society has a long history of spanking as the appropriate response to misbehavior: Spare the rod, and spoil the child. When home visitors work with parents who take for granted that spanking is their right and is the most appropriate form of discipline, the home visitor is confronted with a challenging task: "How can I empower these parents and at the same time inform them of alternative methods of discipline?" Many parents do not know methods other than spanking. Home visitors can suggest that parents can leave the grocery story rather than hit their misbehaving child. Parents can calmly tell their child that he will go to school in his pajamas if he won't get dressed because his dad cannot be late for work. First, the home visitor must find specific parenting that can be affirmed. Second, the home visitor must remember that parents are the ultimate decision makers, and the home visitor merely can share new information. As they chat with parents, home visitors can share some of the negative results of physical punishment. (See Table 3.)

Rewards

Home visitors often are challenged by those parents who rely on rewards to guide their young child. As with the topic of punishment, visitors can inform parents of the negative consequences of excessive use of rewards. They can emphasize that rewarding a child inhibits self-direction. Rewards can undermine a child's motivation: Children learn to act in order to gain a reward, rather than gain pleasure from activities and accomplishments in and of themselves. When a young child repeatedly receives rewards, the absence of reward can feel like punishment. In order for a reward to be an effective way to control childrens'

Table 3. Potential problems in the use of physical punishment

Children learn by observation. Parents are modeling aggression and violence as they physically punish their child.

When they are spanked, children can experience strong underlying messages such as rejection.

Physical punishment does not guide young children toward behavior their parent considers right.

Physical punishment works only as long as the parent is present.

The memory of being hit is remembered more than the misbehavior that triggered the physical punishment.

Physical punishment is no longer an effective control method once the child is an adolescent.

A child who behaves only in response to spanking is being set up for problems in school because many schools do not allow teachers to spank.

behavior, children must be unable to acquire the reward on their own; in other words, they must remain dependent on their parents. In reality, as children grow older, they become increasingly able get their own rewards, for example, earning their own money to go to the movies.

Praise

General evaluative praise responses can have similar negative effects on a young child. Repeated slogans such as "Good boy," "Good job," and "Nice girl" communicate to young children that they are pleasing the adult; thus, they may foster short-term obedience. These comments tell children nothing about themselves, except that they are pleasing the adult. These general praise statements do not contribute to a young child's self-reliance, self-direction, or self-control. One long-term goal is for children to recognize their accomplishments and be pleased with themselves. Home visitors can help parents learn how their specific, positive descriptions of their child's actions are not only rewarding but also are helping their child recognize his or her own accomplishments and feelings of self-worth. Such comments offer encouragement (e.g., "You can put on your shoes and socks without any help! I'm proud of you"). Young children thrive on their parents' recognition of their good behavior. It is a challenging task for home visitors to emphasize both the importance of parents' positive responses to their child's good behavior and at the same time help parents learn ways to be positive using dependence on external rewards or global praise, which fosters dependence.

CONCLUSION

This chapter began by describing how many young parents are ambivalent in directing, redirecting, and setting limits for their young children. Of all possible child-rearing topics, home visitors can be certain that parents will be eager to discuss guidance and discipline. At the same time, home visitors need to recognize that this is an area where parents feel vulnerable. Possibly, parents are disciplining in the manner in which they were parented as a young child. If so, a critique of their methods is a critique of their family heritage. If a child's behavior is out of control, the parent may see this misbehavior as a reflection of his or her own incompetence, and thus be very sensitive. Home visitors need to approach this topic with sensitivity and respect because if parents do not feel respected, they cannot hear and integrate the home visitor's information and guidance.

Table 4. Progression of child development and accompanying parental guidance and discipline

Developmental patterns	Guidance and discipline strategies
Birth–8 months	
Crying as response to discomfort	Positive home climate
Vocalizations, gestures, and body movements	Helping infant self-calm
	Emotional availability
Expressing different temperaments	Observation
	Contingent responsiveness
	Reciprocal communication
	Adapting own behavior to infant's temperament
9–17 months	
Mobility	Home safety precautions
Independence and autonomy	Anticipation of potential problems
Social referencing	Distraction; alternative suggestions
Exploration	Limit setting: Clear behavior expectations
Dependence	Consistency
Biting, hitting, hair pulling	
18–36 months	
Independence and autonomy; clinging dependency	Verbalization of child's feelings and intentions
Exploration	Time-out
Negativism	Giving limited choices
Temper tantrums	Natural and logical consequences
Simple role play	Assigning family responsibilities
Fear	Ignoring minor misbehavior
	Respecting and valuing child's perspective
3–5 years	
Verbal skills	Simple explanations accompanying limits
Cognitive skills	Assisting child in problem solving
Extended role-play	Providing experiences with peers
Aggression	Assisting child in conflict resolution
Whining, lying, swearing, stealing	
Problem solving	

Home visitors need to be knowledgeable of the different guidance and discipline strategies needed for different periods of the baby's and young child's development. Table 4 portrays the progression of baby development and accompanying parental guidance and discipline needed to promote this development. It is important to recognize that parenting behaviors continue to be needed as the baby develops. For example, during the baby's first 8 months, parents need to be emotionally available and responsive and to engage in reciprocal communication. These parenting behaviors remain important strategies in promoting toddlers' and young children's development.

The home visitor's task is indeed complex. First, he or she needs an understanding of babies', toddlers', and young children's development. Second, the home visitor needs knowledge of appropriate guidance and discipline strategies to promote this development. Third, the home visitor needs to be able to develop an accepting, nurturing relationship through which the home visitor can support, affirm, and guide young parents.

7

Communication and Language

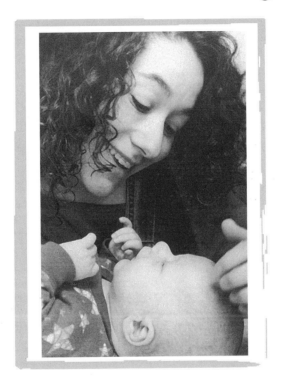

I noticed that people would name some object and then turn towards whatever it was that they had named. I watched them and understood that the sound they made when they wanted to indicate that particular thing was the name which they gave to it, and their actions clearly showed what they meant, for there is a kind of universal language, consisting of expressions of the face and eyes, gestures and tones of voice, which can show whether a person means to ask for something and get it, or refuse it and have nothing to do with it.

Saint Augustine (c. 396–397 A.D./1961, p. 29)

Parent educators know that communication and language are the foundation of a young child's development. The developmental process follows a continuum: Beginning at birth, babies communicate nonverbally with their caregivers; then as toddlers, they develop language; and as preschoolers, they tell stories. Very young babies communicate effectively with their parents, but true mutuality in which complex thoughts and ideas are exchanged awaits developmental changes during the first 3–4 years. This chapter gives a brief developmental overview of communication and language and discusses how home visitors can address these developmental areas in their work with young children and their parents.

COMMUNICATION AND LANGUAGE

Communication is people sending messages to each other. We communicate when we let people know what we want and what we are thinking. Communication can be expressed in many ways: a baby's cry or smile, a parent's encouragement, a singer's style, or a couple's dancing. Beginning at birth, babies learn to communicate when their parents feed, bathe, diaper, dress, and play with them. Language is a specific form of communication: a shared, rule-governed social system that is capable of symbolically representing thoughts. Language makes it possible for people to express and understand a wide variety of messages. For typically developing children, language emerges spontaneously in social settings as a means of communicating.[1]

Language originates from everyday interaction.[2] It can seem like a vocal tennis game, with all of the repetition of words and phrases by baby and parent. Language is not restricted to speech, for it also includes sign language and written words. Not all children learn to talk well, which suggests that there are some fragile elements in language acquisition. Although the ability to learn language is innate, learning language requires an emotional base in order for the baby and young child to have purpose and function to speak. Children need both expressive and receptive abilities to communicate well. *Expressive ability* is the ability to produce vocalizations, gestures, and/or speech, whereas *receptive ability* is the ability to receive and comprehend the communication signals of another. In addition to verbal communication, children learn to communicate via writing. *Emerging literacy* is the young child's understanding of the meaning of written words and increasing ability to use written words to understand and communicate with others.

Communication, language, and literacy focus on meaning. Young children experience meaning through social interaction, as illustrated in the following vignette with Tracy and Mia.

Mia (age 26 months) is placing shapes on a formboard. As she places a tri-angle onto the formboard, Mia says, "There we go."

Mia's mother, Tracy, repeats, "There we go."

Janice comments, "It's so good you repeat."

Tracy says, "I do it so much that Mia will continue repeating until I do, or she'll say, 'Mommy, do it.'"

Janice replies, "It gives her two pieces of feedback: She knows that she is being understood, and she is hearing the way the words are sup-posed to be pronounced without being corrected."

PRESPEECH: BIRTH TO 10 MONTHS

In the prelinguistic phase of language development, birth to 10 months, baby–caregiver interaction is the setting within which babies learn to express their needs, wants, and intentions.

Birth to 3 Months

The newborn is wired for interaction; that is, newborns have strong in-born preferences and behavior tendencies to interact with others. Ba-bies communicate from the first moments of life by giving positive and negative signals. From the beginning, newborns and parents repeti-tively interact. These interactions only take a second or two. The mother moves her eyes and mouth as her baby looks at her or cries. These re-petitive communication patterns are the building blocks of regulation of babies' emotion and behavior.[3]

Babies can see at birth but not in detail; they lack depth perception and the ability to focus both eyes on a single object. Newborns, how-ever, can turn toward a light and recognize contrast. They like circular shapes and prefer looking at the human face. Newborns see best when objects are 8–15 inches away, and they can recognize contrasts and see brightness, color, and motion. At age 2 months, babies can track hori-zontally, follow a moving person, and smile in response to a smiling face. At age 3 months, babies enjoy looking at their own hands and can reach for, grasp, and mouth objects. They also can recognize their par-ents and everyday caregivers.

Babies use nonverbal behavior or movements to produce their first stories or prenarratives. Establishing eye contact is an effective first step. Jervay-Pendergrass and Brown illustrate how a six-week-old tells a story.

Six-week-old Erin Nicole lay in her mother's arm drinking . . . from a bottle. Her bright eyes conveyed delight. Suddenly, however, her facial expression changed; she stopped sucking; and her darkening gaze went first toward her bottle, then away. Something happened! Erin Nicole's mother, momentarily puzzled, took the bottle, and then turned it upside down to make sure that the liquid was flowing. It was not.[4]

Erin Nicole's eye gaze and facial expressions communicated a narrative to her mother, who was able to learn what the difficulty was. Home visitors can help parents learn to read their babies' facial gestures and movements so that they can communicate effectively with them.

At birth, hearing acuity is greater than visual discrimination. Babies are born with a remarkable ability to hear differences between speech sounds. Their ability to hear sounds and voices is a central part of their language learning. Newborns produce sounds that primarily involve crying, but babies have several different cries that represent different kinds of discomfort.

Starting at about 2–3 months, babies show pleasure by cooing; by 3 months, they play with speech sounds, especially as they participate in vocal play with their parents. Play and having fun are key ingredients in baby and parent social interaction.[5] This playful interaction often involves imitation within routines such as dressing. It is the setting in which babies learn what to expect from their parents and in which the parents learn what to expect from their babies.[6] Within these first months, babies learn to read cues from their parents' facial expressions and speech. Similarly, parents learn to read their babies' cues from vocalizations, body movement, and facial expressions. Parents learn that different cries have different sounds and meaning, for example, a soft cry for attention, a steady rhythmic cry for hunger, and a loud shrieking cry for pain.

Beginning with their first visit, even a few weeks after the child's birth, home visitors can help parents understand the meaning of their babies' vocalizations. As parents and the home visitor discuss the baby's sounds, the home visitor can encourage parents to respond to their child's vocalizations, thus promoting the parent–baby vocal play that is crucial for the baby's development of language and communication. The following conversation between Janice and Karyn about Karyn's 6-week-old son, Greg, is illustrative.

Karyn: [Greg] makes moaning noises. Is that normal?

Janice: Yes. You'll enjoy listening to how his sounds change, changing into vowel sounds and then adding consonants. And he'll get responsive. That's something to watch for. You can make sounds, and he'll respond. He's not using words, but he'll understand taking turns. "I can say something, and she'll respond. She'll say something, and I'll respond." And smiling—waiting for you to respond—all that is reciprocal. Babies look for that. . . .Have you tried sticking out your tongue?

Karyn: Yes, and he does that.

Janice: That shows how responsive he is to you.

Janice responds to Karyn's question and in that response provides both developmental information and suggestions to foster Greg's optimal development. Janice's statements are simple and clearly stated within the context of a mother's concern. In these answers, Janice has begun to talk about the most important underpinning of communication and language—namely, the significance of spontaneous give-and-take of baby–mother exchanges.

Ages 4–10 Months

Between 4 and 6 months, babies connect vowel and consonant sounds together in a string of sounds called *babbling*.[7] Babies are so delighted with listening to themselves babble that they practice these vocalizations without an audience. On Janice's visit when Greg was 4 months old, Karyn told Janice that now Greg could say *uh, moo, boo,* but mostly *oh.* Within the context of this mother's spontaneous sharing, Janice affirmed Karyn and provided developmental information and suggestions.

Janice: He's now stringing vowels and consonants together. [To Greg] You're used to having someone talk to you. I can tell. [To Karyn] It's good to imitate his sounds. It's interesting about language development. Babies babble in their own language. You can hear the difference between babies in Japan and America: The sounds coming out are the sounds of their own language.

Karyn: Really!

Janice: He's working on the sounds he needs for English. [To Greg] You are a good talker, and that's the best news!

Janice explains to Karyn that babies change their sounds to sound like their parents' language. This pattern illustrates that hearing and discrimination come before making sounds.

During each visit, Janice and Karyn discuss the progress of Greg's language. When Greg was age 5½ months, Karyn told Janice that Greg now said "ma," but she knew it doesn't mean anything. Janice then explained, "You'll change that for him. As you respond differently to different sounds, he'll learn that some of his sounds do mean something." In the winter, Greg had a series of ear infections. Janice explained to Karyn that it's important to keep close track of Greg's hearing because this will have a major impact on his language. When Greg was age 7 months, Karyn reported to Janice:

Karyn: He doesn't say a lot, primarily "da, da, da."

Janice: That's a change from last time, and he is repeating syllables—that is a big step.

Karyn: Every once in a while he'll say "ba."

Janice: When you think about it, it makes sense, sounds in the front of his mouth: da, ba, ma. And now he is getting to the age when it is appropriate to begin saying what he is doing.

When Karyn reports Greg's pattern of making sounds, Janice provides developmental information to help Karyn understand her son's progress. Karyn started the conversation about language. Seeing Karyn's interest, Janice is able to give a simple suggestion that Karyn can begin describing what Greg is doing. When visiting babies and their parents, Janice helps parents to understand how they stimulate their babies' growing skill in language and communication.

Janice's comments to another mother of a 7-month-old illustrate how home visitors can help promote their child's language development.

Jene (age 7 months) begins babbling, and her mother, Natalie, imitates her sounds. Janice comments, "It's important to imitate her sounds like you just did. That is as rewarding to her as it is to you. What fun to get a response, and to feel connectedness."

Janice's comments affirm Natalie's spontaneous approach to her baby; at the same time, Janice provides an interpretation of the developmental importance of her interaction to Jene's babbling. When imitating, parents follow their baby's lead as they match their baby's behavioral style and tempo. This parental response often encourages the baby to respond, and turn-taking sequences begin. Turn-taking promotes the baby's developing communication skills.[8]

Natalie picks up Jene, who smiles at her. Natalie softly chuckles in response. Janice helps Natalie understand how important these brief spontaneous interactions are for the development of babbling. She says, "Mommy laughs right with you. It's important that you laugh with her. 'I smile. What is Mommy's reaction? I am hurt. What is mommy's reaction to this?'"

Once again, Janice helps this mother recognize how her responsiveness is developmentally very important to her baby.

At age 6 months, babies have 20/60 vision and may not acquire 20/20 vision until they are 7–9 months old. Most of the babies' visual skills now are nearly equal to those of an adult. By 7 months, babies can retrieve a partially hidden object, and by 8 months, they can find and retrieve hidden objects. Eight-month-olds can play Pat-a-cake with assistance, and at age 9 months, they need no assistance. When home visitors talk to parents about how their baby's vision is developing, they can help parents learn how, when, and what to provide for visual stimulation. They also can talk about signs of possible vision problems so that parents can obtain the earliest possible treatment. Most home visiting programs conduct an annual screening which includes the baby's vision.

A very large change takes place between 6 and 10 months. By 5–6 months, babies can make consonant sounds. Between 6 and 10 months, consonant–vowel sequences produce a kind of syllable, often repeated over and over. This rhythmic babbling often has a sentence-like flow. Now babies often sound like they are making a statement or even asking a question.

Between 8 and 10 months, babies can recognize and understand spoken words. Babies can understand individual words before they can talk verbally. This ability to understand is termed *receptive language* and lays the foundation for early speech. Babies can recognize that some of the sounds that they hear always are associated with the same experience, person, or object. They recognize their names and turn toward the speaker. They can understand and respond to "no" when their parents use it forcefully. They can copy nonspeech sounds such as tongue clicking or lip smacking.

By age 9 months, babies' vocalizations and gestures show that their actions are purposeful. Now the babies' sounds are no longer random; rather, their sounds are those of the baby's specific culture. Using gestures or combinations of gestures and sounds, they begin demanding or asking for things. In addition, babies play gesture games with parents, such as Pat-a-cake, and copycat games in which the baby imitates the parent's motor movement, such as the game So Big.

Within the framework of the babies' and parents' action and interaction, home visitors' conversations with parents help them to understand their child's development and their own pivotal role in this development. During the baby's first months, home visitors discuss how different cries signal different kinds of discomfort and how cooing signifies pleasure. Parents are encouraged to play sound and gesture games with their babies, to talk to their babies about the things they and their babies are doing, to read simple stories, and to recite rhymes as they hold their babies close to them. As the infant becomes older, home visitors point out the baby's rising and falling intonation, which is similar to the intonation of sentences, and is a sign that babies are paying attention to the speech around them. Home visitors also call attention to the baby's frequent use of pointing to ask for things (e.g., pointing to a desired cookie, pointing to the arm of a doll to show the parent it is broken). When babies are about 10 months old, home visitors make certain that babies can understand simple directions.

Janice's dialogue with Tracy illustrates how home visitors can help parents understand their child's developing language.

Maggie (age 10 months) makes repetitive sounds in a rhythmic manner as she crawls about the room. Janice asks Tracy, "Does she like to repeat sounds like that often?"

Tracy says, "Yes, it's one of her favorite activities."

As she makes rhythmic sounds, Maggie puts her hand to her mouth. Her mother begins singing softly, "One little, two little, three little Indians . . . ," and Janice sings with her.

Janice comments, "Rhythmic babbling is good for language development, for the muscles in the mouth. The occupational therapist who works with our staff says it's really beneficial to help develop those little muscles they need for talking. Your singing is a wonderful way of encouraging Maggie's exploring with sounds."

In her conversation with Tracy, Janice interprets the significance of Maggie's rhythmic babbling and Tracy's singing and, in so doing, she assists Tracy in understanding her baby's language development.

EMERGENCE OF FIRST WORDS
AND JARGON TALK: 10–15 MONTHS

Around ages 10–12 months, babies make giant strides in all developmental realms—movement, cognition, language, and social-emotional development. Now babies can understand many regularly used words, phrases, and simple directions, such as "Get the ball" and "Don't touch." Understanding language becomes an important underpinning for babies' emerging speech. Babies learn to wave bye-bye and can appropriately clap their hands and roll their hands in Pat-a-cake. They can vocalize along with music and acquire exclamatory speech such as "ouch," "pop," and "uh-oh." In order to resolve uncertainty, when moving toward a new desired goal, babies look back and forth from their desired goals to their parents and, in this way, gain encouragement from their parents. These gestures, termed *social referencing*, indicate significant emotional development.[9]

By age 12 months, infants acquire new skills in the ability to think symbolically, with accompanying gains in communication and language. Toddlers' early words are shaped by their social environments— by the objects and actions associated in their daily activities with important people in their lives. Toddlers differ in the way they develop their first vocabulary. Some toddlers use an expressive style: Their early words are linked to social relationships, such as "hi," "want," and "me." Other toddlers use a referential style: Their early words refer to objects, such as "keys," "ball," and "Mommy."[10]

Once babies reach the first-word milestone, vocabulary growth proceeds slowly. It usually takes 3–4 months for the toddler to add the next 10 words. The baby uses single words for many purposes: labeling people and objects (e.g., "Daddy," "ball"), requesting objects (e.g., "key"), requesting action (e.g., "go"), protesting (e.g., "no"), greetings (e.g., "hi"), and attention seeking (e.g., "see"). Parents delight in sharing with their home visitor their baby's gain in new words.

Karyn: Can you believe that Greg [age 14 months] already can say about 12 words!

Janice: Wonderful!

Karyn: And our favorite word is "trash." We took him to the botanical gardens, and he pointed out each of the trash cans for us. He also loves fans, but the sound he uses for fan isn't an English word, so we don't count that.

Janice: But it is a word if it's spontaneous, consistently used, and you know what it means.

As Karyn shares her son's growth in vocabulary, Janice shares in her delight. Janice also provides developmental information to help Karyn understand her son's developing language.

When beginning to learn words, toddlers continue to use gestures or their body to communicate, especially when they are frustrated. Janice explained this to Karyn.

Karyn says, "Greg does a little head banging. The doctor said to ignore it."
   "He wants to communicate," Janice explains, "but he sometimes can't and gets frustrated."

Karyn then describes how, during his bath, Greg became frustrated and began banging his head against the tub. She figured out he wanted to hold the shampoo bottle. Once she gave it to him, he was fine.

Janice says, "Your analysis is right on target. Babies this age are going to use their bodies when they don't have the words. When he learns to use his arms better, then he'll not use his head. It's like the developmental patterns we talked about when he was a very young baby—development progresses top–down and center–out."

Head banging can be very worrisome to new parents. Janice helps Karyn understand why her toddler might bang his head. Her explanation sparks Karyn's sharing of a recent example of Greg's head banging and her response. Janice not only affirms Karyn's response to her baby, but also provides developmental information so that Karyn could better understand Greg's behavior.

Between 13 and 15 months, toddlers frequently string sounds together as if they are carrying on a conversation. Child developmentalists term this gibberish *jargon talk*. Home visitors can encourage parents to take advantage of their child's jargon talk by responding to whatever they think their baby might be saying, for example, "I know you like the way Mommy is washing your back." This taking turns talking in pretend conversation helps toddlers learn the basics of conversation. Some children, especially those who begin to talk very early, skip this jargon phase. Others continue using jargon along with real words. Jargon usually disappears by 2½ years.

Another parenting strategy that home visitors can promote is termed *parallel talk*. Parallel talk refers to adults describing what the young child or caregiver is doing as the young child acts.

Janice places on the rug a cylinder filled with small film canisters. The cylinder's top has a hole in the center. She places film canisters on the rug next to the cylinder. Greg (age 14 months) puts a canister into the hole.

Janice says about the small canisters that Greg is manipulating, "In it goes . . . turning it around." Greg shakes the cylinder. Janice helps him remove the lid, and he dumps out all of the film canisters. Janice says, "Now it is empty, all gone." She then puts the top on the cylinder, and Greg again begins putting the small film canisters into the hole. Janice remarks, "In it goes. Into the can." As he puts the canisters into the can, Greg looks at his father and babbles, and Janice explains, "Telling Daddy all about it." Greg empties the cylinder once again. Janice repeats, "Now it's empty, all gone."

Janice then begins talking to Greg's mother and father, Karyn and Don. "When Greg is playing, just describe what he is doing. That helps him know you are interested in what he is doing. As you describe for him what he is doing, that is the way he learns words to think. It builds language, connected with experience. Sometimes it might seem kind of boring to you, but developmentally it is very helpful. I also was helping Greg build the concept 'empty' and linking it with 'all gone,' which he knows—building his vocabulary."

Janice is helping Karyn and Don understand that they can foster their child's understanding of language if they describe specifically what Greg is doing as he acts. Janice's comments are made as Greg plays and are stated as both developmental information and suggestion.

WORD COMBINATIONS: 16 MONTHS TO 2 YEARS

For ages 16–24 months, toddlers' understanding of new words and simple directions continues to expand. They rely less on gestures and more on words to understand meaning. They absorb new meanings as they experience new words in everyday conversational interactions. Now they can understand simple and short sentences. They continue to understand many more words than they can say. By 18 months, they can understand much of what is said to them even though they may only speak a few words. Toddlers now understand and enjoy rhymes and songs. They love picture books, can turn the pages, and begin labeling the pictures. They can recognize and point to several body parts.

At around 18 months, there is a rapid increase in vocabulary, which continues through the preschool years. The toddler's and young preschooler's language development follows a predictable sequence. Toddlers combine a word and a gesture, termed a *holophrase,* for example, saying "cookie" while grabbing mother's hand. Then, between 18 and 24 months, they begin using two-word sentences to express an idea, termed *telegraphic speech*—for example, "More milk" or "Daddy go." Toddlers use this telegraphic speech for many purposes: requests (e.g., "stop it"), responses to requests (e.g., "doll mine"), and commenting (e.g., "Daddy hat").

Parents have innumerable opportunities to reinforce and extend their toddler's telegraphic speech.

Janice has just arrived at the home of Shelly and her daughter, Erin (age 22 months). Erin says to Shelly, "Daddy, firehouse." Shelly affirms, "Yes, Daddy is working at the firehouse today." As Erin and Shelly complete the puzzle they had been doing before our arrival, Erin tells Janice, "Daddy cut lawn. Erin swing. Mommy push." Shelly says, "Yes, last night Daddy cut the lawn while Mommy pushed you in the swing."

Shelly has learned from Janice that when she extends Erin's speech she is both affirming Erin and promoting her language development. These expansions often remake Erin's sentences with correct grammar. Shelly's response tells Erin she is interested and encourages Erin to continue talking. During this home visit, Shelly describes to Janice a recent errand she and her daughter have taken. Shelly describes how Erin noticed and named the many items alongside the road as they were driving. She comments, "It's not often that we are in the car that we are not talking. I remember last year, you said how important it is to talk about what we are doing." Shelly has integrated Janice's information and now uses it in her everyday interactions with Erin.

Initially, young children's first ideas emerge as discrete items of thought without relation between the thoughts. The 2-year-old may say "bottle," "go outdoors," and so forth. Not until the third and fourth year does the child form bridges among his or her ideas and thoughts. Connections between a child's ideas depend on the caregiver's ability to understand and respond to the child's ideas.

Toddlers between 19 and 24 months love to label objects and begin to form categories of objects in their mind, for example "truck" for all large vehicles and "dog" for all small four-legged animals. Now, the child can understand simple phrases when visual cues are not present, for example, "Let's go get Daddy" or "Let's go in the kitchen to eat lunch." When parents read to their child, he or she can follow the sequences within simple stories.

Home visitors can help parents learn to tell stories with their toddlers. Kaon's help in telling Justin's story is illustrative:

Justin says, "Zoo."
Kaon responds, "Daddy took you to the zoo yesterday, didn't he?" Justin nods his head. "And what did you and Daddy ride?"
Justin says, "Train."
"You and Daddy rode the train," Kaon says, "and did you see the tigers?" Justin nods yes. "And what did the tiger say?" Justin roars and chuckles in delight.

Parents can tell stories about experiences they have had with their toddlers and in this manner promote their toddlers' thinking and language development. Similarly, they can ask questions. Research on conversations between mothers and toddlers indicates that mothers' asking questions and always responding to their children's speech promotes their children's language. When the adult and the child focus on something together, both the adult and child talk more often and engage in longer conversations. Kathryn Nelson and her colleagues have researched children's language.[11] A key finding of their research is that stories are central to the growth of young children's thought processes and language. Given the intertwining of language and cognitive development, storytelling strengthens young children's cognition.

Within the parents' taken-for-granted everyday child-rearing interactions, parents often may not notice their young child's developmental gains in language. As home visitors interact with a child and parent, they have many opportunities to call attention to the child's growth in language and thinking. When Mia (age 25 months) asks her mother for another drink, Janice comments, "Mia continues to express new concepts, doesn't she, like 'another.'" When, at age 30 months, Erin tells her mother that she can't find a toy, Janice tells Erin's mother, "Using the contraction 'I can't' is complex language use for a 2-year-old." As Erin and Mia talk to themselves as they play, Janice discusses with their mothers that as the children describe to themselves what they are doing or give themselves instructions, they are using their own language to guide their behavior. Parents' increased understanding of their children's progress inspires their understanding, appreciation, and motivation to stimulate their child's development further.

From the beginning, children's language is meant to communicate. At the same time, young children learn to use language in private monologues to make sense of their everyday world and to help them attend to the task they are performing. In other words, young children's private speech is a tool for guiding and regulating self and problem solving.[12] Research indicates that these monologues are vastly different from dialogues. The book, *Narratives from the Crib*, reported the results of a 2-year study of the monologues of Emily and her dialogues with parents before bed.[13] These monologues and dialogues were tape-recorded for 15 months, between ages 21 and 36 months. Most striking was the contrast between monologue and dialogue speech. Emily's monologues were much richer and more varied than were her dialogues with her parents. In her monologues, Emily told stories of daily events that had happened or that she had been told were going to happen. She also recreated stories and created imaginary happenings. Some of her monologues were problem solving, sorting out her everyday world, and often organized around daily events, such as eating, sleeping, and dressing. Nelson, the book's editor, notes that Emily's monologues primarily served "the evident purpose of representing and sorting out her experience, using language to make sense."[14]

The amount of time mothers and child care providers talk to their young children is strongly related to the children's vocabulary growth.[15] Early differences in vocabulary growth seem to be quite stable to school entry. Most adults speak in simpler sentences and simpler vocabulary to children than they do to other adults. This pattern has been termed *motherese*.[16] Typical characteristics of motherese include short and grammatically simple wording, concrete vocabulary, and repeated phrases. As home visitors observe how parents' child-rearing interactions are promoting their child's language, they help the parents recognize these patterns.

Tracy: Mia [age 23 months] started talking at such an early age.

Janice: So many words and sentences. Tracy, I really believe that one of the reasons her language is so good is that there is a pay off for her. When she asks, you respond. You are the best motivation. That's wonderful.

Mia: [As the adults chat, Mia goes to her mother] Tap, Mom?

Tracy: Hammer.

Mia: Go find it.

Tracy: I don't know where it is.

Janice: That is a perfect example. You don't correct her, but merely say the right word, "hammer."

Tracy: Yeah, she knows it goes tap, tap.

Janice explains that Tracy's comment is dependent on what her child says: "When she asks, you respond. You are the best motivation." Tracy's response stimulates her daughter to talk more. In her interpretation of this mother's actions, Janice helps Tracy understand how important she is in Mia's developing language.

Differences in timing of language development is normal.[17] Often girls' language develops earlier than boys'. Young children's speech contains immaturities typical of their age (e.g., errors in pronunciation), and this may be worrisome to parents. Parents frequently share these concerns with their home visitors. They may express a concern about what they call stuttering, but this is often normal dysfluency that almost half of all preschoolers experience as they learn language. Home visitors can help parents understand that their young child may sound as if he or she is stuttering because motor skills have not caught up with thinking skills. They can suggest that parents give their child time and that they try to ignore the stuttering until their child outgrows this normal dysfluency. As parents question and express concern about their young child's immature speech, Janice provides information and suggestions.

Shelly:	I try to get Erin [age 29 months] to say words the right way. Is that stressful for her?
Janice:	Immature articulation is typical of children Erin's age. Let her go. At this age, your goal is communication. If she gets hung up on how words are said, communication won't flow as easily.
Shelly:	Rob's [Erin's father's] family goes crazy and are always correcting her.
Janice:	If someone is hung up about that, try and get her to say it for Erin without correcting, without making her repeat. You don't want to slow her down.

In these conversations, parents learn what they can expect in typical child development and feel reassured that they are promoting their child's language. Home visitors can help parents pay attention to *what* their child is saying, not *how* they are saying it. They can help parents learn that their child learns to talk naturally, not from instruction.

LANGUAGE AND COMMUNICATION: 2–5 YEARS

As toddlers approach 2 years, their ability to understand speech increases significantly. They can understand 200–300 words, as well as simple directions with prepositions, for example, "Put the cookie on the table." Young children can understand and respond to simple questions, for example, "Where is your ball?" If they do not want to do something, they refuse by using "no." New words take on meaning only when attached to emotion and intentionality.

In the second or third year, the young child can deal not only with behavior but with ideas.

She begins to grasp that one thing can stand for another, that an image of something can represent the thing itself. This realization allows her to create an inner picture of her world. Moreover, these symbols can represent not only for her own intentions, wishes, and feelings but those of other people as well.[18]

Now, the young child has gone from an action mode to the symbolic mode. Children can make this transition because of changes in neurology as well as the richness of their affective experiences in relationships with significant adults. This shift requires a long-term involvement of parents who promote interaction, who join the child in conversation and pretend play, and who give the child sheer pleasure in being listened and responded to. Whereas younger babies communicate to get something, children this age enjoy communication for communication's sake.

Parents can help the young child learn to reflect. If a child says, "I want to go to the playground," the caregiver can respond, "What do you want to do at the playground?" If a child says she wants to go out in the rain, the caregiver can ask why and help the child understand what will happen if she goes outdoors in the rain. The ability to make connections among emotions and ideas evolves into the capacity to step back from an experience and reflect on one's own feelings.

Listening is an important skill in language learning. Good listening does not just emerge. As in talking, listening skills are learned gradually through everyday interactions with parents. Home visitors can help parents develop skills to help their energetic 2-year-olds maintain attention when listening. Respectful ways for parents to help their child learn to listen include the following:

- Keep your facial expression interesting.
- Vary your voice tone.
- Be sure to have your child's eye contact before speaking.
- Squat down to your child's eye level so your child can easily look at you as you speak.
- When necessary, distract your child to gain attention, for example, suddenly whisper, or sing a chant.

The children's neurological development continues toward more and more complexity. The increased complexity allows the young child to mentally recreate complex events observed. The child now has a memory that includes not only patterns of action, but also emotions, intentions, and desires. Children this age are developing a rich inner life from their experiences of warmth, dependency, exploration, assertiveness, curiosity, love, empathy, anger, and protest.

During their third year, children learn to understand most adult sentences. They can recognize and name themselves and other familiar people. They can understand and respond correctly to two related directions given at one time, for example, "Pick up your shoes, and put them in your room." They can understand descriptive words such as "big," "heavy," and "fast."

Now, young children can engage in extended simple conversations. By the time they are 2 ½ years old, they talk in three- and four-word sentences. They make simple requests, for example, "Open the door." They love singing songs such as Jingle Bells or Happy Birthday. Children this age have a speaking vocabulary of 300 or more words. As they explore their everyday world, their developing language supports their thinking about this world. Language not only reflects what the child is thinking; it also makes thinking possible.

Young children's simple sentences are creative, but these sentences also follow rules. Children begin using plurals, past tenses, and prepositions in a fairly predictable sequence. Similarly, initial use of questions and negatives follows a predictable progression: using "wh" words at the beginning of the sentence without the auxiliary verb, such as "When mommy come home," and omitting the auxiliary verb with a negative, such as "I no go." In addition, children express different meanings with the same sentence form. The young child may say "Daddy hat" to connote "This is Daddy's hat," which she has picked up off the floor. On another occasion, "Daddy hat" means "Daddy is putting my hat on me." Throughout the preschool years, vocabulary continues to increase, and more complex sentence forms are learned.

In conversation, children as young as 2 years old change the form of their language according to the person with whom they are talking. A toddler will say "Gimme" as he grabs another toddler's cookie, but to his mother, he might say "More juice." Research on children's conversations with younger children demonstrates that 3- to 5-year-olds are quite skilled at using simpler language when talking to younger children.[19] These changes for the purpose of communicating better give clear evidence that very young children can adapt to another person's level: They recognize that other viewpoints exist.[20]

Once young children begin forming sentences, parents can incorporate spontaneous, incidental conversations in their daily interactions within daily routines, such as eating meals together, getting ready for bed, or riding in the car. Conversation includes joint attention and joint activity. In conversation, young children learn both speaker and listener roles. Conversation also involves taking turns. Parent–child interactions in early infancy and games such as Peekaboo promote turn taking, which prepares the way for later conversation. Home visitors can assist parents in understanding the value of conversation for promoting language, thinking, communication, and emerging literacy. They can help parents understand that because conversation symbolizes ideas, thoughts, and feelings, which in turn are grounded in experience, conversation promotes young children's thinking and reading readiness. Furthermore, as young children engage in conversation they experience feelings of connectedness and shared enjoyment with their parents.

Around 3 years old, children love telling stories, and they tell stories that are based on their creative play. For example, they may make up a story about a building that they have constructed with blocks. Stories also often are about the children's everyday experience. Interestingly, the language young children use in stories often is more complex and more advanced than language used in other settings. For example, they show an understanding of hypothetical relationships such as "if, then" or "when x, then y." As young children tell stories about past experiences, they begin to understand the continuity of past and present time. Home visitors can encourage parents to tell stories with their children about experiences that they have shared.

Not all parents know how to have conversations with very young children. Home visitors have many opportunities to model and discuss how to have extended conversations. On Janice's first home visit after Christmas, Erin's (age 33 months) new kitchen set was in the living room.

> Janice says to Erin, "This must be your most special Christmas present."
>
> Erin affirms, "Yes." She then picks up a frying pan and brings it to Janice. "A pan."
>
> Janice repeats, "A frying pan."
>
> "And I have toy pots," Erin adds.
>
> Janice asks, "You have new toy pots?" Erin nods yes and then goes to Janice with her toy potholder glove on her hand. "Does that protect your hand?"
>
> Erin says, "No, it keeps my hand from getting hurt."
>
> Janice replies, "That's what we mean when we say 'protect.'"

As Erin speaks, Janice carefully listens. She asks Erin questions to encourage her to think and to continue talking. Janice has visited Erin and her parents since Erin's birth. Erin looks forward to Janice's visit, and usually, upon Janice's arrival, she is eager to tell Janice stories. In turn, Janice replies in a manner to extend Erin's comments. Over the months and years, Janice has had many opportunities to share with Shelly the value of talking with her child. In turn, Shelly often shares with Janice her conversations with Erin and her delight in Erin's creative verbal constructions.

When parents engage in pretend play with their young children, it provides wonderful opportunities for promoting young children's language.

> Cynthia puts toy pots and pans, dishes, and plastic food on the rug as she asks Willy's (age 21 months) mother, Sally, and grandmother, Donna, "Have you seen any pretend play?"
>
> Sally responds, "Not really."
>
> Donna clarifies, "He pretends to read and to talk on the phone."

Cynthia says, "Both are part of the beginning of pretend play. Pretend play would be a wonderful activity for you to do with Willy. Let's do a little today."

As Cynthia gives herself and Sally a cup, she hands Willy a pitcher as she says to him, "Please pour some coffee for Mom and me." As Willy pretends to pour, Cynthia says to Sally, "See, he is pretending. You will see that he imitates what you are doing." Cynthia and Willy pretend to cook eggs for breakfast. She asks him for some juice and holds out her plastic glass, which Willy pretends to fill. She asks him, "Would you like some juice?"

Willy replies, "Like juice." Cynthia pretends to pour juice for Willy.

Donna adds, "We used to think pretend play was harmful to children."

Cynthia responds, "It is important to use imagination. Pretending helps with Willy's language development. Pretend play also helps with Willy's thinking and planning. He'll begin to pretend experiences from his everyday life."

In this home visit, Cynthia has chosen a pretend-play activity, and she uses this activity to show Willy's mother and grandmother how they can promote Willy's language through playing with him. Sally thinks very concretely, so Cynthia provides developmental information directly related to the experiences that Sally is observing. On a subsequent visit, Sally described how she and Willy have enjoyed pretending to go to the grocery store and cook together.

Preschool children are active questioners. Questioning is an important way for young children to explore the world. When children ask questions based on what they see and wonder about, they have some control over their learning. They actively search for what they want to know. As they ask why, how, and what questions, they are creating connections among different parts of the symbolic self that has emerged. Through children's questions, adults can capture the inventiveness of children's thinking and explorations, for example, "Why do clouds move?" and "Why do churches have steeples?" Home visitors can encourage parents to be active listeners and respectful responders to their child's questions. Home visitors can model this active listening and can use a young child's question as an opportunity to extend their thinking, for example, "Why do you think the clouds move?"

COMMUNICATION AND LANGUAGE DIFFICULTIES

Speech, language, and communication disorders are the most common disabilities in early childhood. Some reports claim as many as 11% of kindergartners have such disorders.[21] Young children are at risk for communication and language difficulties because of biological conditions such as Down syndrome, low birth weight, anoxia, or otitis media, as well as environmental conditions such as poverty, caregiver–child interaction disturbances, or child maltreatment. Prelinguistic communication often can indicate strengths and problems in later language acquisition. Intervention prior to age 3 years can prevent later problems. There is a significant relationship between preschool communication and language disorders and later learning difficulties.

Research indicates strong relationships between communication and emotional and behavioral disorders.[22] For example, Carson, Klee, Perry, Muskina, and Donaghy compared a group of children with expressive language delays with typically developing children at the same age on measures of development and behavioral difficulties.[23] Scores on social and cognitive development measures for children with language delays were significantly lower than scores for typically developing children. Children with language delays exhibited more symptoms of anxiety and depression, withdrawal, sleep problems, and other behavior disturbances.

EMERGING LITERACY

Just as communication and language learning is a social activity, so, too, emerging literacy occurs within a social context—the everyday activities and interactions of parents and their babies and young children. This section uses the term *emerging literacy* to refer to the young child's awareness of print and its functions: Writing is used to express meaning, and the function of reading is to understand meaning. Studies indicate that reading is a process in which the reader draws on previously acquired learning in order to gain meaning from print.[24] Young children become ready for reading by experiencing print in books and on signs and by writing and drawing. Through these processes, they learn that written marks have meaning. Literacy development is gradual and is a part of the total communication process that includes listening, speaking, reading, and writing.[25]

The emotionally satisfying process of reading or reciting rhymes to babies while holding them close is the beginning of their emerging literacy. As babies develop, storybook reading remains a powerful influence on the language development of young children. In addition, the very young child learns that books are a source of enjoyment.

Young children have an easier time learning to read and write when they have experienced meaningful use of written language in their everyday lives. Early and frequent reading to young children can be one of the most important foundations in the growth of reading readiness. Emerging literacy includes listening to stories, reciting stories by memory, asking and answering questions about stories, scribbling, and using other forms of drawing and writing. Many pre-schoolers spontaneously learn to read environmental print, such as advertisement logos, cereal boxes, and tee shirts. When writing and drawing, young children experiment and developmentally proceed through exploratory motorial scribbling, purposeful scribbling that follows conventional writing patterns, mock writing, representational letters, inventive spelling, and finally, conventional spelling and writing forms. The process of learning to write is an early phase in learning to read.

When babies are a few months old, home visitors can integrate story reading with picture books into each visit. With parents who have low literacy, Cynthia's home visits have a central focus on story reading.

Cynthia gives Willy (age 22 months) a picture book of farm animals as she says to him, "Willy, I have a really neat book here." Willy immediately takes the book and sits next to Cynthia, with the book open between his legs. Cynthia shows Willy how their fingers fit through the holes in each picture in the book.

Willy's grandmother, Donna asks him, "How does the cow go?"

He replies, "Moo."

Willy then goes to Cynthia's bag as Cynthia asks him, "Do you think I have more books in here?"

Willy affirmatively replies, "Uh-huh." Cynthia gives him a second book, and he sits down and turns the pages to look at the pictures.

Cynthia says to Sally, "He's changed his approach. Remember how he used to take the book and back into your lap? Now he turns the pages alone. See what he has learned about books?"

Willy says, "Orange."

Cynthia remarks, "Did he say 'orange'?"

Sally explains, "He knows the color orange. He'll sit over there for the longest time." Sally points to the shelf filled with picture books in the next room. As the adults chat, Willy continues to look at his book. As he turns a page, Sally says, "Pumpkin," which he repeats.

Cynthia says, "When you say it, he repeats it back."

Willy says to Cynthia, "More."

Cynthia responds, "You give me your book, and I'll give you another." Willy gives Cynthia his book, and she gives him one that has pictures of trains. "See how he listens," Cynthia says to Sally. "I tell him to bring me a book, and he brings it to me. He understands."

Donna then tells Cynthia that the local store had a sale of children's books, and she bought six for Willy and three for his best friend. Cynthia responds, "You bought a good variety, with good concepts to work on. Willy is using his language a lot more. And he's trying to respond to all my questions. It's good to ask him questions and then wait for his response. I can tell you both talk to him and read to him a lot."

Cynthia has been working with Sally and her son, Willy, for about 18 months. Sally left school in the eighth grade. She married at a young age, and she and her husband live with Donna, her husband's mother. Given Cynthia's consistent pattern of modeling and encouraging conversation and story reading, early literacy is a central part of Willy's everyday life. Community libraries usually have a wide variety of high-quality children's books. These libraries can be a resource for parents who have low incomes to get storybooks for daily use at home.

Babies and young children love these daily story-reading rituals. Young toddlers like Willy often enjoy looking at books themselves and love hearing the same story over and over. Soon, they can repeat it themselves. Parents often express surprise at how quickly their toddlers learn the stories and enjoy pretending to read as they tell the stories to themselves while looking at a book. These activities help the children learn the importance of written symbols. One of the parents with whom Janice works described this process.

Evan loves the book you gave him. I read it over and over to him. His daddy reads it to him, and when nobody will read it to him, he just reads it himself—oh just the pictures, but he knows every animal!

Home visitors assist parents in understanding that their young child also needs numerous opportunities and time to draw and write and a caring adult to talk about these written expressions. Parents learn that having a variety of printed materials, along with a variety of paper and drawing and writing tools, available stimulates their young child's interest in reading and writing. Similarly, their child's understanding of the meaning of writing is enhanced if his or her everyday environment contains a great deal of written language, such as notes, recipes, grocery lists, newspapers and magazines, books, and so forth, and the child sees his or her parents frequently reading and writing.

Often, parents of preschoolers ask home visitors questions about stimulating their child's skill with the alphabet.

Shelly: I have another question about reciting the ABCs. Is Erin [age 34 months] too young to get her to write them? She already knows how to write her name.

Janice: Follow her lead on that. Don't push hard. She's now doing wonderful pictures. Creativity has to be expressed. When you tell her how to make letters, you are telling her how to do things correctly. . . .Let her write her scribbles, and then you can ask her what it says and write down what she tells you. If she is strictly confined to making letters, it doesn't give her the chance to write on her own and then say what it says, which is a significant step in her learning about the meaning of words. That is valuable creativity. She will do much more of it and is still getting her fine motor control.

As Janice works with Shelly, she helps Shelly understand developmentally appropriate writing and drawing activities and the importance of writing down what Erin says about her drawings.

Home visitors can help parents understand how they can promote emerging literacy throughout each day. Beyond reading stories to young children, families' everyday activities also can provide young children with meaningful experiences with written language. Young children see their parents write grocery lists and can suggest items to be included. As children make pictures and tell their parents about them, parents can write these dictations on their children's drawings. When another adult or older sibling reads these dictations on a child's drawings, the child experiences a powerful example of how meaningful letters are.

Home visitors can explain to parents that when they provide play experiences for their children, this play often fosters language, communication, and emerging literacy. For example, as children use words to substitute for objects, talk about what they are doing, and decide what roles they will play, this role-play fosters their language development. As the 3-year-old uses a long scarf tied around her waist to represent a skirt or uses a block for a telephone, she is using symbols—one thing is representing another. These early symbolic experiences help young children understand the symbolic nature of writing. Visitors also can encourage parents to provide toys with which children can refine their small muscle coordination and eye–hand coordination, for example, puzzles, snap-together toys, crayons, and pencils. Developing this coordination assists the child's later ability to discriminate letters and words.

DIFFICULTIES AND DILEMMAS

In many parts of our country, home visitors work with families whose first language is not the same as their own. The United States is a multicultural society. The preceding vignettes have depicted mainstream language usage. In reality, home visitors work with a wide diversity of families with different ethnicities, family interaction patterns, and accompanying language usage. In their work with families, home visitors often need to adapt their process to address unique family patterns. For example, home visitors working in Hispanic cultures must be skilled in communicating in Spanish.

Another dilemma for home visitors can be working in homes in which parents do not spontaneous speak with their babies and young children and who themselves have minimal literacy. Home visitors learn to adapt their approach to address these patterns. Incorporating high-interest story reading into each visit provides parents with opportunities to see their young child's delight in this activity.

During the visit, home visitors can encourage parents to use picture books with their child and can leave several high-interest books for the parents to use between visits. As mentioned in a previous chapter Cynthia uses books often in home visits.

> Books are wonderful because what you can do with a book is to settle down. It settles you in the hope of a quiet time, even in families that seem chaotic. Often, when I have more than one child, I'll start with a book. I'll read it to set the tone for the visit, and usually it is a pleasant time for both the kids and their parents. With my one family that has about 18 children and two mothers living in one home, everyone joins me when I read. One of the things I do for these chaotic families is have things I always do, provide them with some routine. In the time that I am in their home, I try to bring some order. In that living room, for 10 minutes, if I can get everyone around me listening to that book I brought, that to me is powerful, and maybe they will pick up a book and sit down to read to their child and bring order.

A year after this conversation with Cynthia, I interviewed Marquisha, one of the mothers Cynthia had been discussing. Marquisha has six children between ages 3 and 21 years old. Marquisha described to me how her work with Cynthia has changed her parenting.

Marquisha: I think working with Cynthia has made a lot of difference in the way I'm parenting my kids. Now I read to them. I used to read to them just every now and then. If they didn't seem interested, I would just go ahead and put the book down. Working with Cynthia, she helped me to get them interested, to wanting to sit them on my lap and do it the fun way. I'll stop and let them try to read, you know, because they be wanting to read, too. So I stop and let them read a little. They don't know what they be reading, but they know the pictures real good. They learn the pictures, and it helps them learn the story.

Carol: How often do you read to them?

Marquisha: Now I read to them at least once a week. Before, I read to them probably once a year.

Marquisha's oldest three children are between 18 and 21 years old. She described how her work with Cynthia has helped her relationship with her older children.

Marquisha: I can deal with my two older sons better now than what I could. I used to tell Cynthia all the time, "I cannot deal with my sons the way I can with my older daughter because she listens to me more." I just couldn't deal with my boys the way I wanted to.

Carol: What do you think made the difference in terms of how you relate to the boys now as opposed to 4 years ago?

Marquisha: Talking—just talking. I used to talk to them, but mostly discipline talk, and listening to Cynthia talk to my oldest ones helped me understand what I was doing wrong. Now I just sit down and talk to them, or joke with them, something like that.

Carol: Like a good friend.

Marquisha: Yeah. I was doing that with my daughter, but I didn't realize that they needed it, too.

Marquisha was the fourth of nine children growing up in a single-parent family with a low income. Previously, she had three brief experiences in general equivalency diploma (GED) programs. Her oldest brother is her only sibling with a high school diploma, which he received when in the military service. She is very proud that her two oldest children have their GED certificates, and the third is working on it. When I asked Marquisha what are her dreams for her 3-year-old daughter when her daughter turns 20, Marquisha replied as follows.

My dream for Tarina is to see her walk across the stage, which I have never gotten a chance to see. I want to see Tarina walk across the stage, do the things my oldest daughter or I didn't do. But most of all I would like to see her be able to make up her mind to want to do the . . . educational, everything . . . on her own. You know, because in case if I'm not here, I would like to know that my daughter, that I left enough in her mind to motivate her to want to do everything that she want to do, you know, to succeed in life.

CONCLUSION

In their work together, parents and home visitors can interweave communication and language development into their discussions and activities. Parents enjoy sharing their young child's gains in language and appreciate having a friend with whom to share concerns. As home visitors observe and interact with child and parent, they listen, affirm, sup-

Table 1.   Developmental progression of language, communication and emerging literacy and accompanying parenting practices to promote this developmental progression

Developmental patterns	Parenting practices
Birth–3 months	
Watches parents' facial expressions change	Changes facial expressions and voice during interactions with infant
Hears differences in sound and speech	Imitates infant's facial gestures and sounds
Has several different cries	
Makes eye contact with parent when parent is talking	Begins and responds to give-and-take vocal play with infant
Shows pleasure by smiling and cooing	Sings and talks softly during routine activities
4–10 months	
Uses vowels and consonants to babble	Repeats infant's sounds
Laughs and smiles in response to familiar persons	Describes what infant and self are doing during routine caregiving
Babbles rhythmically with sentence-like flow	Plays simple gesture games with infant (e.g., hide and seek with towel)
Playfully imitates nonspeech sounds (e.g., lip smacking, tongue licking)	Reads simple picture books to infant
Understands regularly used individual words	Sings simple rhymes and songs to infant
Recognizes name and turns toward speaker	Encourages infant to respond to his or her name
Plays gesture games such as Pat-a-cake	
Uses gesturing to ask for things	
Understands and responds to "no"	
Enjoys simple picture books	
11–15 months	
Understands simple and short sentences	Continues give-and-take vocal play with infant
Understands simple directions	
Enjoys picture books and simple story books	Identifies infant's body parts, and encourages infant to point to them
Imitates gestures like Peekaboo	Sings simple rhymes, fingerplays, and stories
Waves bye-bye	
Says first words	Reads simple storybooks
Checks to see if parent is looking before exploring on own	Talks about what infant and self are doing
Strings sounds together in gibberish (jargon talk)	Responds to infant's jargon talk as if infant is speaking words

Developmental patterns	Parenting practices
16–24 months	
Has increased understanding of words, simple sentences, and simple directions	Plays simple interactive games like "chase me" and telephone talk
Follows simple directions	Has simple give-and-take conversations with toddler during routine care
Enjoys and understands simple songs, rhymes, and fingerplays	Extends toddler's speech
Uses "no" to protest	Sings simple rhymes, fingerplays, and songs
Uses "hi" and "bye" greetings	Reads familiar storybooks
Uses jargon speech with state, command, and questioning inflections	Has toddler's eye contact before speaking
Uses jargon speech with state, command, and questioning inflections	Actively listens and responds to toddler's talk
Refers to self by name	Encourages and participates in pretend-play with toddler
Names pictures, objects, body parts	
Says two-word sentences	
Makes simple verbal request (e.g., "More milk")	
2–5 years	
Understands and responds to questions	Has extended daily conversations with child
Asks questions, especially about what child sees and experiences	Actively listens and responds to child's talk
Has large increase in vocabulary	Responds to child's questions and invites child to continue talking
Speaks in full sentences	Asks child open-ended questions
Tells simple stories of immediate experiences	Encourages and participates in pretend-play with child
Enjoys songs, fingerplays, and storybooks	Sings songs and fingerplays with child
Enjoys using language in pretend-play alone and with others	Reads storybooks with child
Has extended give-and-take conversation	Provides a variety of writing implementations and paper for the child to use for drawing and writing
Enjoys drawing and writing	
Recognizes frequently seen words such as fast-food advertising	

port, and reassure parents. They provide suggestions, information, and interpretations within the context of their observations, their activities, or parent concerns. As parents become more aware of what to expect of their child, they become more observant of their child's emerging communication and language. With knowledge and understanding, they can promote their young child's communication and language through their child rearing and provision of developmentally appropriate activities and experiences. Table 1 summarizes the developmental progression of language, communication, and emerging literacy and accompanying parenting strategies that can promote this developmental progression.

8

Play, Learning, and Development

Child, how happy you are sitting in the dust, playing with a broken twig all the morning!

I smile at your play with that little bit of a broken twig.

I am busy with my accounts, adding up figures by the hour.

Perhaps you glance at me and think, "What a stupid game to spoil your morning with!"

Child, I have forgotten the art of being absorbed in sticks and mud-pies.

I seek out costly playthings, and gather lumps of gold and silver.

With whatever you find you create your glad games. I spend both my time and my strength over things I can never obtain.

In my frail canoe I struggle to cross the sea of desire, and forget that I too am playing a game.

Rabindranath Tagore (1958, p. 48)

Play is babies' and young children's primary task and is the main way they learn and develop. Babies and young children love to play because play is intrinsically motivating; that is, children play for the enjoyment and satisfaction of the activity itself. Through play, babies and young children understand and gain mastery of their bodies and master their experiences in their everyday world. Unlike adults, who leave their everyday work so they can play for relaxation, young children's primary way of learning is through play; play is children's work.[1]

Babies and young children are by nature curious. In their play, they explore spontaneously. First, they examine their own bodies and then the surrounding world, people, and things. Young children learn through imaginative and active play, which involves people and objects. As they play, they create and make something entirely new. After she described the many steps a young child needs to understand how the telephone works, Margaret Mead observed, "This is the creative moment. The child, like Alexander Graham Bell, has just created the telephone—suddenly, from all the little bits and pieces of slowly understood meanings, the idea of telephone has come up."[2] To explore, to understand, to master, to create—these are some of the central meanings and purposes of babies' and young children's play. According to Piaget, young children gain knowledge and understanding through their actions; that is, each child individually constructs knowledge through action.[3]

Play occurs within babies' and young children's everyday relationships with their parents. Parents make a difference in their child's play in how they interact with their child not only during play times but also within everyday routines such as diapering and feeding. The quality of parent–child interaction is pivotal to the baby's and young child's ability to play. The discussion of the role of the parent and of additional meanings and purposes of play in this chapter unfolds as it tracks the developmental progression of play and the home visitor's role in promoting optimal child and parent development.

Essential features of play include exploration, imitation, repetition, and sensory experiences with a variety of materials and experiences. This chapter discusses each of these features and illustrates them with vignettes.

BODY PLAY: BIRTH TO 12 MONTHS

As their parents playfully interact with them, babies experience approval, connectedness, and shared delight. These interactions often are very brief; for example, a mother moves her eyes and mouth when her baby smiles, or she responds with sounds when her baby coos.[4] These

1- and 2-second exchanges are the beginning of everyday patterns of playful parent–baby exchanges. Even when they do not interact directly with their baby, parents are a stabilizing presence. That is, they give their baby a sense of security: "If I need something, my parent is available." As babies develop, effective parents need to continue being active play partners and to tune into their child's interests, ideas, and feelings. Often communication is achieved through gestures; for example, a parent quickly lifts the baby's arms up to indicate surprise.

Babies' Abilities to Interact Socially

Babies are born with biological readiness for social interaction. From the start, babies are able to begin and end social interactions with others. *Affect*, the term for feeling and emotion in developmental literature, is central to the babies' experiences of relating to others. From their earliest moments, babies' experiences are governed by what is pleasurable and not pleasurable. Newborns can begin and end interactions with others; for example, a newborn can focus on mother's face as she speaks or turn away from mother.

Young infants playfully explore their bodies, beginning with their mouth and hand, and their parents' bodies. A great deal of parents' interaction with their very young baby entails meeting the baby's biological needs: dressing, bathing, feeding, and diapering. During these tasks, skilled parents take time to talk, smile, and cuddle with their baby. As they care for their baby, they can play with him or her by touching, holding, imitating, and playing simple Peekaboo games.[5] A variety of parent behaviors seem to be instinctive.[6] For example, parents in virtually all cultures give exaggerated hellos and imitate their baby's facial and vocal expressions.

Newborns prefer to look at people's faces. By age 8 weeks, they smile, give more direct eye contact, vocalize socially, and are more responsive. They experience longer periods of wakefulness. Active interest in toys and people increases with its accompanying learning and development. For example, when a father approaches his 3-month-old daughter lying in her crib, she smiles, kicks her legs, and moves her arms excitedly. Mutual involvement and attention between baby and parent are essential for the baby's healthy development. These shared interactions provide shared pleasure and a sense of connectedness. Parents and babies communicate by facial and vocal expressions, and the quality of movement, such as how the parent picks up, cuddles, or soothes the baby. Parents and their babies develop patterns of interaction that become highly ritualized; that is, parents approach their baby, respond to their baby's awakening, and smile and coo in a similar manner each day.[7] These playful routines are the same for every parent and baby, yet the particular interactions are unique. In time, parents learn how much activity and which forms of sensation and communication their baby enjoys most, whether it be sound, touch, sight, or movement.

Exploratory Play

During the first year, babies' play is primarily exploratory because they investigate their bodies, objects in their everyday environment, and other people. As they play, babies discover what does and doesn't fit into their mouth and what does and does not feel good. Babies first learn to bring objects to their mouth and explore them with their lips and tongue, and shortly after that, they bring objects before their eyes to look at. With increased motor coordination, they turn small objects about, bang them, and continue to put them in their mouth. Moving, touching, and making sounds are basic components of these play activities. Parents' responses are crucial to the development of these exploratory actions. Parents have the opportunity to encourage babies' play through positive responses; for example, parents can imitate their baby's facial expression or body movements.

Not all new parents understand that beginning at birth, their baby is capable of actively relating to them and that their interactions with their baby are essential for the baby's optimal development. Thus, it helps when home visitors share this developmental information and make certain that parents understand the developmental significance of their active involvement with their baby. Home visitors can model, praise, and encourage these daily patterns of interaction, as in the following vignette.

> Karyn holds her son, Greg (age 4 months), as Janice softly speaks to him. "You're looking right at me. You have very good eye contact." Greg begins cooing, and Janice repeats the same sounds. Janice continues, "You're used to having someone talk to you. I can tell. You are a good talker, and that's the best news! I'd never get any work done if I were your mommy."

This is Janice's second home visit since Greg's birth, and she can observe that this mother and baby interact frequently. As she relates to Greg, Janice both models imitation of Greg's vocalizations and affirms Karyn's talking with her son. Karyn asks Janice what would be good toys to buy for Greg.

> Janice replies, "Small things that he can get a hold of—the kinds of things I see you have. Bright things—things he can get a grasp of—things that

make different kinds of sounds—a variety of different kinds of stimulation to explore. Small kitchen items such as measuring spoons are as good as toys." Janice then moves the ring rattle out of Greg's view, but Greg does not follow it. She says, "Notice how out-of-sight still is out-of-mind." She then puts a rattle in Greg's hand, and he puts it in his mouth. Janice tells Karyn, "That's babies' primary way of exploring. It makes sense, for feeding is so important, and the mouth is the first body part that really works for them."

   Janice stresses that exploration is the primary way young babies play. Within the context of Karyn's questions and Greg's actions, Janice gives developmental information: Greg is too young to track objects when they are removed from his sight, and his mouth is his primary tool for exploration. Karyn tells Janice that each night Greg's daddy has extended play with him for a couple hours and that lots of this play involves moving him about and pretend wrestling.

   Janice says, "For Greg, that's real learning, playing together with Dad, and it's great that dads have different play patterns than moms have."

   Janice returns to Karyn's home when Greg is 5, 7, and 9 months old. Each time, she brings a tub of small assorted kitchen items and toys. As the months progress, Greg continues to make developmental strides. As she and Karyn observe Greg's play, Janice identifies new areas of learning and development. Within the context of Greg's play, she chats with Karyn and gives her developmental information, suggestions, and interpretations of the meaning of Greg's actions.

   Greg (age 5½ months) is seated on the rug while supported by his mother. Janice puts a tub of baby toys next to Greg, who looks into the tub.

Janice: It's important for you to watch to see how he reacts to containers. As he gets older and has eye–hand coordination, he'll immediately dump [the tub].

Karyn: He used just to look at his toys; now he grabs.

Janice: Isn't that neat! It's hard for him to reach in [the tub]. I'm allowing a little bit of frustration, for frustration now helps him deal with frustration later. [Janice gives Greg a rattle, and he puts it in his mouth.] Straight to my mouth. Greg, that's what we want to see. It doesn't mean he's hungry, but exploring.

Karyn: His favorite toys are the small ones.

Janice: Developmentally, it's very predictable what kinds of toys a baby likes. He likes small things because he can hold them and can get them to his mouth.

Janice spontaneously expresses delight in Greg's actions and helps Karyn see meaning in her son's play. Janice explains that Greg's eye–hand coordination will soon allow him to dump things. As she and Karyn watch Greg's approach to the tub of toys, Janice helps Karyn anticipate steps in her son's development and understand the important role of motor development in her son's play. As she observed when Greg was 4 months, Janice again calls attention to how Greg is learning by exploring objects with his mouth. After she leaves Karyn and Greg, Janice writes down what Greg did with these toys so that she can identify changes during the next visit.

Six weeks later, Janice returns to visit Karyn and Greg. She helps Karyn recognize and understand her son's new gains in motor development, and she affirms Karyn's keen observation of her son.

> Janice gives Greg (age 7 months) a tub of toys, and he reaches in the tub and pulls out a toy. She says, "Last time, he didn't get anything from the tub; now he's getting his hand right in there. That's really good." Greg tips the tub, and all of the small baby toys fall out. Janice says, "He's much more secure in the sitting position."
> Karyn affirms, "The last week or so."
> "Your mommy watches close and knows when you've changed," Janice tells Greg. "He handles that toy very well," she tells Karyn. "Notice he takes it in both hands and has lots more freedom with his fingers. He turns it over and turns it back." Greg drops a toy, which rolls to his side, and he turns to find it. Janice says, "You lost it! And he remembered where it was. That's very significant. He dropped and looked for it. This is something to watch for." Greg rolls over on his stomach and reaches for a toy. "You can see how motor development and curiosity are hooked together."

As Greg explores the small objects in the tub, Janice helps his mother see how his actions point to gains in his fine motor skill. Janice links curiosity with motor development to help Karyn understand the manner in which her baby learns through play.

Janice returns when Greg is 9 months old and once again gives him a tub of toys. As Greg plays with the toys, Janice again comments on Greg's actions and how these actions point to Greg's developmental progress.

Karyn: [Greg's] Dad has asked me to ask you what can he do with Greg besides playing and reading books.

Janice: That is really the way a baby learns, in all areas of development. For Greg, that's real learning—playing together. Suggest [to Greg's dad] that he mimic what Greg is doing. Mimicking extends his attention span, affirms his play, and invites him to continue [the play].

Karyn: He plays with Greg about 3 hours each night.

Janice's first home visit with Karyn and her husband, Joe, was during Karyn's third trimester of pregnancy. Joe clearly is very immersed in parenting. Joe also wants to use this home visit program to assist in his parenting. In turn, Janice acknowledges that Joe is a central player in his son's development and gives a helpful suggestion.

In play, babies actively explore the effect they have on objects in their environment. Around 5 months, the baby bangs, drops, and throws objects; this cause-and-effect play makes and organizes the many connections between neurons in the baby's brain. Repetition helps babies learn in an organized way because the same connected nerve pathways in the brain are used over and over. The baby's repeated actions become permanent brain cell connections in the baby's brain and always are available for use.

Beginning at around age 6 months, parents and their babies enjoy playing motion sequence games, such as Pat-a-cake and Peekaboo. Parents often invent new games as their baby gets older. For example, when a baby hits two blocks together, the parent makes a popping sound as she claps, and the sequence is repeated. Beyond the shared enjoyment and connectedness the baby feels in these experiences, these patterned games anticipate the young child's learning to take turns.

Babies usually begin to creep and crawl around 8–10 months of age. Movement offers new ways to explore, and suddenly the baby is cruising or crawling in every possible direction. Travel offers babies new perspectives and new discoveries within their everyday world. They can explore all sides of the living room couch and, with practice, can learn to pull themselves to an upright position. This is the time for home visitors to remind parents that they need to make certain they have child-proofed their home (e.g., put gates on open stairways, put safety latches on low kitchen cupboards that contain cleaning supplies, put plugs on electrical outlets).

PARALLEL PLAY: 12–30 MONTHS

The most striking characteristics of toddlers are their interest in movement, their curiosity, and their strong attempts to be independent. At first, simply walking and climbing are totally absorbing. With movement, toddlers realize they can be independent of their parents. Yet, toddlers have strong security needs of attachment and accompanying feelings of dependence. As they explore their newly found skills in movement and their newly found upright world, toddlers struggle with the ambivalent feelings of independence and dependence. Much of toddlers' play centers around this ambivalence because it is at the core of the toddlers' striving to form their own identity. When toddlers begin games of give-and-take with their parents, it is as if toddlers are exploring what is "yours" and "mine." As they become more sure-footed and begin to run, toddlers explore whether the parent knows where they are in hide-and-seek games.

> Nancy (age 24 months) and Ricky (age 22 months) have been playing in the sandbox, and Ricky's mother, Jean, is seated with them. The children leave the sandbox and run into the garage to hide from Jean. Jean goes to a large tree near the sandbox and calls out, "Where are you? Nancy and Ricky, where are you?" The children laugh gleefully and look out at Jean.
>
> Jean tells the children, "You can't find me?" Jean then walks behind the tree, and the children run toward her. As the children come to the tree, Jean walks around the tree so they can't catch her, as she says playfully, "Where's Nancy and Ricky? Where are you?" The children giggle as they run around the tree with Jean. When they catch her, they race to the garage as they say, "We hide!"

In their spirited hide-and-seek play with Jean, these toddlers are experimenting with their strong feelings of separation and independence. In these games, toddlers also learn turn taking and cooperation.

Movement, Simple Pretend Play, and Continued Exploration

Playing alone, toddlers enjoy dumping and filling containers repeatedly, or piling blocks and knocking them down. These seemingly endless play sequences give the toddler practice in fine motor skill development and eye–hand coordination. In this exploratory play, they are learning about cause and effect: how their own actions have an effect on objects. As they initiate play with toddlers, home visitors provide everyday play experiences and use these experiences to assist parents in understanding the meaning of their toddler's play.

> As she shakes the cans, Cynthia places two cans, each containing plastic poker chips, on the rug next to Cassandra (age 14 months). As she gives the cans to Cassandra, Cynthia says to Cassandra's mother, Samantha, "Let's see how she plays with these toys."

Cassandra throws a chip, and Cynthia says, "She found a new way to play with this."

Samantha puts a chip into the can as she says to her daughter, "Can you do that?"

Cynthia asks, "Mommy made a different sound, didn't she?" Samantha then helps her daughter by supporting one can as Cassandra dumps the chips from one can into the other. Cynthia says, "That's neat, the way you put your hand under hers, and allow her to do it, but help her a little bit." Cassandra puts her hand in the can and shakes the chips. Cynthia says, "Now we're making some new noises."

As she dumps out the chips, Samantha says to her daughter, "Let's try it again." Cassandra puts the chips into the can and looks up to her mother, who nods affirmatively. Cassandra continues the task.

Cynthia says, "Just with a look, you gave her encouragement to do it. You gave her that go-ahead to do it, and she did. See how this finger is coming together with that?" Cynthia demonstrates the pincer grasp with her hand. "That is called the pincer grasp," she says. "The pincer grasp is developing and is really important because you have to have the pincer to be able to write. Another thing, this is good for using her eyes with her hands. In order to pick them up and put them back in the can, she is building eye–hand coordination, which is another skill needed in writing."

As Cynthia talks to Samantha, Cassandra dumps and fills the cans with chips. Cynthia explains, "Lots of time we think this is fun, and we don't recognize it's learning too."

As she watches Samantha assist Cassandra in this new task, Cynthia tells Samantha the importance of what her toddler is doing. She also helps this mother understand how this play fosters Cassandra's pincer grasping and eye–hand coordination—basic skills needed for writing.

At age 12 or 13 months, toddlers typically begin to say their first words. As they gain increased skill in speaking and understanding language, toddlers love naming games. Just as they love to explore their hands and feet as young babies, toddlers love to name the parts of their bodies, pictures in books, and objects in the world about them. This is a period in which toddlers love spontaneous, impromptu games with adults, especially when their bodies are involved.

Jeff (age 18 months) brings the basket of plastic Easter eggs to Sally, his family child care provider. Jeff puts a half-egg on Sally's nose as he says, "Nose."

Sally responds, "On my nose! I'm going to put a purple on Jeff's nose."

> As Sally holds the egg over Jeff's nose, he laughs gleefully. Sally then
> says to Jeff, "And I can make it a hat," as she puts her half-egg on top of
> her head. Sally puts two more half-eggs on her head as she says, "Three
> hats." The hats fall off, and Jeff laughs.
>
> Jeff then puts a half egg on his head as he says, "Hat."

Jeff has initiated a simple pretend game, and Sally is skilled in entering into his play as a play partner. Sally imitates Jeff, who in turn imitates Sally, a common play pattern among young toddlers and adults. Sally encourages and extends Jeff's language—"on my nose"—and takes the play one step further as she puts the egg on her head. In his play, Jeff practices his language and experiences shared enjoyment and connectedness.

Often, an adult can support and extend a toddler's play without being a full participant. In the next vignette, the family child care provider, Jean, is folding clothes in the room where three toddlers, Nancy, Ricky, and Jason, play.

> Nancy (age 19 months) pretends she's getting on a school bus and rides
> past Jean as she says, "Beep, beep."
>
> Jean asks her, "Where is your horn?" Nancy then makes the sound
> of the school bus horn. Jean adds, "Picking up the kids from school? Got
> any kids?"
>
> Nancy says, "Pick up."
>
> Jean affirms, "Picking up the kids." Jean reaches down to the floor,
> picks up a play person, and hands it to Nancy as she says, "Here is one."
>
> Jason (age 28 months) then sees another play person across the room
> and gives it to Nancy as he says, "Here's another people. I find one."
>
> Nancy then rides off as she says, "Go school."

Jean skillfully provides guidance to these young children's play. Nancy has taken the lead, and Jean enters into the play and extends it. Like Sally, Jean promotes Nancy's language as she repeats and extends Nancy's spontaneous comments.

In their work with parents, home visitors can help parents understand that play is the means by which their toddler is learning, and that they can significantly influence their toddlers' play and accompanying learning and development. When parents understand the meaning of their toddlers' playful explorations, independent actions, and negative responses, they will not see these actions as mere signs of the so-called "terrible twos." Instead, they can strive to provide an environment that encourages developmental progress within clear limits. Shelly and Rob, who have had a home visitor since Shelly's third trimester, illustrate this type of learning.

Shelly: It helps to know that these things are going to occur, and what Erin [age 26 months] is doing now is good. This is good that she wants to play with the knobs on the stereo. You know, most people would just say "No" and slap their children's hands, but we knew that was just a way for Erin to investigate things. Instead of correcting her for something that wasn't really going to hurt, we let her do it, and she doesn't play with anybody's knobs when we go to their house. We didn't have to stand there and yell "No" at her because we knew that these things were going to pass and that this was good for her to investigate things. Just those little things that we knew ahead of time, I think, helped us prepare for each step.

Rob: Yes, knowing what's coming up when you see her do something. Knowing, "Hey, this is a stage that this child is going through." And you should pick up on it and work with it rather than put her on a leash!

Toddlers seem to spend most of their day experimenting. They climb into cupboards, twirl to music, scatter their food about their high chair tray, and splash vigorously in the bathtub. Objects in their everyday world become toys, and their approach to experiences is playful during dressing, eating, and bathing, as well during "legitimate" playtimes. Home visitors can assist parents in understanding that their toddler's exploration, experimentation, and testing is their way of knowing and learning. In order to assist parents in seeing and understanding this dominant approach of their toddlers, Janice often brings a "curiosity bag" filled with "beautiful junk" for the toddler to explore.

Janice puts a cloth toy bag on the floor as she says to Mia (age 24 months), "Here is a whole bag for you to explore." Mia sits down and begins to pull items out of the bag as Janice comments to Tracy, "This is basically a bag of junk. It's important to continue to give Mia opportunity to explore and to be creative."

Tracy replies, "When Mia is downstairs with me as I am doing laundry, she is always finding things—anything that is new and different—and she's always asking me, 'What's this, Mommy?'"

Mia has pulled a toy plastic milk bottle out of the bag and begins to shake it. Janice helps Mia begin to open the lid, and Mia finishes opening it and dumps a play person on the floor. She then goes into the bag and removes a car as she says, "Ooooh, car." She puts the play person in the car as Janice comments, "Sure, he can ride in the car."

Mia replies, "I too big."

Tracy affirms, "You are too big to ride in that car."

In each of her visits, Janice emphasizes that Mia is learning as she actively explores her everyday environment. Bringing a bag of everyday "beautiful junk" for Mia to explore helps Tracy observe how her toddler is learning, as well as how to take the toddler's point of view toward objects in her home. As Mia investigates the items, Janice assists Mia, and her actions are powerful models for Mia's mother, Tracy.

> As Mia looks through the bag, Janice comments to Tracy, "Children all have their own style with this bag. Mia is so precise—looking and deciding what she wants. When you think about how her exploring has changed—initially everything went right into her mouth. Now, she explores things with her hands and eyes."
>
> Mia takes a small cosmetic bag but has difficulty unzipping it. Her mother says, "Bring it here, and I'll hold it so that you can unzip it." Mia does as her mother has directed. Janice comments, "It is good that you structure the job so that she could do it herself." Mia unzips the bag and removes a small play figure that she identifies as Cookie Monster.

As Tracy assists her daughter, Janice affirms the manner in which Tracy enables Mia to succeed at a task. With this bag of beautiful junk, Janice models encouragement and uses Mia's play to help Tracy understand how her toddler's curiosity, exploration, and learning are progressing.

Quality of the Home Environment

Janice also helps parents understand that the quality of their home environment makes a difference in their child's play. Homes environments that promote play include

- A relaxed atmosphere with minimal adult directives
- Adequate and safe space
- A variety of objects and toys that promote active participation and creative construction

As Janice brings everyday objects and simple toys to use during her home visits, she helps parents to understand the values of play activities that invite construction, foster eye–hand and fine motor coordination, and encourage imagination and self-expression. Some toys encourage early role-play, for example, dishes, pots, pans, dolls, blocks, and toy trucks.

Role Play

Toddlers not only begin to speak in words but begin pretend role play—two actions that give evidence that toddlers can think symbolically; that is, they can represent actions, objects, and people in their minds. In pretend play, toddlers begin to use meanings other than those usually attached to objects or actions. For example, they pretend to feed a toy dog with a cup or pretend a stick is a horse to ride. Usually, the role play centers around simple themes of everyday home experiences.[8] In these role-play sequences, toddlers replay their familial activities, explore their related feelings and reactions to those experiences, and gain mastery of these feelings. For example, as they rigorously wash their doll's hair, they are gaining control of their own feelings when their hair has been washed. Home visitors can help parents understand the value of this role playing. During their home visits, they can initiate role-play activities with the toddler and encourage parents to join in the play.

Home visitor Winneta has placed a checkered tablecloth and assorted plastic dishes, utensils, and plastic food on the tablecloth. She suggests to Jayla (age 25 months) that they have a picnic.

Jayla brings a plastic hamburger in a bun to Winneta, who says, "Let me have a bite. Mmmmm . . . real good." Jayla then brings her mother, Sheryll, a hamburger, and sits next to her as she pretends to eat a hot dog and potato chips. Sheryll tells Winneta that just as Jayla is pretending to eat her plastic hot dog without a bun, she also eats real hot dogs without a bun.

Winneta explains, "She brings her real world into her pretend play. That's very important. Pretend play helps understanding of her real world."

"My husband plays this with Jayla in her kitchen in her bedroom," Sheryll adds.

Winneta exclaims, "Super!"

Sheryll describes how, the previous night, Jayla took the dustpan and broom and pretended to sweep and then put everything away.

Winneta says, "I encourage you to let her continue to role play. By acting out her experiences, she better understands her feelings about these experiences."

Winneta, Sheryll, and Jayla enjoy an extended role-play sequence during Winneta's home visit. Winneta affirms the role-play that Jayla's dad has with her. Winneta helps Sheryll understand that role playing is an important way for Jayla to understand her everyday experiences.

Jayla's dad works a split-shift work schedule and often is part of Winneta's home visit. In fact, he came home at the end of this visit and read a story to his daughter. Winneta is very committed to involving both parents in her home visits. She explained to me her perspective as follows.

I feel each (parent) has their own style. And they both bring equally important techniques. Maybe Dad might be real interactive and playful and like to do motor things, whereas Mom might like to do more calming things, reading things. I try to tell parents they are both equally important, and their roles are very important even though they are different.

Encouraging Parents to Play with Their Child

An important goal in home visiting is to encourage parents to be partners in play with their young child. As parents enter into their child's play, their child feels affirmed, feels a sense of connectedness, and has an invitation to express him- or herself imaginatively and constructively in play.[9] Many home visitors can play skillfully with a very young child and have constructive conversations with the parents about the child's development and their parenting. Commitment and ability to stimulate parents as play partners is a skill that home visitors develop with experience and professional guidance. The following home visit illustrates this process.

During her home visit, Janice places a box of about 50 small, colored wooden blocks on the floor next to Erin (age 30 months). Once the blocks are on the rug, Erin immediately begins to build a simple structure. Janice then makes the same structure as she says to Erin's mother, Shelly, "One thing I really like to do with blocks is to follow the child's lead."

Shelly asks, "You mean imitate?" Janice nods yes.

Erin then lines up several blocks and puts a second row on top of the first. Janice duplicates the pattern as she says to Erin, "That's a neat building you're making. Is mine like yours?"

Erin smiles and says, "Yeah."

Janice then suggests, "Let's let Mommy build. You build, and Mommy can copy." As Erin begins a new block structure, her mother duplicates it while saying, "Look at mine! It's just like yours." Erin smiles and claps enthusiastically. As Erin and her mother continue building, Janice comments, "One of the nice things with blocks [is] it gives you the opportunity to follow her lead. Children need to be the leader."

Shelly reflects, "I never thought about that. I don't imitate her, even when we color together."

Janice first demonstrated how Erin likes it when Janice mirrors her block building. Shelly then followed Janice's model and clearly enjoyed following her child's lead—the first time she had tried this technique. Several days after this home visit, Janice talked about her rationale for involving parents in play activities with their toddler.

It's a goal for almost every visit, to involve the parent and child together in a play activity. And I definitely involve the parent more when the child is a little older than when there is a baby. I ordinarily initiate the activity with the child, so that I have the opportunity for modeling, because I think modeling is an important aspect of what we do. But then I always like to say, "Give Mom a turn," or "Let's let Mom do it now," or, "We can all do it together." The easy ones are the blocks where the parent mirrors what the child has built. It's also pretty easy to do with dishes. Playdough is really easy. If you have an activity built around the child exploring something, then you have the parent back off. But even then, I will try to reserve time for a book for Mom and her child to read together.

When parents learn to be active participants in their child's play, home visitors can talk about the specific meaning and purpose of this type of parent involvement for their child's development. For example, a parent's active involvement as a play partner gives his child a sense of connectedness and self-worth. The parent is promoting his child's ability to maintain focus—an essential readiness skill for school success.

COOPERATIVE PLAY: 30 MONTHS TO 5 YEARS

During the preschool years, children achieve mastery in play, especially in imaginative constructions and dramatic role-play. Play often stimulates problem solving, for example, figuring out, "How can I prevent the wall of my block building from falling down?"[10] In role-play, children ages 30 months to 5 years can represent real and imagined experiences (e.g., pretending to build an apartment building, to be a Halloween witch, or to put out a fire). In this role-play, children express themselves creatively and feel a sense of power because they are in control of their play. In these experiences, children develop increased sense of competence and self-worth. As home visitors provide these types of play activities for young children, they can help parents understand the developmental meaning and purpose of these experiences.

As young children act out roles, their play is process oriented; that is, the activity is pleasurable in and of itself, and no product is needed. For children 30 months to 4 years old, play themes remain mostly about family situations; however, role-play sequences become more elaborate and extended. Pretend roles are fluid and shifting: One minute, the child is a sister; the next, a mother. These young children have not firmly separated reality and pretend; thus, they dislike being the baby. Because a major task for young children is still separation and identity formation, it is not surprising they most often choose to be the mother.

Most noticeable in preschoolers' play is their delight and complete absorption in role-play sequences. In the following vignette, Amos has had his third birthday the previous week and has started a child care program this week. He engages in a brief role-play sequence in the housekeeping area with his teacher, Dana.

> Amos sets the table and calls to Dana, who is seated at the nearby puzzle table, "Dana, I'll give you some coffee and lunch."
>
> Dana comes to the table as she says, "Good, I like that a lot," and she pretends to eat.
>
> Amos tells Dana, "Now I'll make you a birthday cake." He takes a plate to Dana, and they sing "Happy Birthday." Then, Amos hands Dana a physician's kit as he says, "Now this is your present."
>
> Clapping her hands, Dana replies, "Oh, I love it. Thank you. But now I have to go home. Thanks for the party."
>
> Amos turns to Dana as he tells her, "Now it's closing time."
>
> He takes Dana's hand as Dana asks him, "Now where are we going?"
>
> Amos replies, "We're going home."
>
> Dana questions, "Are you my daddy?"
>
> Amos replies, very seriously, "Yes, and we need to use the seat belts so it won't be dangerous." Amos and Dana leave the housekeeping area hand in hand.

Amos's teacher, Dana, is a full participant in his play, and this role gives Amos respect and a feeling of connectedness. Amos is the leader of the play sequence, and as leader, he is able to act out his everyday world at home and have it affirmed by Dana. Within the play, Amos is able to be creative and enters into conversation that is grounded in his reality. On this, his first week away from home, Amos is able to experience that this is an environment where adults understand and value him.

Development of Abstract Thinking and Pretend Play

Role play of 4- and 5-year-olds no longer centers around family themes. Children this age have a firmer sense of self, can better separate fantasy and reality, and thus know they are pretending. Ghost, monster, and other themes of aggression often surface and give children experiences in mastering their fears. Because children can now use one object to represent another in pretend play, this representation indicates that the child's thinking is moving from the concrete to the abstract.[11] As their representation and language skills develop, children's need for realistic objects to communicate symbolic meaning is lessened. With age and pretend-play experience, children learn to represent imagined objects without using anything concrete. Two role-play sequences of children this age in the playground of their day care center illustrate this point.

Four boys are pretending that the large horizontal concrete pipe is a haunted house. Dan sits on top of the west opening, and J.T. sits on the opposite side. Rob pretends to be a bat and continually makes bat movements with his arms as he runs from one end of the pipe to the other. Chris whispers the magic word to J.T. before he enters the pipe. Chris is a ghost who makes "whoooo" sounds as he moves about the pipe.

Jana and Treeva have just entered the playground and run to the day care sign, which they pretend is a restaurant sign. Jana asks, "What do you want?"

Treeva replies, "An ice cream cone."

Jana pretends to give one to Treeva, who leaves the area as she pretends to lick the cone. Annie comes to the area, and Jana asks, "What do you want?"

Annie answers, "Cherry pie."

Jana responds, "We have only chocolate pie. Do you want some?" Annie nods yes, and Jana pretends to give her some. As Annie leaves, Jana says to herself, "All the children are gone now." Before leaving the area, she calls out loudly, "Anybody want food or drinks?"

As older preschoolers gain greater understanding of both happenings at home and in their community, adults can provide props for children to role-play sequences beyond their homes. Family child care provider, Jean, has structured a post office for her son, Ricky (age 4 years, 1 month), and another child, Nancy (age 4 years, 3 months).

Jean has made a mailbox from a cardboard box, and she has small church offering envelopes for the children to use for their letters. She suggests to Ricky and Nancy that they each get a crayon or a pen and paper and write a letter. As she puts the envelopes on the table in front of the mailbox, Jean says, "Here's our envelopes. Whenever you get your letter done, you can get an envelope. You need to get a big storybook to write on."

Jean gives the children small pieces of paper to write on as she says, "I'm not the one who will write. I am the post officer. I have some stamps [stickers]. Who are you going to write to?"

Ricky replies, "To George Washington."

Nancy replies, "To my mommy [who is in the hospital]."

Ricky brings his mother his paper and asks her to write "George Washington" on it, which she does. Nancy then asks her to write her mother's name, which Jean does. Both children then make pictures on their papers, fold them carefully, get envelopes, and carefully put their papers into the envelopes. Ricky tells his mother, "I'm folding mine good." Jean nods yes. Both Ricky and Nancy then get stamps and put them on their envelopes, and then they place the envelopes inside the box.

Jean has sequenced the tasks clearly for these young children. Each child writes three letters, and, as they make pictures, they tell Jean about the pictures and to whom they are writing. The children remain focused on the task for approximately 30 minutes. This simple role-play activity offers opportunities for fine motor and eye–hand coordination, creativity, and oral communication. Together, Nancy and Ricky experience shared enjoyment in the task. Smilansky's research demonstrated how children's dramatic role play with other children helps them learn to communicate and take the perspective of others.[12] Role play demands joint decision making, such as choosing which child will play which role and what the action will be. In this play, children experience how other children act out being a mother, father, or sibling.

In a home visiting program for families with young children, home visitors need to initiate brief play sequences during each of their visits. Janice explained how she tries to help parents understand the meaning of learning and play.

One way I think our program is important is pointing out to parents that play is important, that when the child is young and trying to do a puzzle or shape sorter, I can talk about that as a way of learning and problem solving for the young child, and I compare a task to how things are going to be different when she gets a little older. Yes, we look at it as maybe just play, but it is very serious problem solving for the child, and I try and help the parent to appreciate that when a child is experimenting and exploring, when they are trying a multitude of the things that they do, when they are pretending, doing private talk, it isn't just silly little play activities. It is something that is very valuable in the total scope of preparing them for the different kind of learning that will happen when they get to the first or sixth grade, and they are sitting at a desk in the classroom. It is all learning, and it just is a different method. It is both serious and necessary for the young child.

Play sequences in Janice's home visit (described next) illustrate how she stimulates children's learning through play. As the children play, Janice helps parents understand that, in their play, these young children are learning about relationships. When Erin is 33 months old, Janice provides a matching game for her.

Janice places an assortment of vehicles and play people on the rug. Then, she makes a long line, about 4 feet long, with red yarn on the living room rug. She suggests to Erin, "Let's see if we can make a parade." She puts a fire truck with a toy fire officer on the front end of the yarn as she asks, "Can you find another fire truck?"

Erin searches and exclaims gleefully, "I found one!"

There is a play fire officer in the truck, and Janice says, "Can you find a [fire officer] to match?"

Erin finds the fire officer as she says, "I found one!" Erin then picks up a racecar driver doll, and puts it into the car. Following Janice's suggestions, she finds the second racecar, puts it behind the first, and puts a driver in each seat.

Janice asks, "Which car will go next?"

Erin picks up the police car and puts it behind the racecars. "How about this one?" she asks.

Janice says, "A police car. How about a driver for it?"

Erin replies, "I can't find one."

"I think she's behind the horse," Janice says. Erin finds it. Janice tells Erin's parents, Rob and Shelly, "That's a great way to reinforce prepositions, such as 'behind,' as she is playing." Erin continues making the parade for several more minutes. As Erin plays, she and Janice talk about "next to," "in front of" and other spatial relationships. Janice explains to Rob and Shelly that matching is an important premath relationship skill.

When Erin's toy parade is completed, Janice initiates a second matching game. This game uses pictures of Sesame Street characters. As they play, Janice explains to Rob and Shelly that first young children learn with concrete objects, then with objects and pictures, and then with pictures alone. The fourth step is letters and numbers. After this visit, Janice described her intent in introducing these games.

My goal is to help parents see that their child is able to pick out things that are alike, to see similarities and differences, and most young children do it spontaneously as they explore. I want parents to be aware of that. It helps me talk about the young child's intellectual development. And I guess what's fun about it is that a child does it spontaneously, and the parent begins to notice what they are doing . . .and the second game gives me a chance to help parents see the difference between using objects, touching and manipulating them, to see things that are alike as opposed to using pictures that are alike. This progression I don't get to with every child, but Erin is very quick. It depends on how they handle the objects in the first game as to whether I pull out the cards.

Toys and Materials to Promote Creative Self-Expression

When parents provide pencils, pens, crayons, felt markers, paint, chalk, playdough, and clay, they invite young children to explore and express themselves creatively.[13] Before age 3, children's drawings primarily consist of scribbling. The activity initially is a motor activity. As children begin to think symbolically and develop motor control and eye–hand coordination, they make representative drawings. When children draw and make something uniquely their own, they feel good about themselves and feel a sense of competency. These also are tools that provide enjoyable releasing experiences.

Construction toys such as blocks and snap-together toys invite another rich medium for imaginative construction. During the preschool years, these constructions become representational (e.g., building a house, a train, or a school). Whether the activity includes creative art or manipulative toys, the child experiences initiative and mastery. There are no rules to follow. In this play, children also learn about spatial relations, such as size, shape, and form.

DIFFICULTIES AND DILEMMAS

Some family patterns trigger difficulties for the home visitor eager to assist parents in understanding how young children learn through their everyday play. One of the most common activities of family life—television viewing habits—can be one of the most problematic for the home visitor. Other challenging family patterns that a home visitor comes into contact with include those parents 1) who did not themselves learn how to play as children, 2) whose primary focus is assisting their young child's academic learning, and 3) whose style is very directive.

Television Viewing Habits

Increasingly, television and videotape viewing is taking the place of young children's active learning through play. It is important for home visitors to be knowledgeable about the impact of television and videotapes on children's play. Dilemmas include both the excessive amount of television watching and the content of children's commercial television programming. As of 1990, children 3–6 years of age watched an average of 4–6 hours of television each day; for children from low-income families, the hours increased by 50%.[14]

Today, the mass media is omnipresent in homes with young children. The average family has 2–3 televisions. In many homes, the television is on during all waking hours. Even when the young child does not pay consistent attention to the television, young children most often have "background media." Anderson and Evans see four possible impacts of background media on the amount and quality of young children's play and interaction.[15]

- Background media may distract the child and disrupt the child's on-going play.
- Very young children often talk to themselves as they play. Re-searches see this private verbalization as the foundation for the de-velopment of verbal thought and internalized self-control. Back-ground language from a television or radio may interfere with this private verbalization during play.
- Background media can enhance the child's attention during play. It may be possible for children to learn to selectively focus their at-tention on their ongoing play and not be open to other stimulation.
- Background media for the very young child may be the foreground for the child's parents, and the parents' focus on television may hinder parent–child interaction.

With deregulation of children's television programs in 1984, for the first time television shows and toys could be marketed together. The dominant theme of both television programming, videotapes, and the related toys is violence.[16] Within 3 years after Reagan's deregulation, the profits from war toys (e.g., Power Rangers) were enormous.[17] By the 1990s, the American Psychological Association (APA) had gathered thousands of studies and had concluded that there was a direct link between the aggression in young children and the violence viewed on television. The APA concluded that television and videotape violence could account for 10% of children's aggressive behavior.[18] Preschool teachers report that, in much of their play, children imitate television characters, resulting in marked increases in violence and aggression and changes in peer interaction.

Young children always have played war games, but in the past, children chose the content of the war play and used their imagination as they invented pretend heroes and enemies. Currently, children's war games most often are imitations of television programming and videotapes. When watching television dominates how children play, creatively acting out one's everyday experience and gaining mastery over these experiences often is no longer the dominant theme in chil-dren's play.

Home visitors have many opportunities to talk about the impact of television in their conversations with parents. They can help parents understand the meaning and purpose of active learning through play, and the distinction between imitating television characters and cre-atively role-playing. They can suggest that parents watch television with their children. As they watch, parents can discuss with their chil-dren what is being viewed or can choose to monitor the programming as being developmentally inappropriate. Unfortunately, parents frequently use television and videotapes as babysitters, that is, as times in which their child is occupied and the parents can do something else in a different part of their home.

In addition to television, the Internet is also a concern for children because it allows children unsupervised access to many inappropriate aspects of American culture, such as graphic news reports and pornography. Video games for both the computer and television, which are often violent, are particularly popular with boys. Studies confirm that boys who played violent video games showed more aggressive thoughts and behavior than boys who did not.[19] Parents now are faced with the challenge of not only monitoring television but also the computer.

In spite of these cautions about television and computer use, home visitors need to be respectful of family patterns. In many American homes, the television is on during a large part of the day; in some homes, it is on all of the time. Thus, this topic demands sensitivity and skill. The home visitor should maintain respect for family patterns and, at the same time, responsibly provide developmental information regarding the impact of television on young children's development. For example, as a child engages in role play with her home visitor, the home visitor can explain to the child's parents that this type of role-play decreases as the time that young children spend watching violent cartoons on television increases. Use of television remains the parents' decision; however, the home visitor can provide appropriate information regarding its developmental impact.

Parents Who Have Difficulty Playing with Their Children

A further challenge that home visitors may face involves parents who do not enjoy or know how to play with their baby or young child. When home visitors are working with parents of very young children, it is important for the home visitors to see whether those parents enjoy playing with their baby or toddler. A parent who does not enjoy playing probably does not know how to play. Parents who were reared in a troubled family may not have extensive joyful childhood play to draw on in their relations with their baby. Spontaneity and having fun is not a given among all parents. Janice spoke with me about this issue as follows.

Janice: Some mothers really don't know how to play with their baby. They know how to do something for their baby, like change her diapers. They may know how to make their baby laugh. They know how to ask their baby questions, but they just don't seem to catch on as to how to play. It's as if they need to be taught. Once a parent is able to enjoy observing her baby and home visitor play together, then the home visitor can go a step further and invite the parent to join in the play.

    This one mom I'm thinking about—I'd invite her on the floor. She'd come down sometimes, but not all the time. We'd do something, and then she'd be back up on her chair, just being apart from, instead of a part of, the activity. That is something that for me as a home visitor has evolved over time, in that I'm better at encouraging parents now than I used to be. But there are just some parents that just won't do it.

Carol: Do you think there are different reasons for the resistance, such as some parents are afraid they'll look silly or others might be too shy?

Janice: I think there's a certain amount of distance that some parents always may have with their children, and they see their role as a directive role and a caretaker, as opposed to a playmate. Getting them to even see themselves as a playmate and then to act that out is real difficult. It's as if they fear they are losing ground in maintaining the respect they want. They fear the authority and response will somehow get muffled.

For these parents, home visitors first have to engage in play with the baby or young child and help the parent see and understand the meaning of this play. Once a trusting relationship between home visitor and parent is firmly established, then the home visitor can encourage the parent to enter into the play. It is through concrete experiences in play with their child that parents can begin to enjoy and value these experiences and then provide them for their child on their own.

Parents Who Do Not Appreciate the Learning Value of Play

In addition to not enjoying play with their children, many young parents may not value play as the primary way their young child learns. Rather, many are eager for their child to excel in more structured learning. One parent remarked that she was more interested that her child "learn his 1–2–3s and ABCs." In fact, 2-, 3-, and 4-year-olds can learn to recognize numbers and letters; however, this is rote learning, without understanding of the meaning of the symbols. For example, many 3-year-olds can count to ten and recognize numerals, but they often do not grasp the concept of what *three* actually means or the concepts of *more than* or *less than*. At first, parents may see their home visitor as their child's teacher, and their expectations are for this person to focus on helping their child's academic learning.

    One of home visitors' first challenges is to help these parents to understand the developmental importance of play as their child's primary means of learning. To do this, the home visitor can use a similar strategy that was discussed for parents who do not know how to play. Once home visitors have established a trusting relationship with parents, they can encourage the parents to enter into play with their child. It is be important to have open-ended materials such as a tub of birdseed or beans or playdough for sensory play. These activities have no rules. The parent can experience her child's delight, and the home visitor can explain the developmental value of the play.

Directive Parents

Some parents are very directive in their interactions with their young child. These parents often are anxious that their child perform in the right manner. Given this concern, it is very difficult for these parents to allow their babies or young children to first explore a toy in their own way. When a home visitor recognizes that a parent has such parenting patterns, he or she needs to explain concretely the meaning and purpose of exploration. As the baby or young child does explore, the home visitor can tell the parent specifically what the child is learning. Janice discussed how she has learned to relate to directive parents during home visits.

> When I first began doing home visits, I had a low-functioning mother. Each visit, she would take over the toy and play with it herself. Then, she would show her child every step of what she was supposed to do. I didn't feel secure enough to jump in and say anything.
>
> Then, I physically got in the mom's way. And then, I would put the toy far away from the mom, and then engage her in conversation so that her baby first could explore. With experience I got better with that—better with talking with the mom who could not let her child explore. When I saw that a mom was overly directive, I started my chatter immediately. I would put a toy down and say, "Let's watch and see what she does with this."

Janice described how she blocked this mother's intrusion into her baby's play. Her blocking is successful only because she is skilled in establishing a relationship with this mother—a relationship that allows, over time, the mother to hear and integrate new developmental information and parenting strategies.

> Directive moms get real embarrassed when their child turns a toy upside down. They are quick to say to the child, "No, that's not the way you're supposed to play with it." Again, I'll be quick to add, "Isn't it wonderful that she wants to explore it from every angle?" I'll also make comments that babies could teach manufacturers many ways that toys could be used.

Janice ties her comments to the baby's actions. Her comments both affirm the baby and parent and inform the parent. The parent's learning is experiential; it is grounded in his or her baby's actions, which Janice observes and interprets.

> I'll tell moms another reason why it is helpful for a child to explore a toy is that it'll extend the time a child plays with a toy, and moms always need time. And finally, I'll suggest that in exploring, the child will get more mileage out of the toy. Then, when a directive mom will let her baby explore, even for half a minute, I'll say, "It's so great the way you let Joey explore!" If an older sibling is part of the visit, I'll talk to the mom through the sibling, as I tell him to let his sister first explore.

Janice does not specifically address parents' directive style. Rather, in each visit, she provides play experiences in which she can affirm the baby's exploratory learning, interpret the developmental purpose of this learning, and affirm both baby and parent. Janice is secure in the knowledge that once she has established a trusting relationship with a parent, over time, the parent will learn experientially to value his or her baby's manner of learning.

Strategies suggested previously can assist home visitors when they work with difficult family situations. At the same time, there are situations in which a family rejects all of a home visitor's approaches. In other words, in some situations, with some families, home visiting just does not work. Given these potential difficulties, home visiting programs need to provide home visitors with a working climate of support and guidance from peers, mentors, and administrators.

CONCLUSION

From infancy through early childhood, play remains the primary method of learning and development. Parents of babies and young children can provide a relaxed atmosphere, space, and interactions that promote and encourage play, learning, and development. In turn, home visitors can help parents develop understanding and skill to promote their baby's and young child's learning and development through play.

This chapter described how babies and young children by nature are curious and spontaneously explore and experiment as they relate to people and to objects. The activity of exploring and experimenting is pleasurable in and of itself; it is intrinsically motivating. As babies and young children explore and experiment, they are playing, which is their primary way of learning. In their play with objects and with people, they often are creative and express themselves imaginatively.

This chapter illustrated and discussed the many ways that home visitors can promote parents' understanding and skill in promoting their child's play. They provide developmental information so that parents can understand the meaning and purposes of their child's play and can anticipate future developmental gains. It is natural that parents may take for granted routine activities such as diapering, dressing, and feeding. Thus, home visitors can be very helpful in discussing how these routine activities are a wonderful environment for playful parent–child interactions. When home visitors observe playful, spontaneous parent–child interactions, they can affirm the parents' actions and describe the meaning of what they are seeing in terms of the young child's learning and development. When they bring small objects and toys with which babies and young children can play, home visitors can help parents see how their child is developing new understanding and skills through their play. They can provide play activities in which they can encourage parents to be active participants and, in this participation, learn how being a play partner benefits their child.

9

Routines, Rituals, and Celebrations

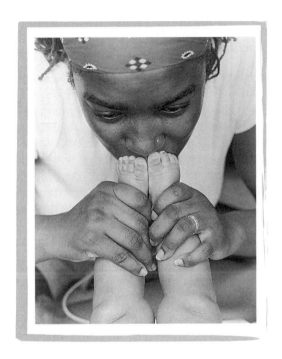

Wee Willie Winkie runs through the town,
Upstairs and downstairs in his nightgown,
Rapping at the window, crying through the lock,
"Are the children in their beds, for it's
now eight o'clock?"

William Miller (1844)

This chapter focuses primarily on the roles of three aspects of family life: 1) everyday family ritual, 2) special family celebrations and traditions, and 3) childhood illnesses. Childhood illnesses are included because they interrupt everyday routines, and the ways parents relate to their children's recurrent illnesses create new rituals. The term *ritual* as used in the chapter refers to the patterns of everyday routines that make up the shared lives of parents and their children. These include mundane practices such as eating, sleeping, bathing, or changing a diaper. It may seem odd to call such everyday happenings *rituals* because they usually are not explicitly recognized or thought out by parents, but in fact, the safe and predictable space that a child finds in these everyday patterns is very much like the familiar space created for adults in traditional rituals, such as religious services, holidays, or birthday celebrations. These rituals help young children to internalize basic processes of morality and emotional regulation and to learn the attitudes, beliefs, and values of their families and cultures.[1] Traditional rituals also play an important role in a child's life and deserve discussion. This chapter calls the more formal or self-conscious traditions *celebrations* to distinguish them from everyday ritual.

Rituals and celebrations are varied. They function in the development of the parent–child relationship in a number of different ways.[2] The elements that go into making a ritual include

- Coordinated practices of family members' interaction patterns[3]
- Predictable, repeated patterns of experience over time
- A means of organizing daily life
- A means of regulating behavior
- An expression of a family's shared beliefs and values
- A means of giving each family member a sense of belonging
- A central element of each family member's sense of identity

Not every ritual or celebration has each of these elements, but the whole structure of ritual and celebration in which a young child lives serves these functions.

Expectations and patterns of the larger culture and family's ethnicity and race influence a family's ritual. For example, the sleep patterns of families in the United States where young children and parents sleep in their own beds is different from many cultures where young children sleep with their parents. Some extended family members may put pressure on young parents to continue their tradition, for example, expecting that a young African American mother will lap-feed her 10-month-old as opposed to sitting the child in a highchair.

Rituals capture and express family members' relationship with one another and express what members mean to each other. They help children and their families make meaning from familiar family happenings. Daily rituals help to shape family relationships because they tell family members who they are to one another. Some familiar rituals are like anchor points during transitions such as birthday cakes and blowing out candles or decorating the Christmas tree. Healthy families have other regular and everyday rituals such as before-bed story reading or family dinnertime. Imberr-Black and Roberts wrote about the meaning of rituals:

They are a lens through which we can see our emotional connections to our parents, siblings, spouse, children and dear friends. . . .They connect us with our past, define our present life, and show us a path to our future as we pass on ceremonies, traditions, objects, symbols, and ways of being with each other.[4]

Fiese identified three dimensions of ritual: communication, commitment, and continuity.[5] Everyday rituals such as breakfast and dinner communicate to young children what needs to be done. Because rituals occur during the same time each day, they contain family members' commitment to each other. As they repeat each day, rituals involve continuity in behavior or the development of family habits.

An evening meal together is a ritual in many families. For example, in many families, everyone has their own place at the dinner table. Family dinner contains both symbols and symbolic actions. Food is one symbol that is different with each family. Food may symbolize nurturance, or it may symbolize the family's connection to a specific ethnic tradition such as borscht soup for Jewish Americans, pasta for Italian Americans, or greens for African Americans. In addition to food, families may have other symbols of dinnertime, such as special china or candlesticks or silverware. When families eat dinner together each day, parents are implementing their deep desire to have shared time together. During dinner, children feel a sense of belonging, connectedness, and predictability.

Many families no longer eat regular dinners together. Older children's team sport events, dancing lessons, and so forth mean that families are not even home during dinnertime. Some parents may not get home from work until well past dinnertime. In other families, rather than chatting together and learning what each family member did that day, family members watch television as they eat. Many American families eat their dinners in restaurants, and in some families, each family member eats whenever he or she wants.

Fiese conducted a longitudinal study examining stability and change in rituals of children from preschool to early school years and found that when dinnertime rituals remained stable, children experienced higher levels of academic success.[6] Fiese also found that when family rituals, such as dinnertime, were disrupted, young children became more vulnerable to developing academic or behavior problems.

Bedtime rituals every night are another time for parents and young children to intimately share. Repetitive bedtime rituals define the parent–child relationship as one of security, comfort, reliability, and safety.[7] As children grow older, they no longer will need to be read to, but they can give their parents a ritual kiss as they say good-night. Some families have weekly rituals, such as a large family breakfasts Sunday mornings, a pizza dinner Friday evenings, or a particular evening when the children cook for the family.

Many families have rituals to say good-bye to each other before they leave their home or greet each other when they return at the end of the day. Parents of very young children often add hugs and kisses to their good-byes and swing their child when they return. These daily rituals mark a boundary between a family and the family's outside world. In these daily rituals, children discover their roles and responsibilities as a family member. As they grow up, they will sense that ritualistic family processes are bigger than themselves. These rituals have elements that are central to spiritual experiences.

When families experience separation or divorce, they have to create new rituals. Visits with the nonresidential parent are most meaningful if ritual is embedded in the transition. During separation or divorce, parents may need to give special attention to a young child's bedtime ritual. When a child returns home to her mother after visiting her father, the mother can regularly have a special ice cream for a before-bedtime treat. Rituals such as this create a bridge that helps the child feel secure.

When young children's family life is embedded in predictability, simplicity, gentleness, and time to share in the ordinary, they may more readily know and experience spirituality. Rituals, even everyday rituals, are full of symbols and include sensory memory—smells, textures and sounds. Symbols provide meaning without words. For example, if a family always has music playing softly during their evening meal, the music signifies that the family dinner is a special and sacred time. Some families create new symbols and new rituals, which often signify new meaning or new relationship possibilities. Parents may invent new rituals (e.g., playing with the child every day before work) while continuing a ritual from their childhood (e.g., eating dinner by candlelight).

Gender roles can often be embedded in the preparation and enactment of rituals. Traditionally, rituals were the mother's responsibility. A slow but steady trend of increased involvement of men in both planning, preparation, and enactment of everyday and holiday rituals shows and symbolizes changing gender roles. With both parents employed full-time, some couples find it helpful to alternate days when one person focuses on household tasks while the other performs young children's bedtime ritual.

Imber-Black and Roberts discussed the function that rituals have in an individual's development:

They . . . enable relating, changing, healing, believing, and celebrating, which are, in fact, major themes in all human existence. Any given ritual, whether it be a daily ritual, a special tradition, a holiday celebration, or a life-cycle ritual, naturally may contain one or more of these elements.[8]

Another ritual for some children is attending religious education or language classes, which introduce children to memorable stories from their religious and cultural traditions. In some families, a special time is set aside to recount stories about an extended family member (e.g., a war hero), a religious figure, or a cultural hero. These stories develop a sense of connection to something beyond the family and encourage a feeling of spirituality. Children realize that they live in a world governed by love, compassion, and something greater than themselves. Investing in family rituals helps young children understand a deeper meaning to life than the unavoidable and mundane. Although there has been a decline in attendance at formal religious services, more people seem to be seeking spirituality. Garbarino and Bedard noted:

It is the decline of the sacred that is most important because with it comes an almost inevitable decline in the structure of adult authority. . . . An important part of the social order derives from recognizing the sacred: to set limits, to define what is done and not done, to give a higher purpose. . . . The issues of sacredness and authority are connected . . . . It is the manifest love rather than the fear of the "wrath of God" that makes a difference—a focus on being a Christlike person rather than a Christian, a Buddha rather than a Buddhist, for example. . . . Spiritual authority is the deepest and strongest authority there is.[9]

In their many conversations with parents, home visitors can explore the family's rituals and the meaning and beliefs expressed in their rituals. What values are parents passing on to their children when they engage in rituals together? Rituals can help young children assume new roles such as setting or clearing the table. Rituals can also help the family change interaction patterns, for example, beginning to have daily dinner together in which each family member is listened to and respected. If a home visitor learns that a family has no ritual, he or she might suggest possible rituals a family might develop, such as eating dinner together or reading stories before a child's bedtime. He or she also can help parents understand how these rituals promote the child's development.

EVERYDAY RITUALS

Principles of development, parenting, and home visiting approaches are relatively similar in each of these everyday rituals. This discussion examines three exemplary routines: 1) sleeping, 2) feeding and eating, and 3) toileting. Following the discussion on everyday rituals is a brief look at the role of more formal celebrations in family life. The chapter continues with a discussion of childhood illnesses and the special challenge that childhood illness presents to the patterns and rituals of everyday life and the ways that these challenges can be met. It concludes with a discussion of some of the dilemmas and difficulties that home visitors experience with regard to everyday rituals and family celebrations.

Sleep

Sleep includes rapid eye movement (REM) sleep and non-REM sleep, each characterized by a different type of brain waves. During REM sleep, the brain is active while the body is quiet and still. Non-REM sleep is the restorative part of sleep when the brain is inactive, but the body may be active. The patterns of alternating sleep stages repeats five to six times during the night. Adequate sleep is very important for the baby's brain to have restorative opportunities necessary for optimal development.

Birth to 3 Months

Newborn babies have a sleep–wake rhythm that was established in utero.[10] Newborns often sleep 15–18 hours each day, in 2- to 4-hour stretches. Because the baby's central nervous system is immature, activities like feeding and sleeping occur at unpredictable times.[11] Newborns have about seven sleeping and waking periods during a 24-hour period.[12] How these cycles change into different patterns is partially dependent on the individual baby's home environment. As parents learn their baby's different states of consciousness, they can begin to prolong their baby's alert states and encourage prolonged sleep states.

In a responsive home environment, sleep–wake cycles more quickly become predictable.

In reality, the total amount of daily sleep babies experience is regulated by the environment. Bottle-fed babies have significantly different sleep profiles than breast-fed babies. Babies who share a bed with their mothers breast-feed almost twice as often as babies who sleep in a separate room. More than half of all American mothers breast-feed their children 3–6 months or sometimes longer.[13] With breast feeding, the likelihood that mothers sleep with their babies increases.

The baby's temperament also affects his or her sleep patterns. Very active babies, or babies who are very aware of sensations, are prone to waking during the night. In night sleep, periods of deep sleep (30–50 minutes) are followed by periods of light sleep (i.e., REM sleep). In deep sleep, newborns can shut out noises around them. During REM sleep, breathing is irregular, and babies move about and are likely to cry out. Between these two cycles, babies often wake up.

Home visitors can help parents learn that their baby's waking up in the middle of the night is normal. Usually at around 3 months of age, babies can learn ways to quiet themselves and return to a deeper sleep. Different babies have different ways of self-comforting, such as finding their thumbs, moving into a new position, or scooting to the corner of their cribs. Babies' ability to soothe themselves—to self-calm—is their important first step in developing independence, which is an essential goal of development.[14] Home visitors can help parents understand the importance of their baby learning to self-calm.

> As Janice speaks with Marta, Marta's 3-month-old infant, Brianna, lies on her back, sucking her thumb. Janice comments, "It's good that Brianna is able to put her thumb in her mouth. Anything she'll do for herself, let her do it. Then, in the middle of the night she won't need you. You can help her do for herself. When she awakens in the night, give her a couple of minutes to calm herself first—to get in the right position and find her thumb."

Janice observes Brianna's ability to suck her thumb and thereby calm herself. She then helps Marta understand the importance of this self-calming skill and how she can help Brianna develop this ability.

Encouraging a baby to sleep through the night requires agreed-on commitment by everyone in the family, both parents and older siblings. To parents, especially those who want to hold and comfort their baby, these night awakenings can be very troubling. Home visitor's can help new parents understand that it is their responsibility to calm their babies and put them to bed; however, it is the *baby's* task to fall asleep. When parents put their baby to sleep by rocking or breast feeding, babies then will need their parents to help them to fall asleep when they awaken during the night. In the following vignette, Janice assists a young mother in mastering this ability to let her baby learn to fall asleep.

Janice: How is Jene (age 3 months) sleeping?

Natalie: She doesn't sleep much during the day. At night, I rock her to sleep, and then she sleeps well, much better than Dvonne [Jene's 3-year-old brother] did as a baby. Dvonne didn't sleep through the night until he was 2½. He would cry whenever his pacifier fell out of his mouth.

Janice: This is the age to concentrate on Jene putting herself to sleep. Think about yourself. If I would fall asleep in my bed and awaken in the kitchen, I would not fall back to sleep. If she falls asleep in your arms and awakens in the bed, she'll expect you to rock her again.

Natalie: I probably cause more problems. I love to hold my babies when they go to sleep. I know it would be easier in the long run. With Dvonne, the minute he would cry, I would go in.

Janice: You can rock her—get her comfortable—but before she is asleep, put her in her bed. When she awakens and cries, let her go for 5 minutes for starters. I know it's harder with Dvonne in the room. Space the time: 5 minutes, then 10 minutes, and 15 minutes. It'll be hard to listen to her cry. Don't talk to her. She needs to realize this is not a social time. It will be helpful to you if she can go to sleep by herself and begin to develop independence.

When Janice visits families with very young babies, she asks parents questions about sleeping and eating. These questions allow Janice to track the baby's developing skills at the same time Janice also learns if parents need helpful information to make these everyday routines the setting for optimal development. Natalie had rocked her first child asleep for his first 18 months. Janice affirms Natalie's desire to rock Jene each evening but stresses that Jene needs to be put in bed prior to falling asleep. Jene needs to learn that her night routine is sleeping in her own bed. Most adults have had the experience of waking up and not being sure of where they are or having trouble going to sleep in a bed not their own. Janice helps Natalie understand this experience as she speaks of what it would be like for an adult to wake up in the kitchen. On her home visiting record, Janice makes a note to herself to remember to initiate discussion with Natalie during her following visits. Janice understands that this will be a major parenting change for Natalie, and she will need her support in the coming months.

During the first 3 months, babies have cycles of eating and sleeping throughout the day and night. By 8 months, 60%–70% of babies are able to self-soothe and return to sleep after a nighttime awakening.[15] Many parents believe that giving their baby food or a bottle will assist in their ability to sleep; however, Ferber warned, "If your child becomes accustomed to being fed at night, her system begins to regard nighttime sleep periods as only naps between feedings."[16] Babies sleep best when their digestive systems are shut down for the night. At the same time, many breast-fed babies feed once during the night until about 12–15 months of age.

Some babies have colic during their first 3 months. Colicky babies cry and cannot be soothed, especially in the late afternoon and evening. When a home visitor works with parents of a colicky baby, first the home visitor makes certain that the parents and physician have checked to see if there may be a physical reason for crying, such as a food allergy or obstructed bowel. Then, he or she works to reassure the parent. Fussy crying periods can be a real threat to new parents, who may feel helpless and may blame themselves when not able to soothe their fussy baby. Usually colic ends by the age of 3 months.

Ages 4–8 Months

Between ages 4 and 8 months, babies will continue to need a morning and afternoon nap. Most babies this age easily accept naps. Home visitors can assist parents in understanding that providing a calm before-nap activity, such as rocking, cuddling, or soft lullabies, assists their child's ability to nap. The brief naps babies have when they are being held or they are riding in a car are not as restorative as napping in their cribs.[17] Babies who do not get enough sleep become overstimulated and irritable. Paradoxically, shortage of naps also seems to make going to sleep at night more difficult. The more tired a baby is, the harder it is for the baby to fall asleep and stay asleep.

At this age, it is good to help babies to associate falling asleep with being in their own bed. In the previous vignette, Janice helped Natalie to understand how she could help her 3-month-old, Jene, fall asleep in her own bed. When Janice returned again, Jene was 5 months old, and her mother reported the following.

Natalie: When it's time to go to bed, I lay her down, and she'll go to sleep.

Janice: That's great!

Natalie: Sometimes she'll cry for a second, and when she wakes up during the night, she begins talking to herself.

Janice: It's great that you have the patience to let her go back to sleep by herself.

Whereas Natalie nightly had rocked her first child to sleep during his first 18 months, now, with help from her home visitor, she could allow her daughter to learn to put herself to sleep and calm herself when she awakened during the night. In response to the news, Janice expressed delight in Jene's new skills and affirmed Natalie's ability to nurture this skill.

By age 4 months, babies' nervous systems are mature enough to allow them to sleep 8–12 hours at night. Some babies need a calming routine so they can relax enough to put themselves to sleep. Home visitors can help parents develop a regular bedtime routine (e.g., singing, reading stories) that is calming and nurturing. It is not too early for parents to begin reading simple stories. The body contact and even tempo of voice tones during story reading provides one of the best calming and nurturing bedtime activities as well as preparing the way for later, when the child will start to develop skills that will lead to reading.

At around 7–8 months, babies' motor development makes significant leaps. Babies can sit up and creep or crawl as they explore toys and other objects with their hands and mouths. With this burst of new skills and the accompanying exploration, babies may suddenly have difficulty calming down for naps and night sleeping. Home visitors can explain to parents how their baby's burst of motor skills is interfering with prior sleep patterns. They can encourage parents to be consistent and firm, with a predictable calming before-sleep routine, such as reading stories. Some parents may need to be reminded that during the night, they may pat the baby or hum to their baby, but they need to make certain that night awakenings do not become social occasions; rather, it is their baby's task to put him- or herself back to sleep.

A small proportion of babies enjoy head banging, head rolling (moving their head from side to side as they lie on their back), or body rocking. These actions are soothing rhythmic patterns of behavior to help themselves fall asleep. These methods of self-calming are normal when they develop prior to 18 months and disappear by around age 3 or 4.[18]

Ages 9–24 Months

During this period, most children will continue to nap. By age 18–24 months, one nap is usually sufficient. With each new leap in development, sleep can become a challenge. Developmental leaps occur at 12 months and again at 18 months. At around 12 months, babies learn to walk and begin saying their first words. The excitement and the frustration of learning these new skills spill over into baby and young toddler's sleeping patterns. Now, the baby can stand. Holding the crib rails while cruising around the crib seems lots more fun than sleeping. A baby who has been sleeping through the night suddenly might begin waking at night. Home visitors often can help parents see that these sleep changes are related to their young child's surges in development. Parents need to be firm with themselves and their baby to make certain that sleep remains the child's task. Bedtime rituals can ease the child's transition to sleep. Some parents find it is helpful to extend the length of bedtime routines, provide a lovey, sit by the baby, or pat the baby's back. But, once again, parents must make certain that night awakenings do not become playtimes.

Again at age 18 months, a new developmental leap occurs. The toddler becomes truly mobile, can speak in two- or three-word sentences, and can begin to enjoy pretend play. It is easy for toddlers to get overexcited and therefore have difficulty settling into sleep. Once again, parents may need to be firm and may need to extend the bedtime routine to calm their toddler. Often, stories after bath time are a calm period of shared enjoyment that assists children in settling down for bedtime.

During the child's first 2 years, sleep difficulties may occur frequently. Some children experience sleep difficulties because they have fears, especially of separation. Others may have difficulties caused by a schedule that is either too active, too inactive, or too unpredictable. During the first 18 months, children may awaken several times during the night. Parents may be overly responsive and may not allow their child to transition during sleep cycles. Some babies and toddlers always are rocked to sleep and never learn to put themselves to sleep. If these children wake up during the night, even when 3–5 years of age, they will expect a parent to sleep with them. Home visitors can inform parents that babies and toddlers never should drink a bottle in bed. Ear infections and damaged teeth can result from babies drinking bottles in bed.

Ages 2–5 Years

Two-year-olds usually need one afternoon nap. When parents arrange for their child's nap to end by 2:30 P.M. or 3:00 P.M., their child can be ready for bedtime in the early evening. At this age, many children talk themselves to sleep. Their talk is often a rehearsal of everything they have done during the day.[19] Just as many adults go over their day's events in their mind before they fall asleep, many toddlers do the same.

Night fears are common for children 2, 3, and 4 years of age. Parents should respect their child's fears. New strategies such as leaving the child's bedroom door open, putting a light in the child's bedroom, and extending the bedtime ritual by adding a quiet snack or story often can be helpful. Home visitors can help parents learn that these night fears are normal and that they, as parents, can make sure their child knows they are available for support.

Children vary with regard to when they no longer need naps. Even though a preschooler does not sleep during the afternoon, it can be very helpful if the child has a brief period of rest. Young children who are comfortable going to bed at night can be comfortable in the afternoon looking at books or quietly playing with toys on their beds.

As preschoolers get older and develop self-care skills, it can be tempting for parents to omit bedtime rituals; however, attention to bedtime rituals remains very important. Preschoolers increasingly encounter new experiences and new people every day; thus they thrive on the predictability and comfort of their special bedtime moments with their parents. Usually, preschoolers know many of their stories, and they like to tell their favorite ones to their parents at bedtime. Evening storytime prior to the time the child enters elementary school also strengthens the child's emerging literacy. Now that bedtime is a little later, parents can add a healthy snack or brief parent–child playtime to the child's bedtime routine. These routines become rituals, and this ritual continuity provides the young child with a sense of predictability, emotional security, belonging, and shared identity.

Feeding and Eating

Principles of parenting are similar for both eating and sleeping times. As the baby grows up, parents and children develop a predictable feeding ritual. Just as it is the task of the baby and toddler to fall asleep, so too is it the child's task to eat. The parent is responsible for what food is offered to the baby, but the baby is responsible for how much is eaten. As the child grows, a continuous push and pull develops between dependence (e.g., being fed) and independence (e.g., feeding oneself). The long-term goal is for young children to feed themselves and to enjoy eating and for mealtimes to be a social occasion for the family. The family mealtime routine becomes a ritual involving communication, connectedness, a shared identity and values.

Birth to 3 Months

During the first few weeks, the newborn sets the feeding schedule. Newborns need support from their parents to master eating. At first, parents need to adjust their feeding to their baby's rhythm, and gradually they learn which cries mean hunger and which mean something else. By the time their baby is 6 weeks of age, parents usually can begin to work toward a regular feeding schedule, which usually is every 3–4 hours. As the baby grows, the number of feedings decreases until, at 20 weeks, four feedings a day are adequate.

The most important part of eating for the baby, other than nutrition, is to experience loving communication during feeding periods.[20] Home visitors can encourage parents to sing, rock, and hug their baby during feeding so that feeding is pleasurable. During feeding, the baby–parent give-and-take interactions are like a dance, with the baby and parent responding to and influencing each other. Babies indicate they are hungry, and their parents respond. The feeding process is babies' first experience in active engagement with their parents. These frequent exchanges are the beginning foundation of the development of attachment.

Feeding can be one of the first challenges for new parents, who may feel very insecure, especially if their baby is colicky. In these situations, home visitors can offer support and guidance that both affirms the parents and provides appropriate suggestions. Karyn's 5-week-old has been colicky, and Janice assists Karyn.

> Karyn tells Janice that Greg's pediatrician has given him formula with iron; however, she thinks it is the iron that is causing the colic. The pediatrician explained that recent studies indicate that some developmental problems may stem from iron deficiency.
>
> Janice responds, "This is one of the tricky things. In my position, visiting many families with babies, I hear so much different advice coming from pediatricians." Karyn then tells Janice that her sister-in-law's pediatrician had given her different information. Janice says, "That is one of the reasons you need confidence in yourself. 'I have chosen this pediatrician, and I feel most comfortable with him.' We add one qualification. You are your baby's mom. If the pediatrician says, 'Don't worry,' and you think differently, keep pushing with your pediatrician. How often does [Greg] eat?"
>
> "Every 2 hours," Karyn says, "but it can vary. At night, sometimes 8 hours and last night, two 4-hour stretches."
>
> "These are helpful stretches for you," Janice says.
>
> Karyn adds, "The pediatrician said no solid food for 4 months, but he seems to be never satisfied."
>
> "The reason is, his stomach is not ready," Janice explains "And it might make him gassy. His digestive system is not very developed. See if the no-iron makes a difference. Push your pediatrician on it. Ask him what is the critical period for the iron. Unless he has had a baby in his own home that is crying all the time, he may not understand."

As a new mother, Karyn is ambivalent about the pediatrician's advice regarding iron. Janice supports Karyn and urges her to respect her own judgment—to recognize that she is the expert when it comes to knowing her son. Janice encourages Karyn to be assertive with the pediatrician and to know that his voice is merely one of many. As with sleep, Janice tracks Greg's feeding pattern. She gives Karyn developmental information so that Karyn can understand the basis for the pediatrician's directive regarding solid food. In the next few home visits,

Janice continues to support Karyn: Her first topic of conversation with Karyn is feeding and Greg's colic. Karyn also knows that if she is feeling especially stressed, she can call Janice.

Ages 4–8 Months

By 4 months, most babies have a predictable schedule of feeding every 3–4 hours. Just as it is the task of babies and young children to fall asleep, so too it is the task of babies to control how much milk they will drink. Parents are responsible for appropriate calm feeding times and for appropriate food, but it is the baby who regulates the amount taken. Home visitors can help parents understand these important divisions of responsibility. When feeding is a calm, predictable, positive, shared time between parent and baby, the foundation for healthy eating patterns is established.

The American Academy of Pediatrics recommends introducing solid food at 6 months of age in the form of cereal with milk. Home visitors can help parents understand that the addition of solid food is a real transition for young babies. It can be problematic for young babies to learn to swallow solid food, to eat with a spoon, and to tolerate different textures. Babies are beginning to have increased eye–hand coordination, and they enjoy exploring with their hands. Thus, they enjoy pushing their bottles, batting the spoon away, or putting their hands in their mouth to help suck their food down. Home visitors can describe these common behaviors that are typical of this transition, so that new parents can know what to expect, and thus can feel comfortable with these gradual changes within feeding patterns. When parents are confident, feeding times can be rituals with happy communication between parent and baby. Home visitors can encourage parents to introduce one solid at a time so that they can learn if their baby has any allergies to certain foods. They also can tell parents to initially expect to see the new food in their baby's stool.

During these months, many babies begin teething. Teething may bother babies because of the swelling around the budding tooth, which feels like a foreign substance in their mouth. It can cause discomfort and the accompanying fussiness and may lessen babies' appetite. To help sooth their baby's discomfort, parents can wipe their baby's gums with a wet cloth after the baby eats. This wiping cleans the plaque off the gums in the same way that brushing teeth does. Such suggestions from home visitors can be reassuring and helpful to young parents, as in the following vignette.

Karyn: Everything goes in his mouth.

Janice: Are his gums swollen? [Karyn nods yes.] Do his gums seem to hurt him?

Karyn: I think so.

Janice: Dentists recommend washing babies' gums after they eat and drink to get off the plaque. This helps the teething process and feels good—to have a soft, damp terry cloth on one's gums . . . Everything in his mouth, that's so good. He's so curious. And there is a connection between mouthing toys and eating later on.

Karyn introduces two topics: teething and exploration through mouthing. Janice uses the topics Karyn introduced to provide helpful developmental and parenting information. Because Karyn has introduced the topics, she is more likely to hear Janice's information and decide to utilize it. Janice not only addresses ongoing issues, such as teething, but she helps Karyn have a long-range developmental perspective. Putting items in his or her mouth is not only the way a curious baby learns but also the foundation for tolerating changing textures of food in the coming months and years. This information can help Karyn be at ease and understand the meaning and purpose of Greg's behavior patterns.

With increasing age, feedings become a playful exploration time for babies. With their increased eye–hand coordination, they explore new activities, such as smearing food across their faces and wanting to hold the spoon. Parents need to allow additional time and have more patience while their babies eat. When parents are in a rush, the food play can be stressful. If parents can take their time and play with the baby, for example, by making the spoon of food an airplane, mealtime can be a time to solidify attachment and playful interaction patterns. By the time babies are age 7–8 months, they can grasp items and enjoy playing with their cups. When a home visitor interprets the meaning of these new baby behaviors, he or she can assist parents in understanding that learning through exploration is as important to their baby as feeding and eating. These interpretations are especially important for very young or needy parents, who may see these exploratory actions as the baby's intentional attempts to upset the parent. When a parent understands that playful exploration during feeding is the normal way babies learn, the parent can allow more time for feeding and know that patience is necessary.

Ages 9–24 Months

As babies' and young toddlers' motor skills develop, so too does their interest in eating independently. If parents provide a variety of finger foods and a toddler cup as a part of each meal, they encourage their child to feed him- or herself. Often, babies and young toddlers allow their parents to feed them while they also are feeding themselves with their hands. Feeding oneself is another independence skill to be mastered. Babies also may want to hold and tap their spoon, though they generally cannot use it properly until age 2 years.

As babies approach age 12 months they can feed themselves chopped or mashed food and can begin to drink from a cup. This age often is a good time for parents to begin weaning from the bottle or breast. Weaning can be a gradual process of replacing nipple feeding with other ways of eating and drinking. Weaning begins as soon as parents introduce solid foods and drinking from a cup. Babies and young toddlers will be so involved in these new experiences that they usually they do not miss nipple feeding during meals. Breast or bottle often can be reserved for early morning or late at night. As home visitors chat with parents, it remains important for them to track how feeding and eating are developing. When Greg is 9 months old, Janice, asks his mother about eating.

Janice: He continues to like to eat and feed himself?

Karyn: Yes! Anything, even though he doesn't have but two teeth. He loves solid food.

Janice: It's important to pay attention to the baby's signals. It'll pay off in the coming months. It's not the teeth that help him chew. It's the jaw. He gets a lot of power from his gums.

Janice continues to initiate conversation about everyday rituals in parenting a baby. In this brief exchange, Janice gives Karyn important developmental information so that Karyn can understand her baby's actions and tune into the meaning of his actions.

Brazelton emphasized that "a rounded diet cannot be the goal for the second year."[21] This is the time during which independence and autonomy are dominant issues, and toddlers become sensitive to adult demands about eating. Brazelton suggested that a minimal daily diet during the second and third year should include the following.

- One pint (16 ounces) of milk or its equivalent in cheese, yogurt, or ice cream
- 2 ounces of protein (e.g., meat, an egg) or cereals fortified with iron
- One ounce of orange juice or other fresh fruit
- One multivitamin, which [can] cover for uneaten vegetables[22]

Because autonomy and negativism are a normal part of babies' development, eating times are the setting for toddlers to test newly discovered independence. Parents can expect toddlers to refuse to eat, spit food out, smash their food, or engage in other exploratory or testing behaviors during mealtimes. Home visitors can help parents understand that these new behaviors are normal parts of development and that parents need to be firm. They can assist parents in understanding that when toddlers lose interest in eating, parents should allow their toddlers to leave the table. Parents can tell their child that the meal is over *until* the next meal and that there are no snacks. Once toddlers learn that there will be no food once they have left the table in the middle of a meal, they will learn appropriate eating behaviors.

Ages 2–5 Years

By age 24 months, most toddlers can use a spoon and a fork, although they occasionally prefer using their fingers. Toddlers usually continue to be messy when eating. Some young children are more sensitive to taste and smell and may react to foods more strongly than others do. Home visitors can reassure parents that it is common for preschoolers to be picky eaters; for example, they may not like things mixed together, such as pot roast or spaghetti with sauce. Young children are more sensitive to the textures and smells of food than are adults, but they outgrow this sensitivity. If a toddler rejects mixed foods, the parent can substitute something nutritious such as crackers and cheese. Parents' attitudes can make a difference. If parents themselves enjoy cooking and eating and provide a relaxed mealtime, their young children probably will adopt this attitude toward eating. Mealtime then can be a special family time of shared enjoyment—a time in which children know their parents are eager to chat with them and with each other. The predictable ritual of these daily meals nourishes children's emotional security and sense of belonging.

Even if parents are enthusiastic about eating, they may find it difficult to accept their young child's emerging independence and negativism. Some parents believe that they will foster malnutrition if their young child misses a meal. Home visitors can give parents important information regarding their child's need for food. Often parents need reassurance that if their child ordinarily has a well-balanced diet, missing a meal will not matter. Janice's conversation with Tracy is illustrative.

Janice has just arrived, and she and Tracy are chatting. Mia (age 28 months) begins fussing, and her mother asks her, "What do you want? Juice?"

Mia says, "I don't want juice!" Tracy and Mia go to the kitchen and return with a small bowl of raisins and cereal.

Janice tells Tracy, "It's good that you give her nutritious snacks. At this age, children often are picky."

"She ate a good breakfast today," Tracy says, "but last night she would not eat dinner."

"How did you feel about it?" Janice asks.

Tracy answers, "I was frustrated. I tried to feed her, but she just didn't want any. So I just let it go. I tried everything."

"Good," Janice says. "It is important to pay attention to the child's natural appetite—knowing, on the one hand, her behavior, and on the other, she is not hungry. If we push, we are denying her own limits. The child should determine how much she eats."

In this discussion, Janice affirms Tracy's parenting. In addition she gives Tracy developmental information to help her learn the significance of her decision so that she can continue ignoring Mia's pickiness and know that her child will be fine if she misses a meal.

It is important for children to develop the rhythm of eating meals when they are hungry, to stop eating when they are full, and to enjoy eating. Home visitors can help parents understand that there are liabilities when they use food for punishment or reward. When food is used as a reward for good behavior, young children learn to connect food with prizes rather than with hunger. When parents withdraw dessert as punishment, they unwittingly teach their child that there is good food and bad food.

Preschoolers enjoy helping their parents prepare meals. When children help cook food, they are more likely to eat it. When young children help set and clear the table and assist in simple cooking tasks, they are contributing members of the family. In these activities, they get a sense of belonging and pride in their new skills.

Our society has an ever-increasing number of working single parents and two-working-parent families for whom time is at a premium. With the accessibility of numerous fast-food restaurants, microwaveable dinners, and prepackaged foods, traditional food preparation and leisurely mealtimes may not be a given part of family life.

Rolanda and Carl each have high-powered professional jobs. Carl takes their 3½-year-old son, Ben, to his day care at 7:30 A.M., and Rolanda picks Ben up at 5:30 P.M. Ben was 36 months old the first time the family's home visitor, Nina, visited them. Nina initiated a conversation about mealtimes.

Rolanda: Well, in truth, we don't eat together as a family. Carl gets home an hour after Ben and I do, and he uses a couple hours to unwind—reading the paper, exercising on the treadmill, that kind of thing, so Ben and I eat simple meals together shortly after we arrive home. It's a pattern that just developed. We've never discussed it much.

Carl: You know, when we first got married 8 years ago, I used to talk with Rolanda about how special it would be to have family dinners. My own father never returned home from his law office until after 8:00 in the evening, so I grew up without experiencing daily dinners with everyone.

Nina: It sounds like beginning a new pattern of eating together might be worth exploring together. Today, many young working parents are developing a repertoire of simple meals, such as pasta, that they can manage to prepare after a long day at work. And, increasingly, grocery stories have prepared meats, such as rotisserie chicken, at reasonable prices. But, the issue is not the type of food; rather, what is important is that children and their parents daily have time together. Every evening, dinners together can provide this shared time.

Rolanda: Now that I think of it, Carl and I hardly ever eat together. Dinners together would be important for our relationship, too.

Given their high-pressure work, Carl and Rolanda had developed a daily pattern that excluded family dinners, and they had never thought much about it. When Nina introduced the topic, they quickly recognized what they and their son were missing. One month later, when Nina returned to visit, Rolanda told Nina that her mother now picks up Ben from his child care on Wednesday and cares for him for several hours. Then, she and Carl can take time to go out to dinner together, a pattern they had maintained for 5 years prior to Ben's birth. Rolanda also explained that she and Carl plan to begin regular dinners with Ben, but this shift is going to take time. Together, Nina and Rolanda brainstormed possible easy meals and ways of preparing some meals during the weekend.

When they talk about eating and mealtimes, home visitors like Nina can help parents understand the developmental significance of good eating habits and family mealtimes. They can talk about how family dinner rituals give each family member a sense of belonging and security. Nina and Rolanda did some problem solving as they discussed possibilities of weekend cooking for weekday dinners and munching on nutritious finger food like carrot sticks and celery with peanut butter instead of making time-consuming salads. Different people and different families have their own eating habits. For adults, eating often is a social occasion—for example, coffee breaks at work and going out to lunch. Home visitors can assist parents in making family meals social occasions that include their very young children.

Toilet Training

Just as it is the child's task to fall asleep and to decide how much to eat, toilet training is also the child's accomplishment. Like sleeping and eating, the learning process initially involves parent and child working together. Likewise, learning independence is a central part of the toileting process.

Unfortunately, many parents feel pressure to train their toddler early. Grandparents may expect the child to train as early as the parent, and some preschools will not accept 2-year-olds unless they are toilet trained. Sometimes, parents think of their child's early toilet training as a sign of their parental competence. There is no correct age for toilet training; however, most children are not ready until after their second birthday.[23]

Because many parents feel pressure and lack confidence in training their toddler, home visitors can assist by helping parents recognize when their child is really ready for toilet training. Experts agree that there are clear signs of readiness for toilet training. Lansky provided a summary of signs of readiness. The child

- Is aware of the "need to go" and shows it by facial expression or by telling the parent
- Can express and understand one-word statements, such as "wet," "dry," "potty," and "go"
- Demonstrates imitative behavior
- Dislikes wet or dirty diapers
- Is able to stay dry for at least 2 hours or wakes up dry in the morning or after a nap
- Is able to pull pants up and down
- Is anxious to please the parent
- Has a sense of social "appropriateness" (Wet pants can be an embarrassment.)
- Tells you he or she is about to urinate
- Asks to use the potty chair or toilet[24]

Home visitors have an important role in helping parents understand that maturity of the child's gastrointestinal tract and central nervous system is necessary for a young child to be ready for toilet training. This maturity allows the child to know the sensations that come before a bowel movement or urination. Girls often are ready before boys, and children with older siblings may learn from them. Any time before age 4 is normal. Children most often gain bowel control before they have bladder control.

All young children need their parents' guidance in toilet training, and often home visitors can provide helpful suggestions. Parents learn to understand that toilet training takes a long time and that accidents are common. One aspect of toilet training is learning a new vocabulary.

Home visitors can encourage parents to use whatever words are comfortable to them when they talk to their toddler about body parts and elimination. Portable potties allow young children to have their feet on the floor, and with a potty, the child does not have to deal with a big, noisy toilet that make things disappear. It helps young children to see others using the toilet. When they begin the toilet training process, parents can comment in a matter-of-fact manner when they see their child having a bowel movement. Parents can remind their child to use the potty, but it is the child's decision to use it. When the child does produce something, parents can enthusiastically praise their child and can leave it in the potty for their child to take pride in the accomplishment. Home visitors can encourage parents to avoid shaming or pressuring their child. Most young children cooperate because they find pleasure in pleasing their parents and in growing up.

Just as home visitor–parent discussions of feeding and sleeping behavior are important, toilet training is an important recurrent topic of discussion during toddlerhood. Janice and Shelly discussed toileting during Janice's visits when Erin was between 18 and 34 months of age. These discussions illustrate how home visitors can support, affirm, and guide young parents.

Janice and Erin (age 18 months) are rolling Erin's beach ball as Shelly says to Janice, "Erin is interested in the potty, especially since her older cousin is being toilet trained."

Erin says, "Potty" and begins to pull down her pants.

Shelly looks at Janice as she says, "Should I?"

Janice responds, "Sure, if she is interested."

Erin and Shelly go to the bathroom. In the bathroom, Erin says, "Mamma?"

Shelly replies, "Mamma sit down, too."

In a couple moments, Shelly and Erin return to the living room. Erin has her diaper and jeans off, and Shelly is carrying the potty, which she puts on the rug. With a small wad of paper in her hand, Erin sits on the potty.

Shelly tells Janice, "Rob and others say I should train her. I tell them she is not ready."

Janice replies, "Good, but you are potty training because your child is interested. This is all a part of it."

Erin quickly loses interest in the potty and gets up. Shelly puts Erin's diaper and jeans on, and Erin and Janice return to playing ball.

Janice does not introduce the toilet-training topic until the child is 2 years old, the age that Janice thinks is appropriate for beginning the process. Janice explained, "By the time the child is 2 years, parents have learned that I prepare them for each step. If I bring it up earlier, they'll think it's time to start." When Shelly initiates the topic, Janice supports her because it is Erin who first had interest in the task.

> Janice has just arrived and Erin (age 23 months) has wheeled her doll carriage into the living room and begins showing Janice her dolls. Shelly suggests, "Tell Janice what we have been doing."
>
> Shelly then whispers to Erin, who says, "Potty. I tinkle in the potty." Erin then bends over and puts her hand between her legs to pantomime as she says to Janice, "Wipe and then put it in the potty. Flush. It go—yeah!" Erin claps, and then continues, "Poo-poo, too—baby one and big one, too."
>
> Shelly tells Janice that every single day for a week Erin has used the toilet completely on her own initiative. Shelly states that she had no intention of starting toilet training this early and had not even bought any books about the topic. Recently, Erin was no longer going to the toilet every single day.
>
> Janice responds, "It's great that you are so relaxed about it. Though children need our help, it is the child's decision to use the toilet."

Janice has three visits between Erin's 18th and 23rd months; however, Shelly does not initiate conversation about toilet training. When she does, Janice affirms Shelly's relaxed manner. Just as Janice encourages Shelly to maintain a relaxed manner and take her cues from her daughter, so too, Janice takes her cues from Shelly when discussing the topic. If Shelly was not relaxed or was pressuring Erin, Janice would initiate the topic. During Janice's next two visits Shelly briefly talks about toileting.

> As Janice picks up her items, she asks Shelly, "Do you have any questions?"
>
> Shelly says, "With regard to potty training, I'm not sure what to do—if it's okay for me to put diapers on Erin or would that be bad to be inconsistent?"
>
> Janice replies, "Consistency is always best, but you need to follow Erin's lead. If she begins wetting, it's appropriate to return to the diapers."

Once again Janice reminds Shelly that it is her daughter who decides when she will use the potty. When Janice visits the next month (Erin is age 25 months), Erin's father, Rob, also is part of the visit.

Rob: [to Shelly] Did you tell Janice that Erin is almost potty trained?

Shelly: I can't keep track of how often she is dry, and if she does have an accident, it's is usually my fault—forgetting before we go out. Most of the time, she says it herself.

Janice: That's wonderful.

Shelly: I find we're reusing and reusing diapers. We use diapers when we leave the house. Like you suggested, I have been real relaxed.

The previous conversation took place during the last visit before Janice's 3-month summer vacation. When Janice returns in the fall, Shelly gives her an update on Erin's toilet training.

Shelly: If I would put her on the potty, she would just whine. She has very few accidents. I said to Rob, when she wants to go, she'll go. I put a calendar on the wall in the kitchen. Now, I put up a star when she goes potty. I ask her if she wants a star, and she'll say, "Yes," and go to the bathroom.

Janice: You're really smart. The decision must be Erin's.

Three months later, Shelly gives Janice another report.

Shelly: Erin (age 34 months) seems to deal well with spontaneity, like if we walk into the bathroom and she needs to go potty, it's fine. It works much better than when I suggest that we go to the bathroom.

Janice: You are really tuning into her cues. This is another part of her growing autonomy, and you know what works, and you use it. You have learned what causes confrontations.

Just like the child's learning to walk or talk, toilet training progresses with stops and starts. Erin is dry for a few days; then she begins having accidents. Throughout these 7 months, Shelly keeps Janice informed on her daughter's toilet training. Janice supports and affirms Shelly's approach. Repeatedly, and in different ways, Janice maintains the theme that toilet training is the child's task, and parents need to remain relaxed. When toddlers experience pressure in toilet training, they may begin to hold onto their bowel movements. Holding back can lead to constipation.

Toilet training is another area in which young children need to become independent at their own speed, and the process can be difficult for parents, who may think of toilet training as their responsibility. Children often are reluctant to follow their parents' timetable, and parents may feel this resistance points to a failure in their parenting ability. Young children's reluctance may stem from parental pressure or immaturity of their intestinal tract or central nervous system. Home visitors can assist parents in this potentially problematic area by providing developmental information so parents can know what to expect from their child, suggestions, support, and affirmation.

Patterns of Mutuality

Patterns of development and of parenting arise across these everyday routines of feeding and eating, sleeping, and toilet training. Each area involves child and parent working together; there is mutuality. In order for these patterns of mutuality to occur, parents need to learn to read the language of their child's behavior, for example, they need to recognize the meaning of different cries, when to stand back, and when to nudge their child forward. Communication—nonverbal facial gestures, body posture and movement, as well as speaking—is integral to these everyday interactions in sleeping, feeding and eating, and toilet training.

Each of these areas involves the *child's* accomplishment: It is the child's task to learn to fall asleep, to decide how much to eat, and to use the toilet. As young children learn to feed themselves, put themselves to sleep, and use the toilet, they are developing increased independence. This process of becoming independent is not always even. Development often occurs in bursts, such as the emergence of new motor or language skills. A burst in one area may lead to unevenness in another; for example, new motor skills may lead to overexcitement and accompanying difficulty in calming down to fall asleep.

As their child grows, parents learn that the different areas of their child's development are intertwined. As motor skills develop, babies can chew and swallow and begin to feed themselves. As their social-emotional and language skills develop, eating times can be pleasurable times of companionship. With increased language and cognitive skill, toddlers can understand and follow directions in eating, sleeping, and toilet-training activities. Because of the emotional bond with his or her parent, the young child is responsive and eager to please. Successes in these everyday rituals are major developmental accomplishments and become a part of the child's identity.

Predictability is central to each of these everyday rituals. Falling asleep becomes a natural part of everyday routine when there is a calm bedtime ritual. When family members regularly come together to eat, eating is enjoyable, and the child feels a sense of connectedness. Regular reminders to use the potty become a part of the child's everyday routine until children can recognize their bodily signals for toileting. In time, the preschooler experiences a predictable rhythm—eating when hungry, sleeping when tired, and toileting according to bodily signals. It is not uncommon for everyday rituals to trigger parents' worry, anxiety, and insecurity. New parents may feel like a failure when their new baby is colicky or when they think their child is not eating enough. Often, parents love the process of putting their child to sleep, but then experience the frustration of nighttime awakenings with seemingly endless crying. Normal patterns of negativism lead to toddlers' refusal to eat or nap. Within these experiences, new parents can feel their sense of parenting competence is eroding.

Within everyday rituals, home visitors can provide important support, affirmation, developmental information, and suggestions to help young parents in their important and challenging parenting tasks. When home visitors prepare parents with information regarding what to expect from their growing baby and young child, parents can develop both confidence in their child's development and confidence in their ability to foster this development. As they observe parent and child behavior, home visitors have the opportunity to interpret the developmental meaning of these actions and to support and affirm the parent. When a parent is feeling insecure or perplexed, home visitors' support and information may assist this parent's understanding of both child and self and thereby offer needed assistance.

FAMILY CELEBRATIONS AND TRADITIONS

Family traditions are regularly occurring events. Some are unique to the family, such as summer vacations and visits with extended families, but others are part of larger religious or national occasions, such as events scheduled for Independence Day, Passover, or Martin Luther King, Jr.'s birthday. *Celebrations* include rites of passage, such as baptism, bar or bat mitzvahs, weddings, graduations, and religious holidays. They are connected to both the culture and the family's ethnic and religious roots.[25] Celebrations often involve symbols that will be important for the rest of the child's life.

Like everyday rituals, family celebrations and traditions involve predictable, repeated patterns of family interactions. They give family members a sense of shared identity, and through celebrations and traditions, family members link past, present, and future. Participating in traditions and celebrations provides connectedness and continuity. Family members feel affirmed and comforted when parts of a holiday celebration are passed on to the next generation. Examples include reading *The Night Before Christmas* on Christmas Eve and attending a block party on Independence Day. Although families differ in the extent to which their traditions and celebrations are child centered or involve people beyond the immediate family, all celebrations and traditions maintain the family's shared beliefs and values.

Some celebrations, such as birthdays and religious holidays, become markers of continuity in a family's life cycle as multiple generations gather together (e.g., great-grandmother attends the baby's first birthday party). Families develop their own style of practicing celebrations. Birthdays can have many important meanings: honoring the aging process, honoring the person who is celebrating his or her birthday, remembering the birth parents, affirming life, or just having fun. Some families go to special restaurants on a birthday or have a treasure hunt for the birthday member to find his or her gifts. Many families remember the birthdays of people who have died or left the family. Often giving and receiving are an integral part of rituals. In some families, all gifts are homemade. In other families, all gifts must be wrapped, each member of a family must receive the same number of presents, or a gift must always be a surprise. Rituals of celebration may not be complete without traditional food and drink, music, gifts, or dress.

As children grow and families change over time, birthday celebrations change. Children may become too old for yearly parties with friends. Most family rituals are flexible so that they can adapt to the increasing age and maturity of the children. As home visitors discuss with parents their family's rituals, some parents may discover that they need to think about how they want to keep or change rituals now that their family includes children.

Yearly family vacations often become rituals for middle- and upper-class families. Families may leave their homes before dawn for long driving trips. Children and parents may play the same games such as identifying license plates or counting cows. With the increase of two parents working, vacations often become a special protected time and space for parents and their children. Family members have an increased amount of shared time—playing on the beach together, cooking together, exploring new restaurants together, or playing games together in the evening, in a leisurely way—that they may not feel they have time for in their complex lives at home.

In their relationships with parents, home visitors have the opportunity to respect and honor each family's tradition and forms of celebration. Frequently, visits occur close to holiday seasons. Janice's visit during December illustrates.

Janice arrives at Natalie's home 1 week before Christmas. Dvonne (age 3½ years) greets her at the door and immediately shows her his Christmas tree. His mother, Natalie, suggests that Dvonne tell Janice where they cut down the tree, and he tells her they cut it down at a tree farm. Natalie places Jene, Dvonne's little sister, on the rug in front of her. Dvonne excitedly tells Janice what he has asked Santa to bring him for Christmas.

Janice tells him, "We ask Santa for what we think we want, but Santa has surprises, too. Santa also likes to have ideas."

As Janice speaks, Dvonne touches the ornaments and gestures for her to look at them.

Janice says, "You are being very careful with the ornaments, and the needles of the tree still feel sharp, so they can hurt your fingers."

Dvonne affirms, "They feel sharp!"

Janice joins in Dvonne's excitement regarding the forthcoming holiday and engages in an extended conversation with him about his ornaments. By the time this exchange is completed, one fourth of the home visit time is consumed, but Janice understands that she must address the excitement of holidays before Dvonne can settle down and let her also relate to his mother and baby sister. As Janice relates to Dvonne, she also models extended conversation for Natalie, who smiles as she observes and listens.

Holidays can be stressful for mothers of very young children. Mary is a young mother of two boys: Gary (age 4 years) and Paul (age 17 months). Mary's home visitor, Linnette, has worked with her since her older son was 6 months old, so Linnette understands that Mary tends to become anxious during holidays. When Linnette visits in late November, she tries to assist Mary.

Linnette: It's getting into the Christmas season, a season that can be stressful for kids and for parents. Before decorating or shopping, it might be helpful for you and Stanley to sit down and see if you can make plans to lessen the stress. Other moms have tried things. One mom, she said that decorating the tree is a family thing. She doesn't have a formal meal that night, but puts out healthy finger foods that the kids like. The kids put ornaments on the low branches. Some moms involve the kids in baking cookies. Small kids love to play with cookie dough.

Mary: Our problem is we have 100 things to do. I took the kids to the mall to see Santa. We waited for an hour for him to show up, and then we waited for the picture taking. By the time she flashed, Gary was not smiling, and Paul was crying. [By the time Mary had finished her story, she was chuckling.]

Linnette: Lots of time, we put stress upon ourselves. Afterwards, we can laugh about it. It's important to plan.

Mary: Like wrapping. I do it after they are in bed, and I find it a relaxing activity.

Knowing that Mary can let holidays become stressful, Linnette begins a discussion of the forthcoming holiday. She speaks of strategies that other mothers use to help make the holiday a relaxing time for family activities. When home visitors develop a partnership in their relations with parents, they find that using examples of other mothers is a helpful way of giving suggestions. Mary is comfortable enough to share a recent stressful experience, and because she knows that she has often shared with Linnette how she gets stressed, she can distance herself from the experience and can laugh about it. The conversation ends as Mary reports a successful holiday experience. This Christmas will be better for the children because Linnette helped Mary make it better for herself. When Linnette visited Mary and her boys after Christmas, Mary eagerly shared holiday events—those that were pleasant and festive, as well as those that were stressful. Linnette shared that Mary's level of stress has decreased in each of the 3 years that she has visited Mary. Linnette's support, affirmation, and assistance no doubt helped.

For many families, the preparation time of celebrations may be as important as the actual celebration. Historically, women have carried the major responsibility for celebration preparation; however today gender roles are gaining increasing flexibility. Mother and father may spend hours together as they bake Christmas cookies or shop for gifts. Young children love assisting in making Christmas cookies and decorating their house for the holidays. Celebration preparations become vibrant patterns of relationship between family members. Often, the elders in a family are the prime keepers of key celebration-making components such as recipes, stories, photos, or other family memorabilia.

Just as everyday rituals give young children a sense of connectedness and security, family celebrations and traditions offer each family member a sense of belonging and shared identity, both to that which is unique to the family and to the extended family and the larger culture. Home visitors can assist young parents in recognizing and understanding the value of these celebrations and traditions for their child and each family member's development. With very small children, parents may experience the task of creating these celebrations and traditions as additional tasks that are not easy to orchestrate and add unwanted stress. In these environments, the home visitor can offer needed support and suggestions.

CHILDHOOD ILLNESSES

Young children get sick, but they cannot tell their parents what is wrong with them. Between ages 1 and 3 years, children average 8 or 9 illnesses a year.[26] Illnesses often make new parents feel anxious, even when illnesses are minor. Parents can be exhausted by the child's increased needs and by their own lack of sleep. Frequent illnesses include colds, nausea and vomiting, and diarrhea, which usually do not need antibiotics or other medicine. Parents can help their children best by letting them build up an immunity to illness. Home visitors support and help parents of sick children when they provide clear guidelines. They can explain that illness will cause fussiness, interrupted sleep, and regression, no matter how skilled a parent may be. Furthermore, they can provide information and suggestions. For example, they can tell parents that clear fluids are important if a child has a fever or diarrhea in order to prevent dehydration. These common illnesses cause breaks in the family's predictable everyday routine. From a developmental perspective, home visitors can help parents understand that they will develop important new rituals with their child during the experience of illness.

Parents' care for their sick child is an intense personal and social experience for both parent and child. A child's illness also is an important experience in social relatedness. When sick, the child's sense of self is changed, and he or she does not feel happy, energetic, or curious. When the child recovers, his or her sense of self is restored, but the child now remembers how bad he or she felt and how nurturing the parent was. During children's illnesses, parents' caregiving changes, too. They more readily accept irritability and make fewer demands on the child. They help reduce the child's discomfort and express empathy. Often, the child's illness is contagious, so children may observe as their siblings or parents go through similar experiences of illness. Then, children can learn how to help in caring for someone else. Illness can be the setting for learning compassion, nurturing, and caring. Initially, the child who is ill experiences increased empathy and caring. When family members then become ill, the child can develop prosocial behavior such as empathy and assisting others.

Home visitors can make certain that parents have basic health and safety knowledge and resources; for example, they understand what is a medical emergency that needs immediate attention, they have phone numbers of a physician and of a poison control center near every telephone in the house, and they have in their home a good first-aid guide. Brazelton defined medical emergencies as those occasions when the child is unconscious, has obstructed breathing, or has convulsions.[27] When children have fever or diarrhea, dehydration is a danger. It is common for children under age 3 to have high fever because their body's regulatory system is immature. If children have more than 6 bowel movements a day, or if they stop urinating, they are getting dehydrated. Not all new parents know this information; thus, it is important that home visitors explain the dangers of dehydration.

Middle-ear infections resulting from colds are quite common during infancy and toddlerhood. Fluid in the middle ear and a loss of hearing often accompany middle-ear infections. With frequent ear infections and accompanying hearing loss, a young child may have immature language skills. Janice is aware that Greg has had several ear infections (before he was 12 months old, he had outpatient surgery to put tubes in his ears to assist the fluid drainage); thus, she regularly initiates a discussion with Greg's mother about this topic.

> Janice asks, "Has Greg continued to have ear infections?" Karyn nods yes. Janice explains, "When he has had ear infections, his hearing is not as good. If you notice a pattern that he is not responding to you, check with his pediatrician."
>
> Janice proceeds with play activities with Greg and Karyn. Before she leaves, she returns to the earlier topic. "Even a couple of weeks after an ear infection, babies are not hearing as well. With ear infections, we encourage you to keep close track of his hearing. This can have a major impact on his language development."

Because Janice has a strong commitment to relate to parents as partners, she usually is not as directive as she is in this vignette. With experience, however, Janice has learned that many new parents do not know this information about ear infections, which is crucial for Greg's healthy development.

Preventable Diseases

Many new parents do not understand the numerous contagious diseases that young children can acquire and that can cause serious long-term disability. Many home visiting programs have a parent handout on preventable diseases. It is important for home visitors to ensure that parents are getting the correct vaccinations and immunizations for their child. If a home visitor works with teen parents, parents who are developmentally slow, parents with mental illness, or parents who abuse substances, the home visitor may need to be rather directive as he or she ensures that the babies and young children get their vaccinations and immunizations. Immunizations for the following diseases are most common, but please check The American Academy of Pediatrics web site at http://www.aap.org or another reliable source for updates.

- Polio is a viral disease that can cause permanent paralysis. Polio vaccine is commonly given at 2 months, 4 months, 15 months, and 4–6 years. In the United States, polio was an epidemic disease until the late 1950s, when a vaccine was developed. Unfortunately, cases of polio still occur because many parents do not immunize their young children.

- Measles can cause respiratory problems, ear problems, and brain damage that can cause mental retardation.

- Rubella, commonly called German measles, is a mild infection in children, but if a pregnant mother catches it from a child, it can cause miscarriage, stillbirth, and severe birth defects.

- Mumps is characterized by painful swelling around the jaw and can lead to other complications such as deafness, central nervous system damage, and kidney inflammation.

- Diphtheria is a bacterial infection that can cause pneumonia, heart failure, and nerve damage.

- Whooping cough is a respiratory infection that can cause pneumonia, brain damage, and death. It is especially dangerous to babies under 1 year old but is less dangerous to older children.

- Tetanus is a noncontagious disease caused by germs found in the soil. It often enters the body through wounds. Tetanus can cause muscle spasms, severe nervous system damage, and death. Individuals should be reimmunized for tetanus every 10 years.

- *Haemophilus influenzae* type b is a contagious bacteria. It is responsible for many infections in children including meningitis, which is the leading cause of acquired mental disability.

- Chicken pox is a contagious infection. Symptoms include a fever and an itchy, blister-like rash that can cover most of the body.

- Hepatitis B is an inflammation of the liver caused by toxic agents in the body. The vaccine is commonly given at birth, 2 months, and 6 months of age.

Massage

Many parents also are not aware that a massage can help infants feel more comfortable during illness. Throughout the world, especially in Asia and Africa, parents massage their babies. Often babies are given a massage with oil after their daily bath and before they go to sleep for the first several months of their lives. In some countries, like India, massaging a baby is a daily routine beginning in the baby's first days of life. Research indicates that after babies are massaged, they sleep more soundly, and the massage relieves gas and colic, which helps heal the baby from congestion and pain.[28]

Americans are just learning that baby massage stimulates respiration, circulation, digestion, and elimination; promotes sleep; and relieves gas and colic.[29] In the United States, there are massage therapy schools in almost every major city. These schools teach parents how to massage their babies. The massage process seems to be mutually enjoyable for babies and their caregivers. Home visitors can share this information with parents and demonstrate the massaging process.

Over the past few decades, research has indicated that massaging high-risk babies can ameliorate some of their symptoms. When they are massaged for a 15-minute period prior to bedtime between 3 and 6 months of age, they become less irritable, fall asleep faster, experience fewer night awakenings, and are able to spend more time in quiet, alert states.[30]

Lead Poisoning

Young children put everything in their mouths, including paint chips that contain lead. When young children ingest lead, the long-term effects can be very serious, including mental retardation, hyperactivity and reduced attention span, impaired hearing, decreased growth, and learning disabilities. Children should be tested for lead at 1 year old and every year thereafter if the family lives in a home built prior to 1978, when lead paint was commonly used. Home visitors can tell parents that children who eat enough iron and calcium absorb less lead. Foods rich in iron include eggs, beans, and lean red meat. Dairy products are high in calcium.

Sudden Infant Death Syndrome

Sudden infant death syndrome (SIDS), or "crib death," is the single leading cause of death of babies less than 4 months old. A baby of a family of any race, religion, ethnic, or cultural group can die from SIDS, and the syndrome occurs in healthy, typically developing babies during the babies' sleep. The death occurs quickly. Because the baby does not cry, the parents do not know it is happening. Babies who seem to be at higher risk for SIDS include:

- Babies who sleep on their stomachs
- Babies whose mothers are younger than 20 years of age
- Babies with low birth weight and/or premature babies
- Babies whose mothers smoked during pregnancy

Since the early 1990s, pediatricians have advised parents to put their babies to sleep on their backs until they are old enough to roll over by themselves, usually at around 4 months old. Still, if a baby is at risk, home visitors can suggest that parents ask their pediatrician about using monitors.

Prematurity

Physicians consider a baby born before the 36th week of pregnancy as premature. In the United States, approximately 1.1% of babies are born prematurely.[31] These babies are often at least 8 weeks premature and usually stay in the hospital until their expected date of birth. Because of the technological improvements and skilled care in neonatal intensive care units (NICUs), babies born at 24–28 weeks old may survive. Babies born very early, however, may have chronic medical problems that involve the brain and lungs, poorly developed motor skills, and delayed development. For the first 4–6 months, they may have feeding and sleeping difficulties. They frequently are irritable and have difficulty calming themselves. Babies with birth weight of less than 5 pounds may have learning problems; cerebral palsy; and impairments in sight, hearing, and lung functions. Premature babies with no serious physiological abnormality usually are discharged from the hospital when they weigh 4–5 pounds, with gestational ages of 37–40 weeks.

Physicians and parents may not know why a baby is born premature, so some mothers feel guilty and blame themselves. Some women with excellent prenatal care have premature babies. At the same time, there are contributing factors to prematurity:

- Toxemia and/or high blood pressure
- Multiple births, such as twins and triplets
- Poor nutrition
- Use of alcohol, tobacco, or other drugs, especially cocaine
- Inadequate prenatal care
- Prior abortions or miscarriages
- Frequent urinary infections

Good maternal health during pregnancy is critical to the health of the fetus, though of course the best care cannot guarantee a successful outcome. Healthy prenatal care includes a balanced diet; avoidance of excessive stress, tobacco, alcohol, and other drugs; and a reasonable amount of exercise. During the last 3 months of pregnancy, the fetus gains weight, completes the maturation of organ systems, and develops early responses to sensory stimuli. Because increased neurological development takes place between 24 and 40 weeks of gestation, immature neurological functioning is common among premature babies. As a result, the baby's heart rate, temperature, muscle tone, and ability to process sensory input may be affected.

Some parents may feel anger, grief, or shame because they did not have the perfect baby that they expected. Some parents may become overprotective because of their babies' initial health problems. A sub-stantive body of research indicates that mothers of premature babies show anxiety and low self-confidence in their caregiving competence during the baby's first year of life.[32] It seems that interactional difficulties between premature babies and their mothers are primarily reflections of the baby's mother's insecurity and low self-esteem.

During early home visits with families of premature babies, home visitors can encourage parents to talk about their fears, confusions, or worries. Often, parents have not had the opportunity to share these concerns with another person. A home visitor can invite parents to talk about their baby's prematurity and any lingering questions or concerns they may have. We know that in order for parents to focus on their baby and promote their baby's development, parents' needs must be met. Since premature babies can be easily overstimulated, home visitors can assist parents in reading the language of their baby's behavior to learn what amount of stimulation their baby can tolerate. Because premature babies initially do not give a lot of positive feedback to their parents, some parents can feel that they are not being effective parents. They often need extra support, encouragement, and acknowledgment of their efforts. Home visitors can reassure parents by reminding them that their baby's age is better reflected by his or her due date instead of his or her delivery date. When home visitors comment positively on the baby's growth and changing behaviors, parents are encouraged and can become more relaxed. In addition, some home visiting programs develop support groups of parents who have had similar experiences with their premature babies.

Allergies

Home visitors also need to consider possible allergies. Asthma and eczema usually are inherited allergies; thus, parents with family history of these illnesses need to watch carefully for possible allergies in their young children. If asthma or eczema begin, parents need immediate help from their doctor because if these conditions are allowed to escalate, young children feel helpless and anxious, which can increase the severity of their illnesses.

If a young child's cold extends beyond 2 or 3 weeks and congestion seems endless, the cold infection may have developed into an allergic reaction. Over the past few months, when Janice has visited Tracy and her toddler, Maggie, Maggie has been congested. Janice helps Tracy understand the possibility of allergies.

Janice asks Tracy if Maggie (age 19 months) has a cold or if it seems to be allergies. Maggie had clear nasal drainage this morning, and her chest seems quite congested.

Tracy answers, "Maggie has had a cold for a little over 3 weeks."

"The allergy count has been very high this spring," Janice explains. "It might be helpful to ask the pediatrician about the possibility of Maggie having allergies."

"I never really thought about allergies," Tracy admits.

Janice then explains that when one of her sons was quite young, he had allergic reactions in the spring. Tracy replies that she will ask the doctor and will watch if being outdoors triggers Maggie's congestion. Janice then initiates play activities with Maggie and her old sister, Mia. Before leaving, she initiates a conversation about using a cold water vaporizer to help Maggie's breathing. Tracy replies that occasionally she uses one to help Maggie's congestion.

Janice says, "My son's pediatrician warned me that the cold water vaporizer builds up mold, which was one of the things Tom was allergic to. If Tom had a cold, the allergies would kick in, and he would have an allergic reaction."

During this visit, Janice gave Tracy information to see that Maggie's recurrent lingering colds and congestion may be due to allergic reactions. This was new information for Tracy. The younger the child is, the more successful allergy treatment can be. Once she had Maggie's allergies confirmed, Tracy could take prevention steps. She eliminated stuffed animals, feather pillows, and throw rugs in Maggie's room. She turned on the air conditioner more often, which protected Maggie from some of the airborne allergens. She also began using antihistamines so that Maggie's breathing would not get obstructed. These steps prevented Maggie from having more symptoms.

Developmental Importance of Illness

New parents, especially parents who find their child's illness a major intrusion in their already complex lives, may not understand the developmental importance of their child's frequent illness. Working parents also feel the pull of conflicting demands when their child is sick: Do I earn a living or care for my child? Home visitors can offer developmental information and suggestions to help parents manage their child's illness as a natural part of growth and development—an experience that provides the child with significant learning about self and other and with development of prosocial behavior. In addition, the visitor can be aware of and sensitive to the parents' feelings and concerns, for example, feelings of inadequacy in the face of illness, fear of their baby's fragility, or anger over the intrusiveness of this illness.

Times when young children are sick are intense interpersonal periods for both parent and child. Children's illness is a time that can test parents' sense of competence and children's sense of security, but when parents successfully nurse their child through illness, they gain a sense of competence, and the child gains an increased sense of being cared for in a safe world.

DIFFICULTIES AND DILEMMAS

As home visitors strive to promote young parents ability to create and sustain healthy everyday rituals, celebrations, and traditions, they may encounter several difficulties. The first problem usually occurs in work with families with low incomes because babies failing to thrive most often live in families of this environment. The second difficulty comes from the modern family's functioning in that the complexities of the modern family's functioning may create obstacles to providing predictable everyday rituals. Third, when parents are trying to bridge two family traditions, each containing unique patterns of everyday ritual, celebrations, and traditions, parents may find that two patterns are not easy to blend. Finally, home visitors may confront family problems that are unique to single parents or to a recently divorced family.

When home visitors work with low-income families with multiple problems, they need to watch for signs of poor growth and development in young babies and toddlers. These signs may be evidence of failure to thrive (FTT) syndrome, the medical term used to identify babies characterized by growth and development failure.[33] FTT is caused by malnourishment, which generally results from parents' inability to see and respond to their baby's needs. FTT is not an organic disease; rather, it is a descriptive phrase identifying babies and toddlers having growth failure. A child with FTT is less than 2 years of age and most often is less than 6 months of age. Beyond failing to gain weight, these babies often have disrupted social-emotional development, delayed psychomotor development, and developmental retardation. Research has shown that malnourishment, especially during the first 6 months can cause permanent brain damage. Babies hospitalized during their first year of life for FTT are likely to be cognitively slow during later years.[34] Children under 2 years of age who experience multiple risk factors such as poverty and low birth weight can be susceptible to FTT. Given the individual differences and fluidity of baby development, recognizing FTT early is one of the most important base line responsibilities of home visitors.

People often see weight gain as concrete evidence of good parenting. When their baby or toddler is diagnosed with FTT, parents often respond defensively. No parent wants to hear from others or admit to themselves that they are inadequate parents. Given this pattern, home

Table 1. Guidelines for effective communication with parents of young children with failure to thrive (FTT)

1. Some parents will not express concern about their child's growth when this child is diagnosed with FTT. Communicating sensitivity to parents' sense of competence while helping parents recognize the needs of their child with FTT requires sensitivity and careful balancing of information.
2. Taking time to learn parents' views of their child's condition is central to parents' trust of the professional.
3. Professionals should expect that many parents will give a medical explanation for their child's failure to gain weight.
4. Professionals should expect that some parents will disagree with the medical diagnosis of FTT, especially when they see their toddler running and climbing.
5. It can be very helpful to focus on the future when discussing the child's condition with the parent. That is, parents can feel supported when a primary focus is how they can improve their child's growth and development.

From Sturm, L., & Drotar, D. (1992). Communication strategies for working with parents of infants who fail to thrive. *Zero to Three, 12*(5), 25–28; adapted by permission.

visitors need to be sensitive when they work with parents of FTT babies and toddlers. Table 1 provides several guidelines for effective communication with parents of young children with FTT.[35].

The second challenge is less life threatening but is also developmentally important. New family structures offer complexities that challenge our society's taken-for-granted notion of family life and threaten parents' ability to develop predictable daily rituals.[36] Home visitors need to be alert to these changes and develop flexibility in assisting parents in exploring new patterns of everyday rituals. As everyday family life in the United States becomes increasingly more complex, it becomes challenging for parents to provide predictable routines for their young children. It is increasingly rare for one parent to be a full-time homemaker. Only 10% of American families consist of two parents with one home full time. About half of the children in the United States will spend time in a single parent home.[37]

Current technology often merges family and work life. With car phones, personal computers, electronic mail, fax machines, and so forth, technology allows adults to bring their work lives into their homes. Television and videotapes have become ready-made babysitters. It is not uncommon for family members to have different daily schedules (e.g., older children engaged in sports or other after-school events, parents traveling out-of-town). These patterns often lead to disruption of families' daily rituals; for example, regular dinner times disappear as different family members are involved in their own tasks. No longer is shared family time a given. Family members, even spouses, share less and less of a common reality. As the home visitor and parents share in activities and conversations, the home visitor can help parents recognize their young child's need for predictable, daily, shared family rituals. Once parents understand this need, the home visitor and parent can brainstorm strategies to make certain these daily family rituals take place.

Home visitors also need to be alert to the complexities that spouses experience in joining their two family traditions, which not all couples think out thoroughly prior to marriage. Many people get married without realizing the challenge of uniting two different family traditions. Traditions such as celebrating a holiday or summer vacations may or may not be complementary. In addition, given the pluralistic nature of our society, beyond merging family traditions, many couples marry across race, ethnicity, and religion. For these couples, rituals take on added meaning because they must blend the traditions of not only two separate childhoods, but also two racial, ethnic, or religious communities. Food for everyday mealtimes may not be a taken-for-granted part of one's day; rather the couple may need to have mindful discussions about the different foods of their respective families. Initially, it may be helpful for menu planning and shopping to be a joint activity of planning and action. Some inter-religious couples may need to made decisions regarding holidays, such as questions of celebrating Chanukah or Christmas. Parents often see their home visitor as a supportive person with whom they can talk through their decision making as they blend two family traditions.

CONCLUSION

This chapter discussed families' everyday routines, childhood illness, and how illness disrupts taken-for-grant daily patterns of family life, and traditional family rituals, which we call celebrations to distinguish them from everyday rituals. Rituals consist of repeated, predictable patterns of interactions among family members that give each family member shared beliefs and values, a sense of belonging, and identity. For young children, everyday rituals of eating, sleeping, diapering, and toilet training are the settings for developmental growth. Although this discussion of these daily rituals may seem very detailed, it is in the detail that the quality of parent–child interaction has an impact on the child's development and sense of self. Initially, daily rituals of eating and going to sleep allow for the child's biological regulation. Intertwined with the interactions in these rituals is regulation of the child's emotion. Development in all areas (e.g., a sense of self, a sense of relatedness, language and communication, and an understanding of the world) occur within parent and child interaction of everyday rituals.

Frequent childhood illnesses can disrupt everyday interactions and can lead to both parents' and children's feelings of insecurity. At the same time, illness can be a setting for enriched social relatedness between family members and young children's learning of nurturance and caring. Regularly occurring family celebrations reflect both unique family beliefs and values and those of the culture. These celebrations provide family members with a sense of belonging and shared identity.

10

∫iblings

I was the eldest of five children. But I have very few memories of my early childhood in which my brother does not play a part. I remember my second birthday party and I remember spoiling my new red shoes by going out in the snow that winter. Then in spring Richard was born, and very soon Margaret and Richard were expected to do everything together.

We used to have our supper together, wearing white nightclothes (with feet) and eating cereal or, on ∫unday night, brownies made of dried remains of ∫aturday's Boston browis bread and baked beans soaked in hot milk. We were taught to sing the same songs together until it became obvious that while Richard's voice was true and clear, I had no voice at all.

Margaret Mead (1972, p. 61)

Relationships with siblings endure longer than any other. The sibling bond generates feelings of intimacy, support, and belonging. The strength of the sibling bond is indicated by the way people use of the terms *brother* and *sister* in religious groups, sororities, fraternities, unions, and service clubs. Communities have "big brother" programs in which men "adopt" boys from single-parent families. Some African Americans greet each other as "brother" or "sister" or refer to each other in conversation as "brother" or "sister," with or without the person's name.

The childhood history siblings share allows them to understand one another's strengths and vulnerabilities more fully than they can understand such personality traits among people outside of the family. Older siblings often act as tutors to young children, teaching them games, skills like how to skip, or what to expect at school. Within this shared history, siblings can provide a lifelong support system and a source of honest feedback, as well as shared responsibilities caring for sick and aging parents.

The sibling bond, however, also contains rivalry and conflict. Although quarrels among siblings are normal, many children in the same family actually spend a large portion of their childhood playing and positively relating with each other. Research indicates that siblings as young as 3 years old can skillfully understand their younger siblings' acts and feelings and can adapt their speaking to accommodate their younger brother's or sister's developmental level.[1]

Once parents have a second child, they encounter unexpected new experiences that can challenge their sense of competence as parents, change their image of family life, and evoke memories of their own childhood struggles. This chapter discusses themes that emerge in families with multiple children. These themes include

1. Preparation for the new infant
2. Parental expectations and comparisons
3. Parents relating differently to their children
4. Children's perceptions of these differences
5. Siblings' patterns of relating, including conflicts and rivalry

The discussion reviews how home visitors can support and affirm parents and their children and provides helpful developmental information, interpretation, and suggested parenting approaches. The chapter explores the skills needed for home visitors to balance their involvement with parents and more than one child.

PREPARATION FOR THE NEW INFANT

Sometimes, parents worry that if they have another child, the older child will suffer because the new baby will distract them from their relationship with their older child. These feelings are strongest before the birth of the second child because the first child has had the parents' exclusive attention. Not surprisingly, the first child may resent the sibling's intrusion and may fear parents' loss of love more than middle children might. But adjusting to a new sibling also offers new learning opportunities. Brazelton stated that there is no ideal time for having a second child. He claimed that once parents "can handle another, the first child can handle one, too."[2] In contrast, White stressed that the ideal spacing of children is a minimum of 3 years because rivalry and resentment are more problematic for first children younger than 3 years old.[3]

The addition of a new child to the family brings significant changes in the older children's everyday life, changes that begin in the months leading up to the birth of the child. It is normal for pregnant women to turn inward and subtly withdraw from their family. Older children notice these changes. Thus, it is helpful for parents to discuss the baby's pending arrival, beginning in early pregnancy, as if the pregnancy were a natural event in the family's development.

Home visitors can offer parents needed support and guidance during this important transition period of family life. As they help parents prepare their first child for the arrival of the new baby, home visitors can also help parents realize that their concerns are normal. The following conversation between Janice and Shelly is illustrative. Shelly is in her second month of pregnancy. She tells Janice that her daughter, Erin (age 32 months), thinks she is having the baby.

Janice: Let it go.

Shelly: She says, "I'm going to have one and you, too, but not Daddy. He doesn't have milk."

Janice: Erin wants to be like you.

Shelly: I'm concerned because she is with me so much. I'm getting Rob to do more with her, like wash her hair.

Janice: You are going to see her really growing up in the next several months—around 3 years.

Shelly: Everybody tells me we're going to have so many problems when there's a new baby.

Janice: It's always an adjustment, and it's always hardest with the first child. The second child is used to sharing attention when another child comes.

Shelly: We've never even spent a night away from Erin.

Janice: My three children are just about the same distance apart. I remember how well my first was able to entertain himself. Erin also is very skilled at that.

Shelly: Now, I think I'll be more worried than Erin. Erin probably will be fine.

Janice: As long as you know there's an adjustment—that nothing is wrong. As long as you are really sensitive to what she is needing. You and Rob are wonderful parents, and you'll continue to be. We'll talk about it more.

Shelly: It's hard to imagine having another one, hard to think it's possible that you can split the time and have the same feelings for the second one.

Janice: You'll experience a whole range of new feelings. I can't even describe the excitement of seeing the two children together. You'll wonder at it— at Erin's sensitivity and at the baby's response.

In the 32 months Janice and Shelly have known each other, they have developed a close personal relationship. Shelly feels comfortable sharing her worries with Janice. In turn, Janice offers reassurance: She reminds Shelly of her daughter's strengths and that Erin will develop new skills in the coming months. She compares Erin's strength to that of the oldest of her own three children and thereby lets Shelly know that she has had similar experiences. Janice is able to interpret the meaning of Erin's behavior. She acknowledges that the new baby will be an adjustment for all family members; at the same time, she affirms Shelly and her husband's parenting skills.

Two months after the previous conversation took place, Shelly shares with Janice what she has learned when she attended two parent meetings that focused on siblings. She reports that Rob has arranged time for activities just for Erin and himself, and she sees them becoming much closer. Shelly describes her plans for rearranging the space in their small home, and Janice replies, "A lot will fall into place. Probably you're better off to let Erin have the same space that she is used to. So much else will be new for her."

As the months progress, Shelly tells Janice about the plans she and Rob are making together and about how they are involving Erin in preparations for the new baby. Over time, Shelly shows more confidence in both Erin's and her own ability to adjust to the birth of her new baby. Janice's visits have offered needed support, reassurance, and guidance during this significant transition in the family's everyday life.

BIRTH OF THE ADDITIONAL BABY

As discussed previously, the birth of a new baby sparks older siblings' fear of losing their parents' love. Because older children go through so many changes in their moment-to-moment experiences, once the new baby arrives, it is normal for these children to feel a large sense of loss. Parents' feelings about their older child change after the new baby's birth. Parents often expect more grown-up behavior, yet they find that suddenly their older child begins acting in babyish ways (e.g., suddenly asking for a bottle, having toileting accidents). Home visitors can reassure parents that it is normal for their older child to regress. Home visitors can suggest to parents possible new patterns of family life in which the older child can participate. For example, parents can create ways in which their older child could help with baby care. Home visitors can call attention to the skills the older child has but the baby does not; in doing so, they affirm the older child. Home visitors also can help parents reassure the older child of their love by setting aside a few moments each day to be with only the older child. Just as they helped parents know what to expect with their first child, home visitors can give information regarding expectations of older siblings' behavior.

Natalie's 3-month-old, Jene, has just fallen asleep in Natalie's arms. Dvonne (age 3½ years) is playing in the back yard.

Natalie: Now he is doing very well. It's helpful that he can enjoy playing outside without me.

Janice: It's nice that he feels that way about his new sister. It indicates what a close relationship you two have. His ability to go play outdoors by himself says good things about your relationship with him. And Dvonne still is in a period of adjustment. His life has changed dramatically and will continue to change, like when she becomes mobile. And he'll sense she is getting more attention because of her doing new things, and how [he has] to adjust again and again.

The first few months can be a relatively easy adjustment for the older sibling because the new infant sleeps a great deal. Janice is helping Natalie understand that, as her daughter matures, Dvonne will begin to experience more intrusion from his sibling. At the same time, Janice gives a clear affirmation to Natalie regarding her role in her son's healthy adjustment and independence.

In her relations with older children, Janice repeatedly affirms the first child in relation to the younger sibling. For example, when Maggie began crawling at age 8 months, Janice told Maggie's 26-month-old sister, Mia, "Look at Maggie crawl! Did you show her how to do that? I bet you showed her all you could do, and she thought, 'Look at my big sister.'" When Dvonne's 4-month-old sister began fussing, Janice said, "Your sister is saying, 'I want to play with you.'" Home visitors often bring special toys for the older child. When Janice begins visiting Marta's second child, Brianna, she brings Brianna's 3-year-old brother, Antoine, a wooden train set. As Janice and Marta chat with Brianna on the floor in the living room, Antoine puts together the train set in the adjoining kitchen. When Antoine joins Janice and Marta, Janice affirms him (e.g., "Only Antoine can play with tiny things because Antoine is old enough to understand. Brianna is still too little.")

Once another child is born, home visitors usually try to divide their attention between the children. If the home visitor has been working with the family since the first child's infancy, the parents have been exposed to the developmental information on infancy. Often, parents maintain their focus on the oldest child because the behaviors of the oldest child are new to the parent. It can be challenging for home visitors to reintroduce infant material in a meaningful and nonrepetitious manner. Sometimes, home visitors can interpret the infants' behavior for the older sibling. Then, the home visitor is both involving the older sibling in the home visit and still providing information for the parent.

> When Janice arrives at Tracey's home, Maggie (age 8 months) is a bit uneasy. Janice explains to Mia (age 26 months), "Maggie knows, 'Someone strange is in my house.' When Janice and Carol come, Maggie is not sure yet—they are not Mia, Mommy, or Daddy. She knows she loves Mia, Mommy, and Daddy. She's not sure of those new people."

Janice both involves the older sibling, Mia, in the home visit and provides information for Tracy, the girls' mother.

PARENT EXPECTATIONS AND COMPARISONS

Every parent has images of what or how they would like their child to be. These images are central to parents' expectations. Tracy's comments are a poignant example.

> When Maggie comes, I want Mia to be as old as I want her to be. I have to remind myself that she is still a baby.

Parental expectations can be powerful influences on their own and their children's behavior. As noted previously, after the birth of a new baby, parents may expect competency from their oldest child while the child is acting like a baby. When their older child behaves immaturely, parents may respond in anger. This anger is not a response simply to their child but to the difference in unstated expectations and the child's action. When home visitors help parents say their expectation out loud, parents often see that they are being unrealistic.

Parents unwittingly have different expectations for each of their children. These expectations stem from factors that are unique for different children and parents. Sometimes more is expected from first children and from sons.[4] Sometimes the first child sets the standard for younger siblings. Although the second child develops differently, parents may set their expectations according to the development of their first child. When parental expectations are not met, parents sometimes feel overwhelmed and inadequate. Often, the child senses these feelings. Shelly's comments to her home visitor are illustrative.

Shelly: I remember the parent meetings on siblings and the leader saying that the first-born always knows the rules. We would never let Erin get by with what her younger brother does.

Janice: And she wouldn't try.

A central way in which people know and understand objects, people, and events is by making comparisons with other objects, people, and events in their lives. It is normal for parents to compare their children. As parents make these comparisons in conversations with home visitors, home visitors can let them know that their comparisons and accompanying feelings are normal. Home visitors can talk about how even though all children progress through similar developmental phases, the timing and speed of development varies for each child. Similarly, they can show that each child has a different personality and temperament and assist parents in understanding that their children are more different from each other than the same. Talking about these differences is natural, but comparisons become problematic when they are judgmental—that is, when one child is deemed good or bad but is just different from the sibling.

Often, the home visitor can make an interpretive comment to help parents to understand their different children's behavior and development.

Natalie: When Jene [age 3 months] is in her crib, I hear her making noises as she sucks her fists.

Janice: How wonderful—by herself. The best possible way.

Natalie: Dvonne needed the pacifier to drop off to sleep, and he'd cry whenever it fell out of his mouth. He still needs his pacifier when going to bed.

Janice: She doesn't need it, for she can calm herself without it.

Natalie: She's such a good baby. Dvonne didn't sleep through the night until he was 3.

Janice: Each child is born with a different temperament; that is, different babies have different manners of sleeping, different levels of activity, and different ways of responding to their parents. It seems as if your children each have a different temperament.

Natalie: That's helpful. I keep talking of Jene being a good baby, but I don't mean that Dvonne is bad.

As Natalie spontaneously compared her two children, she unwittingly thought of her second baby as the "good" baby, in contrast to Dvonne. She might unintentionally communicate these judgments to Dvonne. Janice introduces the idea that each infant is born with a unique temperament that is expressed in different ways of relating to others and different levels of activity, and Natalie begins to understand that her children's differences are not a matter of good versus bad.

When Janice returns home after the visit, she writes a note on the home visit form to remember to continue the comparison topic on future visits in order to make certain that Natalie understands temperament and comparisons. As the months progress, Natalie continues to make comparisons of her children, but in a new manner. She compares Jene and Dvonne nonjudgmentally. For example, when Jene is 6 months old, Natalie describes how Dvonne, when a baby, seemed to manage well when different people beyond his parents were present; however, Jene seems to need to have her mother at her side. In response, Janice is able to explain that this is the age when infants learn to be very aware of different people who are not their parents, and she notes that every child follows a different path in relating to others.

VALUING EACH CHILD AS SPECIAL

Studies provide convincing evidence that siblings not only are different from each other, but also do not experience the same family life in the same way.[5] Faber and Mazlish noted that although it is natural for parents to strive to treat their children equally, in reality, parents unwittingly treat each of their children quite differently.[6] Children are sensitive not only to how their parents treat them, but also to how their parents treat their siblings. Just as it is normal for parents to compare their children, children also compare their parents' treatment of themselves as opposed to their siblings. In contrast to popular opinion, studies indicate that there is no straightforward relationship between a child's birth order and how the child is treated by parents or siblings.[7] In reality, siblings do not need to be treated equally by their parents. Rather, each child needs to feel that parents treat him or her uniquely, that their parents value each of them as special.

As home visitors help parents to be good observers of their infant and his or her older siblings and to gain information on the meaning of their children's actions and development, they play an important role in assisting parents to recognize the specialness of each child. When home visitors are relating to the older sibling, they often can model for the parent ways to affirm the older siblings in relation to their younger sibling. For example, they can invite the older child to give the younger one a toy. The following excerpts from two of Janice's home visits are illustrative.

As Mia (age 21 months) plays at the side of her mother, Tracy, Janice and Tracy discuss Mia's increased vocabulary and ability to express her needs verbally. Janice comments to Mia, "You're teaching Maggie [age 3 months] to talk, too—all those good sounds."

Janice has put on the floor two 10-inch-high cylindrical canisters, each with a circular hole on the lid. Janice empties one canister and dumps out an array of small film cans. Maggie (age 12 months) takes a canister and immediately puts it in her mouth. Mia (age 30 months) skillfully puts the film cans into the canister's circular hole. Janice says to her, "It helps Maggie to learn when you play with what she does. Good, right there in the hole of the can. And Maggie is watching everything you do." Mia smiles proudly as she continues the task.

Janice's comments help Mia feel she is special. When Janice praises Mia's ability to do things better than Maggie, Janice helps to counteract Mia's inevitable ambivalent or jealous feelings. As Tracy observes the way Janice helps Mia feel good, how Mia really helps her baby sister learn, Tracy learns to affirm Mia herself in a more powerful way than she would have if Janice had just made a verbal suggestion. Tracy has not only a clear example but also the concrete results to observe: Maggie's delight.

In an interview, Tracy spoke of the pleasure she gets when she observes Janice and her children.

Tracy: I like the fact that when she does come into my home, she directly interacts with the kids, rather than just sitting down and just talking to me.

Carol: What part of the home visit do you find most enjoyable?

Tracy: Actually, just watching how my kids respond to what Janice is asking them to do. It's exciting to see that they can do what she asks them to do . . . and every time Janice leaves, she tells me, "You are doing a wonderful job." And it makes me feel real good for somebody to come and tell me I am doing so good, and my kids are developing so good.

Mia was born 2 years after Tracy and her husband graduated from high school. Janice's ability to involve Tracy's children in play activities and to discuss how their behavior points to their development helps this young mother recognize her children's strengths. She can believe Janice's verbal praise of her children because she has repeatedly observed her children succeed with Janice, and these repeated experiences allow Tracy to integrate Janice's verbal praise of Tracy as a mother.

SIBLING RELATIONSHIPS

Fighting among siblings is normal. Although some parents focus on the fighting, most siblings also spend a lot of time playing together and interacting with each other in many different ways. For example, siblings do family chores together, walk to school together, join in games with neighborhood friends together, and simply play with each other for hours without fighting. In their hours together, siblings experience a wide range of feelings, both positive and negative. They experience shared interest, affection, caring, and nurturance, as well as jealousy, irritation, control, conflict, and rivalry. The sibling relationship changes as the children's developmental levels change and as each child is able to both enjoy the sibling and be frustrated by a sibling in new ways. Each sibling relationship is unique to each child.[8] That is, each child may experience his or her relationship to a brother or sister quite differently than does the brother or sister. For example, a younger child may view her sister as a good friend with whom she loves to play, whereas the older sister may view the little one as bothersome and intrusive.

The age and developmental level of children is a big factor in the ease with which siblings interact with each other. The most psychologically dangerous period is toddlerhood because when a sibling is born, the toddler is at the age where fear of losing parents' love and being replaced is most upsetting.[9] A 3- to 6-year-old can better understand parents' explanations about the new baby and is more skilled at maintaining focus on play and playing alone. When the youngest child is a toddler, the toddler frequently disrupts the older sibling's play because exploring is the toddler's natural way of relating to the world. Usually, toddlers do not understand their intrusiveness. Because older children can better understand their parents, parents may expect them to be more generous with their younger sibling than is fair or developmentally appropriate. In this case, home visitors can make sure that the parents understand what they are expecting of each child and can help the parent to test whether the expectations are realistic.

Personality and temperament also influence the way in which siblings interact with each other. An older child's temperamental style and personality influence the child's ability to accept a new baby, and later affects how he or she responds to a toddler sibling's intrusions. For example, an even-tempered toddler can be more accepting and patient than a more active, easily frustrated toddler.

Home visitors can assist parents in helping their children get along in many different ways. As previously discussed, Janice modeled skill in affirming the older child's skill level in contrast to the younger sibling and in giving the older child small tasks to help her younger sibling. As the second baby develops, Janice asks if the children are playing together more, and parents often enjoy in sharing small sequences of their children's play.

Tracy: It's fun to see how Maggie [age 18 months] follows along with Mia [age 36 months], with purses, dolls, stuff like that. The other night, they were playing with a Wiffle ball in their bedroom. Mia was trying to get Maggie to play catch, and Maggie was laughing so hard. In the next room, Dave and I chuckled as we listened to them.

Janice: Now that she is three, Mia is getting better and better [at] playing with Maggie. Three-year-olds understand more.

Janice frames these questions positively, and in turn, parents like to describe their children playing together. Janice's frequent questions help parents become good observers of their children's play together. Seeing over time how Janice enjoys their children, the parents will spontaneously share when their children enjoy each other, for example, when an infant begins to enjoy watching her brother's play, or when an older sibling spontaneously assists his younger brother.

Natalie: Dvonne [3 ½ years] will get down on the floor with Jene [age 4 months], and tell her to say "Dada" or say "Mama." He plays with her like that.

Janice: Wonderful. A study I recently read showed that when the first child gets involved with the baby, it makes a difference in the second child's language development. It's going to help.

Janice takes pleasure in Natalie's telling about her children. She also provides developmental information to help Natalie understand the value of her son's interactions with Jene. As the months progress, this kind of exchange between Janice and Natalie becomes a natural part of the home visit.

Sibling Rivalry and Fighting

It is inevitable that brothers and sisters will be jealous and competitive with each other and will fight. When parents are able to stay out of their children's fights, children have a chance to learn to work out problems together. Letting their children fight without interfering is difficult for most parents. It is natural for parents' images of being good parents to be threatened when their children fight. When parents do become engaged in their children's fights, fighting can become the setting for children to manipulate their parents (e.g., by convincing the parents of who is at fault or what a punishment should be).

Home visitors can help parents understand that their children's fights are normal. They also can help parents see these fights as an opportunity for their children to learn social skills, especially conflict resolution skills. Faber and Mazlish (1987) as well as Galinsky and David (1988) provided helpful suggestions for parents to respond to their children's fighting.[10]

If one child is dominating the other, or if one child has an unfair advantage, however, home visitors can help the parents to intervene in a constructive way. Parents can learn when it is most reasonable to withdraw (e.g., when their children are bickering) or when to intervene (e.g., to separate children when a situation is potentially dangerous). Most important, home visitors can provide helpful suggestions for parents to assist their children in learning how to negotiate. For example, the parent can allow each child to state his or her feelings and intentions, or, if the child is quite young, the parent can verbalize feelings and intentions. Then, the parent can help the children figure out solutions to the problem. As home visitors help parents learn to talk about their young children's feelings and intentions, some parents are having their first experience in recognizing and talking about feelings and intentions. When that happens, parents are learning the same significant social skills as their children. Parents and children are developing an increased ability to recognize the perspective of the other, as well as recognize their own feelings and motivations.

PARENTS AND SIBLINGS: BALANCING
THE HOME VISITOR'S INTERACTIONS

When there are two or more mobile children plus their parent in the interactions of a home visit, the home visitor's job becomes more diffi- cult. His or her task may be most challenging when the older child is still a toddler because the toddler may not be mature enough to focus on solitary play activities for an extended time while the home visitor focuses with the infant. As home visitors develop their skills, they learn the art of introducing activities that invite extended involvement for both children. Janice demonstrates remarkable talent in orchestrating sustained involvement of Maggie and Mia, siblings with 18 months of difference in age.

Janice removes from her bag a box filled with several dozen colored 2-inch diameter circular plastic chips, each with either one, two, or five holes in the center. She also removes two cardboard and two plastic canisters, each with a slot on the lid. As she puts the toys on the rig, she says to Mia (age 33 months) and Maggie (age 15 months), "I brought these today. There's enough so that everybody can play."

Mia immediately takes some chips and places them into one of the holes of the canister as she says, "It's like a bank to put money in."

Janice answers, "You are right. It's like a bank to put money in." Mean- while, Maggie uses alternate hands to put chips into a canister that does not have a top. Mia puts two chips into a slot at the same time, and Janice says, "Mia, you did that fast, putting two in at the same time. Wow!" As she watches Maggie open and shut the cigar box containing the chips, Jan- ice says, "Close the box, open the box, close the box." Maggie then places a chip through a large slot of another canister. Janice exclaims, "Good, Maggie; you put it right through the slot!"

As Mia watches, she says, "Yeah, Maggie."

Both children stay included in extended play. Because of Janice's repeated affirmation of Mia, Mia is able to enthusiastically praise her younger sister. As Maggie and Mia play, Janice repeatedly describes the children's play. These descriptions affirm the children's involvement, help them recognize their own successes, and model powerful ways for Tracy to help her children develop their self-worth.

Maggie continues to busily dump several chips into a can and then dumps them out and begins the process again. (Both children have remained fo- cused in play for 15 minutes.)

Janice places a 12-cup muffin tin on the floor, and Mia slowly places one chip into each of the muffin tin cups as Janice says with each placement, "One, one, one," and so forth. Mia then begins placing a second disk into each of the cups as Janice comments, "One more makes two."

When Mia seems to tire of filling the muffin tin, Janice gives her a string with a knot on its end and suggests, "Do you think we could put some of these on the string?" Janice holds up two red chips, one with one hole and one with five holes. She asks Mia which chip looks like the one on the string, and Mia picks the chip with the one hole and puts it on the string. They continue this game until Mia has about 10 chips of the string. Janice comments, "Good, you know all of them that have just one hole."

As Mia and Janice play together, Maggie continues to play with the canisters and chips. Janice asks Tracy if Mia understands "two," and Tracy shrugs as she says, "Try it." Janice suggests to Mia that they can string the two-hole chips and shows her how she can put the string in each of the holes as if she were sewing. Mia then successfully chooses the two-hole chips and puts the string through them. Janice then holds up her string as she says, "Look how nice it is. Maggie, isn't it nice what your sister has made? The ones are on the bottom and the twos are on the top." As Janice speaks, Mia smiles.

Janice then removes two large metal spoons from her bag and shows Mia how she can tap the bottom of the canister with the spoon. Mia seems to enjoy this tapping action. She alternately taps the plastic and the metal bottom of the canisters as Janice comments, "Different sounds. The plastic one is not like this one, is it?" Mia nods her head.

During these activities, each child is able to maintain sustained interest in the same toys. With each child, Janice plays several roles—observing, affirming, clarifying, structuring, and extending the children's action as well as interpreting their actions for the children's mother. These are roles typical of Janice's work with one child and parent, but made more complex with two small children 18 months apart in age.

As the children play, Janice extends and structures new uses of simple materials. She integrates learning into the children's play. Her descriptive comments help these young children learn important concepts. For example, she comments about sameness versus difference of sound and spatial relationships of the one- and two-hole disks on the string. Janice explained her approach as follows.

I think all of that helps parents to see how children's play is legitimate learning. And many times, I can say in a visit, a statement that I heard Burton White say in a training session several years ago, that this is just as serious learning as any child is doing in school. It's neat to see the parents' reaction to that—they'll grin, or say, "Oh, really!" It just makes what the child does seem important to the parents, and it is important.

Learning through play is discussed more fully in Chapter 8.

Although she usually has a general idea of the children's play involvement, Janice also improvises. In our conversation after this visit, Janice commented:

> I have to admit, I just thought of that on the spot. I knew that in the visit, I wanted to differentiate the task for Mia and still follow her lead. And once she started threading, I thought this is the time we can start talking about numbers and help her mom realize that she can be aware of those kinds of things. And I thought, "Oh, that's going to work. I can do it some more."

Janice always has some activity plans before beginning a home visit. She chooses activities that are somewhat open-ended so that she can be flexible in use of materials. This flexibility is especially important when more than one child is present because unpredictable occurrences are more likely during the home visit. Beyond having materials, the home visitor constantly observes, interprets, and evaluates ongoing happenings. This internal dialogue, which sometimes is only in the home visitor's mind, but which often is what the home visitor is saying aloud, allows the home visitor to shift gears when appropriate. Knowing that relationships are more important in promoting development than any specific activity gives the home visitor the security to be flexible.

In some situations, the home visitor has not worked previously with the family's older children. Because the home visiting experience is relatively new, it is not unusual for the older children to be more demanding of attention. For these families, home visitors need to provide play activities specifically geared for the older children and to be prepared to devote some time to these older children.

DIFFICULTIES AND DILEMMAS

Each home visitor has a caseload of families of varying size and varying patterns of relationships. When focusing on siblings, there are two identifiable problem areas that may provoke challenges for the home visitor. First, parents may be carrying their unresolved childhood sibling conflicts or other unpleasant sibling experiences that left emotional scars. A second difficult area entails making home visits in families with several children present.

Ever since Cain asked, "Am I my brother's keeper?" it has been clear that there is tension in sibling relationships. When parents' childhood feelings are extremely problematic, parents may carry them into their own parenting. For example, they may feel helpless and out of control when their children tease each other or fight because these sibling behaviors trigger the parents' own feelings from their negative childhood experiences of living in a family with continual sibling conflict. Other parents live with feelings of being less competent than their siblings or being left out, and these feelings are carried into their interactions with their own children. When these parenting dynamics are operating, the home visitor's role takes on new dimensions. First, home visitors learn to recognize these parent–child dynamics. Once they recognize the dynamics, home visitors need to decide whether this issue can be addressed in the home visitor's work with the parent or whether the family needs a referral to a mental health specialist or other resource.

The home visitor's task can become very challenging when he or she visits homes where there are many children. Sometimes all the children are within one large family; at other times, two different families are living in the same home. To have a successful home visit, the home visitor must be flexible and skilled in working with people of various ages. In these situations, the home visitor often does not know how many people will be present during the visit. Some home visitors go prepared with materials and/or activity ideas for each of the age ranges. Others chose activities that all different ages can enjoy. Cynthia works with many low-income families in which several children always are involved in her home visits. Cynthia shared her approach during these visits.

> It's not as hard as it sounds. You just need to have a couple of good books. Books are wonderful because what you can do with a book is settle down. It settles you in hopes of a quiet time. Lots of times, if I have more than one child, I'll start out with a book and read it just to set the tone—a pleasant time.
>
> The hardest thing is working with two babies. If you have a toddler and a small baby, that is a high level of difficulty because their attention span is real short. So the baby has to have lots of different activities, lots of things to do. Toddlers demand a lot of attention in that respect. Sometimes I think they get the bulk, and in that case, I may actually plan a time when I know that child is napping so I can spend more time with the baby. And you can have some material for each child. So if you get the kids included in that, then you have time to play with the other child and to work with Mom.

Especially when siblings and parents seem to have difficulty with managing kids, I like to do activities where everybody can play, regardless of their age. Then, what you can show Mom is yes, this 6-month-old can play lotto. And it's a time for Mom to hold the baby. Let the baby hold the cards while Mom is still interacting with the 4-year-old and doing the matching. And the baby wants to eat a card, and that's okay because it's cardboard.

The home where I went the other day, I had a 3-year-old, a 4-year-old, an 8-year-old, a 7-year-old, a 9-year-old, and a 13-month-old, and we all played lotto. Everybody had a card. They took turns. The older kids I used to be the callers, and they took turns calling. The 13-month-old got to walk around holding the cards and stacking them because he had extra cards. You can take one activity and make it apply to all the kids because that is what families do. Families don't get up in the morning and say, "Oh well, you are 12 months old, so you are going to do this activity. Okay, George, you are 15 years old," and so forth. Families do what they have to do, and everybody participates, and they all have a place. That's pretty much what I do with siblings.

Cynthia is skilled in involving all children in home visits, regardless of their age. She understands that if she is not successful in this task, parents will not gain much from her work with them because, as she states so clearly, "That's what families do" (i.e., participate in similar activities, regardless of the age span of family members).

CONCLUSION

The birth of additional children brings new family dynamics for both parents and their older children. Parents and their older children experience the push and pull of feelings, some of which are new and uncomfortable. Parents may experience unexpected changes in their feelings and expectations for their older child, challenges in their sense of parental competence, and unanticipated feelings, which may evoke their own childhood struggles as siblings. The older child's everyday predictability vanishes with the arrival of a new baby, and feelings of loss abound. During this transition period of a family, home visitors can listen, affirm both the parents and their children, and provide developmental information and suggestions as needed.

This chapter discusses common patterns of parenting more than one child, for example, having different expectations for each child, unwittingly comparing children, and relating to each child differently. We have seen how home visitors can assist parents in comparing their children nonjudgmentally and valuing each child as unique and special.

This chapter also examines how sibling relationships involve a complex web of interactions that cross over a wide range of feelings—from admiration, intimacy, support, and belonging to jealousy, competition, and rivalry. Each child's unique temperamental style and personality influence the nature of his or her relationships with siblings. Siblings' interactions with each other adjust with changes in their age and developmental level. Fighting usually is a normal part of this relationship; however, it may be quite problematic to the children's parents. Home visitors can help parents understand the different ways their children interact with each other. When parents are uneasy with their children's fighting, home visitors can give helpful developmental information and, when appropriate, assistance in gaining skill in conflict resolution.

Home visitors who deal with families who have more than one child are working in a complex web of relationships—relationships between children, between parents and their children, and between the home visitor and all family members. An essential skill in these situations is the home visitor's ability to orchestrate sustained involvement of young siblings and, at the same time, maintain interactions with their parents.

Two challenges are embedded in the home visitor's work with families with more than one child. First, home visitors need to develop awareness of when parents are bringing unresolved pain from childhood memories of their own siblings into their current parenting and when these parents may need assistance beyond the skills of a home visitor. Second, the balancing of one's interactions in homes with many children during a home visit demands great care and skill.

11

The Psychologically
Vulnerable Family

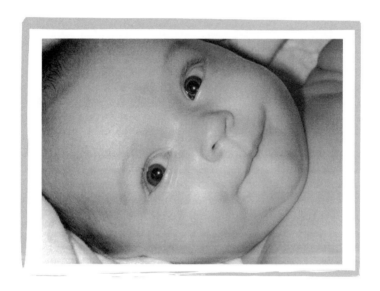

This uniqueness transforms the minus of the handicap into the
plus of the compensation.

Oliver Sacks, (1996, p. xvii)

Throughout the United States, many families live with high levels of chronic stress. A significant number of these families are coping with more than one stressor, such as low income, parental mental illness, domestic violence, or substance abuse. Given this reality, it is not surprising that many home visitors are confronted with babies, young children, and parents with significant problems. The unhealthy environments and family situations in which many babies and young children are raised can cause them to develop relationship problems and developmental difficulties or delays. When a family is vulnerable psychologically, the children and parents are at risk for increased internal and external problems. Internal problems include psychological illness and substance abuse, and external problems include situations such as unemployment and inadequate housing. This chapter discusses environments that place babies and young children at risk for unhealthy adaptations and in turn create challenges for their caregivers.[1] It closes with a discussion of resilient children.

PREDICTING CHILD OUTCOMES

Every baby and young child learns to adapt to his or her environment, but some adaptations also serve as limitations. A baby's adaptation to a violent home environment may be self-protective for the baby, but this adaptation may severely limit the baby from experiencing his or her full potential. For instance, it may be a good thing for a young child living in a violent environment to be fearful because it will prevent him or her from talking to potentially dangerous strangers, but living a life based on fear will seriously inhibit the number of trusting relationships the child has the opportunity to form. As Pawl stated, "Babies learn to adapt, but it may mean they never do the tango, only the two step."[2]

One negative experience does not carry a major risk for a child to develop a mental disorder; however, multiple negative factors do carry a greater risk. The number rather than the nature of risk factors is the best indicator of possible problems.[3] Mental disorders usually are not solely caused by environmental problems. There are genetic and biological factors as well. In some cases, gene–environment interactions cause the development of mental disorders, especially with regard to antisocial problems, depression, and anxiety disorders. In young children, mental disorders usually manifest themselves as relationship problems. Environmental risks for babies seem to be more indicative of future problems than intrinsic (i.e., genetic) risk factors.[4]

In a longitudinal study in Rochester, New York, researchers assessed the effects of 10 environmental risk variables on the development of 4-year-olds of various socioeconomic groups. One conclusion from this study was that the number of risk factors rather than the socioeconomic level itself was the prime determinant of psychopathology within each socioeconomic level. In addition, the same outcomes often were the result of different combinations of risk factors.[5] Sameroff and Fiese identified income and marital status as the two risk factors that make a major difference because these factors are strongly associated with a combination of other risk factors.[6]

This chapter describes a transactional model that assumes that developmental outcomes are not a function of the individual child or the child's experiences separately. Rather, the *interaction* of child and environment determines the outcome. Therefore, a difficult home environment does not necessarily mean that the child will be unhealthy.[7] Home visitors should not assume that a baby or young child will bring problems to the child care program just because of his of her unhealthy sociocultural environment. Nevertheless, they need to be aware of the potential problems a difficult home environment can create for a child and be prepared to work with babies and young children who do bring problems into the caregiving setting.

FAMILIES WHO ARE PSYCHOLOGICALLY VULNERABLE

This section addresses the issues and concerns of families who are psychologically vulnerable and the effect of such a family situation on children. Specifically, marital discord and divorce, mental illness, substance abuse, domestic and community violence, and child maltreatment are addressed. The reason family problems affect children so much is that the family is the child's main context for interaction. Children depend on their families for physical, emotional, social, cognitive, moral, and spiritual development.[8] They observe family interactions and listen to family stories and in doing so develop working models of relationships that then guide their behavior. As children mature, they continue to internalize memories that help to stabilize the parent–child relationship. Reiss clarified this dynamic:

The pivotal concept in this perspective is that not only are the coherence, stability, and substance of the relationship represented by these internalized structures, but the stability and coherence of the relationship itself may be located and conserved through time by such structures.[9]

Given the pivotal impact of parent–child relationships on the child's developing self, parental stress and even absence can lead to problems.

Marital Discord, Separation and Divorce

Home visitors inevitably will work with families experiencing marital discord, separation, and/or divorce. As part of long-term social, economic, and demographic shifts, the American family has changed dramatically. Since the mid-1980s, nearly half of all children in the United States have spent some time living in a single-parent home.[10] Many of these families include a single mother and extended family members or new male partners. Many single parents still believe that marriage will lead to a happy life, and, consequently, they remarry. Two thirds of divorced women and three fourths of divorced men eventually remarry.[11]

Children from intact families with chronic marital discord frequently have more behavioral problems than children from separated but conflict-free families.[12] This may be because parents immersed in marital discord may be less emotionally available to their young children. Belsky, Woodworth, and Crnic examined the consequences of troubled family interaction. The researchers observed 64 families rearing their first-born sons in the child's second year of life and again in the child's third year of life. The likelihood of children's externalizing problem behavior (e.g., anger, aggression, noncompliance, and hyperactivity) at 3 years of age was related to chronicity (i.e., ever present disorder) of troubled family interaction. The authors found, "It is not 'troubled' family interaction at any particular time during the toddler years that principally fosters the development of problematic child behavior, especially of the externalizing variety, but rather the chronicity of such experience."[13]

In addition, Heiniccke, Guthrie, and Ruth's research indicated that children from families where the parents were experiencing marital discord but chose not to divorce were more likely to externalize control, act uncontrollably, and possess more anti-social characteristics as opposed to prosocial.[14]

Divorce is a transitional process, not a legal relationship, and children are an integral part of the process. Every divorce includes stress and many changes for each family member, some expected and others not. Family systems theory posits that the behavior of each family member has an effect on the behavior of every other family member.[15] Separation and divorce lead to disruptions in each individual's relationships with family members. A family is like a mobile: Move one mobile piece, and the entire mobile shifts.

Babies and young children are bound to suffer when their parents separate and/or divorce. Even when marital discord occurs in the original family, young children dream of having their parents together with them again. Very young children especially have difficulty understanding their parents' separation and divorce. When one parent leaves, a young child might wonder, "If one can leave me, will the other also?" Very young children do not have a clear understanding of fantasy and reality, or the ability to differentiate clearly between self and other. Thus, a young child might feel somewhat responsible for his or her parents' separation and divorce, and wonder, "Did the parent leave because he (or she) doesn't love me?"

A young child whose parents are having marital difficulty or separation may regress, for example, resume bed wetting, have sleep difficulties, suddenly be intolerant of frustration, or cling to adults. Home visitors can help by listening and by offering reliability, support, and nurturing. They can reassure children that they are not to blame for their parents' difficulties, and they can protect the children from their fear of desertion. Reading picture books about divorce also can help young children gain understanding of their pain.

Mothers' Mental Illness

Constantino defined mental illness as "the relative inability (assuming physical health and a reasonable living environment) to experience fulfillment (or happiness) in self, in work, and in love."[16] Babies and young children can be at risk if either of their parents have mental illness. This section, however, focuses solely on mothers' mental illness because the vast majority of research has centered around maternal mental illness and because mothers are usually the primary caregivers. A mother's psychological disturbance does not necessarily lead to inappropriate parenting and resulting child difficulties. For some mothers, the bond with their children may be the most stable part of their lives, yet the task of child rearing can be more difficult for a mother dealing with mental illness.

Research indicates that child rearing by a parent with mental illness may create developmental risks for the child through both genetic and environmental factors.[17] Mental illness can be inherited and is clustered around specific diagnoses such as depression or schizophrenia.[18] At the same time, however, the vast majority of individuals with mental illness do not have a family history of the illness. Risks for children should not be surprising because often a mother with mental illness is unavailable, both physically and emotionally. For example, the often taken-for-granted preverbal interaction between baby and mother in routine caregiving may not exist.

The two most common mental illnesses experienced by mothers are depression and schizophrenia, with depression being the most common. Symptoms of depressed mothers include a negative mood, loss of pleasure, low energy, apathy, problems with sleep and appetite, and negative views of self. Women are twice as likely to be at risk for depression as men.

How does depression affect parent–child interaction? From birth, babies demonstrate sensitivities especially oriented toward human stimulation. From very early on, caregivers and babies interact both to regulate babies' biological functions such as sleep and feeding and to support emotional and social development. Research indicates that depressed mothers' parenting often is impaired in ways that may be problematic for their children's development.[19] Depressed mothers are more disengaged, more negative, and less likely to respond to their babies' cues.[20] They express very little positive emotion. Thus, when mothers are depressed, home visitors need to see if their babies are experiencing themselves as effective communicators. Clark and Fenichel described some problematic depressed mother–child interactions.

Many depressed mothers respond to their babies and toddlers' fussing, tugging or even biting, but not to smiles or positive bids for attention. Babies who have learned from their mothers that only negative strategies get a response are not likely to endear themselves to other adults. Moreover, many passive babies may simply withdraw from social interaction altogether when their depressed mothers don't respond to their bids for attention.[21]

When young babies of depressed mothers develop emotional and behavioral regulation, they repeatedly use their mother's facial expression; thus, many babies of depressed mothers have a negative emotional expression themselves. These babies have more difficult temperaments, greater irritability, and more difficulty in self-calming (i.e., they are depressed themselves). Rutter summarized the literature that describes depressed mothers' difficulties in interacting with their young children as follows.[22]

- The mother's depressed mood may lead to her baby mirroring this depressed affect.[23]
- A depressed mother may be insensitive and slower to respond to her child's cues and needs.[24]
- Depression can impair a mother's ability to discipline her child appropriately.[25]
- Depression often is associated with family discord, and this marital conflict may impinge adversely on young children. [26]

Brain research shows that early caregiving experiences influence the growth of brain interconnections and the maturation of the frontal limbic system of the brain, which regulates psychological states and ability to cope with stress.[27] This research points to the risk of children of depressed mothers to a predisposition for psychiatric disorders. Jones, Field, Lundy, and Davalos studied the brain activity of babies whose mothers were depressed and babies whose mothers were not.[28] They found that even in babies as young as 1 month of age, electroencephalogram (EEG) activation indicated that infants of depressed mothers exhibited greater frontal lobe EEG asymmetry as compared with other babies. This asymmetry, the authors observed, was related to more frequent negative facial expressions, less activity, and more erratic sleep of the 1-month-old babies of depressed mothers.

Babies are particularly sensitive to the negative effects of maternal depression between 6 and 18 months of age. Studies have found that when babies are exposed to their mothers' depression during this time, they often have emotional and cognitive difficulties during the preschool and early school years, regardless of their mothers' depression status during these later years.[29] Seifer and Dickstein's research indicated that parental mental illness can be related to negative child outcomes, such as children's cognitive deficits, delinquency, or poor social adaptation.[30] Several research studies have indicated that maternal depression has been related to higher rates of insecure attachment.[31]

Stern described four ways that babies adjust to living with an emotionally unavailable mother. Each of these methods of adapting continues to develop over time. That is, the pattern or style of relating to the world and to the self that begins in the first few months between the depressed mother and her baby may remain the baby's pattern and style throughout the rest of the child's life.

- Some babies learn to "turn their mother on." Sometimes they are successful in reaching their emotionally unavailable mother. Stern described these babies as spark plugs that can stimulate the mother. The baby becomes an anti-depressor.[32] Sometimes the baby's vocalizing, smiling, and gesturing works, and the mother is reanimated, even though depressed. This infrequent response is good reinforcement for the baby's behavior. These babies often develop into charmers who are skilled in capturing people's attention.

- When the mother is not responsive, some babies turn away, become curious, and seek stimulation elsewhere. These babies develop their own ability to stimulate themselves with external objects and events.

- Some mothers are aware that they are not responding to their baby enough, and they make a huge effort to overcompensate in bursts. Stern suspects that the baby can discriminate these forced interactions from an easy flow; yet, they are so eager for relationship that they adjust their behavior accordingly. Although the desires of both baby and mother are very real, "a false interaction between a false mother and a false baby" occurs.[33]

- Some babies, in their desire to be with the mother, identify and imitate the mother's depression. These babies have low levels of activity and negative or minimal facial expressitivity.[34]

When studying the effects of maternal depression on babies and young children, one needs to also consider the familial context in which this development occurs. Stresses such as marital discord, unemployment and low social class, and lack of informal social support increase the probability that maternal depression will result in negative mother–child interaction and negative child outcomes.

When maternal depression occurs in a marriage experiencing marital harmony, mothers are more likely to sustain positive, healthy interactions with their babies and young children, and the children are less likely to develop problematic consequences.[35] When babies of depressed mothers have other caregivers who are not depressed, these caregivers can be a protective factor.

Consider the following example of how Jean's work with Nancy (age 11 months) helped her to counteract the effects of her mother, Gail's, depression.

Gail and her family lived in a rural town of 3,000 people. She was 26 years old and the wife of Gary, a short-distance truck driver. Gail was the eleventh child of a mother who committed suicide when Gail was 10 years old. From the time she was an adolescent, Gail had suffered from severe depression; she was hospitalized at least once a year and took several medications. Due to Gail's depression, Gary cooked all the family dinners, and Nancy spent all her waking hours in a playpen by herself.

Gail decided to enroll in a project that provided her with a family caregiver, Jean, who began caring for Nancy when Nancy was 11 months old. At this time, Nancy had no verbalizations and little if any affect. Jean cared for Nancy 4½ days a week, and Gail came to Jean's home one morning a week. Jean cared for Nancy until Nancy entered kindergarten. At that time, Gail began working as a nurse's aide at a nursing home, and Jean cared for Nancy in the afternoon after kindergarten.

At Jean's home, Nancy helped Jean cook simple items such as biscuits or muffins. Sometimes, when Jean returned Nancy to her home, she would teach Gail to bake brownies and cook simple meals. After 1 year in Jean's care, Nancy was spontaneously talking and was emotionally expressive. In fact, by the time she was 3 years old, her behavior showed that she possessed a quick intellect. Nancy grew up to be a spontaneous, happy teenager.

When child care providers are skilled in providing affect regulation, physical intimacy, spontaneous conversation, and contingent responses, they promote healthy social and emotional development that can compensate for the actions of the baby's depressed mother, such as how Jean was able to encourage Nancy to communicate and participate in tasks such as cooking.

Postpartum Depression

In their early contact with families of newborns, home visitors can head off some later problems if they look for postpartum depression. Symptoms include difficulty in eating and sleeping and lack of energy and affect. About 15% of mothers have postpartum depression following childbirth, and it can cause disruptions in mother–baby interaction. Being a new mother is always a challenge, and for some new mothers, it can be overwhelming. After childbirth, new mothers typically experience heightened family and family-of-origin issues as they move into parenthood. They need to make adjustments in their sleep schedules, in how they and their spouse allocate roles, and in deciding what employment now means to them. No matter how many children a mother has, each baby has a unique style, needs, and strengths, so every postpartum experience is different. Home visitors can help by listening and supporting the mother. If prolonged, the home visitor can seek psychological consultation for the parent.

Parental Substance Abuse

Many babies exposed prenatally to parental substance abuse are likely to experience ongoing parental substance abuse after birth. When home visitors work with babies and young children of parents who are substance abusers, it is important to understand the different effects of different substances. For example, crack-cocaine users tend to be jumpy and full of vitality, whereas alcohol abusers are more likely to be listless, with little energy.[36] This section discusses the effects of drug abuse (e.g., abuse of cocaine, marijuana, heroin, and other street and prescription drugs) and alcohol abuse on both the person abusing the drug and the child.

Children Exposed to Drugs

Norinne (age 32 months old) entered a child care center on her second birthday. Her mother is addicted to cocaine and lives in a home where there is a steady traffic of drugs. Norinne's health record gives no evidence of prenatal drug exposure. Although she spent her first year of life with her mother, she now lives with her 4-year-old sister, her father, his girlfriend, and her three children. Her father reports that at home she rarely eats; however,

Harriet, her teacher, reports that at the center she acts as if she is unable to get enough to eat. About once or twice a month, Norinne's mother brings her to the center. On these days, Norinne repeatedly asks for her mother.

Harriet reports that often Norinne has no facial expression and seems depressed. Her speech is clear, but she rarely talks. She relates to her peers only with unprovoked aggression. She frequently has toileting accidents and puts everything into her mouth. Each day, Norinne spends long periods of time playing in the water table. Whenever possible, Norinne clings to her older sister. She is quite aggressive with dolls. For example, one time she entered the housekeeping area and picked up a doll, saying, "Sleepy baby." Then, she rigorously hit the doll's stomach, saying, "I'm going to hit your butt!" To counter Norinne's behavior, Harriet had to enter the housekeeping area and talk to her softly. They left the area with Norinne carrying the doll. Harriet then read a story to Norinne.

Harriet reports that the only time that Norinne is emotionally expressive is when she is alone and playing with the dolls. On most occasions, she only expresses anger and aggression. Norinne has lived in an environment of drug use and drug dealers. Her teachers do not know if she has experienced or witnessed violence. Norinne's chaotic home life during her first year with her mother has caused her a great deal of anxiety, which often is externalized into aggressive behavior demonstrated with dolls.

To address Norinne's high level of anxiety, Harriet has water play available, and Norinne plays in water quietly each day for about 20 minutes. Harriet also ensures that she gives Norinne focused one-on-one time each day, often reading her a storybook.

This vignette illustrates the unusual and aggressive behavior that many children who are exposed to drugs experience. Child care providers and home visitors must work to provide peaceful, calming activities for these children, such as when Harriet read Norinne a story.

Given the surge of cocaine use since the mid-1980s, most research on babies who have been exposed to street and prescription drugs prenatally are studies of cocaine-exposed infants.[37] This research provides no consistent pattern of anomalies in prenatally exposed babies. Some studies show the impact of cocaine on child behavior and development, whereas other studies show no impact. Some studies indicate that prenatal exposure may result in birth defects, growth retardation, and developmental problems such as difficulty in information processing and attention difficulties. At present, it is not certain what effect prenatal substance abuse has on the developing fetus because research studies on the issue are quite complex. First, it is difficult to know for certain that a drug is solely responsible for a child's maladaptive behavior or development. Second, most cocaine-using mothers are poly-drug users (i.e., they also use alcohol, cigarettes, marijuana, and other street or prescription drugs) so it is difficult to determine whether the effects on a child's development are a result of a specific drug or a combination of drugs. Third, some children have psychological disturbances or live in a maladaptive environment and also deal with such risk factors as domestic violence, unemployment, or lack of social support. In other words, prenatally exposed babies as well as babies with parents who are still using drugs have multiple risks.

Lester and colleagues reviewed 188 research studies conducted on prenatal cocaine exposure.[38] They learned that 15 different neuro-behavioral measures were used in these studies. Therefore, it is difficult to compare the studies. Only 7% of the published literature has followed children beyond infancy. Another confounding factor is the fact that women who are substance abusers have higher rates of mental health problems, family disorganization and violence, physical illness, and difficulties in parenting. It is hard to say how substance abuse causes problems when it occurs most often in the midst of other problem-creating factors. We know that young children can be resilient; however, resilience has not been applied to the study of drug-exposed babies.[39]

Many infants exposed to drugs in the womb are born prematurely. Studies have been unable to show whether prenatal exposure to drugs causes the prematurity and low birth weight or whether the prematurity is caused by the mother's multiple stressors.[40] Because most studies of babies exposed to drugs have been only done on low-income families, other risk factors such as unemployment and inadequate housing get mixed up with the effects of drugs like cocaine.[41]

Zuckerman and Brown noted that prenatal effects of drugs often can be seen in the central nervous system of the fetus, for these substances cross the placenta and the blood-brain barrier.[42] Mayes, Bornstein, Charwarsk, Haynes, and Granger investigated the relationship between cocaine exposure and infants' regulation of arousal in response to novelty.[43] Thirty-six babies exposed to cocaine prenatally and twenty-seven babies with no exposure participated in the study at 3 months of age. The researchers measured the babies' behavioral states, emotional expressiveness, and attention to regulation of arousal. Compared with the group of babies with no prenatal drug exposure, babies exposed prenatally were more likely to cry and express negative emotions on novel stimulus presentation.

The consequences of prenatal drug exposure depend on many factors, such as the type of drug, the timing and dose of exposure, emotional state of the baby, mothers' mental illness, and other unhealthy habits or environmental stressors. Zuckerman and Brown noted that many babies exposed to drugs prenatally have difficulty in regulating arousal; and such babies may not elicit adequate caregiving.[44] That is, their mothers may be less likely to respond to their cues for food or stimulation. Immediately after delivery, exposed babies have behavioral abnormalities detected in the Brazelton Neonatal Behavior Assessment Scale (NBAS), such as increased irritability, low responsiveness to visual stimuli, decreased consolability, tremors, and low muscle tone.

Research on new treatment options for drug-abusing women and their children is just beginning. These studies indicate that drug-abusing women in treatment need effective case management, drug counseling, and school/job training as well as guidance in their parenting skills.[45] Home visitors can assist drug-abusing mothers in finding effective treatment programs and support their continued participation in these programs.

Children Exposed to Alcohol

Similar to children exposed to drugs prenatally, babies and children exposed to alcohol prenatally frequently live in environments of chronic stress caused by factors other than alcohol (e.g., low income, parental unemployment, parental mental illness). These children also are likely to experience ongoing parental substance abuse.

Extensive research has demonstrated that prenatal exposure to alcohol causes serious maladaptation in development. Fetal alcohol syndrome (FAS) is the term used to describe the disabilities that result from prenatal alcohol exposure. Birth defects caused by prenatal alcohol exposure indicate the impact that alcohol has on the formation of the fetus's brain and body. The central nervous system and brain are especially sensitive to effects of prenatal alcohol exposure Characteristics of babies and young children with FAS include specific physical abnormalities, such as characteristic facial features like thin upper lip, short nose, flat midface, and flattening of the jaw; low muscle tone; and central nervous system dysfunction characterized by mental retardation, hyperactivity, impulsivity, and/or seizures. Olson, Burgess, and Streissguth described preschool children with FAS as follows:

[The children are] often alert, talkative, and friendly. They have been described as typically short and skinny, with butterfly movements, but a generally vigorous appearance. These children may have severe temper tantrums and difficulty making transitions. More than half show hyperactivity and many are oversensitive to touch and other stimulation. Attentional deficits, fine motor difficulties and developmental delays also are seen.[46]

Because much of babies' neurological development occurs after birth, however, children with FAS can make progress when they receive competent caregiving and adequate nutrition.[47]

Children are also affected by their parents' ongoing alcohol abuse. Eiden and Leonard (1996) studied 55 mothers and babies (ages 12–24 months old) and found that paternal alcoholism has an impact on both family functioning and the mother–baby relationship as early as infancy.[48] Fathers' alcoholism was linked to maternal depression, marital dissatisfaction, and the poor quality of the babies' attachment to their mothers. Wives of alcoholics had higher depressive symptoms and lower marital satisfaction compared to wives of nonalcoholic husbands. Sixty-seven percent of infants whose fathers were heavy drinkers had insecure attachment with their mothers.

Working with parents who abuse alcohol can be frustrating for caregivers who see the problems the drinking is having on the children. Consider Consetta's frustration when working with LaDonna.

LaDonna is a 20-year-old mother of two preschoolers, age 3 and 4 years. During the day, her children are cared for by Consetta, a therapeutic family child caregiver. After LaDonna spends one morning at Consetta's home with her children, Consetta writes in her journal:

> LaDonna told me that her children need to improve their speech. Throughout the morning, she was quite open about her drinking habits. She says she is trying to "cut down" somewhat. But then she goes on to say that her idea of having a restful day is to get drunk, have the children take naps with her while she passes out. She seems unable to grasp the concept of "what if they get up and hurt themselves while I am sleeping?" Rather, she insists that they always just keep sleeping, so it is okay for her.

Consetta reports that on some days, the children are ready when she comes to take them to her home. On other days, their mother is sleeping, and the 4-year-old is cooking eggs and toast for their breakfast. Some days when she arrives, mother and children all are asleep together.

Once they are able to develop a trusting relationship with parents, home visitors may have the opportunity to help a parent utilize community resources for treatment and other needed assistance. Knowledge of accessible substance abuse treatment centers is a first prerequisite in order for home visitors and directors to serve as a resource for parents. In reality, many of these families need comprehensive, multidisciplinary interventions to assist them with their chronic problems. Thus, if the resources are available, home visitors might want to consider making referrals to agencies that can provide the help these families need. If a home visitor suspects that a child is in danger at home, he or she needs to be vigilant in checking the child for signs of maltreatment as well as informing her administrator about this concern. Every early educator is mandated to report evidence of child maltreatment.

Community Violence

Psychologically vulnerable families often live in poverty. Poverty rates have increased in the last three decades. In 2000, the median family income in the United States was $38,000 a year; poverty for a family of 4 was defined as earning less than $16,400 a year.[49] Poverty often leads to exposure to community violence.

The United States has the highest incidence of violence of any industrialized nation in the world. The murder rate in the United States is five times that of England and 10 times that of Spain.[50] In 1993, 22 per 100,00 homicide victims in the United States were males 15–24 years old, whereas all other Western industrialized nations had 5 homicides or less per 100,000 males of the same age group.[51] With both the high incidence of violence on television and the increased frequency of homicides in our nation, it is reasonable to speak of violence as being part of the inner psyche of each American.

As researchers and clinicians, Cicchetti and Lynch noted, "Violence, in fact, is becoming a defining characteristic of American society."[52] In urban, low-income neighborhoods, violence is epidemic. Young children are both victims and witnesses of episodes of domestic and community violence.[53] Karr-Morse and Wiley provided data on incarceration in America in 1997.

If our present rates of incarcerating continue, one out of every twenty babies born in the United States today will spend some part of their adult lives in state or federal prison. An African-American male has a greater than one in four chance of going to prison in his lifetime, while a Hispanic male has a one in six chance of serving time. . . . And our prison population has exploded. California, for example, is now spending more on its criminal justice system than on higher education.[54]

Child development experts believe that children in America today may be the most fearful in history.[55] Continual violence in a community may lead to young children feeling helpless and hopeless. Healthy parents provide a holding environment for their babies and young children, but a constant barrage of violence in a community may result in parents communicating a sense of helplessness to their young children. As a result, many babies and young children are growing up without a basic sense of trust and security that is the basis for healthy development.

Adults think that babies and young children who witness violence are too young to understand what happened and will not remember the violent event, but clear evidence shows that babies, toddlers, and older children do not forget traumatic events.

The ability to re-see or, occasionally but less frequently, to re-feel a terrible event or series of events is an important common characteristic of almost all externally generated disorders of childhood. Re-seeing is so important that it sometimes occurs even when the original experience was not at all visual. Visualizations are most strongly stimulated by reminders of the traumatic event, but they occasionally come up entirely unbidden. . . . Even those who were infants or toddlers at the time of their ordeals and thus were unable to lay down, store, or retrieve full verbal memories of their taumas, tend to play out, to draw, or to re-see highly visualized elements from their old experiences.[56]

In addition to remembering a visual picture of a traumatic event, children can recall the verbal aspect of traumatic experiences that occurred when the children were as young as 2½ years of age.[57] An additional concern for children under 6 years old is their confusion of fantasy and reality. This confusion can put them at even greater risk of having specific fears, nightmares, and disturbing fantasies.

When young children live in an unpredictable, violent environment, it becomes the fabric of their lives, and they are unable to gain feelings of either safety or security, two essential milestones of early development. These experiences have a significant impact on children's development in the present and continue to do so in the future.[58] Researchers and clinicians have poignantly described how young children's exposure to violence leads to social-emotional problems that can be lasting.[59] Studies provide convincing evidence that community violence increases the risk of family disruption and parental stress and thereby increases the probability of child maltreatment.[60] The younger the child, the greater the threat to healthy development when he or she is exposed to violence. Osofsky identified behaviors associated with young children's exposure to violence which include

* Reexperiencing the traumatic event—often in the form of nightmares and in repetitive play sequences
* Traumatic-specific fears, such as the dark, strangers, being alone, specific animals, or vehicles
* Sleep disturbances

- Bed-wetting
- Low tolerance of frustration, aggression, and impulsivity
- Selective inattention
- Lack of curiosity and lack of pleasure in exploring
- Depression and perpetual mourning
- Lack of a sense of trust and security
- Avoidance of intimacy
- Sensitized hyperarousal state[61]

These symptoms are similar to those of posttraumatic stress disorder (PTSD). In fact, studies of young children exposed to violence point to clear associations between the exposure to violence and the occurrence of PTSD.[62] If experiences with violence are chronic, young children may develop a permanent pattern of hyperarousal or numbing, which can become the precursor to learning and behavior problems. With prolonged stress, the brain's chemical profile can be altered by changes in hormone levels, which affect information processing and can lead to maladaptive behavior.[63] Prolonged and frequent periods of stress seem to have lasting effects on alteration of a child's brain from the third trimester of pregnancy to 24 months of age. Damage appears greatest for those areas of the brain that control emotion regulation.

Many individual differences influence how a small child experiences a traumatic event. Young children's caregivers differ in the quality and amount of soothing they provide after a trauma has occurred. Often, the caregiver is not emotionally accessible and responds to the child's experience of stress inappropriately. The amount of distress experienced may depend on how the child perceives the caregiver's affect.[64] Babies and young children also have different sensory sensitivities, and these sensitivities influence how a child responds to an event.

Osofsky (1996) identified factors that can influence young children's response to traumatic events:

Intensity: Witnessing someone pushing another person is likely to result in a less severe traumatic response than witnessing a shooting.

Proximity to the event: The research of Pynoos and others on sniper attacks in school yards suggests that a child who is a first hand witness to a violent event is likely to be much more strongly affected than a child who is shielded from full sight of the violence or only hears about the event.[65]

Familiarity with the victim, perpetrator, or both, strongly increases the intensity of a child's response to witnessing violence. The developmental status of the child affects his or her response and capacity to cope with the impact of violence. . . .

Chronicity of exposure to violence: It is likely that experiencing violence repeatedly over the years may be devastating to the social and emotional development of young children, who learn, from what they see, that violence is a usual and acceptable way to respond to other people.[66]

Maurice is a child who lives in a traumatic environment. With help from his teacher, Jerri, his needs are being addressed.

Maurice (age 4) lives with his single mother who abuses both drugs and alcohol. Maurice was prenatally exposed to drugs. An array of adults come in and out of Maurice's home, with violence frequently erupting. The last time Jerri made a home visit, adults were throwing bricks at each other.

Maurice's teachers report that during snack time, he seems to fear that he will not get enough food, and he eats as much as possible. In addition, he engages in unprovoked aggression throughout the day, is unable to participate in any group activity, and has nightmares when sleeping during naptime. In the classroom or during gross motor play, Marice is able to maintain focus in an activity only if Jerri is at his side. Otherwise, he runs about or engages in unprovoked aggression. In other words, Maurice can function appropriately when Jerri is able to "shadow" him. This shadowing seems to contain his excessive anxiety and resulting lack of self-control.

The child care center is working with the special school district to have Maurice evaluated for placement in special education for the following year. Jerri also is assisting Maurice's mother in gaining support through her community's mental health center and arranging for a psychiatric evaluation to determine if medication could help Maurice.

It is critical for home visitors of young children to be aware of the effects of violence, to be able to note signs of these effects in children, and to have knowledge of how they can work with these at-risk children. Home visitors can help by

- Providing a calm, safe, nurturing environment for children who have witnessed or experienced violence.
- Ensuring that each child under their care has a loving, trusting relationship with them.
- Focusing on inner experiences, on feelings, their own and the children's.

Child Maltreatment

Children age 3 and younger comprise 26% of all indicated child maltreatment reports and comprise 77% of child fatalities that occur to children of all ages.[67] The most common forms of child maltreatment are neglect (45%), physical abuse (15%), and sexual abuse (16%).[68] Behavior patterns of very young children that most often spark maltreatment are incessant crying, negativism, and pants wetting or soiling. External signs of physical abuse are bruises, lacerations, scars, and burns.[69] Young children often experience multiple forms of abuse; for example, physical and sexual abuse often occur together. Mrazek identified the following factors that are highly correlated with child maltreatment:

- Negative maternal attitude toward pregnancy
- High level of perceived social stress
- Low socioeconomic status
- Lack of financial resources
- Parent's low intelligence
- Parent's criminal record
- History of parent's own child maltreatment[70]

Egeland and Sroufe conducted a prospective, longitudinal investigation of 270 children from birth through 5 years of age.[71] Their study provided lucid documentation of the progressive decline in functioning of maltreated children, with the greatest decline among those children raised by psychologically unavailable mothers. Because maltreatment most often occurs along with other risk factors, maltreatment affects children differently.

Studies indicate that babies who have been maltreated consistently are far more likely to be insecurely attached than are babies who have not been maltreated.[72] Many young children with a history of maltreatment develop not only negative representational models of their attachment figures but also negative representations of themselves. Moreover, the young children often disconnect from their actual emotional experience. Toth, Cicchetti, Macfie, and Emde clarified, "Maltreated children often act compulsively compliant with their caregivers (e.g., ignore their own needs in order to care for and please the parent) and display insincere positive affect."[73]

Research studies report that maltreated young children tend to be more aggressive with peers and siblings.[74] These children also are less likely to show sadness in witnessing a peer's distress or remorse when attention is called to the impact of their aggression. These traumatized children also have difficulties in affect regulation. They seem to be less flexible, less able to adjust their emotions to external cues, and have a "tilt" toward negative emotions.[75] Not surprisingly, they also have difficulty in self-understanding and self-esteem.

When maltreatment is chronic, young children develop brain pattern changes as well as changes in behavior similar to those mentioned among children exposed to violence. Some maltreated children respond to anxiety by being hypersensitive; others dissociate. Karr-Morse and Wiley wrote, "Instead of providing the foundation for self-control, for empathy, and for focused cognitive learning, abuse in earliest life undermines all three."[76]

Karr-Moore and Wiley's book, *Ghosts from the Nursery*, clearly articulates how maltreatment from gestation through the second year of life is a precursor to the growing epidemic of violence by children in the United States.

The last three decades have provided us with research that brings to light a range of more subtle toxins profoundly influencing our children's earliest development: chronic stress or neglect, which affects the development of the fetal or early infant brain; early child abuse and neglect, which undermine focused learning; chronic parental depression; neglect or lack of stimulation necessary for normal brain development; early loss of primary relationships or breaks in caregiving . . . through the interplay of the developing brain with the environment during the nine months of gestation and the first two years after birth, the core of an individual's ability to think, feel, and relate to others is formed. Violent behavior often begins to take root during those thirty-three months as the result of chronic stress, such as domestic or child abuse, or through neglect, including preingestion of toxins. . . . Maltreatment of a baby may lead to the permanent loss or impairment of key protective factors—such as intelligence, trust, and empathy—that enable many children to survive and even overcome difficult family circumstances and later traumas.[77]

Sexual abuse of children can range from excessive exposure to pornography, to living in sexually explicit environments, to physical acts of abuse, such as fondling, oral copulation, vaginal intercourse, or sodomy. Sexual abuse can result in children having thoughts pervaded with sexuality; engaging in inappropriate sexual behavior, such as excessive masturbation and disturbing toileting patterns (e.g., sniffing underwear or wearing soiled underpants, repeatedly stuffing the toilet until it overflows); or molesting other children.[78] Such characteristics were displayed by Charetta (age 3 years). These signs prompted her teacher and a group counselor to approach the topic of sexual abuse with her mother.

Charetta is the only daughter of 33-year-old Keona. When Charetta was 8 months old, Keona divorced Charetta's father, Joe, who is a self-employed plumber. Keona works as an executive secretary for a large corporation, and she and Charetta live in a comfortable home in the suburbs. Joe lives with his parents and four adult brothers, three of whom use and sell drugs.

Keona and Joe are one of five couples who attended a parenting group. Joe stated that, "Charetta is the apple of my eye. My reason for living." On some days, prior to Keona picking up her daughter from the child care center, Joe takes Charetta for an hour or so in the afternoon, then returns her to the center. On Sunday, Joe takes Charetta to his mother's home to be with him.

During the first week of the parenting sessions, Charetta's teacher, Jean, told the group counselor that Charetta was masturbating persistently throughout the day. Jean, Keona, and the counselor then met to discuss Charetta's behavior. Keona commented that she, too, had noticed Charetta's increasing masturbation.

Keona then arranged for Joe to have visits with her daughter only when she was present. With help from Charetta's child care director, she also arranged for Charetta to have weekly play therapy with a child psychiatrist for 1 year. Charetta's masturbation ceased. Now, at 7 years old, she is a bright, high-achieving second grader.

When a home visitor suspects that a child in her or his care has been physically or sexually abused, as in Charetta's case, the first step is to have a confidential conversation with the child's parent. Then, the home visitor can assist the parent in obtaining a medical evaluation of the child and psychotherapy to help heal the child. In most families where child maltreatment occurs, family therapy can assist every family member. Once a home visitor's suspicion regarding a young child's maltreatment has been confirmed, he or she is mandated to report the maltreatment to the state protection agency.

THE RESILIENT CHILD

Most of this chapter has addressed the environmental problems that are part of many babies' and young children's lives, but young children are not always victims of their fate. The literature describes children living in the midst of chronic stress and deprivation who have been able to overcome this deprivation and maintain healthy development because they are resilient.[79] Each psychologically vulnerable family is different from other families suffering similar difficulties. As Tolstoy wrote, "Happy families are all alike. Every unhappy family is unhappy in its own way."[80] Similarly, each child responds to family difficulties in his or her unique way; in fact, some children are resilient enough that their family difficulties do not substantively damage their development.

Resilience refers to adapting successfully and functioning competently despite experiencing chronic stress or adversity, or following exposure to prolonged or severe trauma.[81] Like competence, resilience changes over time and context. Further, children may be resilient to some stresses but not to others. Some children may manage to avoid failure in the face of poverty or violence but experience real deprivation in the capacity for intimate relationships. Yes, some children are resilient, yet some environments are too much for anyone.

Wolin and Wolin identified seven strengths that they see as part of the selfhood of resilient children:

INSIGHT: the habit of asking tough questions and giving honest answers

INDEPENDENCE: drawing boundaries between yourself and troubled parents; keeping emotional and physical distance while satisfying the demands of your conscience

RELATIONSHIPS: intimate and fulfilling ties to other people that balance a mature regard for your own needs with empathy and the capacity to give to someone else

INITIATIVE: taking charge of problems; exerting control; a taste for stretching and testing yourself in demanding tasks

CREATIVITY: imposing order, beauty, and purpose on the chaos of your troubling experiences and painful feelings

HUMOR: finding the comic in the tragic

MORALITY: an informed conscience that extends your wish for a good personal life to all of humankind[82]

Each resilient child does not have all seven of these strengths. Karr-Moore and Wiley discussed two protective factors that resilient children often have. First, they have "effortful control; that is they are able to choose one behavior while inhibiting another; thus they are able to focus on important information in school. Second, they have an affiliative or social personality and can generate relationships."[83]

Resilient children often figure out how to locate allies outside their families, and home visitors can serve as allies for children from troubled families. Resilient children often have the capacity to see themselves as separate from their troubled parents and to intuit that their family is not what it is supposed to be. When their home visitors are loving, predictable, and available, these home visitors can be models to help young children learn that there is a different way to relate than the way that they experience at home.

When home visitors recognize that a baby's or a young child's daily life at home is immersed in stress and adversity, they can ensure that they give these young children loving care and a sense of safety and security. In their interactions, home visitors can provide a trusting, predictable relationship. Many of these children live in homes where they have no control over events. The home visitors can ensure that these children experience a sense of efficacy by being quick to respond to the children's initiatives, and by providing opportunities for the children to make choices.

CONCLUSION

Every baby has the right to interact routinely and consistently with an admiring, supporting, and loving caregiver in a relationship that provides security and intimacy. Unfortunately, many babies and young children are at risk for not realizing their potential because of their families' extreme deprivations. As Elshtain noted, "Familial ties and models of child rearing are essential to establish the minimal foundation of human, social existence. . . .The family's status as a moral imperative derives from its universal, pan-cultural existence in all known past and present societies."[84] Young children in these troubled families may fail to achieve a strong sense of self and optimal development because their relationship with a primary caregiver is not strong enough to contain and nurture them.

Garbarino wrote about social toxicity as a current threat in contemporary culture to children's well-being and survival.[85] A socially toxic environment contains widespread threats to the development of identity, competence, moral reasoning, trust, hope, and the other features of social maps that make for success in school, family, work, and community. Many changes in recent decades put young children at risk. Young children are spending endless hours watching violent television and videos and playing violent games. Many do not have relaxed daily dinners or ample time to play with their parents. The United States is not a society that puts its children first or seems to understand that nurturing all our children is building our society's future.

Many parents are hungry for the help and support that home visitors can provide. Focus on inner experience is the most effective tool home visitors can bring to their work with babies and young children who have limitations. Home visitors can focus on the child's feelings and on his or her inner experience. When a baby does not respond or when a toddler has a tantrum, home visitors can ask themselves,

"What is this child feeling? What is the child trying to express?" At the same time, home visitors need to consider how their experiences with children and parents make them feel. They need to imagine that they were in the position of the children and parents and explore how they would feel. They should ask themselves, "How does it feel to be vulnerable? How does it feel to be angry? How does it feel to be helpless?" The home visitor then can use the energy from the feelings to marshal the strength to be patient, nurturing, and respectful in order to help the child and parent.

III

Person
and
Profession

12

Personal History and Professional Competence

Every life has its own significance. This lies in a context of meaning in which every moment that can be remembered has an intrinsic value and, yet, in the context of memory, it also has a relation to the meaning of the whole. The significance of an individual existence is quite unique and so cannot be fathomed by knowledge; yet, in its way, like Leibniz's monads, it represents the historical universe.

Wilhelm Dilthey (1961, pp. 88–89)

Throughout this volume, it is clear that who the home visitor is as a person plays a large part in his or her approach. Home visitors' commitment, perspective, values, decision making, and patterns of relating all have roots in their unique personal histories. In other words, in home visiting, personal and professional identity are intertwined.[1]

Chapters 1–10 presented observations of how Janice and Cynthia conduct home visits. This chapter first explores how these two women see their home visiting work as part of the meaning and purpose they find in their lives, how they have grown professionally, and what resources have promoted that professional growth. The next section discusses the interaction between their personal histories and their home visiting. There is no formula to predict or explain the way that a person's life history influences who that person is today. Nevertheless, a very important way in which a person's past and present interact in the present is in the process of remembering, retelling, and actively integrating his or her personal history because retelling a past event involves interpreting it and making it your own. (Think about the stories you retell the most often and how the re-telling tells you the importance, both about who you were and what life was like then, and who you are now and what life currently means to you.) These stories help us to reflect on who we are, both in our relationships with others and in our understanding of ourselves.[2] Thus, although there is no formula for the process through which someone's personal life history influences his or her professional life, by presenting two life histories as told by Janice and Cynthia as they reflected on their own experiences, perhaps this chapter can provide a window into this process.

In order to learn how home visitors' professional work is connected with their childhoods and present personal lives as adults, I conducted life history interviews with Janice and Cynthia, the two exemplary home visitors discussed in this book. Janice and Cynthia each told me in four interviews about their childhoods and adult lives.[3] They began by telling me about their early childhoods and families. As they progressed beyond their stories of early childhood, their stories expanded to include extended family, friends, schooling, religion, and community. Later, they described their adult personal lives and career paths, from their first jobs to their current work.[4] Throughout the interviews, I occasionally asked a question, either to clarify or to extend their descriptions.

Prior to these interviews, I had observed and discussed Janice's home visits with her for 4 years. I had known Cynthia also for 4 years and worked with her in my role as action researcher for 18 months. In working together with Janice and Cynthia, I had many lengthy conversations and several interviews with both women. So, by the time Janice and Cynthia sat down for life history interviews with me, we knew each other quite well.[5] The interviews, structured by these women's remembrances and by their understanding of their personal and professional lives, were informal. As they told me about their life experiences, I felt the freedom to ask questions or to comment on similar experiences in my own life.

These personal and professional histories of Janice and Cynthia should not be regarded as case studies or blueprints. Rather, I present the voices of Janice and Cynthia, as they reflect on their own development as people and professionals, for readers to use as a resource to think about how this type of reflection and development works. In considering how these home visitors reflected on their histories and integrated them into their work, the reader is challenged to think about how this process works, both in the home-visiting profession in general and in the reader's own professional development.

Janice and Cynthia's self-portrayals begin with each woman's description of her home visiting work. First, she identifies the personal meaning and purpose she finds in her work with parents and their infants and young children. Second, she describes her growth in understanding and skill. Third, she discusses what has helped her to grow professionally. Janice's and Cynthia's reflections capture some of the ways that home visiting can be meaningful, that home visitors can grow over time, and that resources available for professional development can play a role in the home visiting process. There is no single way in which home visitors find meaning in their work, grow as professionals, or use the available resources for professional development. But reading the stories of Janice and Cynthia can provide a range of possibilities and can indicate how one's work and resources can be *actively* and *reflectively* used.

Not all competent professionals grew up in families in which parents had strong family values and gave their children consistent, loving care. Prior to my life history interviews with Janice and Cynthia, I was unaware that each woman had a healthy, happy childhood family life, though their families are quite different from each other. Therefore, the chapter closes with a conversation with another a home visitor, Karen, who uses her recognition and resolution of her painful childhood as a building block for her professional competence. She turned childhood pain into professional strength.

JANICE DISCUSSES HER HOME VISITING WORK
Personal Meaningfulness of Home Visiting

The strength and happiness of Janice's childhood family life and commitment to her husband and children are themes that blend into her home visiting work. The strongest passions in her personal life are school, babies, and parenting. Home visiting blends these passions.[6]

Serving families as a home visitor in Parents as Teachers [PAT] has been a privilege for me. I believe it to be an extension of who I am as a person, not just as a professional. Family and children always have been—and continue to be—the most important part of my life. Therefore, to be able to promote strong family life and understanding children as part of my career seems at times like a dream.

PAT has given me something in my life that I love to do. I knew all along with my own babies that I really loved that stage of development. And it gives me a chance to renew that joy for myself.[7] Work is just fun. It gives me a lift every time I do it. Yes, I get frustrated when things aren't going well with a child. But every situation, and I truly mean this, every child, every situation, there will be parts of the visit that I truly enjoy. There has not been a child, not a parent that I have ever worked with—and I've had some pretty difficult situations—that I've not been able to say, "This is good, that's good, or whatever," because it is there, and I truly enjoy little children. Part of the joy is being with very young children who aren't tainted yet. It helps me to keep a more positive outlook on the rest of my life. It helps me stay happy. When other things are sort of bearing down, I have this picture of Erin [one of the children I work with] in my head, doing something especially darling. It helps alleviate other stresses in my life.

I also am intrigued with child development. Intellectually, I find it very fascinating to learn about something in a course, to read about something in a book, and go into a home and see it happen right there in front of my eyes. I truly enjoy education, and being able to convey this knowledge is just fun. I mean, I liked it when I was a classroom teacher, but doing one-on-one adult education and have a baby to play with at the same time—what could be better for somebody who loves to teach, but not in a formal classroom manner?

Relationships always have been very important to me. I would never be happy working quietly in front of a computer in a cubicle in an office. I like being a play partner with children. I like getting to know parents better and better over several years of service. I like sharing ideas with my colleagues. It feels good to me when I can jointly solve a problem with another person (parent or staff member), especially when that means a smoother period of life for a child.

Home visiting continues themes integral to Janice's personal life history and counterbalances stresses that she encounters. She loves home visiting because it is sheer fun for her. Furthermore, this enjoyment can balance those parts of her life that can be stressful. Since she was a child, Janice has used her intellect to be an active learner. She always has loved teaching. Child development stimulates her intellect, and working with parents continues her love of teaching.

Janice also knows that she is making a difference in people's lives, that her work has meaning beyond just herself.

> I love the process. You definitely can see results from the information you convey. You get feedback from the parents and from the child. You know it's good. You know that you are making a difference. I think most people like to see results from their work. If you can see that in another human being, that's really valuable.

I have observed Janice working with young parents and their babies and young children for 4 years. I can better understand her home visiting style now that she and I have completed four life history interviews. I often have been impressed at her ease and very soft manner as she relates to a baby and parent, her spontaneous and genuine delight in a child's action, and her openness when she shares her own parenting experiences.

Professional Development Over Time

Since she first began home visiting, Janice has enjoyed her work. At the same time, she is aware of the many changes in her professional development over the course of 10 years.

> I'm getting better at it now that I am aware of more detail and better at understanding development. I understand the significance of certain parts of development better, and thus I can convey this better. And my increase in child development knowledge has helped me, especially where development is not progressing quite normally. I am better at seeing subtle things that indicate progress, and I can suggest activities that will help that progress. I know it's going to make a difference because, with experience, I've seen it.
>
> I don't think my basic approach has changed. From the very beginning, I have conducted my home visits in a very integrated way rather than thinking about specific things I was supposed to accomplish. I was never lesson-plan oriented. I always knew there was certain information that I needed to convey, but I didn't have an outline in my head as to how that hour was going to go. I always used the child's action to talk about development—when I would see the child do something, I would point that out. Because, from the beginning, I had learned how important it is to hook information to something that is important to the parent. Certainly, the baby is very important to the parent. If I can hook developmental information to what we both see as being significant, something they might not have even noticed, this will help a mom appreciate her child's development. I've always taught development that way.

The third place my developmental knowledge has changed is in understanding premature babies. The in-service training that I have gotten through Parents as Teachers made all the difference in the world in my ability to provide meaningful service to families with premature babies. It's incredible how much preemies are on their own timetable. And working with families of preemies for 3 full years has given me increased understanding to share with other families.

Also, in the beginning, I thought I had to take a zillion activities because, if something didn't work, I wanted to be sure to have something else to do. I don't take so much stuff anymore because I realize that no matter how much I bring, the child will go through all of it anyway. When they get through all of it, they'll go do their own thing or bring their own toys, and we'll play with that. So, since that's going to happen anyway, I might as well not have so much stuff. Also, the other advantage is the child will focus more and spend more time with an appropriate activity or two that I now bring. The game is no longer "Let's go through the bag." The game is "Let's really do this activity." I'm also better at tuning into each child's tempo, and that is different for each child and different for each age.

And finally, my relationships with parents have changed. I think my relationships with parents always have been pretty solid. It certainly is better with families that I have a chance to spend the full 3 years with. And there always are certain families where it's going to click and certain families where it's not going to click as well.

I know my families are comfortable with me, and I'm not really sure why. I know I always would enjoy staying longer, and I always feel like they would like to have me stay longer. But I don't. I stick to a schedule because I know realistically that's what it needs to be for them and for me.

I guess the difference has been sort of in the general comfort level as far as I feel like I don't have anything to prove. The confidence I have in my own ability to do this job sort of takes any pretense away. And I am much more comfortable with silence than I used to be.[8] I used to feel like I needed to talk all the time. Now, I realize that the parent can be comfortable, and I can be comfortable just watching the child play and waiting for something to happen that we can talk about. It used to be that I couldn't do that—it would just be too scary—but now I can do it.

The pattern that definitely has changed is the way I respond to parents' questions. It's typical for parents to ask questions about their child's behavior and how to manage this behavior. It used to be that if a parent asked me a question, I thought I had to answer it. Now, I usually will remember to say, "What have you tried?" They'll talk about what they have tried, and I'll say, "What else have you tried?," and in this manner let the answer come from the parent instead of from me. Often, I can say to them, "That's really a good idea. Just stick with it, and give it more time." That's so much more powerful than my saying an answer. And sometimes I'll expand on their idea and give them something to read.

In her 10 years as a home visitor, Janice has gained new professional knowledge, skill, and understanding of herself. Gaining increased knowledge in child development and in understanding premature infants, for example, has helped Janice's skill in observing and interpreting behavior and in her giving information to parents. The process of doing home visits over time has led to improved skill, for example, visits no longer involve a series of activities; instead, the child can have extended focus in only one or two activities, and Janice can be more involved with the parent as well as the child. Janice speaks of how her increased self-confidence has allowed her to slow down. She is comfortable with silence as she and the parent watch the infant play. These observations can be the basis of helping the mother understand the developmental meaning of his or her infant's actions and what to expect next. Being comfortable with herself, Janice no longer feels she has to answer each parent's question; rather, a question can be the basis for helping parents problem-solve on their own.

I think the most difficult for me is talking to men and convincing men of [what] I believe in. Yet, the first year that I was on the school board, I was the only woman, so I had to be forceful, and I found that when I talk about something that I believe in like early childhood education, I can talk to anybody. As a child growing up, I was shy with boys. In college, I always was shy with boys. I'm just not always comfortable with men. It was fun to have all sons, and that has helped me professionally. All of a sudden, I was with boys and fathers, doing a lot with boys and fathers in Cub Scouts and athletics.

Resources for Professional Development

Each home visitor has a different way of teaching and learning. Janice speaks clearly about what she thinks has helped her most over the course of her career. In the chapter on professional development (Chapter 4), Janice described how sharing her work with colleagues has helped her. She also spoke of how helpful the regularly scheduled PAT in-service sessions have been in terms of deepening her knowledge base and expanding her processes.

I have had the opportunity to hear some well-known professionals in the field of early childhood, and several really have impacted how I work, one of them being T. Berry Brazelton. Brazelton gave me a new view of infants. Initially, I was thinking much more along the cognitive line that we had learned from Burton White, who intrigued me also. But when I heard Brazelton talk about all the things that infants could do and the relationships between infants and their parents, it was a new understanding for me. It opened many new avenues of thought in terms of how I work with parents and help them understand their baby.

Very early in my career, I heard Sally Provence talk about the importance of building rapport with a family, beginning with your phone call, and the importance of sharing enough of yourself with parents so that they understand who you are as a person, and that you really do share some common ground.

I'm a firm believer that professionals should access every opportunity to learn from leading authorities in the field.[9] It's not good enough to have one person on the staff go hear somebody and bring back their notes. If you're really going to get it, you've got to hear somebody yourself. I think the reason for this is, in the work that we're doing, we are doing person-to-person work, not book-to-person work. And to see how experts who are experts in engaging people can engage me on a personal level means that, if I am going to access any of their skills, I have to experience it.

Given her keen intellect and love of learning, Janice actively engages in new learning that national experts provide. She gains new ways of thinking and new skills in the same way that the parents she works with learn from her.

As previously discussed, home visiting is a craft, and professional growth occurs best through doing and reflecting on that doing. Janice described how she has always been self-reflective.

A lot of my reflection probably is just part of my growing. I always think about situations that have occurred in my own parenting experience with my own three children. I would think about things and wonder if I could do it better the next time if a similar instance occurred or do it better the next time with my younger child. That's the kind of person I am.

As a child, Janice's family's daily conversations at dinner and before bedtime were the anchor points of each day. These times in which family members reflected together on daily happenings seem to parallel Janice's ease in being self-reflective about her work and parenting.

As discussed in Chapter 1, Janice maintains boundaries in her work and thereby recognizes when she does not have the expertise to work with some of the problems a parent may share. In these situations, she offers empathic listening and support to parents. Just as she gives to parents, Janice's husband listens and supports her when she feels frustrated in her work.

I talk to my husband about situations that I find frustrating in my job. Sometimes, when you're talking about frustrations, you don't need anybody to give you answers. You just need somebody to sit there and nod their head and give you a hug. It is a skill or an art to be able to shield yourself, given the burdens of the job, because parents sometimes share more than you wish they would share. And if you are a sensitive person, and I am very sensitive, it's hard to just listen and walk away from it. I do listen, and I do walk away from it, but I can't get it out of my head a quickly as I wish I could. And that's because it's the kind of job where if you don't have some way to take care of yourself and somebody who will listen, it's too stressful.

Janice talked about the work she and I did together and about how it influenced her home visiting.

The kind of observation of my work you did when you would go into a home with me was very helpful. You would go into a home with me and with the parents' permission write down everything that was said during a home visit, and then we'd go back over what you had written. I know I became more aware of giving interpretive comments of the developmental meaning of a child's action, once you pointed this out to me. And then I was able to work towards giving interpretive comments more frequently.

But also, it was the time that I could take privately to read through what had occurred during the home visit. It helped me to appreciate what really had gone on. A home visitor doesn't remember everything that she has said or a parent has said. For example, it certainly helped me to appreciate the necessity to wrap up before I leave the home so that the parent really will have a parting thought. Over the course of the hour, she may not have realized [my message] because so much goes on. Our program is now teaching coordinators how to do what you have done.

Janice ended her discussion of influences on her work by returning to her own parenting.

There is always professional development that makes you do your job well, but I think there also is a very personal development that makes you do your job well. I think a lot of why I enjoy the work I do and why I have confidence in myself doing this job is because I really enjoyed my own motherhood. I enjoyed my children as babies. I enjoyed them as toddlers, young children, and the teen years that always are a new challenge. And now I enjoy them as young adults. I look at my children and see how successful they are in their relationships with other people and how successful they've been in school. It gives me the confidence in this job to think, "Yeah, I think I did a pretty good job as a mother. My children are really great."

So, it gives me the confidence to talk about some of these child-rearing issues in a very sincere way. I'm not just talking about it because I've read it in book. I'm talking about it because I've experienced it in my own life, and the results have been positive. Because I have the personal experience, I think that makes me more credible.

A give-and-take mutuality seems to characterize Janice's parenting and her work life. Just as her parenting influences her home visiting, so, too, her home visiting work influences her parenting. Five years before I conducted these life history interviews, Janice told me how working as a home visitor helped with her parenting of her teenage children.

PAT helps me keep a focus on development, even though my children are older. It helps me structure my thinking about my children in terms of their development. And the parenting techniques I talk about with the mothers of little ones, I find I really use with my teenagers, only adjust up a little. And when I go to parenting workshops at the high school, I hear them saying the same kinds of things that I am telling parents of toddlers. And I can say to the parents of my babies that these are techniques that you will use all the way through your parenting because you do.

Janice's personal style makes the interplay between her own parenting and home visiting possible. She is quite self-reflective about all her experiences and tends to approach both family and her professional experiences in a thinking, cognitive manner.

JANICE'S PERSONAL AND PROFESSIONAL HISTORY
Childhood Family

Janice grew up in Nathan, a middle-class suburb of a large midwestern city, Centerville. She was the older of two daughters in a family where children and adults were very close, within both her nuclear and extended family. Janice described her childhood family life as being routine, predictable, and traditional.

I remember growing up in a very modest and predictable environment. My mother was a homemaker; my dad went to the office. My dad went to work at the same time every morning and got home at 5:15 every single night. Mother cooked, cleaned, and dusted the furniture every day. Dinner was the same time every night, mashed potatoes every night. We'd sit around the table, and everyone would share happenings of the day. In the summer, conversation would happen again around 10:00 P.M. Everybody would be back out in the kitchen talking again. Lots of sharing about things going on in other families, families within our family, job stories and Navy stories from

Dad. And we were very active in the church. Dad was on the vestry, so I guess there'd be stories about church activity. . . . Just lots of conversation.

And every Sunday, like clockwork, after church we went to my father's mother's house—a ritual. She was my only grandparent. We would always have the same dinners. Even now, when I walk into anybody's house and smell pot roast, immediately I think of Sundays walking into my grand-mother's house after church. After dinner was over, we would clear the table, do the dishes, and spend the day together. That was Sunday, a fam-ily day.

Predictable daily routines, lengthy daily family conversations, and gatherings of extended family each Sunday anchored Janice with a firm sense of connectedness and security.

When Janice was 7 years old, her parents adopted a baby girl. Jan-ice describes her sister as follows.

We weren't playmates, but I spent a lot of time with her because I loved the way she laughed. I just had fun playing with her, even though it wasn't play-mate kind of play. She was my baby sister. She was bright and creative, but she never really could accept the success that I had in school and felt like she always was trying to be my sister instead of being herself. She was much more resistant to authority. As a teenager, Sherry had a different peer culture than I did—1965 versus 1958. She was incredibly rebellious, and my parents did not know how to deal with it. They had some very difficult times. Bottom line is Sherry moved out. She moved to Oregon and has maintained her distance ever since.

As a child, Janice never questioned her parents' love and adora-tion for their daughters.

I always had the strong feeling that my parents really adored us. They al-ways spoke to us in a very respectful way. I don't remember any harsh words. I don't remember being punished. We just always understood what was expected.

Shared time with extended family was an important part of Jan-ice's childhood. Her mother was one of seven children, and her father had a twin brother. Everyone lived in Centerville. Each year, Janice and her family had holiday and birthday celebrations with her moth-er's siblings and their spouses and children.

This was a family that truly knew how to have fun, and that probably gave me my sense of family. As I was growing up, we always had family birthday parties for every cousin's birthday, every single year. And there were very

large holiday parties that were family-oriented and fun. They had quite wonderful parties because everybody loved music and sang all the time. That's
my memory of what it was like to grow up in this family. We'd sing, dance,
and party in the front room. And lots of just playing the old-time parlor
games like the Pig in the Parlor. That's the context in which I grew up.

Janice shared that she had been sorry that her own children did
not have the same kind if extended family experiences with "lots of
laughing, lots of playing, and the old-time parlor games." At the same
time, as a full-time homemaker, she could create much of her family
patterns and parenting parallel to her childhood family life. Her children
had predictable routines and shared time among family members, just
as Janice had as a child. After she gave birth to her first child, she was
a full-time homemaker for 17 years.

I never will understand how some people can buy into what I see as a very
narrow view of what it means to be a woman. I think that there is too much
setting aside the whole concept of motherhood and marriage. My view of it is
that. . . it is your obligation to yourself to head out in a career. That negates
what for me is a very important part of my life. My experience has been that
you can have both. I think you can have a rewarding professional experience, take time out for a rewarding family experience, and come back at
another stage in your life and have a rewarding professional experience. I
think doing that has helped my family be more stable.

I remained home for 17 years without objection. Granted, that's the
way I grew up; and that may be more difficult for young women now. I'm not
so sure of that because I think we don't take a realistic view of how important parenthood is. One of my objections to the feminist movement is the
whole emphasis on moving away from what the children need, from what
the family needs.

Schooling

Citizens in Janice's childhood community of Nathan were part of the
first-generation postwar middle class. Nathan residents valued education, and parents expected that their children would be better educated
than they were and, in turn, be successfully employed. Janice spoke of
her love of school and how early schooling influenced her choice of career in teaching.

Janice: Education was valued highly in my family. My mother was one of only
           two in her family to graduate from high school, the same high school as

my dad. As long as I can remember, it was assumed that I would go to college, to Metropolitan University, and as early as second grade, I knew I wanted to be a teacher. It took scholarships and loans and lots of hard work to make it happen, but I graduated Phi Beta Kappa.

I loved school. It was just my favorite place to be, my favorite thing to do. I can remember every single teacher I had in grade school. Those grade school teachers—I can remember stories from every single year.

Carol: What do you mean, stories?

Janice: Things stick in my mind. Like in kindergarten—all the way through school, I was tall. In kindergarten, I was always in the back row. At the tables, I was in the back row. It frustrated me that we always were learning to write other people's names and never got to write my name. That's just the way they taught. They'd demonstrate one person's name on the chalkboard, and everybody would practice over and over and over again. The fact that my name was Janice didn't matter. We all learned to write Mary.

I had the same teacher for first and second grade. She was wonderful. She absolutely was the person who made me want to become a teacher. She had a wonderful sense of humor and was so much fun to be with. I loved learning.

As Janice talked about her schooling, her detailed description of each of her elementary school teachers from 30–40 years before was amazing. Two teachers, the one who taught first and second grade and her sixth-grade teacher, became lifelong models who triggered her love of education. Both her teachers and her parents had high expectations for her, and she excelled throughout school.[10]

In high school, Janice was in accelerated classes, and she continued to love all aspects of school.

Nathan at that time was considered one of the better districts, and my high school education was excellent. People really valued education. Everybody was expected to work. Everybody was expected to do well. Everybody was expected to learn. I was very well prepared for college.

I was editor of the high school newspaper. I drove my mother crazy because of the hours I kept. I always was very busy because I was incredibly active in all kinds of things in high school. I did tons of term papers in high school and had lots of homework—burning the midnight oil.

Janice also spoke of having fine teachers at Metropolitan University, and once again, she loved school. She lived at home.

It never entered my head to go any place other than Metropolitan University. I knew how special it was. I was the first person in my family or my extended family who graduated from college.

After graduation, she looked forward to returning to the classroom as a primary teacher.

Friendships

Janice's life revolves around relationships. As a child, she experienced family-like intimacy with close friends. During her childhood, Janice had several special friends, many of whom she still feels close to.

At my last high school reunion . . . we had a group of people from my elementary school at the same table. Several of us still are friends, and several of us were the key people who put together the high school reunion. Suzi is my closest friend, since first grade.

Janice also spoke of creative play with friends in the neighborhood.

Two little girls close to my age lived across the street until I was about 10. We used to play together all the time, and we usually played things like office or school. And we played movie stars and dress-up. TV and that kind of stuff just wasn't in my life. We had to create our own fun, and it was a very happy time.

Religion

Religion has played a significant role in Janice's childhood and adult life.

My grandmother, Mawie, on my dad's side was very, very religious, very faithful. We are Episcopalian. I grew up going to Sunday school every single Sunday. I taught Sunday school for years, through high school and college. I think I mentioned earlier that after church we would go to my grandmother's, so that ritual of Sunday was very important.

I started going to church again regularly when we came back to Centerville and returned to church where we absolute fell in love with the minister. He was both very warm and very humorous. We started going back there every single Sunday. My children were reared going to church every Sunday.

Janice clearly holds faith as important.[11] She spoke of the influence of having a pastor who could translate religion meaningfully for her.

Janice's grandmother, Mawie, was her model in religious faith. Mawie had a leadership role in the church in a time when it was rare for women to be leaders. Janice described how Mawie had regular prayers that she recited to give her strength. When Janice was a child, Mawie always told her, "When you can't figure something out, pray about it." Janice told me that, in fact, now she feels like she has a very personal relationship with God. "In difficult times in my life, I really will say, 'I can't handle this. Please help me.' And I gain the strength to deal with the situation."

Marriage, Work, and Parenting

Janice met her husband when they both were sophomores at Metropolitan University. She got married and started a new job shortly after graduation.

> When I met Joe, I fell for him so fast. He was serious about his studies, an engineering major, and he was very good to me. We went together 3 years and decided we would get married. He was very kind, always treated me well. We never quarreled. I perceived him as very much like my father. He treated me similarly.
>
> When we married, we moved to Northton, where Joe was in graduate school. We had a wonderful life in Northton. I got a job in the wealthiest suburb on the South Shore, Bentley. I taught first grade, and I felt like I had died and gone to heaven. I had a wonderful class, flexibility, good support, and many new friends, other young teachers. I loved teaching!

Janice has been able to continue her love of teaching as she works with parents of infants and young children in home visiting.

In October of Janice's second year teaching at Bentley, she learned that she was pregnant. She had been taking oral contraceptives, so the pregnancy was a total surprise to her and Joe.

> The news was like a lightning bolt.[12] I was devastated. I could not imagine it. I was the one teaching with my husband in graduate school. This is not the way my life was planned. When I told Joe, he couldn't believe it either. We couldn't even be excited about it at first because we were so stunned. It never even dawned on me that I would go back to work after this baby was born.[13] My baby was due the middle of March, and the pregnancy put Joe on the fast track. He finished his Ph.D. 3 years after graduating from college.

Janice's life was planned at first by her parents and later by Joe and herself. Having a baby was not part of the plan. Once Janice integrated this dramatic life-cycle change, her teaching plans were put aside so that she could give total devotion to parenting.

In April, Janice gave birth to a baby boy, named Brett. One year later, Joe received his Ph.D., and they returned to Johnston, a city adjacent to Janice's childhood hometown, where her parents still lived. When Brett was 4 years old, Janice gave birth to another son and then, 3 years later, another son. She loved being a homemaker and mother. She returned to her childhood schooling and church interests by becoming very active in her children's schools and teaching Sunday school. Janice felt continuity between her own family and the family in which she grew up.

Janice has worked part-time for 5 years and full-time for 10 years for PAT. She always has been hard-working and thinks nothing of working a full day and then spending the evening at one of her children's concerts or sporting events. During the weekend, she sometimes cares for her two grandchildren, who live 5 minutes from her home.

CYNTHIA DISCUSSES HER HOME VISITING WORK
Personal Meaningfulness of Home Visiting

I asked Cynthia if she could talk about what her home visiting work has meant to her.

Cynthia: I think it's meaningful work. Again, it's not something I consciously chose to do. I think we follow a path that feels comfortable to us—not that it isn't challenging and frustrating at times—but, for the most part, when I go into a home and sit down and talk to people, I feel comfortable.

And I can use my intellect, although it may not seem that way to someone on the outside looking in. I get to use it with the family as I am watching the dynamics and helping people process, and I reflect on what I've done and how I've done it, why I've done it. I do a lot of that. I will leave a home visit, and I can tell by my spirits how that home visit went. Sometimes I fly high out of a home visit. I feel like I made some progress with this person; it was a good experience for both of us. I like to think that the adult and child I leave feel the same way—high. This was a good thing that just happened.

Then, there are others that I leave and I feel like the slug of the earth. It just didn't go well. I didn't say the right thing. I should have known better. I missed this. So, I know by how [high] my spirit is soaring as to how that visit went. I could leave it at that, or I can take the time—I even do it as I'm driving or as I go out walking—[to] replay the visit in my head. I can almost repeat it verbatim. I remember the look the mom shot the kid or the kid shot the mom. I'll just play it in my head, and I'll think, "Well, what if I'd done this, or what if I'd done that?" Again, the chance to sit and talk to other people who do this kind of work is so important. We never get enough of that.

So I get "stuff" from my home visits, from my interactions with people. It may be a way of correcting the child. I've watched a mom just touch a certain part of the baby's hair to caress, and I've actually gone home and done it with my child. There is a reciprocity. I think there has to be that reciprocity. You have to have an understanding that this is not a one-way street. I'm not just going into a home just to do things with people. I am going into homes to have a relationship. They give me as much as I give them.

Carol: Can you give an example?

Cynthia: I have taken exact words, verbatim, from another home visitor—from Janice—words that I read from one of [her] home visit observations: her explanation of language. I now use it. It's mine. I can't create everything, so I take things from people. My home visits still look very different from Janice's, even though we may have several phrases in which we use the exact same words.

           I know I make a difference, and parents will tell me that. It's taking the time to sit back and think about it—to think about what that person was like 3 years ago, to be able to do the Denver [Developmental Screening Test] for the child and see that the child is growing, is developmentally appropriate. Maybe it's not the way you want it, but it could have been worse. What has been consistently the most difficult for me is not being able to find the key or not being there when that person needs me.

Professional Development over Time

For the past 5 years, Cynthia has worked as a home visitor with primarily low-income, at-risk families. This is her first home visiting position. Cynthia sees home visiting as deepening the level of her involvement with low-income families. She also is aware of her increased level of knowledge and skill. She described how she has grown in her home visiting role.

Cynthia: When I started home visiting, I had been working in [the] early childhood [field] about 12 years. I had some experience working with parents, but not in the home setting. When I first went on home visits, I would talk to parents about their children; my visit was child-focused. The PAT curriculum, the manual, says this is your lesson, and this is what you are going to do. I really didn't deal that much with the parents. It was more the child and how the child felt and how the child was developing. With time, and especially with the kind of families I work with, I still focus on the child and talk about the child, but I'm much more aware of the relationship between the parent and child and the parent as a person and how that person deals with everyday life. Some new home visitors actually will sit there and almost read from the lessons, but as you grow and develop your skill and become more knowledge-able of development and of the many different ways to promote devel-opment, you merely use the written materials to reinforce information with the parent.

It's such an interesting profession. You are privy to a person's innermost life. You get to see where they live, what possessions they have, how they arrange them, how they arrange their life. Then, you watch their interactions with their baby. When I think about that, I get a little afraid sometimes.

Carol: Afraid in what way?

Cynthia: Well, because it's that person's private world. I don't want to invade that private world, and I don't want to be an intrusion into someone's private world. I guess that's where the balance is.

Carol: Maybe it's being cautious.

Cynthia: Maybe, but I tend to think of caution as negative. I don't mean fear like, "Oh, my gosh, what am I going to do?" or "I'm going to be hurt," or that kind of thing, but just that I'm very aware that this is a person's private life that I'm seeing. I want the person I'm talking with to know that I value their privacy, that I understand that what they are sharing with me is private. Actually, it is a gift when somebody shares something that is private.

Cynthia spoke very specifically about how she has changed her approach with increased experience in home visiting.

Cynthia: My visits have changed over the years. When I first started, I was con-cerned about how I'd do with the child. You know, would the child respond to me? Would I be able to get the child to play? Over time, I realized that my job isn't to play with the child but to involve the parent with the child so that there's more interaction. Then, I'm able to talk with the parent about how the parent interacts with the child.

When I first started home visiting, I spent more time playing with the child. The play would end, and we'd go to the next section of the lessons, which is review what we've been talking about. It was much more Step A, Step B, Step C, Step D. Now, it melds together, though I do try to summarize at the end, summarize important things to re-member.

I still play with the child and often do model. Not just model. I play with the child because it is fun, and through that play, the parent is more likely to want to participate because it is fun. And if it looks like fun and sounds fun, it must be fun. I found that most parents want to play with their kids, but they may not be sure exactly how to do it.

So if we can spend 20 minutes where everybody is having fun and the parent feels successful and the child is having a good time and parent and child are interacting, then I'll physically back off. We all will be sitting on the floor, and the parent, child, and I will be playing. Then, I'll back out of the play so that the parent and child are playing together. Then, I can observe and can give the parent feedback on what's going on, on what they are doing.

I use the written materials—the parent handouts—to help parents see what they already know how to do because I'll observe them as they play with their child. Toward the end of the visit, when I summarize, I'll say, "Here are the handouts for language development. Look here, your child already is doing these things. We heard him today." Then, I'll summarize, "Remember when he said, 'Ba ba?' He is using those sounds. Then, when you responded to him, that is one of the most important things you can do. It says it right here." I relate the written material back to what has happened in our visit. That's been part of my growth. I wasn't able to do that at first. It makes the parent feel good: "I must be a good parent if I can do these things."

When I first started home visiting, I relied on those written materials. I thought it was all in the manual. I felt that if I just read it long enough and memorized it, I'd know every answer to any question any parent would ask me. Now, there are all kinds of questions I can't answer. I don't know why that child sleeps 12 hours and then he's awake 2 and then sleeps 8 more. I don't have definite answers for all these things, and that's okay. I'm much more comfortable saying to a parent, "Well, I'm not really sure. What do you think?," instead of feeling that I have to give the answer. It is not my child. It's their child, and they probably have the answer. They just need some help pulling it out or taking a look at it from a different point of view.

Now, I'm more aware of what I don't know, and I'm comfortable with that. I used to feel that I alone was responsible for this child's development. Now, I'm comfortable with knowing that "No, I'm not totally responsible; what I'm responsible for is supplying information and being there and interaction with the parent and the child. But it's not my responsibility to make sure that child develops in a certain way. That's the parent's responsibility."

And I have grown in my ability to accept that not all people want my service; not all people are ready to accept it. There are homes I'll never get in.[14] There are homes I'll get in once and never be invited back. There are other homes I can be in all the time but never get past a certain point. I really believe that people take from me what they need, not what I want to give them. When I first started, I thought I had things to give them and they needed to take them. Now, I feel I have things to offer, and they'll take what they need, what they're able to take at that time. That's what I've learned. Patience is a virtue, one that I've never had.

Carol: Patience with your families or with yourself?

Cynthia: Patience with everything. I've learned that when you're working with families over time, changes flow and changes may never come. Giving parents time to be able to do things and giving myself time and knowing that if something doesn't happen tomorrow, that's okay. It may happen the next day, and I've learned to wait for that next day.

Like Janice, when she first began home visiting, Cynthia focused primarily on the baby or young child. I was not surprised to hear each woman describe her initial inclination to focus on the children, because these two women had years of prior experience with babies and young children. With time, Cynthia learned that the greatest gift she could give the parents was to involve them in play with their children and to help them to see the meaning and purpose of this involvement. Cynthia enjoys playing with little ones, and she skillfully generates this pleasure in parents as she invites them to play. Initially in her approach, she moved from one step to another as she followed the lesson plan. Now, like Janice, she has an integrated approach. She involves parent and baby, and she shares developmental information and interpretation in terms of the baby's and parents' actions. She also integrates the parent handouts—the written materials. As she summarizes the visits, she notes what the parent and baby did that directly relates to the written materials. Cynthia has learned that she cannot be all things to all people—that parents will take what they are able to take from her—and she can be at peace knowing some families will reject her services.

Resources for Professional Development

Cynthia has been working in the field of early intervention for almost 20 years. She feels that during her first few jobs, she developed skills by "dealing with the task at hand and learning by trial and error." I asked her if, over the years, other people or experiences have influenced her professional development.[15]

Cynthia: A person who has been influential in my work was one of my professors at graduate school. Every time we moved, there were new courses needed for certification, or I even had to repeat a course. When I arrived at Dr. Frank's office at the University of Alabama, I learned that they were going to take away all the hours I had completed at the University of Florida. I sat crying in his office. He made three phone calls, and they made some exceptions for me and wrote a special program for me. It wasn't that he did me the favor but that he cared. I had been in so many colleges at that point where nobody wanted to listen to my story, nobody really cared: Just give me your money and go to class and abide by these state rules. This man was different. The thing I always remember about Dr. Frank was when you walked in that door, and he was terribly busy, he took time to listen to what you had to say and responded as a human being. I think he was as pleased as I was when I finally got my master's [degree]. For years after I left there, I sent him a poinsettia every Christmas.

He taught me to slow down and to listen to people and to see people as people, not as a means to an end. That's what I took from that man. It's so easy when you get busy and caught up in things to look at the people you work with as a way to get the job done, rather than a person, a human being with hopes and dreams and problems at home. I think we forget that too often. It helps me to be more compassionate, to remember to stop and say to my Even Start home visitor, Terry, "How is Lori doing? How's the toilet training going?" rather than "Do you have the report done that I need?" Dr. Frank helped me learn to relate to people as people rather than just co-workers. The truth is, a lot of people have influenced me. I've always been one to sit back, watch, and observe. I take things from others and put them into my own repertoire. But as far as influencing me, I can tell you exactly what Dr. Frank gave to me, his gift to me.

The other thing I want to say about why this work is meaningful to me is because I've made the statement that I go in and have things to offer and people take from me what they need or are ready to take. I think the same of myself. I take from the people I work with on an everyday basis. I take things for myself. For example, I take your knowledge. I take your ability to synthesize and to look at things from a different perspective, and I make that my own. I play with it. You have given me a new way to look at things. It may be something as simple as the way someone has arranged flowers in a vase, but it catches my eye, and I may use it in my own home. It may be a phrase, the way they put their words together, and I like the way that sounds, and it becomes my own.

Carol: Cynthia, since you have begun home visiting, do you have anybody with whom you can discuss your work?

Cynthia: Yes, in that respect I have a lot of support. I can share with Margaret [di-
           rector of the district's early education], with Dan [the clinical psycholo-
           gist who regularly works with staff], and being able to talk to you has
           been helpful. I do have people to talk to about certain things. I'm the
           kind of person who pretty much needs to talk about something to fig-
           ure it out.[16] I process by talking, and Bob [my husband] knows that
           about me. As I said before, Bob calms me down. And especially when
           I'm struggling with supervision issues, he helps me process and think
           things through. Mostly, he listens to me. I spent a lot of years pretending
           I could handle anything. Now, I am able to say I have a problem. That's
           my personal development and growth. Many things have contributed
           to that. The people I've mentioned, different books I've read, and being
           able to sit and talk about the work with families we do with other home
           visitors, who often encounter similar problems.

Relationships always have been at the center of Cynthia's life, in
childhood, and in her work. Not surprisingly, she sees her professional
development emerging through relationships with significant people.
Cynthia has learned that she need not always excel, that she need not
have all the answers and, in fact, can be comfortable with problems.
She knows she needs individuals with whom she can talk about her
work. She feels fortunate to have several colleagues, as well as her
husband, who listen and offer supportive feedback.

I asked Cynthia how she avoids burnout and what keeps her
going.

I always find a new twist, something new to do within my job. This year it
was Early Head Start, a new collaboration to put together. In my 9 years in
this district, I have had 4 different jobs, not significantly different, but enough
to give me a challenge. I need a challenge.

    I also have learned to recognize my limits. I can recognize my own
needs and have become better at voicing my needs, for example, speaking
with Margaret, the director of early education. I also do things for myself such
as leave work on time, walk, and work in the garden. For fun, for just me, I
go to the botanical gardens and just walk, or I go to our little library. I smell
the books and browse, read the magazines, and go home with 6 or more
books.

I then asked Cynthia what she thinks has been her greatest contribution.

I am inordinately positive and caring. In the area of staff development, I have
grown many good teachers, caregivers, and home visitors. I'm surprised at

my skill almost daily! I have a good sense of what I can do. But I am surprised when I get feedback that I'm good at something. I have had to learn acceptance of others and patience. That's just where some people are, but I still don't accept mediocrity.

I have had to learn not to feel that I have to know and be everything. I seek help; yet, it is not easy to do. In Even Start, Dan, our psychological consultant, and Margaret, our early education director, helped me a lot. Margaret was at each Friday training session; thus, I did not feel that I was shouldering all the responsibility. She always was very supportive.

CYNTHIA'S PERSONAL AND PROFESSIONAL HISTORY

Childhood Family

Cynthia, like Janice, grew up in a very close nuclear and extended family; however, the daily life of this family of seven children was not "like clockwork." They lived in a small rural town, Florence, 1 hour from the closest metropolitan area. Cynthia's father owned a bar in town, and her mother was full-time homemaker until Cynthia was 9 years old. Then, her mother taught Spanish in the town's high school. Cynthia is the fifth of seven children.

Cynthia: I was the start of the second family. My mom had me at 40 and 2 more by the time she was 43. My oldest sister was 17 when I was born. I was raised in an extended family.

Carol: A nuclear family that seemed extended.

Cynthia: Right. But we also had grandmas and grandpas. We lived in this huge house. First, my mother's mother lived with our family when I was very young, and I also grew up with my mother's father living in our home. And there always was a new baby in our family. And as a teen, I had a lot of experience with young children. I did a lot of taking care of them. That's pretty much how I grew up—in a litter.

Cynthia grew up in a family that loved babies and chose a career path continuing her early love of babies and small children. Family celebrations with singing, laughter, and game playing were a central part of her childhood. While Janice's family rituals stayed about the same, Cynthia's daily family life and celebrations always changed.

Holidays always were celebrated with food, decoration, and ceremony. We were raised Catholic, so Christmas and Easter especially were religious holidays, but also fun holidays. Who was there as a family always changed because of the differences in ages and who was and wasn't available at that time. The celebrations always included a lot of food, a lot of noise, a lot of laughter, playing games, and a lot of music. My older sisters both played the piano, had good voices, and sang.

Though her parents did not finish college, they valued learning, and they instilled that value in their seven children.

Reading was extremely important. My mother read to us from the time we were babies, and my father read to us from about age 6 to 12. He'd take the three of us—the little ones. Every night after dinner, for a half hour, he'd read nonfiction to us. He had a love of history. I remember all the presidents' lives. He'd read those children's books to us. It was just such a nice, special time.

My mom and dad had such a love of learning. They both were very determined that all of us would grow up well educated and go to college. I always knew—that was the expectation, that you will go to college, and you will do well in school. You had no choice, and that's what we did.

Beyond a love of learning, Cynthia's parents "had a love of their fellow man." Cynthia explained:

They displayed this love in different ways for different things that were important to them. I remember when I had my mom as a teacher. She was so understanding of these other kids, especially the ones having difficulty. And when Mom died last summer, about 10 of her high school students from about 30 years ago came to the funeral. They loved her. Mom cared about people, understood people, and took time for them.

My dad displayed caring for other people in an entirely different way. He was "the local pawn shop." When someone was in trouble, he'd bail them out of jail and pay for it. If someone didn't have money, they'd bring him their TV, and he'd give them 20 bucks and keep it until they could pay him back. In their own way, both Mom and Dad were very generous people. I grew up with that tolerance of other cultures right from the start. It just always was there, that you are accepting of people who are a little bit different or have different ideas. You don't have to agree with them, but that doesn't have anything to do with the respect you feel for them as a person.

As I listened to Cynthia describe her parents' tolerance, understanding, and assisting people, I reflected on how these themes are central to Cynthia's work as a home visitor and coordinator of Even Start, a program serving families with very low incomes. Although the individual members living in Cynthia's family might have changed, the patterns of her family's daily life were consistent. Dinnertime was one of these consistent patterns.

> At dinnertime, everyone was expected to be there. You knew you had to be home at a certain time for dinner. Then, you had conversation. Sometimes, you had arguments because my mom and dad had such different opinions politically. So, we would listen and learn both sides. Mom was a Democrat, and Dad was a Republican. They would have lively arguments.
>
> Dinner was a time of discussion. My dad might come home with a story from the bar. They were always interesting stories. We learned a lot about human nature and the kinds of things that can happen in families. You recapped your day, what was going on, or what was important. It wasn't so much a time of planning what was going to happen next as a time to be together.

Cynthia grew up in a small town, and Janice grew up in a large metropolitan area. As young children, dinnertime for both involved daily extended conversation about ideas and happenings of family members. As children, both women found a sense of security and connectedness in these daily rituals; yet, there were substantive differences between the two families. Janice experienced very predictable, conservative thinking within her family's daily dinner that always involved the same four family members. Cynthia experienced lively arguments and a wide range of perspective taking as she ate with an ever-changing family constellation.

Cynthia also had a different relationship with her siblings. Whereas Janice was the oldest child in her family, Cynthia was a middle child and was influenced by her much older sister.

> My mom was pregnant a very short time after she had me and then pregnant again. Corrina was a sophomore in high school when I was born. The first 3 years of my life, she pretty much took care of me. In our family, the older kids always bore responsibility for the younger kids. I got to do all kinds of things that most very young babies don't get to do. I hung out with a teenager; so it was great fun.
>
> We all grew up at a very young age with family responsibility. The daily chores of cooking and cleaning with a very large family take a lot of time and organization. At 8, I started doing the laundry with my older sister for our weekly responsibility. I couldn't go to movies until I had washed the floors on Saturday morning. Everybody had their jobs.
>
> We used to do all kinds of things we weren't supposed to do. Like one time we tried to persuade my little sister, Annie, that there really was a tooth fairy. My sister, Liz, who is 5 years older than I am, dressed me up like a fairy,

and I went out on a narrow ledge outside Liz's window and tried to convince this kid that I was the tooth fairy. She was maybe 3, and I wasn't very old. She took one look and said, "Oh, that's just Cynthia." I was dancing two stories up on a ledge, and I shouldn't have been doing that.

We did all kinds of things. We'd sneak out at midnight. My older sister would go swimming in the lake in the moonlight, and she'd take me. I was 3 years old. They'd swim, and I'd sit on the edge and watch. It was wonderful. Then, when the second litter grew up, we'd sneak out of the house while everybody was sleeping and go down to the lake and swim.

For Cynthia, risk taking was just what you did as a child. As an adult, Cynthia continues be comfortable with risks. At the same time, she sometimes feels fearful.

Cynthia: In my work, I have pursued different kinds of positions with more responsibility and a chance to do things in a different way. I have actively sought positions and pushed myself, and sometimes there is risk involved. At the time, I'm thinking, "You don't want to do that." But there's something inside me that makes me do it. I just do it anyway. Until now. Now, I've gotten to the point where I don't think I have to run around taking chances anymore to know who or what I am.

Carol: When you go on home visits in dangerous neighborhoods, do you have the frightening feelings that you remember having as child?

Cynthia: No. It's funny that I don't because I've thought that I probably should. Why am I not afraid? I know some people who work in dangerous neighborhoods are very afraid, and some just won't do it. Maybe it's just stupidity. I feel safe. No, I'm not stupid about it. I feel aware that there could be danger. I don't go to these neighborhoods at night or after 3:00 P.M.

Carol: Well, you seem to have had a childhood, beginning at 3 years, involving risk-taking.

Cynthia: That's probably true, though I've never thought about it much.

Cynthia spoke of her mother as a very strong woman who had a major influence on her life. She poignantly described her mother's gifts and how she influenced her development.

I was crazy about my dad, but I lost him at 19. I said to my son the other night, "I only knew my dad 19 years." I looked at him and said, "You're 13 years old already. I only knew my dad 19 years. That's only 6 more years." But I knew my mom 41 years, so I had more time to know her as a person. I never knew my dad as a person like I grew to know my mother.

My mother had a formidable strength. Yes, she was bossy, and everybody was half afraid of her, but she had love and compassion. I think of her love of life, her sheer delight in a bite of a peach. She would just howl with laughter at things her kids said. No one entertained her more than her own children. She absolutely loved being with them. She waited for the minute we would walk in the door to tell her a story. She would give you her undivided attention at the moment to hear your story. Then, she would make sure that everybody else knew about our accomplishments.

And her love of learning. I was able to watch the different things she could do and realize that while your talents are gifts, they also have to be nurtured and take work. She helped me understand that. It doesn't just happen; you have to work to develop your talents.

And she worked hard throughout her life. She worked hard at learning. I mean even up to the bitter end, she played Scrabble and wanted to win. Half-blind, she would get this big magnifying glass to be able to study the dictionary to learn new words to beat [her friend] May Kabias. They had a Scrabble club. Up to her last day, she still was trying to learn new words to beat May Kabias.

And she never lost her love of gardening. She watched birds. She taught me to appreciate nature. When I was growing up, I hated pulling those weeds. I would cry, "You can't make me go out in that garden," but you know, that taught me something, too. It taught me that you can bring order to the chaos of weeds. I took great pleasure in how it looked when I was done, when I got all those weeds removed. I learned the names of the plants, and I knew how to take care of them because I spent a lot of time out there with Mom. That has become important in my life. I need my time in my garden.

Although I only observed and interviewed Cynthia for 18 months, as I listened to her describe her mother, I reflected on how the descriptions matched what I know of Cynthia. During several meetings, I listened to her tell me stories of a 39-year-old Even Start mother who lived with her sister and their 12 children and 4 grandchildren in a home bordering on chaos, and I sensed her caring and compassion. On Friday, during a break from interviewing, she told me she was looking forward to a day of gardening on Saturday. She shared with me the pleasure she gets in the unusual names of her irises.

Schooling

Cynthia attended a Catholic elementary school and public high school. She described school as being very easy for her. Throughout her childhood, close friendships and time with her large family occupied her far more than did school. There was nothing remarkable about school;

it was just something she did, and she didn't have to work hard to get all As.

> I remember my high school years as just a lot of fun. School wasn't hard for me at all. I started working my sophomore year in high school at a pizza place. I worked one or two nights during the week and on the weekend. That gave me spending money, my clothes money, things like that. I never had to work really hard. I learned things quickly.

Cynthia has a keen intellect that her parents nourished by reading to her since she was a baby and by engaging extended daily conversations and debates at dinner. As I listened to her brief description of school, I thought of how much more stimulating her life at home had been than at school. I also reflected on the stark contrast between Cynthia's and Janice's schooling experiences. Cynthia's small-town elementary and high schools were unexceptional, and she sailed through with ease. Janice's teachers had higher expectation, and she worked very hard to excel.

Given her family's decreased income, Cynthia could not choose which college to attend, and her courses in college seemed as unremarkable to her as her experiences in grade school and high school.

> I wanted to go to the main state university, but we couldn't afford it. I didn't want to go into education. Everyone else in my family was a teacher, and I didn't want to be a teacher. But, at the time, my dad gave me no choice. If he sent me to the main state university, then my younger brother and sister couldn't go to school because there wouldn't be enough money. They had 3 kids to try to get through college; and all of us were going to be in college a year or two together. Dad said that he wanted [me to go] to Southeastern University, and he wanted me to take a teacher [education] scholarship because women need [to have teaching as a backup].[17]

Friendships

Cynthia continues contact with her close friends of early childhood and adolescence, friends whom she shared many happy hours of playful abandon.

> I was just talking to one of my childhood friends two nights ago. Her mother is in the hospital dying. It made me think back to my first memory of Lane Kabias. We were both in diapers and were crawling under a dining room table, one of those gate-leg tables where the sides come down. When I think about Lane, that's the first image that comes to me. Our mothers were dear friends. They were gardener friends and avant garde in this small town.

What the moms had in common was that tolerance of what is different. Lane and I have remained friends. Lane now lives in Chicago, and we talk to each other a couple times a year. She was one of my dearest friends.

Already in high school, Cynthia's actions seemed to mirror her parents' tolerance of difference.

Even though I came from a big family, I always had friends at school. I had friends from pretty much all walks. I had West-Ender friends who were the kids on the wrong side of the track. I didn't really hang around with them because I didn't drink and that kind of thing. But I was respectful of them, and they knew it. I would help them with schoolwork.

Jean Bath became one of my best friends. She was loud and obnoxious and totally hysterical. Jean and I stayed friends through all the years, and I lost her 2 years ago when she died at the age of 38 of pancreatitis. She was one of my best and dearest friends.

Another good friend was Rose Matthews. She also became my friend in high school, and we ended up at the same college. We were kind of like a rat pack: Jean, Rose, and I. Rose continues to be a good friend of mine. I see her probably two or three times a year, whenever I go back to Florence.

All the friends I have mentioned spent hours at my house. Our home was the hangout. Poor Mom and Dad—how they could stand it I'll never know. I mean, we were the last of seven kids. Our home was across the street from the pizza place where I worked, so we'd close the pizza place, and everyone would come over to my house. Mom and Dad must have been deaf by that point. We would stay up 'til 1:00, 2:00, or 4:00 in the morning. I remember my high school years as lots of fun.

Throughout childhood and adolescence, Cynthia was immersed in a caring and loving web of relationships. Her parents modeled caring and compassion in their personal and work lives; teenage siblings were primary caregivers when she was very little; and life-long childhood friends are remembered within a circle of love and caring.[18]

Religion

Cynthia was raised Catholic and attended a Catholic grade school in Florence.

Cynthia: In grade school, I spent a lot of time in religion class. I went to church every day. My parents were quite active in the church. I loved the old Latin Mass and the symbolism and incense. The mysticism was to me more prevalent then because you didn't understand the Latin. It's like it was shrouded in a mystery, and to me that made more sense. So, when I think of religion and church, those are the things come to my mind.

Carol: Symbols, images, and mystery.

Cynthia: Yes. And the celebrations. The Catholic Church is great for celebrations. The priests dress up in fancy vestments. They use incense. I think that's important in my life—celebrations in my life. And the religious celebration matched my family life. We carried it into the home. Growing up, religion had a strong influence.

Carol: And sin?

Cynthia: And sin—oh yes, mortal sin. I was scared to death. I remember growing up scared to death they'd catch me doing something awful. And you know, interestingly, I still have that need to confess. I don't actually go to confession anymore, but if I do something I think is wrong, I have to tell somebody. I still have that ingrained in me. Once I confess, I'm fine.

I do have a strong faith in God. My belief in God has influenced my life. In fact, today I had a conversation with one of our Even Start mothers who has been very depressed. We talked about how hard it is when you're depressed to keep moving forward. I said, "You know, I don't look at this as the only part of my life. I really do believe that something comes after this. And that makes daily life, the troubles, and ins and outs not quite so difficult. They are difficult, but this is just a piece of it, not the whole shebang. If I mess this up, there's still something else out there. I think of life as a dress rehearsal for who knows what comes next. I think that for me that makes a difference, and it helps me put things in perspective." She looked at me and nodded.

I've chosen to work with people in a certain way, and I think that probably the way I was raised and my beliefs in a caring and nurturing God probably influence the kind of work I do.

Carol: Do you and Bob continue the Catholicism of your childhood?

Cynthia: I hate to say this, but I don't like to give up my Sunday morning. But I never miss a Christmas or Easter. Being Catholic is great because as long as you go Christmas and Easter, you've got it made. I've never missed. I have a foot in the door.

Cynthia has a strong faith in a tolerant, caring, nurturant God. She is very clear that she strives to continue to be tolerant and caring in her professional life. Her religion has a sense of mystery, symbolism, images, and celebration that Cynthia embraces. Like Janice, she gains strength through her religion, but in a different way. Janice spoke of God giving her strength through prayer in difficult times; Cynthia spoke of trust in an afterlife helping her come to terms with difficulties.

Marriage, Work, and Parenting

Cynthia and her husband, Bob, both grew up in Florence. Bob's brother was Cynthia's classmate, and she knew him well. Bob is 4½ years older than Cynthia. She did not meet him until she was in college and he was in the U.S. Naval Academy.

> Bob would come back home for basketball games. Our brothers played on the same team. We met at one of the games and began dating. I graduated from college in December, and we married in February.
>
> When we were first married, we moved very frequently. First, he was stationed in Texas; then, the Navy moved him to Germany for 3 years. So, we ended up in this little, tiny Navy base. Here I was, 21 years old, an officer's wife. Bob was a junior officer, and we were thrown in with older people. I came from a generation that was burning bras and wearing blue jeans. The military was still old guard. Officers' wives were to wear gloves and hats and go to teas. The wives seldom worked. It was awful!
>
> The only job I could find was teaching 4-year-olds. I had no idea how to teach 4-year-olds or what a preschool curriculum looked like. So I flew by the seat of my pants. I did enjoy this, but even at that time, I knew I didn't want a steady diet of teaching preschool. Actually, I've never wanted a steady diet of classroom teaching in any shape or form. For me, it's too confining, too limiting. But I do have a genuine affection for children, and I realized that. The other thing it made me realize is how families impact development.[19] I began that realization in that base nursery. There were so many little kids whose parents were young and poor. I got interested right then in the family and how the family works and how to help kids with early intervention.

Cynthia's interest in young children, family, and early intervention for at-risk children began with her first position; yet, Cynthia speaks of classroom teaching as being "too confining, too limiting." As I listened to Cynthia describe classroom teaching as too confining, her feelings made sense. Cynthia also has described to me the ever-changing daily pattern of her childhood family life and her love of impromptu fun and excitement. In contrast, Janice felt totally fulfilled teaching first grade in a small, very wealthy suburb.

After 3 years in Germany, Bob and Cynthia moved to Florida, where they stayed for 10 months.

Cynthia: That's where I taught Spanish in an inner-city high school to Cubans, which probably started my risk taking and living dangerously because it was crazy. At that time, teachers were getting beat up in the hallways. I was about 25 years old, looked 12, wore jeans and platform shoes to school so I would blend in and look like one of my kids. It also was scary because I hadn't used my Spanish for 3 years, and I had to teach first-year Spanish through fourth-year Spanish.

Carol: A new environment, like Germany, but with a lot more risk taking—and you were able to do well?

Cynthia: Well, yes. But, by that time, Bob decided that he didn't have much of a career in the Navy, with me as his wife. I mean, that was really part of the decision.

Carol: I'm not sure I understand.

Cynthia: Well, at that time, the wife was expected to have parties, not a career, and to kowtow. That isn't the only reason for Bob's decision, but it was clear to both of us that I was not going to be just an officer's wife; I wanted a career also. I had one [officer] tell me that it was my duty to rub elbows with the big brass. I told him something like, "If I could find somebody to watch his kid [because I worked at the nursery], that I'd be there. Otherwise, Bob was perfectly capable of rubbing elbows on his own."

Cynthia was a woman in her early twenties whose life experience prior to moving overseas had been growing up in a small town and graduating from a rural state university. Yet, Cynthia knew who she was and felt secure in her values and competence, so she could refuse to act in a manner that she thought violated her temperament and basic principles. As I listened to Cynthia describing her determination to remain true to her self, I reflected on her secure, loving childhood that allowed her to know who she was.

Bob and Cynthia then moved to New Jersey, where Bob worked in a chemical company and Cynthia found a position in Head Start.

Cynthia: Head Start was the only job offered me. I was a home visitor for special needs children. My caseload included Puerto Rican families, so I got to use my Spanish. I learned very quickly about families and family dynamics and child development. And then there was an opportunity to move up, so I interviewed and got the job—but then we moved again. Bob's company moved him from New Jersey to their plant in New Mexico.

We were in New Mexico for about 3 years. Again, I worked for Head Start. They hired me as their handicap coordinator. I coordinated services for special needs kids. I could use my Spanish with the large Mexican population. Head Start hired me even though I was pregnant.

I liked that job. I did that until our son was born, then I went back on a part-time basis. Then, I decided I needed to get my master's [degree], so I also started going to the state university. I decided to major in early education. I completed 6 hours, and then we moved again.

We returned to Florida, and I didn't work for the first 18 months. I went to school and was a full-time mommy and didn't do real well with it. All my classes did not transfer; so I had to take the same classes again.

Carol: Cynthia, given your dislike of the classroom, having to repeat education classes, and our culture's negative stereotype of education [e.g., education classes are concrete and simplistic; people choosing education are not very bright, especially today when women can choose any other field; professors who teach education are not as intelligent as professors in other areas], how have you dealt with this?

Cynthia: I have real mixed feelings. Part of me wholeheartedly agrees that our education system doesn't, for the most part, educate very well. I have experienced it firsthand. I've been in a lot of different schools. Not that I've been in the best schools, but I've hit enough of them that I worry about the level of education in this country. Especially now that our son is in school, I see that he is getting even less than I did. But I have been in education now for so long. Most of the people in education that I have met truly care about kids and want to be good at what they do and work hard to do that.

In every state I have lived, I have to take their courses to be certified, and it has been such a waste of time and money. I should have 3 Ph.D.s by now. [I've] gone to school all but two years of my adult life; and I'm 42. When I moved here, I had to take six classes to get state certification and I already had a master's [degree].

Carol: Did the teacher education courses you have taken over the years make a difference or influence you, either in terms of knowledge or skill?

Cynthia: In my undergraduate work, they just threw in 20 hours of education at the very end, and that didn't help a bit. I would say that mostly what has helped over the years has been teacher training on the job. Once you have a position, you seek information. The one thing my teacher training did supply was some resources, some books that I have used. I doubt it really had much impact on how I think or how I do things.

During their first 10 years of marriage, Cynthia and Bob lived in six very different communities across the United States and in Germany. In each area, Cynthia was able to get an early childhood position working with low-income families. She often was in an administrative role where she could be independent and creative. The positions seemed to match her personal style. Each involved young children and families, and in each she could make a contribution. As a reflective, bright young woman, Cynthia was able to develop skills on the job through what she termed *trial and error.*

After her son, Andrew, was born, Cynthia worked part-time. When Andrew was in first grade, Cynthia began working full-time, and she always has had the summers off. Unlike Janice, Cynthia never considered being a full-time homemaker, but combining career and family has not been easy.

> It's been difficult. I remember standing on a stranger's doorstep and knocking on that door to ask this stranger, asking if she'd watch my baby, who was about a year old. And it just struck me, I'm going to ask a total stranger to watch my baby! I couldn't do it. I went home and told Bob, "We've got to figure something else out." And eventually we found a neighbor who we knew. I remember getting in my car at the end of the day with utter terror in my heart that I would get to that babysitter's and my baby wouldn't be okay. We didn't have car phones then. Now, I really like my car phone because when I'm stuck in traffic, I can call my son.
>
> He answers the phone, and I know he's okay. I really sympathize with working moms because I've experienced that fear myself, and it's awful. It's also something I chose to do in spite of its being awful. I chose to work and didn't necessarily have to. Financially, we probably could have made it.
>
> I have given up opportunities to do things as far as my career that I'll never get back. But I chose to do that because I wasn't willing to give up the time with my child. I don't regret that, but I mourn it sometimes. I wish I'd had the chance to do whatever I wanted to do. Parenting is important to me. I understand that awful feeling of having to leave your child day after day. I'm a working mother. I have been all along. It's an important piece of me to be able to work and contribute and use my skills. But I also bear the guilt of leaving my kid.

Parenting and relationships are central themes in Janice's and Cynthia's personal histories. Both women are exceptionally competent home visitors, but they are quite different in many ways. Each woman also has a unique personal history. Both women loved and respected their mothers, though their mothers were very different models. Janice's mother was a quiet, even-tempered homemaker with two daughters. Cynthia's mother was a strong, talented woman who loved lively arguments with her husband, had a passion for writing poetry and gardening, and taught school when three of her seven children were under 10 years old. Janice's husband changed employers only once in the first 27 years of their marriage, whereas Cynthia's husband's career brought seven moves in 15 years.

For 7 years, Cynthia lived 2 hours from Florence. Thus, she often could spend weekends with her mother, with whom she remained close throughout her adult life. Her mother died 1 year prior to our interviews. I asked Cynthia if she thought her parenting of Andrew resembled the parenting she received from her mother and father.[20]

> Sure, I think it has. At the same time, I made conscious choices not to do some of the things my parents did, but it doesn't always work, such as not lecturing, not yelling. I grew up in a yelling family, so I've had to really work not to do that. I am trying to control myself. But when I'm tired, I feel myself slipping into those old patterns. They are hard to break.
>
> I think the positives I have provided for my child are things I grew up with, a strong sense of routine. My mom was a drill sergeant. You did this, and you made sure this happened. Even though she drove me nuts, I also could count on it. It was there. And the feeling that you are special, that you are important in this world, that you can do things in the world. I feel that all that came from my mom and dad. And the love of reading. The importance of education. The expectation that you will do well. There's no question about it. And with Andrew, I've maintained this stance.
>
> But the difference between my childhood and Andrew's is that he can tell [me what he thinks]. He will say to me, "I think you care too much about that. Who cares if I get an A or B on that? It's okay, Mom. It's okay if I get a B." I wouldn't have dared to say that to my parents.

Cynthia grew up with clear parental expectations of excellence, and she continues this theme in her parenting. In spite of family members coming and going in her childhood home, it was a place of daily ritual and routine like Cynthia provides for Andrew.

Cynthia explained the difference between her husband's temperament and personal style and her own and how he has assisted her personally and professionally.

> Bob calms me down. He keeps my feet on the ground. He's very pragmatic and is excellent with people issues. When I'm struggling with how to deal with a supervising issue, he's helpful. He listens to me, helps me process and think it through. He nurtures our son in a way you often don't see in men. He's the one who will put Andrew's vitamin out in the morning. I don't even think about it half the time. He'll take Andrew to the Dairy Queen at 9 o'clock at night, but I'll tell him to wait until tomorrow.

He gives a lot. He's a very calm man. He doesn't get upset about things, but he doesn't express himself. He stifles his emotions whereas I wear him out screaming sometimes. I think there are times he'd love to just shut me up, just as there are times I would love to make him mad, to see him rant and rave. But he knows me, and I know him. He's known me for 20 years, and he loves me. Bob listens to me. I guess I'm the kind of person who pretty much needs to talk about something to figure it out. I process by talking, and so he knows that about me. We go on walks at night, and he lets me talk.

Like Cynthia's parents, Cynthia and Bob have significant temperament and personal style differences. But, as with Cynthia's parents, both lead lives where caring, compassion, and tolerance are dominant themes in their lives.

During our first 10 years of marriage, we moved a lot. When we lived in England for 3 years, we loved to explore England every Saturday. We would hit a new small town and a pub for lunch. When [we were] in Germany, we explored Europe. We'd go to a little town and learn the history of the place. Now, we have lived in the same city for 11 years, and we continue to enjoy using our weekends to go to a [bed and breakfast] in a small town and explore its history.

Since our son was born, lots of my spare time is with him. He's very athletic so I go to all his games. I also have been a volunteer in grade school, middle, and high school. My six siblings are spread out across the country. I try to see all of them at least once a year. Usually, I am the one going to them.

The themes of connectedness and relationships have been central throughout Cynthia's career path.[21] During the last 5 years, these themes have become even more dominant in her home visiting work. Between the spring of 1990 and the fall of 1993, Cynthia was a home visitor. In the fall of 1993, she became an Even Start Coordinator. The Even Start program serves approximately 40 low-income families. Beyond administering the program, Cynthia continues to do home visiting with approximately six families.

CHILDHOOD PAIN TO PROFESSIONAL COMPETENCE

Unlike Janice and Cynthia, many home visitors do not have happy childhoods. In fact, some may have grown up in very troubled families; however, having a troubled childhood does not mean that people cannot be competent home visitors. Often, in coming to terms with their own pain, home visitors gain sensitivity to others, and they find insights into their own lives that can be a resource when they help others. They may understand and be more sensitive because they could not take anything for granted as a child.

Adults carrying pain from their childhood may have achieved resolution in different ways. For example, some adults may come to terms with their childhood pain through reading about ideas and concepts. This process may be varied. Some read novels, biography and autobiography, history, or therapeutic literature; some become well educated in one specific field of knowledge and practice. Other people may learn alternative attitudes, values, and behavior from those outside their families—for example, by spending time with families of childhood friends, or by learning from older adults who are role models. Some use psychotherapy to come to terms with their troubled childhoods.

Whatever means home visitors use to grow, it is important that they understand that each individual must find his or her own path. For example, a home visitor abused as a child may find in God the parent she wished for; her client's path, however, must be the client's own, and the client may not find resolution in a religious faith like that of the home visitor.

Because relationships are central to the process of home visiting, it is common for work with some families to trigger the home visitor's own childhood pain. When this happens, home visitors may respond unwittingly more to what has been triggered by their own histories than by the needs of the child and parent they are serving. Karen is a home visitor who serves low-income families. As a child, Karen had a very angry mother who directed much of her anger toward her. Karen's description of her work with a family illustrates how sometimes painful memories can be triggered for home visitors.

Karen: One mother is a real challenge to me in lots of ways and probably the family comes closest to my situation when I was growing up. The mother is trying hard, but she has a lot of problems. People have said that she has been mentally ill, and she probably still is. She has had some counseling and therapy in the past, but not presently.

She is very negative with her daughter, who recently turned 3. This mom has had a really rough time when she was young, and she has become angry and hardened because of it. She is a very rude person. The mother is treating her daughter, I assume, the way she was treated. She is not one who is easy to like, and what I had as a child was a very angry mother.

Carol: So when you are sitting in her living room, Karen, what is going through your mind?

Karen: I really have to detach from it, but when I leave, it hits me. When I get away, the feelings start coming back. I have been this little girl. I identify with what is going on with the little girl. That is tough for me.

Carol: Has there been anyone in the program with whom you can talk about this family?

Karen: Yes, when Dan [the program consultant, a clinical psychologist] was at our team meeting, I found that I ended up needing to say some things about what was going on in that family. When I spoke, I didn't realize it was kind of rolling around in me. I just talked about what was going on during a visit one day and how that little girl was being affected. And I was very angry. Dan told me that I was blaming the mom, which I was.

At the time, it felt terrible for a professional to say that to me. Dan said, "You can't work with this family if you are blaming the mom and putting guilt on her." I sat back and thought, "Well, she needs to be blamed because she is wrong." That was one of the best things that has happened because putting blame was exactly what I was doing, and it was getting in the way of things. I stepped back and thought, "I need to be there for this mom and this little girl and see how we can work with this to make things different." Because the mother has told me several times that she doesn't want things to be the way they are. She doesn't want her daughter to be afraid of her.

And in my next visit, I told this mom that she can change things, that she can make a difference, and I believed it as I told her. I told her that it is very hopeful to see somebody with a daughter this young who has had some problems and is saying "I don't want to do this." I encourage her and tell her she can change and make it different, that she doesn't have to keep doing things the way she had been. I feel that when I first told her that, that's when we really connected. I think she holds on to that hopeful talk.

Carol: And you, too?

Karen: Yeah, we both do. So I don't know what is going to happen. She is very difficult to talk with, and she can be very rude. But I work hard to find something positive. For example, she told me that sometimes she puts on music and has this dance with her little girl. And I told her that's a great thing to do, and maybe you can do this when you recognize that you are getting angry.

When Karen was able to process happenings with this family with her team, the team leader interpreted her actions and gave her a new understanding, not just of the family, but of her response to this family. Once Karen recognized that she was angry and was blaming the mother, she understood how unproductive her approach was. She then became proactive and spoke directly to this mother about how the mother could change. Karen's clear statement of hope became the beginning of a new phase in their relationship—a relationship that continued to be difficult, but one in which Karen knows she can help make a difference.

It always is important for home visitors to strive to recognize their vulnerabilities, that is, to be alert for experiences may trigger unresolved childhood issues. For Karen, being with an unstable mother who raged at her 3-year-old rekindled the feelings of Karen's own childhood memories with her mother. With the help of supervision, Karen was able to step back and ask herself what was happening. Once she recognized her vulnerability, Karen could move forward and approach the mother differently.

Home visitors cannot assume resolutions they have found will fit the parents with whom they work. For example, the home visitor who has achieved resolution of childhood pain through becoming well versed in a particular area may experience vulnerability when she works with a parent or child experiencing pain similar to that of her own childhood. The home visitor may respond intellectually as she strives to problem solve with the parent. Her intellectual approach may protect herself but may miss where the parent or child is emotionally.

Although parents may look forward to the home visitor's visit, the home visitor may dread it because it is too familiar to her own childhood past. For example, one home visitor, Anna, has a sister with Down syndrome. Anna's mother told her as a child that her sister was a special blessing from God and was the chosen recipient of God's love because she would remain a little child who was fit for the kingdom of God. This religious view implied that Anna's resentment of her sister was sinful. As a child, Anna felt anger for her sister's interference, for her mother's preoccupation with her sister, and later, for having to remain at home to be with her sister, who could not be alone. She felt guilty for all of these feelings because to her they indicated a lack of faith in God's wisdom.

Now, Anna works with a couple who is coming to terms with their 1-year-old child with Down syndrome. The parents are angry that they do not have a perfect child. They feel cheated because they had waited so long for this child and had dreamed of a perfect child. After amniocentesis showed that his child would have Down syndrome, the father had wanted to abort the child. The mother briefly considered this idea but then could not bring herself to do it. She is, however, unable to clearly state religious or philosophical reasons for her choice. These parents' conflict over the abortion continues: the father still thinks he was right even as he begins to bond with his daughter. The mother's anger at his request for abortion continues to be strong, even though she knows her child is not the one she had dreamed of having. In this complex network of emotions, Anna discovered that she is having difficulty with these parents' conflicts because she wants the answers to seem as simple to these parents as they seemed for her mother. At the same time, she has trouble separating the parents' resentment toward their child from the resentment she once felt toward her sister. Discussions with other home visitors or Anna's supervisor may help Anna to examine her feelings about working with the family.

Not all home visitors actively work towards ensuring that their own personal history does not confuse them as they relate to the visit. Even if a home visitor is sensitive to this possibility, sometimes it takes an outsider to identify the dynamics. Given this complexity in home visiting relationships, supervision becomes very important in assisting home visitors' skills in self-reflection and relating to families.[22]

CONCLUSION

This chapter has portrayed rather fully the life histories of two home visitors, Janice and Cynthia, and how they see their home visiting work as giving meaning to their lives and how their personal histories are intertwined with their home visiting. Each woman's home visiting grows out of her childhood history. Relationships with family and friends, to whom they continue to connect, were central to their childhoods and are the core of their home visiting work. As an adult, each woman has strong commitments rooted in her childhood. Janice's adult life expresses a strong commitment to education and her family; Cynthia's, to helping others and to her family. Each woman's early life was situated in an environment—neighborhood, community, and society—that impacted her development. Nathan was a suburb that valued education highly, a dominant theme in Janice's life. Although Cynthia's family highly valued education, the small rural community Cynthia lived in did not challenge her educationally; rather, school was just something she did as a child. Coming from a conservative family and community and being 10 years older than Cynthia, Janice did not consider continuing to work after she had her first child. In contrast, it never dawned on Cynthia to remain home for an extended time once she had her child.

Each person has her own values, attitudes, beliefs, and ways of relating to others. These patterns are rooted in personal history, in which childhood relationships are intertwined with present patterns. When the home visitor experiences strong emotions before or after a visit or feels confused or conflicted when she is there, it sometimes helps to ask if the drama being played out in the family or with the family and herself is similar to a drama the home visitor has experienced in her own family. For example, Karen discovered that her blaming the mother of a 3-year-old was in reality her reexperiencing her own mother's behavior when she was 3 years old. Just as a home visitor's problem often is a response to his or her own childhood, a person's strength is also a part of a childhood pattern. When she shared her childhood history with me, Cynthia discovered that her ability to move in and out of dangerous neighborhoods is not too far from the risks she and her siblings took as very young children.

Both Karen and Cynthia were able to see these connections between current struggles at work and personal history as they talked them over with another person. For Karen, it was the team facilitator; for Cynthia, it was me as an interviewer doing research. Most people understand themselves best when they are reflecting on their experiences with someone else. That is why peer support and supervision are central dynamics for promoting high-quality home visiting.

Home visiting is a relatively new profession. Builders know what they need to construct a house. When they go to work, teachers know what the day's plans are. In contrast, home visitors never know what to expect as they enter a family's home. As in Janice's and Cynthia's work with families, home visiting can be rewarding work; simultaneously, it can be very difficult and untidy.

Central to the home visiting process is the evolving relationship between home visitor and child and parent; development of both parent and child occurs through and within these relationships. The process is different for each family and can be known only as the relationships evolve over time and they develop mutuality in their collaborative work together. The child and parent develop in relationship to each other. Parents develop in their relationships with their home visitor, and the home visitor develops in relation to his or her personal history, to the families he or she visits, and to his or her professional peers and supervisors.

Resources

Books for Parents About Parenting

Brazelton, T.B. (1974). *Toddlers and parents: A declaration of independence.* New York: Dell Publishing.

Brazelton, T.B. (1983). *Infants and mothers: Differences in development.* New York: Dell Publishing.

Crockenberg, S., & Leerkes, E. (2000). Infant social and emotional development in family context. In C.H. Zeanah, Jr. (Ed.), *Handbook of infant mental health* (2nd ed., pp. 60–90). New York: The Guilford Press.

Gowen, J.W., & Nebrig, J.B. (2002). *Enhancing early development: Guiding parents of young children.* Baltimore: Paul H. Brookes Publishing Co.

Greenspan, S., & Greenspan, N.T. (1989). *The essential partnership: How parents and children can meet the emotional challenges of infancy and childhood.* New York: Penguin Books.

Greenspan, S., & Lewis, N.B. (1999). *Building healthy minds: The six experiences that create intelligence and emotional growth in babies and young children.* Cambridge, MA: Perseus Books.

Imber-Black, E., & Roberts, J. (Eds.). (1992). *Rituals for our times: Celebration, healing and changing our lives and our relationships.* New York: Harper Collins.

Lieberman, A.F. (1993). *The emotional life of the toddler.* New York: The Free Press.

Pruett, K.D. (1997). How men and children affect each other's development. *Zero to Three, 18*(1), 3–11.

Children's Play

Biber, B. (1984). *Early education and psychological development.* New Haven: Yale University Press.

Bruner, J.A., & Sylva, K. (Eds.). (1976). *Play: Its role in development and evolution.* New York: Basic Books.

Carlsson-Paige, N., & Levin, D.E. (1990). *Who's calling the shots? How to respond effectively to children's fascination with war play and war toys.* Philadelphia: New Society Publishers.

Dau, E. (1999). *Child's play in early childhood settings.* Paul H. Brookes Publishing Co.

Erikson, E. (1950). *Childhood and society.* New York: W.W. Norton.

Fein, G., & Rivkin, M. (Eds.). (1973). *The young child at play: Reviews of research* (Vol. 4.). Washington, DC: National Association for the Education of Young Children.

Galinsky, E., & David, J. (1988). *The preschool years: Family strategies that work—from experts and parents.* New York: Ballantine Books.

Greenspan, S.N., & Greenspan, N.T. (1989). *The essential partnership: How parents and children can meet the emotional challenges of infancy and childhood.* New York: Penguin Books.

Children's Books About Toilet Training

Allison, A. (1999). *Toddler's potty book.* Los Angeles: Price, Stern, Sloan.

Frankel, A. (1992). *Once upon a potty.* New York: Barrons.

383

384   Resources

Cultural Diversity

Aber, J.L., Jones, S., & Cohen, J. (2000). The impact of poverty on the mental heath and development of very young children. In C.H. Zeanah, Jr. (Ed.), *Handbook of infant mental health* (2nd ed.). New York: The Guilford Press.

Brunson Phillips, C. (1995). Culture: A process that empowers. In J.R. Lally (Ed.), *Infant/toddler caregiving: A guide to culturally sensitive care.* Sacramento: California State Department of Education.

Garcia, E.E. (1994). Addressing the challenges of diversity. In S.L. Kagan & B. Weissbourd (Eds.), *Putting families first: America's family support movement and the challenge of change* (pp. 243–275). San Francisco: Jossey-Bass.

Lynch, E.W., & Hanson, M.J. (1997). *Developing cross-cultural competence: A guide for working with children and their families* (2nd ed.). Baltimore: Paul H. Brookes Publishing Co.

Mallory, B.L., & New, R.S. (1994). *Diversity and developmentally appropriate practices: Challenges for early childhood education.* New York: Teachers College Press.

Nai-Lin Chang, H., & Pulido, D. (1994). The critical importance of cultural and linguistic continuity for infants and toddlers. *Zero to Three, 3*(2), 13–17.

Polk, C. (1994). Therapeutic work with African-American families. *Zero to Three, 3*(2), 9–11.

Early Risk

Cicchetti, D., & Lynch, M. (1993). Toward an ecological/transactional model of community violence and child maltreatment: Consequences for children's development. *Psychiatry, 56,* 95–118.

Garbarino, J. (1990). The human ecology of early risk. In S.J. Meisels & J.P. Shonkoff (Eds.), *Handbook of early childhood intervention* (pp. 78–96). New York: Cambridge University Press.

Garbarino, J. (1992). *Children in danger: Coping with the consequences of community violence.* San Francisco: Jossey-Bass.

Goodman, S.H., Radke-Yarrow, M., & Teti, D. (1993). Maternal depression as a context for child rearing. *Zero to Three, 13*(5), 10–16.

Helfer, R., & Kempe, C.H. (1976). *Child abuse and neglect: The family and the community.* Cambridge, MA: Ballinger.

Kaplan, M.D., & Pruett, K.D. (2000). Divorce and custody: Developmental implications. In C.H. Zeanah, Jr. (Ed.), *Handbook of infant mental health* (2nd ed.). New York: The Guilford Press.

Kaufman, J., & Henrich, C. (2000). Exposure to violence and early childhood trauma. In C.H. Zeanah, Jr. (Ed.), *Handbook of infant mental health* (2nd ed.). New York: The Guilford Press.

Kempe, C.H., & Helfer, R. (1980). *The battered child.* Chicago: University of Chicago Press.

Klein, N.K., & Campbell, P. (1990). Preparing personnel to serve at-risk and disabled infants, toddlers, and preschoolers. In S.J. Meisels & J.P. Shonkoff (Eds.), *Handbook of early childhood intervention* (pp. 679–699). New York: Cambridge University Press.

Luby, J.L. (2000). Depression. In C.H. Zeanah, Jr. (Ed.), *Handbook of infant mental health* (2nd ed.). New York: The Guilford Press.

Main, M., & Goldwyn, R. (1984). Predicting rejections of her infant from mother's representation of her own experience: Implications for the abused-abusing intergenerational cycle. *Child Abuse and Neglect, 8,* 203–217.

Schore, A.N. (1998). Early organization of the nonlinear right brain and development of a predisposition to psychiatric disorders. *Development and Psychopathology, 9*(4), 505–633.

Seifer, R., & Dickstein, S. (2000). Parental mental illness and infant development. In C.H. Zeanah, Jr. (Ed.), *Handbook of infant mental health* (2nd ed.). New York: The Guilford Press

Sugar, M. (1992). Toddler's traumatic memories. *Infant Mental Health Journal, 13*(3), 245–251.

Everyday Routines

Anders, T., Goodlin-Jones, B., & Sadah, A. (2000). Sleep disorders. In C.H. Zeanah, Jr. (Ed.), *Handbook of infant mental health* (2nd ed., pp. 326–338). New York: The Guilford Press.

Brazelton, T.B. (1992). *Touchpoints: The essential reference. Your child's emotional and behavioral development.* New York: Addison-Wesley.

Cole, J. (1983). *Parents' book of toilet teaching.* New York: Ballantine Books.

Ferber, R. (1985). *Solve your child's sleep problems.* New York: Simon & Schuster.

Jones, S. (1992). *Crying baby, sleepless nights:Why your baby is crying and what you can do about it.* Boston: The Harvard Common Press.

Lansky, V. (1984). *Toilet training.* New York: Bantam Books.

Pediatric Nutrition Practice Group. (1992). *Quality assurance criteria for pediatric nutrition conditions: A model.* Chicago: American Dietetic Association.

Satter, E. (1983). *Child of mine: Feeding with love and good sense.* New York: Bell Publishing.

Satter, E. (1992). The feeding relationship. *Zero to Three, 12*(5), 1–9.

Weissbluth, M. (1987). *Healthy sleep habits, happy child.* New York: Fawcett Columbine.

Welford, H. (1987). *Toilet-training and bed-wetting: A practical guide for today's parents.* Rochester, VT: Thorsons Publishing Group.

Family Rituals and Celebration

Imber-Black, E., & Roberts, J. (1992). *Rituals for our times: Celebrating healing, and changing our lives and our relationships.* New York: HarperCollins.

Lieberman, S. (1984). *Let's celebrate: Creating new family traditions.* New York: Putnam Publishing Group.

Wolin, S.F., & Bennet, L.A. (1984). Family ritual. *Family Process, 23,* 401–420.

Guidance and Discipline

Brazelton, T.B. (1992). *Touchpoints: The essential reference. Your child's emotional and behavioral development.* Reading, MA: Addison Wesley Longman.

Brazelton, T.B., & Cramer, B.G. (1990). *The earliest relationship: Parents, infants, and the drama of early attachment.* Reading, MA: Addison Wesley Longman.

Clewett, A.S. (1988). Guidance and discipline: Teaching young children appropriate behavior. *Young Children, 43*(4), 26–36.

Gartrell, D. (1987). Punishment or guidance? *Young Children, 42*(3), 55–60.

Gordon, T. (1989). *Discipline that works: Promoting self-discipline in children.* New York: Penguin Books.

Greenberg, P. (1988). Avoiding "me against you" discipline. *Young Children, 44* (1), 24–29

Honig, A.S. (1985). Compliance, control, and discipline. *Young Children, 40*(2), 50–58.

Miller, C.S. (1984). Building self-control: Discipline for young children. *Young Children, 39*(7), 15–19.

Snyder, M., Snyder, R., & Sndyer, R., Jr. (1980). *The young child as person: Toward the development of a healthy conscience.* New York: Human Science Press.

Soderman, A.K. (1985). Dealing with difficult young children: Strategies for teachers and parents. *Young Children, 40*(5), 15–20.

Thompson, R.A., & Calkins, S.D. (1996). The double-edged sword: Emotional regulation for children at risk. *Development and Psychopathology, 8*(1), 163–182.

Thompson, R.A., Flood, M.F., & Lundquist, L. (1995). Emotional regulation: Its relations to attachment and developmental psychopathology. In D. Cicchetti & S.L. Toth (Eds.), *Emotion, cognition, and representation: Rochester symposium on developmental psychopathology* (Vol. 6, pp. 261–298). Rochester, NY: University of Rochester Press.

Home Visiting

Bromwich, R. (1981). *Working with parents and infants: An interactional approach.* Austin, TX: PRO-ED.

Burch, P., Palanki, A., & Thompson, S. (1994). *Home visiting.* Boston: Institute for Responsive Education.

Cochran, M., Deann, C., Dill, M.F., & Woolever, F. (1984). *Empowering families: Home visiting and building clusters.* Ithaca, NY: Family Matters Project, Cornell University.

Doan-Sampon, Wollenburg, K., Campbell, A. & the Portage Project Staff. (1993). *Growing: Birth to Three.* Portage, WI: Portage Project.

Gowen, J.W., & Nebrig, J.B. (2002). *Enhancing early emotional development: Guiding parents of young children.* Baltimore: Paul H. Brookes Publishing Co.

Johnson, E.G., Strickland, C.S., & Thompson, S. (1993). *Home visiting: A tool kit for quilting.* Boston: The League of Schools Reaching Out, Institute for Responsive Education.

Klass, C.S., Pettinelli, D., & Wilson, M. (1993). Home visiting: Building a bridge between home and school. *Equity and Choice, 10*(10), 52–56.

Morra, L.G. (1990). *Home visiting: A promising early intervention strategy for at-risk families.* Report to the Chairman, Subcommittee on Labor, Health and Human Services, Education, and Related Agencies, Committee on Appropriations, U.S. Senate, Washington, DC, United States General Accounting Office.

Parents as Teachers. (1989). *Parents as Teachers program planning and implementation guide.* St. Louis: University of Missouri, St. Louis.

Parents as Teachers. (1990). *Born to learn: Prenatal to age three curriculum. Implementation guide.* St. Louis: Parents as Teachers National Center.

Provence, S., & Apfel, N.H. (2001). *Infant-Toddler and Family Instrument.* Baltimore: Paul H. Brookes Publishing Co.

Wasik, B.H., Bryant, D.M., & Lyons, C.M. (2000). *Home visiting: Procedures for helping families.* Thousand Oaks, CA: Sage Publications.

Home Visitors' Professional Development

Almonte, B.E. (1994). Professionalization as culture change: Issues for infant/family community workers and their supervisors. *Zero to Three, 15*(2), 18–23.

Fenichel, E. (1991). Learning through supervision and mentorship to support the development of infants, toddlers and their families. *Zero to Three, 12*(2), 1–8.

Illness

Brazelton, T.B. (1992). *Touchpoints: The essential reference. Your child's emotional and behavioral development.* New York: Addison-Wesley Publishing Co.

Dawson, P. (1992). Should the field of early child and family intervention address Failure to Thrive? *Zero to Three, 12*(5) 10–14.

Parmelee, A.H., Jr. (1993). Children's illnesses and normal behavioral development: The role of caregivers. *Zero to Three, 13*(4), 1–8.

Sturm, L., & Drotar, D. (1992). Communication strategies for working with parents of infants who fail to thrive. *Zero to Three, 12*(5) 25–28.

Villarrel, S.F., McKinney, L., & Quackenbush, M. (1992). *Handle with care: Helping children prenatally exposed to drugs and alcohol.* Santa Cruz, CA: ETR Associates.

Infant-Toddler Development and Caregiving

Bernstein, M.H., & Bornstein, H.G. (1995). Caregivers' responsiveness and cognitive development in infants and toddlers: Theory and research. In P.L. Mangione (Ed.), *Infant/toddler caregiving: A guide to cognitive development and learning.* Sacramento: California State Department of Education.

Brazelton, T.B. (1974). *Toddlers and parents: A declaration of independence.* New York: Dell Publishing.

Brazelton, T.B. (1983). *Infants and mothers: Differences in development.* New York: Dell Publishing.

Brazelton, T.B., & Cramer, B.G. (1990). *The earliest relationship: Parents, infants, and the drama of early attachment.* New York: Addison Wesley.

Chess, S., & Thomas, A. (1987). *Know your child: An authoritative guide for today's parents.* New York: Basic Books.

Field, T. (1995). Supporting cognitive development through interactions with young infants. In P.L. Mangione (Ed.), *Infant/toddler caregiving: A guide to cognitive development and learning.* Sacramento: California State Department of Education.

Lally, J.R. (1995). Discovery in infancy: how and what infants learn. In P.L. Mangione (Ed.), *Infant/toddler caregiving: A guide to cognitive development and learning.* Sacremento: California State Department of Education.

Landy, S. (2002). *Pathways to competence: Encouraging healthy social and emotional development in young children.* Baltimore: Paul H. Brookes Publishing Co.

Pruett, K. (1999). *Me, myself, and I: How children build their sense of self: 18 to 36 months.* New York: Goddard Press.

Language, Communication, and Emerging Literacy

Barclay, L., Benelli, C., & Curtis. A. (1995). Literacy begins at birth: What caregivers can learn from parents of children who read early. *Young Children, 50*(4).

Bates, E., O'Connell, B., & Shore, C. (1987). Language and communication in infancy. In J.D. Osofsky (Ed.), *Handbook of infant development* (2nd ed., pp. 149–203). New York: John Wiley & Sons.

Bruner, J. (1985). *Child's talk: Learning to use the language.* New York: W.W. Norton.

388 Resources

Devine, M. (1991). *Baby talk: The art of communicating with infants and toddlers.* New York: Plenum Press.

Dole, J.D., Duffy, G.G., Roehler, L.R., & Perons, P.D. (1991). Moving from old to the new: Research on reading comprehension instruction. *Review of Educational Research, 6*(2), 239–264.

Fields, M.V., & Lee, D. (1989). *Let's begin reading right: A developmental approach to beginning literacy.* Columbus, OH: Merrill.

Galinsky, E., & J. David. (1988). *The preschool years: Family strategies that work—from experts and parents.* New York: Ballantine Books.

Hart, B., & Risley, T.R. (1995). *Meaningful differences in the everyday experience of young American children.* Baltimore: Paul H. Brookes Publishing Co.

Hart, B., & Risley, T.R. (1999). *The social world of children learning to talk.* Baltimore: Paul H. Brookes Publishing Co.

Heath, S.B. (1983). *Way with words: Language, life, and works in communities and classrooms.* New York: Cambridge University Press.

Lee, P. (1989). Is the young child egocentric or sociocentric? *Teachers College Record, 90*(3), 279–291.

Mahoney, B., & Powell, A. (1988). Modifying parent–child interaction: Enhancing the development of handicapped children. *Journal of Special Education, 22*(1), 82–96.

McCartney, K., & Robeson, W.W. (1992). Emergence of communication: Words, grammar, and first conversations. In J.R. Lally, P.L. Mangione, & C.L. Young-Hold (Eds.), *Infant/toddler caregiving: A guide to language development and communication.* Sacramento: California State Department of Education.

Nelson, K. (1973). Structure and strategy in learning to talk. *Monographs of the Society for Research in Child Development, 38*(Serial No. 149).

Nelson, K. (Ed.). (1989). *Narratives from the crib.* Cambridge, MA: Harvard University Press.

Prizant, B.M., Wetherby, A.M., & Roberts, J.E. (2000). Communication problems. In C.H. Zeanah, Jr. (Ed.), *Handbook of infant mental health* (2nd ed.). New York: The Guilford Press.

Sach, J. (1992). Emergence of communication: Earliest signs. In J.R. Lally, P.L. Mangione, & C.L. Young-Hold (Eds.), *Infant/toddler caregiving: A guide to language development and communication.* Sacramento: California State Department of Education.

Shatz, M. (1994). *A toddler's life: From personal narrative to professional insight.* New York: Oxford University Press.

Thal, D.J. (1992). Emergence of communication: Give and take between adult and child. In J.R. Lally, P.L. Mangione, & C.L. Young-Hold (Eds.), *Infant/toddler caregiving: A guide to language development and communication.* Sacramento: California State Department of Education.

Neuroscience

Blakeslee, S. (1995, August 29). Brain's early growth may be crucial. *New York Times*, pp. B5–B6.

Chugani, H.T. (1997). Neuroimaging of developmental nonlinearity and developmental pathologies. In G.R. Lyon (Ed.), *Developmental neuroimaging* (pp. 187–195). San Diego: Academic Press.

Fenichel, E. (2001). From neurons to neighborhoods: What's in it for you? *Zero to Three, 21*(5), 8–15.

Nelson, C.A. (2000). The neurobiological bases of early intervention. In J.P.

Shonkoff & S.J. Meisels (Eds.), *Handbook of early intervention* (2nd ed., pp. 204–230). New York: International University Press.

Nelson, C.A., & Bosquet, M. (2000). Neurobiology of fetal and infant development: Implications for infant mental health. In C.H. Zeanah, Jr. (Ed.), *Handbook of infant mental health* (2nd ed., pp. 37–59). New York: The Guilford Press.

Schore, A.N. (1994). *Affect regulation and the origin of the self: The neurobiology of emotional development.* Mahwah, NJ: Lawrence Erlbaum Associates.

Schore, A.N. (1998). Early organization of the nonlinear right brain and development of a predisposition to psychiatric disorders. *Development and Psychopathology, 9*(4), 505–633.

Shonkoff, J.P., & Phillips, D.A. (2000). *From neurons to neighborhoods: The science of early childhood development.* Washington, DC: National Academy Press.

Shore, R. (1997). *Rethinking the brain.* Chicago: Family and Work Institute.

Super, C., & Harness, S. (1997). The cultural structuring of child development. In J.W. Berry, P.R. Dasen, & T.S. Saraswathi (Eds.), *Cross-cultural psychology: Vol. 2. Basic process and human development* (pp. 1–40). Boston: Allyn & Bacon.

Pregnancy and Prenatal Care

Abrams, B. (1994). Eating for two: Nutrition during pregnancy. *March of Dimes babies and you* (pp. 1–6, 19). White Plains, NY: March of Dimes Birth Defects Foundation.

American Academy of Pediatrics & American College of Obstetricians and Gynecologists (1992). *Guidelines for perinatal care* (3rd ed.). Elk Grove Village, IL: Author.

Auman, G.M.E., & Baird, M.M. (1993). Risk assessment for pregnant women. In R.A. Knuppel & J.A. Drukker (Eds.), *High risk pregnancy: A team approach* (pp. 8–35). Philadelphia: WB Saunders.

Brott, A.A., & Ash, J. (1995). *The expectant father.* New York: Abbeville Press.

Chamberlain, D. (1998). *The mind of your newborn baby.* Berkeley, CA: North Atlantic Books.

Curtis, G.B. (1997). *Your pregnancy week by week.* Tucson, AZ: Fisher Books.

Driscoll, J.W. (1996). Psychological adaptations to pregnancy and postpartum. In K.R. Simpson & P.A. Creehan (Eds.), *AWHONN's perinatal nursing* (pp. 61–72). Philadelphia: J.B. Lippincott.

Eisenberg, A., Murkoff, H.E., & Hathaway, S.E. (1996). *What to expect when you're expecting.* New York: Workman.

Flanigan, G.L. (1996). *Beginning life.* New York: DK Publishing.

Nilsson, L., & Hamberger, L. (1990). *A child is born.* New York: Dell Publishing.

Remich, M. (1994). Promoting a healthy pregnancy. In E.Q. Youngkin & M.S Davis (Eds.), *Women's health: A primary care clinical guide* (pp. 383–392). Norwalk, CT: Appleton and Lange.

Satt, B.J., Zelen, S.L., & Satgt, L.A. (1995). *A sound beginning.* Agoura, CA: A Sound Beginning.

U.S. Department of Health and Human Services. (1992). *Myself, my baby: Health diary.* Washington, DC: U.S. Government Printing Office.

Wayland, J., & Rawlins, R. (1997). African American teen mothers' perception of parenting. *Journal of Pediatric Nursing, 12*(1) 13–20.

Sexuality Education

Bernstein, A. (1977). *The flight of the stork.* New York: Delacorte Press.

Brick, P., Davis, N., Fischel, M., Lupo, T., Marshall, J., & MacVicae, A. (1989).

Bodies, birth and babies: Sexuality and education in early childhood programs.
Bergen County, NJ: Center for Family Life Education, Planned Parenthood.
Calderone, M., & Johnson, E. (1988). *The family book about sexuality.* New York:
Harper and Row.
Calderone, M., & Rame, J. (1982). *Talking with your child about sex.* New York:
Ballantine Books.
Gordon, S., & Gordon, J. (1982). *Did the sun shine before you were born?* New
York: Ed-U Press.
Gordon, S., & Gordon, J. (1983). *Raising a child conservatively in a sexually per-
missive world.* New York: Simon & Schuster.

Siblings

Dunn, J., & Plomin, R. (1990). *Separate lives: Why siblings are so different.* New
York: Basic Books.
Faber, A., & Mazlish, E. (1987). *Siblings without rivalry: How to help your children
live together so you can live too.* New York: W.W. Norton.
Galinsky, E., & David, J. (1988). *The preschool years: Family strategies that work—
from experts and parents.* New York: Ballantine Books.

Television

Carlsson-Paige, N., & Levin, D.E. (1990). *Who's calling the shots? How to respond
effectively to children's fascination with war play and war toys.* Philadelphia: New
Society Publishers.
Jordan, A.B., & Woodard, E.J.H., IV, (2001). Electronic childhood: The availability and use of household media by 2- and 3-year-olds. *Zero to Three,
22*(2), 4–9.
Levin, D.E., & Carlsson-Paige, N. (1994). Developmentally appropriate television: Putting children first. *Young Children, 49*(5), 38–44.
Linn, S., & Poussaint, A.F. (2001). The truth about Teletubbies. *Zero to Three, 22*
(2), 24–29.

Endnotes

Chapter 1

1. Bronfenbrenner discussed this type of reciprocal two-person relationship as a primary dyad. In primary dyads, two people coordinate their activities with one another within a mutuality of positive feeling. This mutuality motivates young children to engage in progressively more complex patterns of interaction and increasingly complex learning processes. Bronfenbrenner wrote that the primary dyad continues to exist for both participants even when they are not physically together. Bronfenbrenner, 1979, pp. 56–66.

2. Garbarino wrote poignantly of how parenting "depends in large measure on the character and quality of the social environment in which we bear and raise our children" (p. xv). Garbarino identified and discussed the array of relationships connecting child, family, and social environment, and how these relationships influence parent and child development. Garbarino, 1992.

3. A large proportion of community-based home visiting programs use paraprofessional home visitors. Musick and Stott identified dilemmas of paraprofessional helping and explored new methods of educating these individuals. Musick & Stott, 1993, pp. 651–657.

4. Weissbourd provided a provocative overview of traditional parent education and a history of the development of family support programs. Weissbourd, 1987, pp. 38–56. Weissbourd also discussed the emergence of the current family resource moment in Weissbourd, 1994, pp. 28–48. In his historical overview of the first 32 years of parent education in America, Schlossman described U.S. public policy with regard to new knowledge in the behavioral sciences. He also found parallels between parent education of the 1960s and the origin of the parent education movement in the late 19th and early 20th centuries. Schlossman, 1976, pp. 436–467.

5. Pawl, 1995.

6. Freeman described how many families can organize around problems. Problems can have useful purposes and can organize family members in a way that allows members to feel connected around the problem. For example, a child's problem can provide a focus and stabilize a marital relationship. Freeman, 1992.

7. Weiss argued that home visiting programs are a "necessary but not sufficient" service to at-risk families with multiple problems. Parents whose multiple, complicated problems are so great that

they interfere with the parents' attention to their child often are beyond a home visiting program that does not have broader social services. Weiss, 1993, pp. 113–128. Schorr provided detailed descriptions of successful intervention and prevention programs for at-risk families and discussed the approaches needed to "break the cycle of disadvantage." L.B. Schorr & D. Schorr, 1988.

8. In a discussion of a home visiting program for families at risk with children from birth to 3 years, Bromwich indicated that the reciprocal positive feelings of parent educators and home visitors was strongly related to the effectiveness of their program's intervention. Bromwich, 1981.

9. Crockenberg & Leerkes, 2000.

10. Osofsky & Thompson, 2000, p. 57.

11. Winnicott, 1957, p. 302.

12. Fox, Calkins, & Bell, 1994.

13. Nelson & Bosquet, 2000.

14. Wakschlag & Hans, 2000.

15. Osofsky & Thompson, 2000, pp. 63–64.

16. Wakschlag & Hans, 2000, p. 134.

17. Wakschlag & Hans, 2000, p. 135.

18. Schorr & Schorr, 1988.

19. Leopold, 1999, p. 1.

20. Brownlee, Hotinski, Pailthorp, Ragan, & Wong, 1999.

21. Talan, 2000, p. 1.

22. Wasik, Bryant, and Lyons provided an overview of characteristics of teenage parents and effective home visiting approaches for working with such families. Wasik, Bryant, & Lyons, 1990, pp. 193–199. Since 1978, the Prenatal/Early Infancy Project has provided nurse home visiting to new teen mothers and their babies. The program has been helpful in improving mothers' and babies' health and has assisted them in using community resources. The program resulted in a decrease in second pregnancies and an increase in mothers' finishing school and gaining employment. Olds, 1981, pp. 173–197.

23. McDonough has spent many years guiding teenage parents with low incomes in Chicago. McDonough first forms a positive alliance with the parent. She uses educational and behavioral psychology to improve mothers' parenting. Her work always focuses on expanding the parent's strength. After parent and child play together, McDonough and parent watch the videotape of this

play sequence. McDonough picks out a positive strength and elaborates on it. Once the positive alliance is formed and the parent can recognize her strengths, the parent often begins talking about her own difficulties nondefensively. McDonough, 1993, pp. 414–426.

24. Wakschlag & Hans, 2000, p. 132.

25. Schon discussed how practitioners, with the help of coaching, learn primarily by doing. He emphasized the power of reflection in action, especially reciprocal reflection in action between coach and practitioner. Schon, 1987, pp. 26–32.

26. Fraiberg, Adelson, & Shapiro, 1975. Pawl and her colleagues Judith Pekarsky and Alicia Lieberman continued Selma Fraiberg's work at the Infant-Parent Program, San Francisco General Hospital, Department of Psychiatry. See Lieberman, Silverman, & Pawl, 2000; Lieberman, 1991; Lieberman & Pawl, 1993.

27. Lieberman, Silverman, & Pawl, 2000.

Chapter 2

1. Bruner discussed how language is the way we "sort out our thoughts about things" (p. 72). He wrote that narratives, or stories, give meaning to experience. If we want to understand people, Bruner claimed, we need to understand the ways in which people construct their world in narrative. Bruner, 1986, pp. 44–78.

   Anderson wrote that, in telling stories, we are not only informing others but forming ourselves. "When one expresses oneself one is in the process of realizing one's identity." Anderson, 1992, p. 89.

2. Penn discussed how concepts of the future and concepts of change are one. She wrote of the power that families have by imagining new solutions in the future and thus facilitating change. Penn, 1985.

3. Bronfenbrenner explained primary dyads as those two-person relationships in which people are engaged in a joint activity. Bronfenbrenner claimed that, once two people participate in a joint activity, they are likely to develop positive feelings toward each other and engage in mutuality. Joint activity, mutuality, and positive feelings promote the young child's learning and development. Bronfenbrenner, 1979, pp. 56–60.

4. Wasik, Bryant, and Lyons discussed their problem-solving model of home visiting. They identified seven stages of problem solving: defining problems, selecting goals, generating alternatives, considering consequences, decision making, implementation, and evaluation. Wasik, Bryant, & Lyons, 1990, pp. 139–146.

5. Greenspan and Greenspan urged parents of young children to spend 30 minutes each day in "floor time" with their child. Greenspan and Greenspan suggested that parents follow their child's lead so that the child can set the emotional tone of the play and can feel both affirmed and connected. Greenspan & Greenspan, 1989, p. 29.

6. Garbarino described the primary threat to the modern world as the "weakening of traditional sources of social pluralism—a wide range of people and groups surrounding the family which shared basic commitment to the family." Garbarino, 1992, p. 313.

7. Bronfenbrenner, 1979, pp. 209–236; Cochran, Larner, Riley, Gunnarsson, & Henderson, 1990.

8. Stern found that a mother of a newborn needs a supporting matrix that serves two functions: 1) physical protection of the mother from the everyday maintenance of family life and 2) a maternal supportive expert force educating the mother on "how to do it," validating and modeling what motherhood is. Stern noted that fathers can fulfill the first function, but only "experts," women who have "been there before" can fulfill the second function. Stern, 1994.

9. Kagan & Neuman, 2000, p. 340.

10. Bronfenbrenner and Neville discussed how the emotional attachment and complexity of the young child and the child's caregiver relationship is enhanced by the other adults who assist, encourage, nurture, and affirm the caregiver. Bronfenbrenner & Neville, 1994, p. 14.

11. Osofsky & Thompson, 2000, p. 60.

12. Wasik et al., 1990, pp. 69–90.

13. O'Hearn Family Outreach Project Members, 1995.

14. Home visitors learn the Parents as Teachers curriculum when they attend a 1-week training institute sponsored by the Parents as Teachers National Center, 2228 Ball Drive St. Louis, MO, 63146. Home visitors can purchase the Portage Project curriculum through the Portage Project, 626 East Slifer Street, Portage, WI, 53901.

Chapter 3

1. Shonkoff & Phillips, 2000, p. 65.

2. Garcia provided a demographic overview of the United States' diversity and the vulnerable populations within this diversity. He

identified standards for effective services and recommended qualities of professionals working with these populations. Garcia, 1994.

3. Coll & Magnuson, 2000, p. 97.

4. Lewis, 2000, pp. 95–97.

5. Coll & Magnuson, 2000, p. 97.

6. Lewis, 2000, p. 94.

7. Heath, 1983.

8. Coll & Magnuson, 2000, p. 104.

9. Garbarino, 1992, p. 187.

10. Garbarino, 1992, p. 194.

11. Coll & Magnuson, 2000.

12. Garbarino, 1992.

13. Fitzgerald & Montanex, 2001, pp. 31–32.

14. Woodworth, 1996.

15. Bronfenbrenner and Neville discussed how the emotional attachment and complexity of the young child and the child's caregiver relationship is enhanced by the other adults who assist, encourage, nurture, and affirm the caregiver. Bronfenbrenner & Neville, 1994, p. 14.

16. Woodworth, 1996, p. 23.

17. Aber, Jones, & Cohen, 2000.

18. Garbarino wrote about how low-income people, given their lack of employment and impoverished neighborhoods, often have minimal informal support systems. He wrote that these support systems are the "staff of life in childrearing." Garbarino, 1992, p. 313.

19. Shonkoff & Phillips, 2000, p. 268.

20. Fenichel, 2001, p. 12.

21. Aber et al., 2000, pp. 115–118.

22. Tong, 1998.

23. National Center for Health Statistics, 1998.

24. Smith & Wells, 1990.

25. Smith & Wells, 1990.

26. Weiss, 1993.

27. Garbarino & Ganzel, 2000, p. 77.

28. Osofsky & Dickson, 2000, pp. 20–21.

29. Groves, Lieberman, Osofsky, & Fenichel, 2000, pp. 11–13.

Chapter 4

1. Schon discussed "indeterminate zones of practice" (p. 6), that is, indeterminate, uncertain, and unique situations that are central to professional practice and cannot be handled solely by applying knowledge or strategies stemming from traditional professional knowledge. Schon argued that at the core of competency in these indeterminate zones of practice is artistry, a kind of knowing in action. Conditions needed for professional development, then, become learning by doing, with access to coaches, who help increase skill in reflection on practice (p. 25). Schon, 1987, pp. 3–4.

2. Fenichel, of ZERO TO THREE: National Center for Infants, Toddlers and Families, emphasized that increased understanding of one's own emotional responses in home visiting is a central aspect of professional development:

By attending to her own affective experience, the worker may be able to learn more about what children and families are feeling. As the supervisee's own emotional responses are acknowledged and respected, she may become increasingly able to acknowledge, respect, and respond sensitively to the emotional experiences and expressions of infants, toddlers, families and colleagues. (Fenichel, 1992, p. 5)

3. Larner & Halpern, 1992; Musick & Stott, 1993.

4. Bruner, 1986; Dewey, 1916; Rogers, 1969.

5. Mead, 1934, pp. 135–226.

6. In Holly's report of an interview study of 60 teachers in the United States and England, she noted that what teachers consider most important is the time to discuss with colleagues, and connecting professional development content with their everyday teaching. Holly, 1989.

7. Norton, 1994.

8. Garbarino & Ganzel, 2000, p. 79.

9. Garbarino & Ganzel, 2000, p. 21.

10. Cochran and his colleagues compared how networks function in African American and Caucasian families in the United States, as well as families in Sweden, Wales, and Germany. Cochran, Larner, Riley, Gunnarsson, & Henderson, 1990.

11. Gilligan, 1982; Gilligan & Brown, 1992; Loevinger, 1976.

12. Kaplan & Pruett, 2000.

13. Smith, Wigginton, Hocking, & Jones, 1991.

14. ZERO TO THREE: National Center for Infants, Toddlers and Families is an interdisciplinary organization of researchers, theorists, and practitioners working with infants, toddlers, and their families. A primary goal of ZERO TO THREE is to promote the continued education of professionals in this field. The organization publishes a bimonthly bulletin, *Zero to Three*. See Fenichel, 1992.

15. Bertacchi & Coplon, 1989; Gilkerson & Young-Hold, 1992; Shanok, 1991.

16. Bertacchi & Stott, 1992.

Chapter 5

1. Greenspan, 1992; Sameroff & Emde, 1989; Stern, 1985.

2. Sroufe, 1989.

3. Winnicott, 1965, p. 39.

4. Emde, 1989; Stern, 1985, pp. 26–33.

5. Emde & Robinson, 2000, pp. 163–164.

6. Greenspan spoke of six developmental levels from birth to 5 years. Greenspan's developmental levels provide indicators of observable behavior that point to the infant's and young child's increased emotional and behavioral capacities. Greenspan, 1992. Greenspan's developmental levels occur within the same age levels that Stern described as changes in sense of self. Whereas Greenspan's levels are behavioral, Stern's levels point to internal experiences. Stern, 1985, pp. 26–33.

7. Chugani, 1997.

8. Schore, 1994; Shore 1997; Sroufe, 1996.

9. Schore, 1994.

10. Schore, 1998.

11. Crockenberg & Leerkes, 2000.

12. Crockenberg & Leerkes, 2000, p. 64.

13. Gowen & Nebrig, 2002, p. 85.

14. Sammons, 1989, pp. 10–11.

15. Sammons, 1989.

16. Crittenden, 1993.

17. Pruett, 1997.

18. Chess & Thomas, 1987.

19. Stern discussed how the behavior of newborns gives evidence of four qualities of sense of self: self-agency, self-coherence, inner affectivity, and self-continuity. These qualities describe experiences that are integrated. Stern, 1985, pp. 70–94.

20. Stern called this cross-modal transfer of information *amodal perception*. Babies experience a correspondence across vision and touch and across hearing and vision. For example, a 3-week-old blindfolded baby sucks a specifically shaped pacifier. Then, the blindfold is removed, and two different shaped pacifiers are placed in front of the baby. The baby will look more at the pacifier he or she sucked—touch and vision are joined. This cross-modal transfer allows the newborn to experience self-coherence. Stern, 1985, pp. 47–54.

21. Emde, 1989.

22. Emde, 1989, p. 37

23. Brazelton & Cramer, 1990, p. 98.

24. Bowlby introduced the concept of *internal working models* (IWM), memories of interactions with one's parent, as a way of explaining how the infant's sense of self emerges from relationships with parents. Bowlby, 1969, 1973.
    Stern stated that many of an infant's specific memories of similar interactions with parent become organized into a generalized memory, which he terms *remembered interactions generalized* (RIGS). Stern, 1985, pp. 97–99, 114–119.

25. Ainsworth and Bowlby identified infant behaviors such as crying, cooing, smiling, and clinging as *proximity-seeking*—bringing their parents in closer contact. Bowlby explained that these infant proximity-seeking behaviors are essential for survival. Ethological studies of animal social life support Bowlby's biological explanation for infant attachment behavior. Ainsworth, Blehar, Waters, & Wall, 1978. *Bonding* is used in the psychological literature to refer to mother's maternally sensitive period, shortly after birth. Bowlby, 1969, 1973. There is some research evidence to suggest a maternal sensitive period immediately following delivery. Klaus & Kennel, 1976. *Attachment* refers to the parent–infant relation that develops progressively throughout the infant's first year. There also is some research evidence to suggest that, for fathers, early contact also helps to create a stronger initial bond between fathers and their infants. Park & Tinsley, 1981.

26. Infant specialists term these parent responses *contingent responsiveness*—the parent is emotionally available to the infant, and thus, the infant's behavior sparks the parent's response. Brazelton & Cramer, 1990, pp. 123–24.

27. Thompson, Flood, & Lundquist, 1995, p. 87.

28. Zeanah & Boris, 2000, p. 356.

29. Stern and his colleagues in Geneva, Switzerland, conducted micro-analytic interviews with mothers, who were asked to recall what they felt, thought, and did during an interaction with their infants. The mother's experiences involved not only their interactions but also their past and future representations. Stern noted, "The mother, in the parenting situation, is necessarily operating in at least two subjective spaces: the behavior interaction and her representational life." Stern, 1995, p. 52; see also Bennett, Lefcourt, Haft, Nachman, & Stern, 1994.

30. Thompson et al., 1995, p. 99.

31. Sroufe, 1989.

32. Zeanah, Larrieu, & Zeanah, 2000, p. 15.

33. Crandell, Fitzgerald, & Whipple, 1997.

34. Garbarino & Bedard, 2001, p. 39.

35. Shonkoff & Phillips, 2000, p. 238.

36. Galinsky, Howes, Kontos, & Shinn, 1994.

37. Gunnar et al., 1996.

38. Greenspan, 1999, pp. 51, 52.

39. Stern stated that the developmental leap at ages 7–9 months is a new sphere of relatedness, termed *intersubjective relatedness*. That is, babies discover that their parents also have inner states of experience and that these inner states are shareable (i.e., intersubjectivity). A new form of experiencing connectedness emerges. Stern identified three states of intersubjectivity, or shared mental states: *shared joint attention, shared intention,* and *shared affective states.* Stern, 1985, pp. 128–133.

    Greenspan wrote of the baby reaching a third developmental level in which the baby can start and respond to two-way presymbolic gestural communication, which Greenspan termed *opening and closing circles.* Greenspan, 1992, p. 5.

40. Emde, 1989, p. 43.

41. Greenspan, 1999, p. 96.

42. Greenspan, 1999, p. 138.

43. Stern, 1984, pp. 3–4. Stern termed this interactive process *affect attunement*. Stern used the term *vitality* to describe how feeling qualities are communicated. Vitality "is captured in such terms as exploding, surging, fading, fleeting" (p. 11). Stern suggested dance and music as examples of vitality changes. Vitality in this sense can be thought of as the quality of feeling being expressed. Different experiences may be joined as long as they share the same quality of feeling that Stern calls vitality. For example, the baby joins a parent's soothing by voice and by touch because each have the same quality. As these experiences are joined by the same quality of feeling, young babies experience their empathic responsiveness and thus experience communication.

44. Erikson, 1950, pp. 72–80.

45. Tronick, Cohn, & Shea, 1986, p. 12.

46. Winnicott called attention to these objects that young children become passionately attached to and called such objects *transitional objects*. Winnicott, 1971, pp. 1–25. Brazelton termed these objects *loveys*. Brazelton, 1992, pp. 171–172.

47. Shore, 1997.

48. Sroufe, 1996.

49. Shonkoff & Phillips, 2000, p. 112.

50. Greenspan and Greenspan discussed how playing as a partner can influence the emotional development of one's baby and young child. The Greenspans emphasized the importance of the baby's active discovery and parents' following their baby's lead in play. Greenspan & Greenspan, 1989.

51. Feldman & Greenbaum, 1997.

52. Stern called this developmental leap of toddlers *the sense of verbal self*. Stern emphasized that the young child's learning to speak creates "a new type of 'being-with,' between adult and child . . . the infant and mother create a being with experience using verbal symbols—a sharing of mutually created meanings about their personal experience." Stern, 1985, p. 172.

53. Erikson, 1950, pp. 80–85.

54. Shonkoff & Phillips, 2000.

55. Greenspan, 1997, p. 101.

56. Greenspan, 1999, p. 208.

57. Shonkoff & Phillips, 2000, p. 163.

58. Beeghly and Cicchetti examined the impact of low social status and child maltreatment on 30-month-olds' emergent self–other understanding. This research provided evidence that these children had significantly less language that reflected their internal states and understanding of self and other. Beeghly & Cicchetti, 1994.

59. Shonkoff & Phillips, 2000, p. 241.

60. Howes's 3-year study of toddlers' peer relationships in child care indicated that very young children, when given the opportunity, can develop a range of social skills. In the early toddler period, young children demonstrated abilities in give-and-take reciprocal roles as they played with each other. These children were ages 16–33 months at the outset of Howes's study. As they engaged in social pretend play in the late toddler period, these children skillfully communicated with each other. Those most socially competent formed friendships that remained stable over the years. Howes, 1988.

61. Shonkoff & Phillips, 2000, p. 168.

62. Stern stated that this developmental leap is marked by young children's ability to narrate their own life stories. Stern claimed that this narrative ability is universal across cultures, innate, and no different than walking and talking. Stern stressed the importance of this new developmental leap is that narratives are "a dynamic laboratory in which the child is constantly working on who he is, defining, redefining who he is, and constantly updating." Stern, 1991. Greenspan described the 36-month-old's ability to "create logical bridges between different emotional ideas, (e.g., "Hit bad guy because he did bad thing"). Greenspan, 1993.

63. Piaget called this lack of perspective-taking *egocentrism.* Piaget, 1969, p. 32.

64. Lee, 1989.

65. Cauley & Tyler, 1989.

66. Erikson, 1950, pp. 90–92.

67. Koenig, Rubin, Klin, & Volkmar, 2000, p. 302.

68. Greenspan, 1992.

69. Fraiberg, 1980; Fraiberg, Adelson, & Shapiro, 1975. The literature of child battering provides evidence that a mother's childhood experience of her own mother as rejecting is related to her own rejection of her baby. Main, Kaplan, & Cassidy, 1989.

70. Shonkoff & Phillips, 2000, p. 383.
71. Shonkoff & Phillips, 2000, pp. 383–384.

Chapter 6

1. Sameroff & Emde, 1989; Sameroff & Fiese, 2000; Shore, 1997.
2. Sameroff & Emde, 1989; Shore, 1997.
3. Greenspan, 1997, p. 113.
4. *Illustrated Oxford Dictionary,* 1998.
5. Thompson & Calkins, 1996, p. 163.
6. Galinsky & David, 1988, p. 7.
7. Honig, 1985.
8. Brazelton, 1992, p. 254.
9. *Random House Dictionary of the English Language,* 1973, p. 409.
10. Vygotsky described the social nature of young children's learning and development. He said that the adult guides the young child by providing a zone of proximal development. Vygotsky explained that the zone of proximal development "is the distance between the actual developmental level as determined by independent problem solving and the level of potential development as determined through problem solving under adult guidance or in collaboration with more capable peers." Vygotsky, 1978, p. 86.
11. Stern stated that emotions are a temporal experience, not a static event outside of time. Emotional experiences have a temporal contour, which Stern termed a temporal feeling shape. The temporal feeling shape depends on which emotions and which motivations are involved in the experience. Stern illustrated the temporal feeling shape with the universal parent game "I'm Gonna Getcha." This game includes increasing suspense, retarding the beat, and then the unexpected "gotcha!" Throughout the game, the baby experiences waves of excitement, suspense, and pleasure. According to Stern, listening to music also is a temporal experience, not a static event. Stern, 1995, pp. 63, 85.
12. Dahl explained that the neurobehavioral systems involved in the regulation of arousal, attention, and emotion overlap with the regulation of sleep. Inadequate sleep influences the emotional state of a baby and young child as well as his or her ability to attend. Babies who experience repeated emotional disturbances or high levels of arousal have difficulty sleeping. Although most babies and young children are deep sleepers, sleep deprivation of

young children at risk has substantive effects in weakening goal-directed behaviors and the ability to regulate emotions. Dahl, 1996.

13. Thomas & Chess, 1977.
14. Chess & Thomas, 1987, pp. 56–60.
15. Brazelton & Cramer, 1990, p. 123.
16. Stern, 1985, pp. 220–223.
17. Reiss, 1989.
18. Mahler, Pine, & Berman, 1975.
19. Stern, 1985.
20. Shonkoff & Phillips, 2000, p. 243.
21. Fabes & Eisenberg, 1992.
22. Mayer, 1985.
23. Noll, 1991.
24. Greenspan, 1999, p. 275.
25. McGee and colleagues studied a sample of preschool children during a 12-year period, and their findings indicated long-term troublesome consequences of preschool hyperactivity. Preschool children who are hyperactive show continued problem behavior during elementary school and adolescence. Hyperactivity seems to be significantly related to poor language skills among preschoolers and lower cognition and reading ability in primary school. A strong association thus appears to exist between limited language skills and inattention and difficulties in cognition. Similar findings are reported by McGee, Partridge, Williams, & Silva, 1991; Stattin & Magnusson, 1996.
26. Shaw, Gilliom, & Giovannelli, 2000, p. 398.
27. Shaw et al., 2000.
28. Karr-Morse & Wiley, 1997.
29. Garbarino & Bedard, 2001.

Chapter 7

1. Bates, O'Connell, & Shore, 1987, pp. 151–168.
2. Heath, 1983, pp. 73–148.
3. Stern, 1995, pp. 59–78.
4. Jervay-Pendergrass & Brown, 2000, p. 28.
5. Stern, 1977, p. 74.
6. Bates et al., 1987, pp. 151–169.

7. Devine provided a practical guide for parents to understand developmental milestones in their infant's and toddler's language and communication development as well as parenting activities to foster this development. Devine, 1991.

8. Mahoney and his colleagues have developed Transactional Intervention Program (TRIP) for children from birth to 3 years old who have disabilities. TRIP promotes parents' communication and offers an approach to playing with their young children. Turn taking and interactive matching are two instructional strategies used in this program. Mahoney & Powell, 1988. Using a mental health perspective, Greenspan did similar work with parents of very young children. Greenspan termed the give-and-take interaction as *opening and closing circles.* Greenspan, 1992.

9. Emde, 1989, p. 45.

10. Nelson, 1973.

11. Nelson & Gruendel, 1986.

12. Berk & Winsler, 1995, pp. 34–49.

13. Nelson, 1989.

14. Nelson, 1989, p. 16.

15. Huttenlocher, Haiglet, Bryk, Deltzer, & Lynos, 1991.

16. Schachter & Strage, 1982.

17. Bates emphasized that between birth and age 3 years is the window of maximum opportunity for neural development and maximum plasticity for language development. Bates, 1994.

18. Lee, 1989.

19. Greenspan, 1997, p. 75.

20. Lee, 1989.

21. Prizant, Wetherby, & Roberts, 2000, p. 283.

22. Carson, Klee, Perry, Muskina, & Donaghy, 1998.

23. Prizant et al., 2000, p. 286.

24. Dole, Duffy, Roehler, & Pearson, 1991.

25. Heath, 1983, pp. 190–235.

Chapter 8

1. Erikson, 1950, p. 222.

2. Mead, 1962, p. 7.

3. Piaget, 1963.

4. Stern explained the developmental significance of these micro-events: "To the extent that these interactions are purely social with no other goal in mind, they consist of mutual microregulation of affect and activation. . . .They are the basic step of an interaction regulatory process." Stern, 1995, p. 63.

5. Bruner & Sherwood, 1976.

6. Emde, 1989.

7. Erikson, 1977, pp. 85–92.

8. Erikson wrote that "dramatic play in childhood provides the infantile form of the human propensity to create model situations in which aspects of the past are re-lived, the present re-presented and renewed, and the future anticipated" Erikson, 1977, p. 44.

9. The role of parent as active participant in young children's play is a relatively new insight among developmental and early education theorists and researchers. Historically, developmental theory promoted adult roles as providers of settings, observers, and periodic participants in children's play who participate as the explicit need arises, for example to implement a rule in conflict situations. Since the mid-1980s, theory and research across the mental health and educational fields emphasize the developmental value of adults' active role in young children's play. Greenspan and Greenspan provided a convincing discussion of how parents' active engagement as play partners with their baby and young child enhances their child's social and emotional self. Greenspan & Greenspan, 1989.

10. Duckworth, 1972.

11. Piaget, 1962.

12. Smilansky, 1968.

13. Biber, 1984.

14. Carlsson-Paige & Levin, 1990.

15. Anderson & Evans, 2001.

16. Carlsson-Page & Levin, 1990.

17. Carlsson-Page & Levin, 1990, p. 12.

18. Garbarino & Bedard, 2001, p. 191.

19. Garbarino & Bedard, 2001, p. 203.

Chapter 9

1. Kubicek, 2002, p. 4.

2. Wolin & Bennett, 1984.

3. Reiss, 1989.

4. Imber-Black & Roberts, 1992, p. 4.

5. Fiese, 2002, p. 10.

6. Fiese, 2000.

7. Imber-Black & Roberts, 1992, p. 151.

8. Imber-Black & Roberts, 1992, p. 28.

9. Garbarino & Bedard, 2001, pp. 153, 168.

10. Brazelton, 1992, p. 381.

11. Weissbluth, 1987, pp. 84–87.

12. Ferber, 1985, p. 32.

13. McKenna, 2000, p. 16.

14. Sammons, 1989.

15. Anders, Goodlin-Jones, & Sadah, 2000, p. 328.

16. Ferber, 1985, p. 82.

17. Weissbluth, 1987, p. 119.

18. Ferber, 1985, p. 196.

19. Essays in the book *Narratives from the Crib* discussed a 2-year study of monologues of a child between 15 and 23 months as she was going to sleep. The reports showed that monologues have greater complexity than the child's dialogues with her parents just prior to sleeping. The studies find these monologues help the child to understand her daily experience. Nelson, 1989.

20. Satter, 1992.

21. Brazelton, 1992, p. 141.

22. Brazelton, 1992, p. 141.

23. Brazelton, 1992, p. 190.

24. Lansky, 1984, p. 9.

25. Wolin & Bennett, 1984.

26. Parmelee, 1993.

27. Brazelton, 1992, p. 313.

28. Field, 2000.

29. Field, 1993.

30. Field, 2000.

31. Minde, 2000, p. 176.

32. Minde, 2000, p. 183.

33. Dawson, 1992.

34. Dawson, 1992, p. 21.

35. Sturm & Drotar, 1992.

36. Gergen, 1991.

37. Kaplan & Pruett, 2000, p. 533.

Chapter 10

1. Dunn & Kendrick, 1982; Lee, 1989.

2. Brazelton, 1992, p. 199.

3. White, 1985.

4. Galinsky, 1987, p. 187.

5. Dunn & Plomin, 1990.

6. Faber & Mazlish, 1987, p. 99.

7. Dunn & Plomin, 1990, pp. 283–284.

8. Dunn and Plomin provided autobiographical and biographical materials of famous people to illustrate remarkable differences in the affection, interest, control, and dominance of brothers and sisters—differences not linked to birth order. Dunn & Plomin, 1990, p. 90.

9. Lieberman discussed the difficulties that toddlers have when displaced by a new baby. Lieberman, 1993, pp. 165–168.

10. Faber & Mazlish, 1987, pp. 162–176; Galinsky & David, 1988, pp. 284–288.

Chapter 11

1. McDonough and her colleagues implemented an interaction guidance approach in their work with at-risk families with such conditions as poverty, mental illness, substance abuse, violence, poor education, and inadequate family support. The goals of their interaction guidance approach were to assist families in gaining enjoyment from their child and in developing an understanding of their child's behavior and development through interactive family play experiences that were videotaped and discussed. McDonough, 2000.

2. Pawl, 1997.

3. Sameroff & Fiese, 2000, p. 137.

4. Zeanah et al., 2000.

5. Sameroff & Fiese, 2000, p. 137.

6. Sameroff & Fiese, 2000, p. 141.

7. Researchers have observed 24-month-old toddlers of depressed and nondepressed mothers in three play sessions involving two mothers and their children. Researchers also documented mothers' child-rearing practices and mothers' reports of children's behavior at age 5 and 6 years. Depressed mothers who could anticipate their children's needs and used respectful, reasoned control methods, as well as provided structure and organization during their children's play, had 5- and 6-year-old children who had fewer instances of aggression. In contrast, depressed mothers who were more inconsistent, negative, and/or unresponsive had 5- and 6-year-old children who exhibited a lot of aggression and other externalizing problems. Zahn-Waxler, Ianotti, Cumming, & Denham, 1990.

8. Sameroff & Fiese, 2000, p. 144.

9. Reiss, 1989, p. 192.

10. Kaplan & Pruett, 2000.

11. Kaplan & Pruett, 2000.

12. Pellegrini & Notarius, 1988.

13. Belsky, Woodworth, & Crnic, 1996, p. 480.

14. Heiniccke, Guthrie, & Ruth, 1997.

15. Kerr & Bowen, 1988.

16. Constantino, 1993, p. 3.

17. Constantino, 1993; Luby, 2000.

18. Seifer & Dickson, 2000, p. 146.

19. Berkowitz & Senter, 1987; Dodge, 1990; Luby, 2000; Murray, 1992; Seifer & Dickson, 1993.

20. Seifer & Dickson, 1993, p. 150.

21. Clark & Fenichel, 2001, p. 49.

22. Rutter, 1990, pp. 61–62.

23. Field, Healy, Goldstein, & Guthertz, 1990.

24. Bettes, 1988; Cox, Puckering, Pound, & Mills, 1987; Stein, Bucher, Gath, Bond, & Cooper, 1989.

25. Davenport, Zahn-Waxler, Adlend, & Mayfield, 1984.

26. Gottlieb & Hooley, 1988; Rutter & Quinton, 1984.

27. Schore, 1997.

28. Jones, Field, Fox, Lundy, & Davalos, 1997.

29. Nelson & Bosquet, 2000.

30. Seifer & Dickson, 1993.

31. Seifer & Dickson, 1993.

32. Stern, 1995, p. 102.

33. Stern, 1995, p. 104.

34. Stern, 1995, pp. 99–105.

35. Shonkoff & Phillips, 2000, p. 254.

36. Jones-Harden, 1997.

37. Mayes, Bornstein, Chawarsk, Haynes, & Granger, 1996; Myers, Olson, & Kaltenbach, 1992; Zuckerman & Brown, 1993.

38. Lester & Tronick, 1994.

39. Lester, Boukydis, & Twomey, 2000.

40. Behnke & Eyler, 1994; Lester & Tronick, 1994.

41. Myers et al., 1992, p. 3.

42. Zuckerman & Brown, 1993.

43. Mayes et al., 1996.

44. Zuckerman & Brown, 1993.

45. Lester et al., 2000, pp. 169–170.

46. Carmichael Olson, Burgess, & Streissguth, 1992, p. 25.

47. Zuckerman & Brown, 1993.

48. Eiden & Leonard, 1996.

49. Aber et al., 2000.

50. Wallach, 1993.

51. Osofsky, 1993.

52. Cicchetti & Lynch, 1993, p. 96.

53. Richters & Martinez, 1993.

54. Karr-Morse & Wiley, 1997, p. 8.

55. Children's Defense Fund, 1994.

56. Terr, 1991, p. 12.

57. Sugar, 1992.

58. Terr, 1991; Zeanah & Burk, 1984.

59. Osofsky, 1993; Pynoos & Eth, 1986; Terr, 1991; Wallach, 1993; Zeanah, 1993.

60. Cicchetti & Lynch, 1993; Richters & Martinez, 1993.

61. Osofsky, 1993.

62. Garbarino, 1992; Osofsky, 1993; Scheeringa & Greenbauer, 2000; Terr, 1991; Zeanah, 1993.

63. Karr-Morse & Wiley, 1997.

64. Drell, Siege, & Gaenbauer, 1993, p. 93.

65. Pynoos, 1985.

66. Osofsky, 1996, p. 8.

67. Kaufman & Henrich, 2000, p. 195.

68. Kaufman & Henrich, 2000.

69. Mrazek, 1993.

70. Mrazek, 1993, p. 162.

71. Egeland & Sroufe, 1981.

72. Kaufman & Henrich, 2000; Toth, Cicchetti, Macfie, & Emde, 1997.

73. Toth et al., 2000, p. 783. Toth, Cicchetti, Macfie, & Emde administered 10 narrative story stems to 107 preschool children, 72% of which had experienced multiple subtypes of abuse, and 27% of whom were nonmaltreated children from families receiving Aid to Families with Dependent Children (now called Temporary Assistance for Needy Families), similar to the families of maltreated children. Maltreated children's stories include negative maternal representation, negative self-representation, and were less responsive and more controlling with the examiner. Toth et al., 1997, p. 786.

74. Cicchetti, Ackerman, & Izard, 1995.

75. Kaufman & Henrich, 2000, p. 197.

76. Karr-Morse & Wiley, 1997, p. 164.

77. Karr-Morse & Wiley, 1997, p. 15.

78. Gil & Johnson, 1993.

79. Werner & Smith, 1992; Wolin & Wolin, 1993.

80. Tolstoy, 1960, p. 1.

81. Cicchetti & Rogosch, 1997, p. 797.

82. Wolin & Wolin, 1993, pp. 5–6.

83. Karr-Moore & Wiley, 1997, pp. 144–147.

84. Elshtain, 1981, pp. 326–327.

85. Garbarino & Bedard, 2001.

Chapter 12

1. Since the 1980s, there has been a growing literature analyzing the relationship of teachers' careers and their childhood history and adult personal life. See Ball & Goodson, 1985; Goodson, 1992; Nias, 1989; Raymond, Butt, & Townsend, 1992; Smith, Kleine, Prunty, & Dwyer, 1986.

2. Anderson, 1991; Bruner, 1986; White & Epston, 1990.

3. Bruner described a person's story, or narrative, of his or her life as being a cognitive act of thought involving not only memory but also interpretation. A narrative is a construction in the present. Narratives of past experiences are shaped by experiences and understandings that have occurred since the remembered experience. They also are shaped by anticipations of future experience. Past, present, and future each play a role in the composition of a narrative, and the narrative unites the three. Bruner, 1987, pp. 13–15. This perspective on time was discussed by William Dilthey and his student, George Herbert Mead. Dilthey, 1961; Mead, 1934.

4. Clandinin and Connelly wrote of personal experience methods as focused in four areas: inward (i.e., thoughts, feelings, values, attitudes), outward (i.e., the environmental context), and backward and forward (i.e., past, present, and future). Clandinin & Connelly, 1994, p. 417. Sociologist Mills argued for the integration of biography, history, and social structure. Mills, 1959. The philosopher Dilthey spoke of one's life preserving "the relation between the outer and something inner, which is the meaning of that life." Dilthey asserted that biography cannot capture this relation without including the sociocultural context of that period. Dilthey, 1961, p. 91.

5. Sociological research in the 1980s and 1990s emphasized the central role of the relationship of researcher to participant. Denzin discussed how writing a biography involves both subjective and intersubjective understanding of experiences, of the person studied and of oneself. In other words, understanding is an intersubjective hermeneutic process. Denzin, 1989.

6. Nias emphasized the personal nature of teaching. Following George Herbert Mead's understanding of the inescapably social nature of self, Nias emphasized how teachers' assumptions, passions, and schemata are rooted in experiences from birth. It follows that many of a teacher's satisfactions are tied to the teacher's identity and sense of self. Nias, 1989.

7. Noddings identified *joy* as the basic human emotion experienced within relatedness and the fulfillment a person experiences when caring for others. Noddings, 1984, pp. 6–7.

8. Schon discussed those fields, such as teaching, in which the worker is a craftsperson, an artist; thus, most of the learning is in the doing. In these professions, framing problems and improvising are essential components of the professional's practice. Schon, 1987, p. 13.

9. Jackson wrote about teachers' development through prolonged reflection on teaching from different perspectives. "The goal is to articulate and broaden the context." Jackson, 1992, p. 73.

10. Bruner argued that most learning is a "sharing of culture. It is not just that the child must make his knowledge his own, but that he must make it his own in a community of those who share his sense of belonging to a culture." Bruner, 1986, p. 127.

11. Butt, Raymond, McCure, and Yamagishi discussed the powerful interaction of person and private and public contexts over time and how this interplay affects a teacher's personal and professional life. Butt, Raymond, McCure, & Yamagishi, 1992, p. 62.

12. Literature on personal biography describes times in a person's life cycle that are termed *critical incidents, turning points,* or *epiphanies.* These critical incidents are key events in a person's life around which pivotal decisions are made, which in turn lead persons in specific directions. Critical incidents may be extrinsic, such as a historical event like the Vietnam War, or intrinsic, like an unexpected pregnancy. For example, Denzin, 1989, pp. 69–71; Measor, 1985.

13. Bruner stated that experience and memory of experience are powerfully structured by deeply internalized cultural *notions,* what he termed *folk psychology.* He argued that we can interpret meaning only if we situate that meaning in the larger cultural context in which specific meanings are created. Bruner, 1992.

14. Seligman and Pawl discussed four broad categories of obstacles they have experienced when they do therapeutic work in the homes of parents experiencing multiple difficulties. The categories include socioeconomic and sociocultural variables, prior experience with professionals and social agencies, the family situation, and personal history and psychology. Seligman & Pawl, 1984.

15. Schon explained the artistry of good coaching and the importance of coaches "who initiate students into the 'traditions of the calling' and help them, by 'the right kind of telling,' to see on

their own behavior and in their own way what they need most to see." Schon, 1987, p. 17.

16. Nias argued that crucial to a teacher's identity are reference groups that help one by offering support in defining the value, meaning, and understanding of one's work. Nias, 1992, pp. 115–116.

17. Bruner discussed how meaning and symbols are public and communal rather than private and individual. He argued that to understand a person is to locate that person in a cultural and historical time and place. Bruner, 1992, pp. 10–11.

18. Noddings argued that "ethical caring depends not upon rule or principle but upon the development of an ideal self . . . in congruence with one's best remembrance of caring and being cared for." Noddings, 1984, p. 94.

19. Rogers argued that significant learning is acquired through experiencing practical problems. Rogers, 1969, pp. 158–162.

20. Beginning with Freud, therapy literature discusses the transference as the adults' replication of childhood relationship with parents in their relationships with their own children or spouse or with other significant people. For example, Basch, 1980; Fraiberg, 1980; Kerr & Bowen, 1988.

21. Beginning with her classic work, *In a Different Voice*, Gilligan's research explores women's psychological development. Gilligan argues that women have different views of self and morality and different ways of understanding and experiencing relationships than do men. Women see relationships as webs of connectedness, whereas men think in terms of images of hierarchy. Whereas men view morality in terms of the logic of justice, women's view is in terms of the ethic of care. Gilligan, 1982.

22. Shanok discussed the supervisory relationship as the context within which to learn by reflection with a confidante whom one feels secure enough to expose one's vulnerabilities. Shanok, 1991.

References

Aber, J.L., Jones, S., & Cohen, J. (2000). The impact of poverty on the mental health and development of very young children. In C.H. Zeanah, Jr. (Ed.), *Handbook of infant mental health* (2nd ed.). New York: The Guilford Press.

Ainsworth, M.D.S., Blehar, M.C., Waters, E., & Wall, S. (1978). *Patterns of attachment.* Mahwah, NJ: Lawrence Erlbaum Associates.

Anders, T., Goodlin-Jones, B., & Sadah, A. (2000). Sleep disorders. In C.J. Zeanah, Jr. (Ed.), *Handbook of infant mental health* (2nd ed., pp. 326–338). New York: The Guilford Press.

Anderson, D.R., & Evans, M.K. (2001). Peril and potential of media for infants and toddlers. *Zero to Three, 22*(2), 10–16.

Anderson, T. (Ed.). (1991). *The reflecting team: Dialogues and dialogues about the dialogue.* New York: W. W. Norton.

Anderson, T. (1992). Relationship, language and pre-understanding in the reflecting process. *Family Therapy, 12*(2), 87–91.

Ball, S.J., & Goodson, I.F. (1985). *Teachers' lives and careers.* Philadelphia: Falmer Press

Barrie, J.M. (1911). *Peter Pan.* London: Penguin Books.

Basch, M.F. (1980). *Doing psychotherapy.* New York: Basic Books.

Bates, E. (1994, December). *Normal and abnormal variation in early language development.* Paper presented at the Frontiers of Infancy Research, ZERO TO THREE, National Center for Clinical Infant Programs' Ninth National Training Institute, Dallas, TX.

Bates, E., O'Connell, B., & Shore, C. (1987). Language and communication in infancy. In J.D. Osofsky (Ed.), *Handbook of infant development* (2nd ed., pp. 149–203). New York: John Wiley & Sons.

Beeghly, M., & Cicchetti, D. (1994). Child maltreatment, attachment, and self system: Emergence of an internal state of toddlers at high social risk. *Development and Psychopathology, 6*(1), 5–30.

Behnke, E., & Eyler, F.D. (1994). Issues in prenatal cocaine use research: Problems in identifying users and choosing an appropriate comparison group. *Infant Mental Health Journal, 15,* 146–157.

Belsky, J., Woodworth, S., & Crnic, K. (1996). Trouble in the second year: Three questions about interaction. *Child Development, 67,* 556–578.

Bennett, S., Lefcourt, I.S., Haft, W., Nachman, P., & Stern, D.N. (1994). The activation of material representations. *Infant Mental Health Journal, 15*(4), 336–347.

Berk, L.E., & Winsler, A. (1995). *Scaffolding children's learning: Vygotsky and early childhood education.* Washington, DC: National Association for the Education of Young Children.

Berkowitz, C.D., & Senter, S.A. (1987). Characteristics of mother–infant interactions in nonorganic failure to thrive. *Journal of Family Practice, 24,* 377–381.

Bertacchi, J., & Coplon, J. (1989). The professional use of self in prevention: 1–7. *Zero to Three, 11,*(2), 1–7.

Bertacchi, J., & Stott, F.M. (1992). A seminar for supervisors in infant/family programs: Growing versus paying more for staying the same. In E. Fenichel (Ed.), *Learning through supervision and mentorship to support the development of infants, toddlers, and their families: A source book* (pp. 132–140). Washington, DC: ZERO TO THREE: National Center for Clinical Infant Programs.

Bettes, B.A. (1988). Maternal depression and motherese: Temporal and intonational features. *Child Development, 59,* 1089–1096.

Biber, B. (1984). *Early education and psychological development.* New Haven, CT: Yale University Press.

Bowlby, J. (1969). *Attachment and loss: Vol. 1. Attachment.* New York: Basic Books.

Bowlby, J. (1973). *Attachment and loss: Vol. 2. Separation, anxiety, and anger.* New York: Basic Books.

Brazelton, T.B. (1992). *Touchpoints: The essential reference. Your child's emotional and behavioral development.* Reading, MA: Addison Wesley Higher Education Group.

Brazelton, T.B., & Cramer, B.G. (1990). *The earliest relationship: Parents, infants, and the drama of early attachment.* Reading, MA: Addison Wesley Higher Education Group.

Bromwich, R. (1981). *Working with parents and infants: An interactional approach.* Austin, TX: PRO-ED.

Bronfenbrenner, U. (1979). *The ecology of human development: Experiments by nature and design.* Cambridge, MA: Harvard University Press.

Bronfenbrenner, U., & Neville, P. (1994). America's children and families: An international perspective. In S.L. Kagan & B. Weissbourd (Eds.), *Putting families first: America's family support movement and the challenge of change* (pp. 3–17). San Francisco: Jossey-Bass.

Brownlee, S., Hotinski, R., Pailthorp, B., Ragan, E., & Wong, K. (1999, August 9). Inside the teen brain: Behavior can be baffling when young minds are taking shape. *U.S. News & World Report.*

Bruner, J.S. (1986). *Actual minds, possible worlds.* Cambridge, MA: Harvard University Press.

Bruner, J.S. (1987). Life as narrative: 11–32. *Social Research* (54), 1.

Bruner, J.S. (1992). *Acts of meaning.* Cambridge, MA: Harvard University Press.

Bruner, J.S., & Sherwood, V. (1976). Peekaboo and the learning of rule structures. In J.S. Bruner, A. Jolly, & K. Sylva (Eds.), *Play: Its role in development and evolution* (pp. 268–276). New York: Basic Books.

Buber, M. (1958). *I and thou.* New York: Charles Scribner's Sons. (Original work published 1923)

Butt, R., Raymond, D., McCure, G., & Yamagishi, L. (1992). Collective autobiography and the teacher's voice. In I.F. Goodson (Ed.), *Studying teachers' lives* (pp. 51–98). New York: Teachers College Press.

Carlson, V.J., & Harwood, R.L. (2000). Understanding and negotiating cultural differences concerning early developmental competence: The six raisin solution. *Zero to Three, 20*(3), 19–24.

Carlsson-Paige, N., & Levin, D.E. (1990). *Who's calling the shots? How to respond effectively to children's fascination with war play and war toys.* Philadelphia: New Society Publishers.

Carmichael Olson, H., Burgess, D.M., & Streissguth, A.P. (1992). Fetal alcohol syndrome (FAS) and fetal alcohol effects (FAE): A lifespan view, with implications for early intervention. *Zero to Three, 13*(1), 24–29.

Carson, D.K., Klee, T., Perry, C.K., Muskina, G., & Donaghy, T. (1998). Comparisons of children with delayed and normal language at 24 months of age on measures of behavioral difficulties. *Infant Mental Health Journal, 19*(1) 59–75.

Cauley, K., & Tyler, B. (1989). The relationship of self-concept to prosocial behavior in children. *Early Childhood Research Quarterly, 4,* 51–60.

Chess, S., & Thomas, A. (1987). *Know your child: An authoritative guide for today's parents.* New York: Basic Books.

Children's Defense Fund. (1994). Living in fear: National poll tops children's list of worries. *Children's Defense Fund Reports, 2,* 1–2.

Chugani, H.T. (1997). Neuroimaging of developmental nonlinearity and developmental pathologies. In G.R. Lyon (Ed.), *Developmental neuroimaging* (pp. 187–195). San Diego: Academic Press.

Cicchetti, D., Ackerman, B.P., & Izard, C.E. (1995). Emotions and emotional regulation in developmental psychopathology. *Development and Psychopathology, 7*(1), 1–10.

Cicchetti, D., & Lynch, M. (1993). Toward an ecological/transactional model of community violence and child maltreatment: Consequences for children's development. *Psychiatry, 56,* 95–118.

Cicchetti, D., & Rogosch, F.A. (1997). Equifinality and multifinality in developmental psychopathology. *Development and Psychopathology, 8*(3), 597–600.

Clandinin, D.J., & Connelly, F.M. (1994). Personal experience methods. In N.K. Denzin & Y.S. Lincoln (Eds.), *Handbook of qualitative research* (pp. 4113–4127). Thousand Oaks, CA: Sage Publications.

Clark, R., & Fenichel, E. (2001). Mothers, babies, and depression: Questions and answers. *Zero to Three, 22*(1), 48–56.

Cochran, M., Larner, M., Riley, D., Gunnarsson, L., & Henderson, C.R., Jr. (1990). *Extending families: The social networks of parents and their children.* New York: Cambridge University Press.

Coll, C.G., & Magnuson, O.K. (2000). Cultural differences as sources of developmental vulnerabilities and resources. In J. Shonkoff & S. Meisels (Eds.), *Handbook of early intervention* (2nd ed.). New York: Cambridge University Press.

Constantino, J.N. (1993). Parents' mental illness and the primary health care of infants and children. *Young Children, 13*(5), 1–9.

Cox, A.D., Puckering, C., Pound, A., & Mills, M. (1987). The impact of maternal depression on young children. *Journal of Child Psychology and Psychiatry, 28,* 917–928.

Crandell, L.E., Fitzgerald, H.E., & Whipple, E.E. (1997). Dyadic synchrony in parent–child interactions: A link with maternal representation of attachment relationships. *Infant Mental Health Journal, 18*(3), 247–264.

Crittenden, P.M. (1993). Characteristics of neglectful parents: An information processing approach. *Criminal Justice and Behavior, 20,* 27–48.

Crockenberg, S., & Leerkes, E. (2000). Infant social and emotional development in family context. In C.H. Zeanah, Jr. (Ed.), *Handbook of infant mental health* (2nd ed., pp. 60–90). New York: The Guilford Press.

Dahl, R.E. (1996). The regulation of sleep and arousal: Development and psychopathology. *Development and Psychopathology, 8*(1), 3–28.

Davenport, Y.B., Zahn-Waxler, C., Adlend, M.C., & Mayfield, J. (1984). Early childrearing practices in families with a manic depressive parent. *American Journal of Psychiatry, 141,* 230–235.

Dawson, P. (1992). Should the field of early child and family intervention address failure to thrive? *Zero to Three, 12*(5), 20–23.

Denzin, N.K. (1989). *Interpretive biography.* Thousand Oaks, CA: Sage Publications.

Devine, M. (1991). *Baby talk: The art of communicating with infants and toddlers.* New York: Kluwer Academic/Plenum Press

Dewey, J. (1916). *Democracy and education.* New York: Macmillan.

Dilthey, W. (1961). *Pattern and meaning in history: Thoughts on history and society.* H.P. Rickman (Editor and Introduction). New York: HarperCollins Publishers. (Edited from Volume VII of Dilthey's collected works, written in 1910)

Dodge, K.A. (1990). Developmental psychopathology in children of depressed mothers. *Developmental Psychology, 26*(1), 3–6.

Dole, J.D., Duffy, G.G., Roehler, L.R., & Pearson, P.D. (1991). Moving from old to the new: Research on reading comprehension instruction. *Review of Educational Research. 61*(2), 239–264.

Drell, M.J., Siege, C.H., & Gaenbauer, T.J. (1993). Post traumatic stress disorder. In C.H. Zeanah, Jr. (Ed.), *Handbook of infant mental health* (pp. 291–304). New York: The Guilford Press.

Duckworth, E. (1972). The having of wonderful ideas. *Harvard Educational Review, 42*(2), 217–231.

Dunn, J., & Kendrick, C. (1982). *Siblings: Love, envy, and understanding.* Cambridge, MA: Harvard University Press.

Dunn, J., & Plomin, R. (1990). *Separate lives: Why siblings are so different.* New York: Basic Books.

Egeland, B., & Sroufe, L.A. (1981). Attachment and early maltreatment. *Child Development, 52*(1), 44–52.

Eiden, L.A., & Leonard, K.E. (1996). Paternal alcohol abuse and mother–infant relationship. *Development and Psychopathology, 8*(2), 307–323.

Einstein, A., & Infeld, L. (1996). *The evolution of physics.* New York: Simon & Schuster. (Original work published 1938)

Elshtain, J.B. (1981). *Public men, private women: Women in social and political thought.* Princeton, NJ: Princeton University Press.

Emde, R.N. (1989). The infant's relationship experience: Developmental and affective aspects. In A.J. Sameroff & R.N. Emde (Eds.), *Relationship disturbances in early childhood: A developmental approach* (pp. 40–47). New York: Basic Books.

Emde, R.N., & Robinson, J. (2000). Guiding principles for a theory of early intervention. In J.P. Shonkoff & S.J. Meisels (Eds.), *Handbook of early intervention* (2nd ed., pp. 160–178). New York: International University Press.

Erikson, E. (1950). *Childhood and society.* New York: W.W. Norton.

Erikson, E. (1977). *Toys and reasons: Stages in the ritualization of experience.* New York: W.W. Norton.

Faber, A., & Mazlish, E. (1987). *Siblings without rivalry: How to help your children live together so you can live too.* New York: W.W. Norton.

Fabes, R.A., & Eisenberg, N. (1992). Young children's coping with interpersonal anger. *Child Development, 63*(1), 116–128.

Feldman, R., & Greenbaum, C.W. (1997). Affect regulation and synchrony in mother–infant play as precursors to the development of symbolic competence. *Infant Mental Health Journal, 18*(1), 4–23.

Fenichel, E. (1992). Learning through supervision and mentorship. In E. Fenichel (Ed.), *Learning through supervision and mentorship to support the development of infants, toddlers, and their families* (pp. 1–8). Washington, DC: ZERO TO THREE: National Center for Clinical Infant Programs.

Fenichel, E. (2001). From neurons to neighborhoods: What's in it for you? *Zero to Three, 21*(5), 8–15.

Ferber, R. (1985). *Solve your child's sleep problems.* New York: Simon & Schuster.

Field, T. (1993). Infant massage. *Zero to Three, 14*(2), 8–12.

Field, T. (2000). Infant massage therapy. In C.H. Zeanah, Jr. (Ed.) *Infant mental health*. New York: The Guilford Press.

Field, T., Healy, B., Goldstein, S., & Guthertz, M. (1990). Behavior state matching and synchrony in mother–infant interactions of nondepressed versus depressed dyads. *Developmental Psychology, 26*, 7–14.

Fiese, B.H. (2000). Family matters: A systems view of family effects on children's cognitive health. In R.J. Sterberg & E.L. Grigorenko (Eds.), *Environmental effects on cognitive abilities* (pp. 390–397). Mahwah, NJ: Lawrence Erlbaum Associates.

Fiese, B.H. (2002). Routines of daily living and rituals in family life: A glimpse of stability and change during the early child-raising years. *Zero to Three, 22*(4), 10–13.

Fitzgerald, H.E., & Montanex, M. (2001). Fathers as facilitators of infant mental health: Implications for Early Head Start. *Zero to Three, 22*(1), 25–28.

Fox, N.A., Calkins, S.D., & Bell, M.A. (1994). Individual differences in response to stress and cerebral asymmetry. *Developmental Neuropsychology, A6*, 677–696.

Fraiberg, S.H. (1980). *Clinical studies in infant mental health*. New York: Basic Books.

Fraiberg, S.H., Adelson, E., & Shapiro, V. (1975). Ghosts in the nursery: A psychoanalytic approach to the problems of impaired mother–infant relationships. *Journal of the American Academy of Child Psychiatry, 14*, 378–421.

Freeman, D.S. (1992). *Family therapy with couples*. Northvale, NJ: Jason Aronson.

Galinsky, E. (1987). *The six states of parenthood*. Reading, MA: Addison Wesley Higher Education Group.

Galinsky, E., & David, J. (1988). *The preschool years: Family strategies that work—from experts and parents*. New York: Ballantine Books.

Galinsky, E., Howes, C., Kontos, S., & Shinn, M. (1994). *The study of children in family child care and relative care*. New York: Families and Work Institute.

Garbarino, J. (1992). *Children and families in the social environment*. New York: Aldine de Gruyter.

Garbarino, J., & Bedard, C. (2001). *Parents under siege: Why you are the solution, not the problem, to your child's life*. New York: The Free Press.

Garbarino, J., & Ganzel, B. (2000). The human ecology of early risk. In J.P. Shonkoff & S.J. Meisels (Eds.), *Handbook of early childhood intervention* (2nd ed., pp. 76–93). New York: Cambridge University Press.

Garcia, E.E. (1994). Addressing the challenges of diversity. In S. Kagan & B. Weissbourd (Eds.), *Putting families first: America's family support movement and the challenge of change* (pp. 243–275). San Francisco: Jossey-Bass.

Gergen, K.J. (1991). *The saturated self: Dilemmas of identity in contemporary life*. New York: Basic Books.

Gil, E., & Johnson, T.C. (1993). *Sexualized children: Assessment and treatment of sexualized children and children who molest*. Rockville, MD: Launch Press.

Gilkerson, L., & Young-Hold, C.L. (1992). Supervision and the management of programs serving infants, toddlers, and families. In E. Fenichel (Ed.), *Learning through supervision and mentorship to support the development of infants, toddlers, and their families: A source book* (pp. 113–119). Washington, DC: ZERO TO THREE: National Center for Clinical Infant Programs.

Gilligan, C. (1982). *In a different voice*. Cambridge, MA: Harvard University Press.

Gilligan, C., & Brown, L.M. (1992). *Meeting at the crossroads: Women's psychology and girl's development*. Cambridge, MA: Harvard University Press.

Goodson, I.F. (1992). *Studying teachers' lives*. New York: Teachers College Press.

Gottlieb, I., & Hooley, J.M. (1988). Depression and marital distress: Current states and future directions. In S. Duck (Ed.), *Handbook of personal relationships* (pp. 543–570). New York: John Wiley & Sons.

Gowen, J.W., & Nebrig, J.B. (2002). *Enhancing early development: Guiding parents of young children*. Baltimore: Paul H. Brookes Publishing Co.

Greenspan, S. (1992). *Infancy and early childhood: The practice of clinical assessment and intervention with emotional and developmental challenges*. Madison, CT: International Universities Press.

Greenspan, S. (1993, December). *Toward a new vision for the developmental assessment of infants and young children*. Paper presented at the plenary session of the National Center for Clinical Programs' Eighth Biennial Training Institute, Washington, DC.

Greenspan, S.I., with Benderly, B.L. (1997). *The growth of the mind and the endangered origins of intelligence*. Reading, MA: Addison-Wesley.

Greenspan, S.I., with Breslau Lewis, N. (1999). *Building healthy minds: The six experiences that create intelligence and emotional growth in babies and young children*. Cambridge, MA: Perseus Books.

Greenspan, S., & Greenspan, N.T. (1989). *The essential partnership: How parents and children can meet the emotional challenges of infancy and childhood*. New York: Penguin Books.

Groves, B.M., Lieberman, A., Osofsky, J.D., & Fenichel, E. (2000). Protecting young children in violent environments: A framework to build on. *Zero to Three, 20*(5), 9–13.

Gunnar, M.R., Brodersen, L., Nachmias, M., Buss, K., & Rigatuso, J. (1996). Stress reactivity and attachment security. *Developmental Psychobiology, 31*(1), 65–85.

Heath, S.B. (1983). *Ways with words: Language, life, and works in communities and classrooms*. New York: Cambridge University Press.

Heiniccke, C.M., Guthrie, D., & Ruth, G. (1997). Marital adaptation, divorce, and parent–infant development: A prospective study. *Infant Mental Health Journal, 18*(3), 282–299.

Holly, M.L. (1989). Teacher professional development: Perceptions and practices in the USA and England. In M.L. Holly & C.S. McLoughlin, *Perspectives on teacher professional development* (pp. 172–203). London: The Falmer Press.

Honig, A.S. (1985). Compliance, control, and discipline. *Young Children, 40*(2), 50–58.

Howes, C. (1988). Peer interaction of young children [Special issues]. *Monographs of the Society for Research in Child Development, 53*(1).

Huttenlocher, J., Haiglet, W., Bryk, A., Deltzer, M., & Lynos, T. (1991). Early vocabulary growth: Relating to language input and gender. *Developmental Psychology, 27*, 236–248.

Illustrated Oxford dictionary. (1998). New York: Oxford University Press.

Imber-Black, E., & Roberts, J. (Eds.). (1992). *Rituals for our times: Celebration, healing and changing our lives and our relationships*. New York: HarperCollins Publishers.

Jackson, P.W. (1992). Helping teachers develop. In A. Hargreaves & M.G.B. Fullan (Eds.), *Understanding teacher development*. New York: Teachers College Press.

Jervay-Pendergrass, D., & Brown, C. (2000). Something happened!: Life stories from birth to three. *Zero to Three, 20*(3), 25–31.

Jones, N.B., Field, T., Fox, N.A., Lundy, B., & Davalos, M. (1997). EEG activations in 1-month-old infants of depressed mothers. *Development and Psychopathology, 9*(3), 491–507.

Jones-Harden, B. (1997). You can't do it alone: Home visitation and psychologically vulnerable families and children. *Zero to Three, 17*(4), 10–16.

Kagan, S.L., & Neuman, M.J. (2000). Early care and education: Current issues and future strategies. In J.P. Shonkoff & S.J. Meisels (Eds.), *Handbook of early intervention* (2nd ed., pp. 339–360). New York: International University Press.

Kaplan, M.D., & Pruett, K.D. (2000). Divorce and custody: Developmental implications. In C.H. Zeanah, Jr. (Ed.), *Handbook of infant mental health* (2nd ed.). New York: The Guilford Press.

Karr-Morse, R., & Wiley, M.S. (1997). *Ghosts from the nursery: Tracing the roots of violence.* New York: The Atlantic Monthly Press.

Kaufman, J., & Henrich, C. (2000). Exposure to violence and early childhood trauma. In C.H. Zeanah, Jr. (Ed.), *Handbook of infant mental health* (2nd ed.). New York: The Guilford Press.

Kerr, M.E., & Bowen, M. (1988). *Family evaluation: An approach based on Bowen theory.* New York: W.W. Norton.

King, M.L., Jr. (1963, August 29). Speech delivered on the steps of the Lincoln Memorial, Washington, DC.

Klaus, H.M., & Kennell, J.H. (1976). *Maternal–infant bonding.* St. Louis: Mosby.

Koenig, K., Rubin, E., Klin, A., & Volkmar, F.R. (2000). Autism and pervasive developmental disorders. In C.H. Zeanah, Jr. (Ed.), *Handbook of infant mental health* (2nd ed., pp. 311–325). New York: The Guilford Press.

Kubicek, L.R. (2002). Fresh perspectives on young children and family rituals. *Zero to Three, 22*(4), 4–9.

Lansky, V. (1984). *Toilet training.* New York: Bantam Books.

Larner, M., & Halpern, T. (1992). Lay home visiting programs: Strengths, tensions, and challenges. In E. Fenichel (Ed.), *Learning through supervision and mentorship to support the development of infants, toddlers, and their families: A source book.* (pp. 91–99). Washington, DC: ZERO TO THREE: National Center for Clinical Infant Programs.

Lee, P. (1989). Is the young child egocentric or sociocentric? *Teacher's College Press, 19*(3), 379–391.

Leopold, S.A. (September 15, 1999). Differences in adult and adolescent brain activity. *OLR Research Report.*

Lester, B.M., Boukydis, C.F.Z., & Twomey, J.E. (2000). Maternal substance abuse and child outcome. In C.H. Zeanah, Jr. (Ed.), *Handbook of infant mental health* (2nd ed.). New York: The Guilford Press.

Lester, B.M., & Tronick, E.Z. (1994). The effects of prenatal cocaine exposure and child outcome. *Infant Mental Health Journal, 15*(2), 107–120.

Lewis, M.L. (2000). The cultural context of infant mental health: The developmental niche of infant–caregiver relationship. In C.H. Zeanah, Jr. (Ed.), *Handbook of infant mental health* (2nd ed., pp. 91–108). New York: The Guilford Press.

Lieberman, A.F. (1991). Attachment theory and infant–parent psychotherapy: Some conceptual, clinical and research considerations. In D. Cicchetti (Ed.), *Rochester symposium on developmental psychopathology* (Vol. 3, pp. 261–287). Rochester, NY: University of Rochester Press.

422 References

Lieberman, A.F. (1993). *The emotional life of the toddler.* New York: The Free Press.

Lieberman, A.F., & Pawl, J.H. (1993). Infant–parent psychotherapy. In C.H. Zeanah, Jr. (Ed.), *Handbook of infant mental health* (2nd ed., pp. 427–442). New York: The Guilford Press.

Lieberman, A.F., Silverman, R., & Pawl, J.H. (2000). Infant–parent psychotherapy: Care concepts and current approaches. In C.H. Zeanah, Jr. (Ed.), *Infant mental health* (2nd ed., pp. 472–484). New York: The Guilford Press.

Loevinger, J. (1976). *Ego development.* San Francisco: Jossey-Bass.

Luby, J.L. (2000). Depression. In C.H. Zeanah, Jr. (Ed.), *Handbook of infant mental health* (2nd ed.). New York: The Guilford Press.

Mahler, M.S., Pine, F., & Berman, A. (1975). *The psychological birth of the human infant: Symbiosis and individuation.* New York: Basic Books.

Mahoney, G., & Powell, A. (1988). Modifying parent–child interaction: Enhancing the development of handicapped children. *Journal of Special Education, 22*(1), 82–96.

Main, M., Kaplan, N., & Cassidy, J. (1989). Security in infancy, childhood and adulthood: A move to the level of representation. In I. Bretherton & E. Waters (Eds.), Growing points in attachment theory and research (pp. 66–106). *Monographs of the Society for Research in Child Development, 50.*

Mayer, M. (1985.) *I was so mad.* Racine, WI: Western.

Mayes, L.C., Bornstein, M.H., Chawarsk, K., Haynes, O.M., & Granger, R.H. (1996). Impaired regulation of arousal in 3-month-old infants exposed prenatally to cocaine and other drugs. *Development and Psychopathology, 8,* 29–42.

McDonough, S.C. (1993). Interaction guidance: Understanding and treating early baby–caregiver relationship disturbances. In C.H. Zeanah, Jr. (Ed.), *Handbook of infant mental health* (pp. 414–426). New York: Guilford Press.

McDonough, S.C. (2000). Interaction guidance: An approach for difficult-to-engage families. In C.H. Zeanah, Jr. (Ed.), *Handbook of infant mental health* (2nd ed., pp. 485–493). New York: The Guilford Press.

McGee, R., Partridge, F., Williams, S., & Silva, P.A. (1991). A twelve-year follow-up of preschool hyperactive children. *Journal of the American Academy of Child and Adolescent Psychiatry, 30,* 224–232.

McKenna, J.J. (2000). Cultural influences on infant and childhood sleep, biology, and the science that studies it: Toward a more inclusive paradigm. *Zero to Three, 20*(3), 9–18.

Mead, G.H. (1934). *Mind, self, and society from the standpoint of a social behaviorist* (Vol. 1). Chicago: University of Chicago Press.

Mead, M. (1962). *A creative life for your children.* (Headliner series no. 1). Washington, DC: Children's Bureau, U.S. Department of Health, Education, and Welfare.

Mead, M. (1972). *Blackberry winter.* New York: Simon & Schuster.

Measor, L. (1985). Critical incidents in the classroom: Identities, choices, and careers. In S.J. Ball & I.F. Goodson (Eds.), *Teachers' lives and careers* (pp. 61–77). Philadelphia: Falmer Press.

Mills, C.W. (1959). *The sociological imagination.* New York: Oxford University Press.

Minde, K. (2000). Prematurity and serious medical conditions in infancy: Implications for development, behavior, and intervention. In C.H. Zeanah, Jr. (Ed.), *Handbook of infant mental health* (2nd ed.). New York: The Guilford Press.

Mrazek, P.J. (1993). Maltreatment and infant development. In C.H. Zeanah, Jr.

(Ed.), *Handbook of infant mental health* (pp. 159–170). New York: The Guilford Press.

Murray, L. (1992). The impact of prenatal development on infant development. *Journal of Child Psychology and Psychiatry, 33*(3), 543–561.

Musick, J.S., & Stott, F. (1993). Paraprofessionals, parenting, and child development: Understanding the problems and seeking solutions (pp. 651–667). In S.J. Meisels & J.P. Shonkoff (Eds.), *Handbook of early childhood intervention.* New York: Cambridge University Press.

Myers, B.J., Olson, H.C., & Kaltenbach, K. (1992). Cocaine-exposed infants: Myths and misunderstandings. *Zero to Three, 13*(1), 1–5.

National Center for Health Statistics. (1998). *Health, United States, 1998 with socioeconomic status and health chart book.* Hyattsville, MD: Author.

Nelson, C.A., & Bosquet, M. (2000). Neurobiology of fetal and infant development: Implications for infant mental health. In C.H. Zeanah, Jr. (Ed.), *Handbook of infant mental health* (2nd ed., pp. 37–59). New York: The Guilford Press.

Nelson, K. (1973). Structure and strategy in learning to talk. *Monographs of the Society for Research in Child Development, 38*(Serial No. 149).

Nelson, K. (Ed.). (1989). *Narratives from the crib.* Cambridge, MA: Harvard University Press.

Nelson, K., & Gruendel, J. (1986). Children's scripts. In K. Nelson (Ed.), *Event knowledge: Structure and function in development* (pp. 21–46). Mahwah, NJ: Lawrence Erlbaum Associates.

Nias, J. (1989). Teaching and the self. In M.L. Holly & C.S. McLoughlin (Eds.), *Perspectives on teacher professional development* (pp. 155–171). Philadelphia: Falmer Press.

Nias, J. (1992). Reference groups in primary teaching: Talking, listening, and identity. In S.J. Ball & I.F. Goodson (Eds.), *Teachers' lives and careers* (pp. 105–119). Philadelphia: Falmer Press.

Noddings, N. (1984). *Caring: A feminine approach to ethics and moral education.* Berkeley: University of California Press.

Noll, S. (1991). *That bothered Kate.* New York: Puffin.

Norton, D.G. (1994). Education for professionals in family support. In. S.L. Kagan & B. Weissbourd (Eds.), *Putting families first: America's family support movement and the challenge of change* (pp. 401–440). San Francisco: Jossey-Bass.

O'Hearn Family Outreach Project Members. (1995). When families lead: The Patrick O'Hearn Family Outreach Project. In A. Palanki & P. Burch (Eds.), *In our hands: A multi-site parent–teacher action research project* (pp. 117–134). Boston: Center on Families, Communities, Schools & Children's Learning.

Olds, D.L. (1981). Improving formal services for mothers and children. In J. Garbarino & S.H. Stocking (Eds.), *Protecting children from abuse and neglect.* San Francisco: Jossey-Bass.

Osofsky, J.D. (1993). *Working with infants, toddlers, and caregivers exposed to violence. Tales from two cities: Boston and New Orleans.* Paper presented at the Eighth Biannual Conference of the ZERO TO THREE National Training Institutes, Washington, DC.

Osofsky, J.D. (1996). Islands of safety: Assessing and treating young victims of violence. *Zero to Three, 16*(5), 5–8.

Osofsky, J.D., & Dickson, A. (2000). Treating traumatized children: The costs of delay. *Zero to Three, 20*(5), 20–25.

Osofsky, J.D., & Thompson, M.D. (2000). Adaptive and maladaptive parenting: Perspectives on risks and protective factors. In J.P. Shonkoff & S.M. Meisels (Eds.), *Handbook of early intervention* (2nd ed.). New York: Cambridge University Press.

Parents as Teachers National Center. (1993). *Program planning and implementation guide.* St. Louis, MO: Author.

Park, R.D., & Tinsley, B.R. (1981). The father's role in infancy: Determinants of involvement in caregiving and play. In M.E. Lamb (Ed.), *The role of father in child development* (2nd ed.). New York: John Wiley & Sons.

Parmelee, A.H., Jr. (1993). Children's illnesses and normal behavioral development: The role of caregivers. *Zero to Three, 13*(4), 1–9.

Pawl, J. (1995). The therapeutic relationship as human connection: Being held in another's mind. *Zero to Three, 15*(4), 1–5.

Pawl, J. (1997). Untitled paper presented at the plenary session of the Building a Good Beginning Project for Every Child conference, St. Louis.

Pellegrini, D.S., & Notarius, C.I. (1988). Marital processes as childhood risk factors: Implications for intervention and prevention. In E.D. Hibbs (Ed.), *Children and families: Studies in prevention and intervention* (pp. 497–509). Madison, CT: International University Press.

Penn, P. (1985). Feed-forward: Future questions, future maps. *Family Process, 24*(3), 299–310.

Piaget, J. (1962). *Play, dreams and imitation in childhood.* New York: W.W. Norton.

Piaget, J. (1963). *The origins of intelligence in children.* New York: W.W. Norton. (Original work published 1952)

Piaget, J. (1969). *The language and thought of the child.* New York: Meridian Books.

Prizant, B.M., Wetherby, A.M., & Roberts, J.E. (2000). Communication problems. In C.H. Zeanah, Jr. (Ed.), *Handbook of infant mental health* (2nd ed., pp. 282–297). New York: The Guilford Press.

Pruett, K.D. (1997). How men and children affect each other's development. *Zero to Three, 18*(1), 3–11.

Pynoos, R.S. (1985). Children traumatized by witnessing parental violence. In S. Eth & R.S. Pynoos (Eds.), *Posttraumatic stress disorder in children.* Washington, DC: American Psychiatric Press.

Pynoos, R.S., & Eth, S. (1986). Witness to violence: The child interview. *Journal of the American Academy of Child Psychiatry, 25,* 306–319.

Random House dictionary of the English language (unabridged). (1973). New York: Random House.

Raymond, D., Butt, B., & Towsend, D. (1992). Contexts for teacher development: Insights from teachers' stories. In A. Hargreaves & M.D. Fullan (Eds.), *Understanding teacher development* (pp. 143–161). New York: Teachers College Press.

Reiss, D. (1989). The represented and practicing family: Contrasting visions of family continuity. In A.J. Sameroff & R.N. Emde (Eds.), *Relationship disturbances in early childhood: A developmental approach.* New York: Basic Books.

Richters, J., & Martinez, P. (1993). The NIMH community violence project: Children as victims and witnesses to violence. *Psychiatry, 56,* 7–21.

Rogers, C.R. (1969). *Freedom to learn.* Columbus, OH: Charles E. Merrill.

Rutter, M. (1990). Commentary: Some focus and process considerations regarding effects of parental depression on children. *Developmental Psychology, 26*(1), 60–67.

Rutter, M., & Quinton, D. (1984). Parental psychiatric disorder: Effects on children. *Psychological Medicine, 14,* 853–880.

Sacks, O.T. (1996). *An anthropologist on Mars: Seven paradoxical tales*. New York: Alfred A. Knopf.

Saint Augustine. (1961). *Confessions* (R.S. Pine-Coffin, trans.). New York: Penguin Books. (Written c. A.D. 396–397)

Sameroff, A.J., & Emde, R.N., (Eds.). (1989). *Relationship disturbances in early childhood: A developmental approach*. New York: Basic Books.

Sameroff, A.J., & Fiese, B.H. (2000). Transactional regulation: The developmental ecology of early intervention. In J.P. Shonkoff & S.J. Meisels (Eds.), *Handbook of early childhood intervention* (2nd ed., pp. 135–159). New York: Cambridge University Press.

Sammons, W.A.H. (1989). *The self-calmed baby: Teach your infant to calm itself—and curb crying, fussing, and sleeplessness*. New York: St. Martin's Press.

Satter, E. (1992). The feeding relationship. *Zero to Three, 12*(4), 1–9.

Schachter, F.F., & Strage, A.A. (1982). Adults' talk and children's language development. In S.G. Moore & C.R. Cooper (Eds.), *The young child: Reviews of research* (Vol. 3). Washington, DC: National Association for the Education of Young Children.

Scheeringa, M.S., & Greenbauer, T.J. (2000). Posttraumatic stress disorder. In C.H. Zeanah, Jr. (Ed.), *Handbook of infant mental health* (2nd ed., pp. 369–381). New York: The Guilford Press.

Schlossman, S.L. (1976). Before home start: Notes toward a history of parent education in America, 1897–1929. *Harvard Educational Review, 46*(3), 436–467.

Schon, D.A. (1987). *Educating the reflective practitioner: Toward a new design for teaching and learning in the professions*. San Francisco: Jossey-Bass.

Schore, A.N. (1994). *Affect regulation and the origin of the self: The neurobiology of emotional development*. Mahwah, NJ: Lawrence Erlbaum Associates.

Schore, A.N. (1997). Early organization of nonlinear right brain and development of predisposition to psychiatric disorders. *Development and Psychopathology, 9*(4), 594–633.

Schore, A.N. (1998). Early organization of the nonlinear right brain and development of a predisposition to psychiatric disorders. *Development and Psychopathology, 9*(4), 505–633.

Schorr, L.B., & Schorr, D. (1988). *Within our reach: Breaking the cycle of disadvantage*. New York: Doubleday.

Seifer, R., & Dickson, S. (1993). Parental maternal illness and infant development. In C.H. Zeanah, Jr. (Ed.), *Handbook of infant mental health* (pp. 120–142). New York: The Guilford Press.

Seifer, R., & Dickson, S. (2000). Parental maternal illness and infant development. In C.H. Zeanah, Jr. (Ed.), *Handbook of infant mental health* (2nd ed., pp. 145–160). New York: The Guilford Press.

Seligman, S.P., & Pawl, J.H. (1984). Impediments to the formation of the working alliance in infant–parent psychotherapy. In J.D. Call, E. Galenson, & R.L. Tyson (Eds.), *Frontiers of infant psychiatry* (Vol. II, pp. 232–237). New York: Basic Books.

Shanok, R.S. (1991). The supervisory relationship: Integrator, resource, and guide. *Zero to Three, 12*(2), 16–19.

Shaw, D.S., Gilliom, M., & Giovannelli, J. (2000). Aggressive behavior disorders. In C.H. Zeanah, Jr. (Ed.), *Handbook of infant mental health* (2nd ed., pp. 397–411). New York: The Guilford Press.

Shonkoff, J.P., & Phillips, D.A. (2000). *From neurons to neighborhoods: The science of early childhood development*. Washington, DC: National Academy Press.

Shore, R. (1997). *Rethinking the brain*. Chicago: Family and Work Institute.

426 References

Smilansky, S. (1968). *The effects of socio-dramatic play on disadvantaged preschool children.* New York: John Wiley & Sons.

Smith, H., Wigginton, E., Hocking, K., & Jones, R.E. (1991). Foxfire teacher networks. In A. Lieberman & L. Miller (Eds.), *Staff development for education in the '90s: New demands, new realities, new perspectives.* New York: Teachers College, Columbia University.

Smith, L.M., Kleine, P.F., Prunty, J.P., & Dwyer, D.C. (1986). *Educational innovators: Then and now.* Philadelphia: Falmer Press.

Smith, L.M., & Wells, W.M. (1990). *Difficult to reach, maintain and help urban families in PAT: Issues, dilemmas, strategies, and resolutions in parent education.* Final report submitted to the Smith Richardson Foundation. St. Louis: Washington University.

Sroufe, L.A. (1989). Relationships, self, and individual adaptation. In A.J. Sameroff & R.N. Emde (Eds.), *Relationship disturbances in early childhood: A developmental approach* (pp. 70–94). New York: Basic Books.

Sroufe, L.A. (1996). *Emotional development: The organization of emotional life in the early years.* London: Cambridge University Press.

Stattin, H., & Magnusson, D. (1996). Antisocial development: A holistic approach. *Development and Psychopathology, 4*(8), 617–647.

Stein, A., Bucher, J., Gath, D., Bond, A., & Cooper, P.J. (1989). *The relationship between postnatal depression and mother–child interaction.* Unpublished manuscript.

Stern, D.N. (1977). *The first relationship: Infant and mother.* Cambridge, MA: Harvard University Press.

Stern, D.N. (1984). Affect attunement. In J. Call, E. Galenson, & R.L. Tyson (Eds.), *Frontiers of infant psychiatry* (Vol. II, pp. 3–14). New York: Basic Books.

Stern, D.N. (1985). *The interpersonal world of the infant: A view from psychoanalysis and developmental psychology.* New York: Basic Books.

Stern, D.N. (1991). *Infant observation and the formation of psychic structure: The Institute for Psychoanalysis Conference.* Chicago: Erikson Institute & The Institute for Psychoananalysis.

Stern, D.N. (1994). *The world of infant research and adult psychotherapy.* Paper presented at the eighth annual Cape Cod Summer Symposia, Eastham, MA.

Stern, D.N. (1995). *The motherhood constellation: A unified view of parent–infant psychotherapy.* New York: Basic Books.

Sturm, L., & Drotar, D. (1992). Communication strategies for working with parents of infants who fail to thrive. *Zero to Three, 12*(5), 25–28.

Sugar, M. (1992). Toddler's traumatic memories. *Infant Mental Health Journal, 13*(3), 245–251.

Tagore, R. (1958). *Collected poems and plays.* New York: Macmillan.

Talan, J. (2000, April 4). Study seeks answer to mystery of brain development, growth. *Augusta Chronicle.*

Terr, L.C. (1991). Childhood traumas: An outline and overview. *American Journal of Psychiatry, 148,* 10–20.

Thomas, A., & Chess, S. (1977). *Temperament and development.* New York: Brunner/Mazel.

Thompson, R.A., & Calkins, S.D. (1996). The double-edged sword: Emotional regulation for children at risk. *Development and Psychopathology, 8*(1), 163–182.

Thompson, R.A., Flood, M.F, & Lundquist, L. (1995). Emotional regulation: It's relations to attachment and developmental psychopathology. In D. Cicchetti & S.L. Toth (Eds.), *Rochester symposium on developmental psychopathology: Vol. 6. Emotion, cognition, and representation* (pp. 261–287). Rochester, NY: University of Rochester Press.

Tolstoy, L. (1960). *Anna Karenina*. New York: Bantam Books.

Tong, S. (1998). Lead exposure and cognitive development: Persistence and a dynamic pattern. *Journal of Pediatrics and Child Health, 34*(2), 114–118.

Toth, S.L., Cicchetti, D., Macfie, J., & Emde, R.N. (1997). Representations of self and other in the narrations of neglected, physically abused, and sexually abused preschoolers. *Development and Psychopathology, 9*(4), 781–796.

Tronick, E.Z., Cohn, J., & Shea, E. (1986). The transfer of affect between mothers and infants. In T.B. Brazelton & M.W. Yogman (Eds.), *Affective development in infancy* (pp. 11–25). Norwood, NJ: Ablex Publishing.

Twain, M. (1947). *The adventures of Huckleberry Finn*. Cleveland, OH: World Publishing. (Original work published 1885)

Vygotsky, L.S. (1978). *Mind in society: The development of higher psychological process*. (M. Cole, V. John-Steiner, S. Scribner, & E. Souberman, Eds. & Trans.). Cambridge, MA: Harvard University Press.

Wakschlag, L.S., & Hans, S.L. (2000). Early parenthood in context: Implications for development and intervention. In C.H. Zeanah, Jr. (Ed.), *Handbook of infant mental health*. (2nd ed., pp. 129–144). New York: The Guilford Press.

Wallach, L.B. (1993). Helping children cope with violence. *Young Children, 48* (4), 4–11.

Wasik, B.H., Bryant, D.M., & Lyons, C.M. (1990). *Home visiting: Procedures for helping families*. Thousand Oaks, CA: Sage Publications.

Weiss, H.B. (1993). Home visits: Necessary but not sufficient. In R.E. Behrman (Ed.), *The future of children* (pp. 113–128). Los Altos, CA: Center for the Future of Children, The David and Lucile Packard Foundation.

Weissbluth, M. (1987). *Healthy sleep habits, happy child*. New York: Ballantine Books.

Weissbourd, B. (1987). A brief history of family support programs. In S.L. Kagan, D.P. Powell, B. Weissbourd, & E.F. Zigler (Eds.), *America's family support programs* (pp. 38–56). New Haven, CT: Yale University Press.

Weissbourd, B. (1994). The evolution of family resource management. In S.L. Kagan & B. Weissbourd (Eds.), *Putting families first: America's family support movement and the challenge of change* (pp. 28–48). San Francisco: Jossey-Bass.

Werner, E.E., & Smith, R.S. (1992). *Overcoming the odds: High risk for children from birth to adulthood*. Ithaca, NY: Cornell University Press.

White, B. (1985). *The first three years of life*. New York: Prentice Hall.

White, M., & Epston, D. (1990). *Narrative means to therapeutic ends*. New York: Norton.

Winnicott, D.W. (1957). *Mother and child: A primer of first relationship*. New York: Basic Books.

Winnicott, D. (1965). *The maturational processes and the facilitating environment*. New York: International Universities Press.

Winnicott, D. (1971). *Playing and reality*. New York: Basic Books.

Wolin, S.J., & Bennett, L.A. (1984). Family rituals. *Family Process, 23*, 402–420.

Wolin, S.J., & Wolin, S. (1993). *The resilient self: How survivors of troubled families rise above adversity*. New York: Villard Books.

Woodworth, R.S. (1996). It's not the same the second time around: Grandparents raising grandchildren. *Zero to Three, 16*(4), 21–26.

Zahn-Waxler, C., Ianotti, R.J., Cumming, E.M., & Denham, S. (1990). Antecedents of problem behaviors in children of depressed mothers. *Development and Psychopathology, 2*, 271–291.

Zeanah, C.H., Jr. (1993). The assessment and treatment of infants and toddlers exposed to violence. *Zero to Three, 14*(3), 29–37.

Zeanah, C.H., Jr., & Boris, N.W. (2000). Disturbances and disorders of attachment in early childhood. In C.H. Zeanah, Jr. (Ed.), *Handbook of infant mental health* (2nd ed., pp. 353–368). New York: The Guilford Press.

Zeanah, C.H., Jr., & Burk, G.S. (1984). A young child who witnessed her mother's murder: Therapeutic and legal considerations. *American Journal of Psychotherapy, 38*(1), 132–145.

Zeanah, P.D., Larrieu, J.A., & Zeanah, C.H., Jr. (2000). Training in infant mental health. In C.H. Zeanah, Jr. (Ed.), *Handbook of infant mental health* (2nd ed.). New York: The Guilford Press.

Zuckerman, B., & Brown, E.R. (1993). Maternal substance abuse and infant development. In C.H. Zeanah, Jr. (Ed.), *Handbook of infant mental health.* New York: The Guilford Press.

Index

Page references followed by *t* indicate tables. References followed by *n* indicate endnotes.